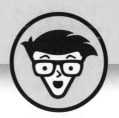

Digital SLR Photography

ALL-IN-ONE

by Robert Correll

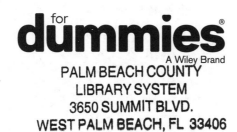

A Wiley Brand

Digital SLR Photography All-in-One For Dummies®, 4th Edition

Published by: **John Wiley & Sons, Inc.,** 111 River Street, Hoboken, NJ 07030-5774, www.wiley.com

Copyright © 2021 by John Wiley & Sons, Inc., Hoboken, New Jersey

Published simultaneously in Canada

No part of this publication may be reproduced, stored in a retrieval system or transmitted in any form or by any means, electronic, mechanical, photocopying, recording, scanning or otherwise, except as permitted under Sections 107 or 108 of the 1976 United States Copyright Act, without the prior written permission of the Publisher. Requests to the Publisher for permission should be addressed to the Permissions Department, John Wiley & Sons, Inc., 111 River Street, Hoboken, NJ 07030, (201) 748-6011, fax (201) 748-6008, or online at http://www.wiley.com/go/permissions.

Trademarks: Wiley, For Dummies, the Dummies Man logo, Dummies.com, Making Everything Easier, and related trade dress are trademarks or registered trademarks of John Wiley & Sons, Inc. and may not be used without written permission. Photoshop is a registered trademark of Adobe, Inc. All other trademarks are the property of their respective owners. John Wiley & Sons, Inc. is not associated with any product or vendor mentioned in this book.

For general information on our other products and services, please contact our Customer Care Department within the U.S. at 877-762-2974, outside the U.S. at 317-572-3993, or fax 317-572-4002. For technical support, please visit https://hub.wiley.com/community/support/dummies.

Wiley publishes in a variety of print and electronic formats and by print-on-demand. Some material included with standard print versions of this book may not be included in e-books or in print-on-demand. If this book refers to media such as a CD or DVD that is not included in the version you purchased, you may download this material at http://booksupport.wiley.com. For more information about Wiley products, visit www.wiley.com.

Library of Congress Control Number: 2020946710

ISBN: 978-1-119-71170-4

ISBN 978-1-119-71171-1 (ebk); ISBN 978-1-119-71172-8 (ebk)

Manufactured in the United States of America

SKY10021740_101520

TECHNICAL STUFF

When you see this icon, you know that technical information lurks nearby. If that's not your cuppa tea, skip it.

Where to Go from Here

First, have a look at the table of contents. Next, jump to somewhere in the book that looks interesting or has information you want to know right now. Then go out and take some pictures. Rinse and repeat.

If you're new to photography, though, I suggest starting at the beginning and reading the first minibook in order. When you've finished that, you should be able to turn to any place in the book and not feel overwhelmed.

Lastly, when you have a minute, go to dummies.com to type **Digital SLR Photography All-in-One For Dummies Cheat Sheet** in the Search box. The Cheat Sheet is full of information you might find valuable.

The more photos and movies you shoot with your dSLR, the more you learn about your camera, lens, and how to operate them. Don't be afraid to take bad shots to get better. Go out and start shooting!

1
Pursuing Digital SLR Photography

Contents at a Glance

Consumer dSLRs

Compared to more expensive cameras, consumer-level dSLRs are less expensive, smaller, lighter, more convenient, and less intimidating. They have a plethora of automatic modes and are easy to use. They use different image sensors, processors, and other technologies than more expensive dLSRs. This limits their performance, by comparison, but makes them affordable.

Consumer dSLRs are great cameras for the beginner or cost-conscious consumer. They range from entry-level models priced under $400 (see Figure 1-6) to more advanced consumer-level models that cost near $1,000. At this level, cameras are most often sold as kits. This means that a basic zoom lens is sold with the camera body. The lens increases the overall cost slightly compared to buying the body only, but most people like the convenience of having everything they need to get started in one box. These dSLRs are made from polycarbonate and their image sensors are cropped-frame.

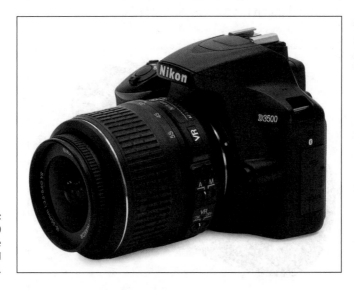

FIGURE 1-6:
The Nikon D3500 is a good example of an entry-level consumer dSLR.

If you want more features and a bit more performance out of your dSLR, shop at the high end of this category. You will find cameras that have higher maximum ISO speeds, better, articulated monitors, faster frame rates, and more options compared to entry-level models. They are also often slightly larger.

REMEMBER

All dSLRs can take fantastic photos. Don't let the consumer or entry-level distinction make you think they are toys. They're not — especially when combined with a good lens. These cameras just aren't designed to perform in *all* situations or to be as customizable as more expensive cameras.

Mid-range models

Mid-range dSLRs are priced roughly between $1,000 and $1,500. They include a mix of enthusiast- and pro-level features. This makes them a great choice for photographers who want a serious upgrade from a consumer-level camera and an inexpensive back-up option for professionals.

Mid-range dSLRs often have faster maximum shutter speeds than the less expensive models, as well as faster flash sync speeds, faster frame rates, better viewfinders, depending on the manufacturer, slightly larger LCD monitors with greater pixel counts, more professional setup options, a better autofocus system with more autofocus points, more custom shooting modes, more precise metering, and better battery life. They're also sealed against the weather and may have a top LCD panel to display shooting information.

Although this level of camera is considered light by professional standards, these cameras are larger and heavier than consumer dSLRs. Magnesium alloy is often used to strengthen the camera body. Figure 1-7 shows the Canon EOS 90D.

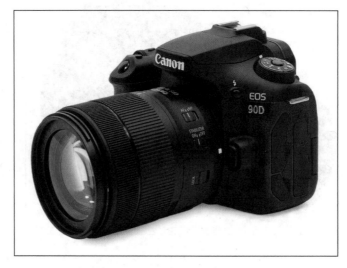

FIGURE 1-7: Mid-range cameras add even more power and features.

Professional cameras

Professional dSLRs are designed to excel in a professional setting. They have all the bells, whistles, features, and performance that pro photographers need. These cameras are large and rugged. They weigh more than lower-level dSLRs and are made from magnesium alloy, are weather sealed, and have more features than consumer or mid-range models. They also shoot faster, focus better, and provide more reliable metering. You'll find flagship (the best model a company sells) cropped-frame and full-frame (see Figure 1-8) dSLRs at this level.

AF Selection modes

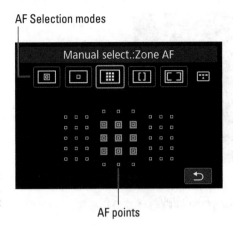

Manual select.:Zone AF

AF points

Here are a few examples: The consumer-level Canon T8i has 45 AF points. The similarly priced Nikon D7500 has 51 AF points. Both cover the same basic area. Less expensive or older cameras might have fewer points, and they might be more centrally located in the viewfinder. More expensive cameras may have more AF points, more sensitivity, and a larger number of selection options. The Canon 5DS has 61 and the Nikon D850 has 153 AF points, respectively.

Movies

Digital SLRs also shoot movies (Figure 1-13 shows this in action). Full HD video is the standard format. Most cameras also have an HD option, which is smaller than Full HD. Support for older VGA is diminishing. 4K video is now available on new cameras. Here are their sizes:

>> Most 4K movies are 3840 x 2160 pixels in size, which is twice the height of Full HD.

>> Full HD movies are 1920 x 1080 pixels.

>> HD movies are 1280 x 720 pixels.

>> Standard definition (SD) movies are 640 x 480 pixels.

When you look at your camera's movie specs, look for how much control you have over movie settings, especially exposure and shutter speed, as well as different movie sizes, compression settings, formats, and frame rates.

Don't confuse frame rates with shutter speed. The frame rate is how many frames per second the movie plays back at. Frame rate also affects how the movie is recorded. Common settings are 24, 30, 60, and 120 fps for NTSC and 25, 50, and 100 fps for PAL video systems.

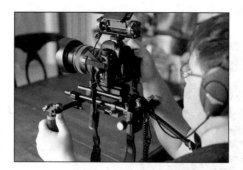

FIGURE 1-13:
Shooting a video with a professional Canon dSLR and extensive rig.

Shooting modes and scenes

Digital SLRs have at least one fully automatic mode and a handful of "classic" shooting modes (sometimes called *exposure modes*). The classic modes include programmed autoexposure, aperture-priority, shutter-priority, and manual. You might see these four called PASM modes. Bulb mode, which is an open-ended exposure, may not be on the mode dial. When it isn't, it should be accessible as a function of shutter speed.

Cameras like the Pentax K-1 Mark II have ingenious modes like sensitivity priority automatic exposure, through which you set the ISO as you would aperture or shutter speed, and shutter- and aperture-priority automatic exposure (think manual mode with Auto ISO).

Most cameras have several scene modes that help you take photos of specific subjects. You select the subject or shooting conditions, and the camera sets itself up to capture them most effectively. Standard scenes include Portrait (see Figure 1-14), Landscape, Action, and Close-up. Additional scenes vary from camera to camera and often include Night Portrait, Child, Candlelight, Sunset, Pet, Surf & Snow, Fireworks, and Food.

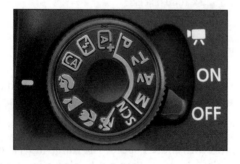

FIGURE 1-14:
This camera has several scene modes right on the dial.

Many cameras have even more user-friendly modes designed to automate the camera and make shooting easier. Examples modes include Sweep Panorama, various automatic HDR (High Dynamic Range) modes, time-lapse, multiple exposures, and more.

TIP

When comparing cameras, carefully investigate the automatic shooting modes and scenes they offer.

In-camera processing

Most dSLRs allow you to process JPEGs and Raw files in-camera (the Raw file is converted and saved as a JPEG). You may be able to resize photos, crop them (see Figure 1-15), modify the exposure, white balance, and color profile, and perform many other retouching tasks. Being able to touch up photos in the camera means not having to use a computer and complicated software to accomplish these tasks. I think they are incredibly useful features for most photographers to have.

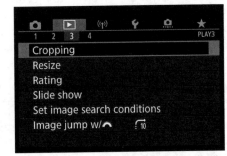

FIGURE 1-15:
Look for in-camera processing features like cropping.

Filters and other creative effects

Look for fun filters and other special effects to add pizzazz to your photos. They help you express your creativity without having to mess around with a computer. Each manufacturer has its own names. Canon calls them Creative Filters; Nikon has Filter Effects; Sony uses the term Picture Effects; and Pentax lists its effects as Digital Filters. Some specific examples include Toy Camera (always a fun filter to use), Miniature, High-Key, Retro, Replace Color, Monochrome, Pop Color, Posterization, Soft Focus, and many HDR effects. I'm applying a creative Toy Camera effect to a photo in Figure 1-16.

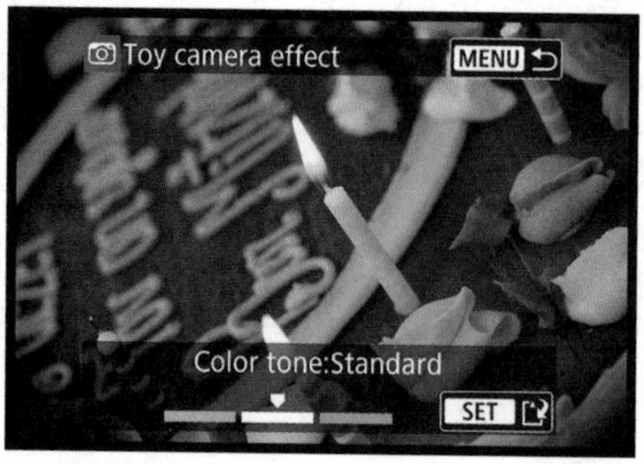

FIGURE 1-16:
Creative effects
and filters
help make
photography
more fun for
everyone.

Media

Digital cameras store photos and movies on memory cards. Be sure to look at your camera's specifications before buying new memory cards to confirm compatibility. For specialty cards such as FlashAir, check that company's website for compatible cameras. Here are several popular card types currently in use:

>> **SD cards** are the most prevalent type of memory card. They're reasonably small and thin. There are several types of SD cards (SD, SDHC, and SDXC), speed classes, and bus interfaces, each with different capabilities. UHS-II cards are newer and much faster than UHS-I type SD cards. Some cameras support the much smaller microSD format card.

>> **CF (Compact Flash) cards** are an older memory card design, larger than SD cards. They perform well and are often used in high-end cameras.

Newer formats include CFexpress, XQD, and CFast cards. These are high-performance variants with much faster read and write speeds. They are meant to support 4K video recording.

>> **Memory Stick** cards were created by Sony and are still used in some cameras. There are different versions of Memory Stick media. A few variants currently in use are the Memory Stick PRO-HG Duo, Memory Stick PRO Duo, and Memory Stick XC-HG Duo.

Viewfinder specs

Take a look at two specifications relating to viewfinders:

>> **Frame coverage:** This specification, given as a percentage, identifies how much of the scene the viewfinder sees compared to the image sensor. Some dSLR viewfinders may have only about 95 percent coverage. This can be a

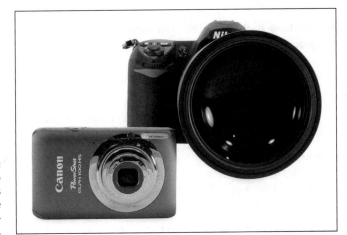

FIGURE 1-26:
The ability to change lenses is a strength of the dSLR over a compact camera.

>> **Focusing is a strength.** Digital SLRs have world-class autofocusing technology and features. This is an important point. If you've tried to capture action or focus on a specific point using a smartphone or tablet, you know how frustrating it can be. Digital SLR autofocus technologies work with precision and flexibility to enable you to reliably focus on what you want, when you want.

>> **The viewfinders are awesome.** The worst dSLR viewfinder is larger, clearer, brighter, and better (see Figure 1-27) than any viewfinder you'll find on a compact or super-zoom camera, assuming that it even has one. Many don't, which makes you rely exclusively on the monitor on the back. Under many conditions, monitors are okay. However, they don't work well in bright light. In addition, smartphones and tablets seem to suffer from display lag at the worst time when taking photos. Digital SLR viewfinders outperform monitors on most devices. And if you want to use the monitor on the back of the camera, you can.

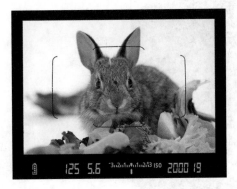

FIGURE 1-27:
Digital SLR viewfinders just work; rabbit not included.

>> **They have flash.** Most dSLRs have a built-in flash (see Figure 1-28) that is capable of lighting your scenes and subjects. All dSLRs have a hot shoe on top of their viewfinder, which enables you to mount an external flash (and other accessories) that you can rotate, swivel, and bounce. Try that with your iPad.

>> **There are plenty of price points.** Digital SLRs are not the most expensive camera option. Although some are extremely pricey, many consumer models cost less than most tablets. In fact, most entry-level dSLRs cost less than a new iPhone.

>> **You can make money with them.** Become a semi-pro or professional photographer with your dSLR. Start a studio. Become a wedding photographer. Make money selling news photos, sports photos, nature photos, the stars, advertising photos, stock photos, or artistic prints.

>> **You're in control, but you don't have to be.** Digital SLRs enable you to control the camera as much or as little as you want. If you're new to photography, you can pick up an entry-level consumer model and start taking photos *right away*. If you're a professional, you have access to cameras with tremendous features and the power you need to succeed.

In the final analysis, my advice is this: Don't spend years messing around with point-and-shoot cameras, smartphones, or tablets struggling to take better photos. If you're interested in photography or making quality movies, pick up a dSLR or dSLT and start taking gorgeous pictures and movies today that you'll treasure for a lifetime.

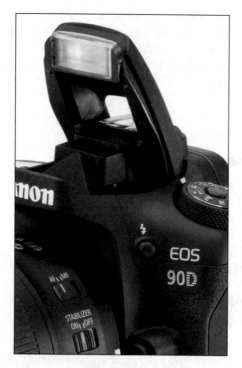

FIGURE 1-28: Pop up the flash for extra light.

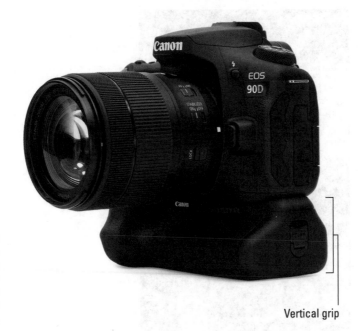

FIGURE 2-8:
This Canon
camera looks
mighty
impressive
with a grip
attached.

Vertical grip

Gripping the Camera

Mastering your grip pays dividends in the form of sharper, clearer photos when shooting handheld. You have a more stable platform to shoot from, you make image stabilization more effective, and you can use slower shutter speeds and not shake the camera. The following sections talk about positions you can work on.

TIP

No matter what grip you use, try to maintain good posture. Don't hunch, bend over improperly, or hold the camera at arm's length. You'll tire easily and possibly hurt yourself. Hold the camera close so that you can support it easily.

Standard grip

The standard grip is shown in Figure 2-9. Use your right hand to grip and support the camera. Slide your right pinky finger underneath on smaller cameras for more support. Your ring and middle fingers squeeze the grip while your index finger works the top controls. Your thumb provides support at times but also works controls on the back of the camera. Your left hand supports and operates the lens. It is also available to work controls on that side of the camera.

REMEMBER

If you have an external flash, you can use either hand to operate it while using the other to hold and support the camera.

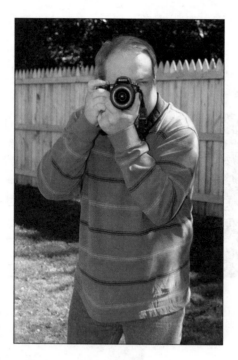

When you're ready to take the photos, support the weight of the lens with your left palm. At times, you may be more comfortable supporting the entire weight of the camera with your left hand so that you can remove your right hand from the grip and work various dials, buttons, and controls. When you're ready to take the picture, move your right hand back into position on the grip to press the shutter button.

To promote good posture and add some stability, lock down your left elbow towards or against your stomach. Look through the viewfinder or watch the back monitor to frame and focus.

Vertical grip

For a vertical grip, your hands and fingers stay in the same place as you twist the camera. If I'm using autofocus and not zooming in and out, I use my left hand to support most of the camera's weight (see Figure 2-10), and my right hand stabilizes the camera vertically and takes the picture. My right elbow is extended in this pose. If you are in a tight space or around other people, you should pull it in close to your body to avoid bumping them. Your right wrist will feel a bit cramped, but if you practice at it you'll be fine.

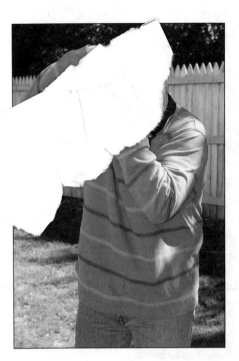

FIGURE 2-10:
Vertical grip.

Over-the-shoulder grip

A well-known photographer promotes a grip style in which you point your left shoulder toward the subject and use it to support the weight of the camera. Hold the camera with your right hand. Bring your left hand up to rest on the back of your right hand, stabilizing and securing it. You have to turn your head toward the camera. I've tried this technique and can't quite seem to get comfortable with it, but it is rock-solid.

Live View grip

Gripping the camera when using Live View is a different feeling. It feels comfortable and natural. You don't have to hold the camera close to your face and body as you do when you're looking through the viewfinder. Hold the camera away from your face so that you can see the monitor. If you wear glasses, this position is much easier than looking through the viewfinder. When zooming or focusing, move your left hand back to the lens to operate these controls. Your right hand doesn't change at all. Figure 2-11 shows me checking the composition.

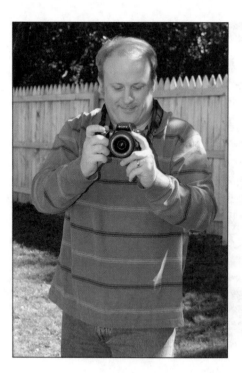

FIGURE 2-11:
Working in
Live View.

TIP

Using the touchscreen with this grip is much easier because your face isn't plastered up against the camera. You can more easily keep track of what's going on around you to catch the action and stay safe. You're also able to interact better with your subjects. However, this position is much harder to stabilize, so I recommend using faster shutter speeds than you would when using the viewfinder.

Providing Additional Support

The best way to stabilize your camera is with a good tripod. You'll be able to take advantage of longer shutter speeds without worrying about camera movement blurring your photos. One-legged monopods offer less support but are much more mobile.

You can mount different heads on tripods and monopods. Some pan and tilt. Others are a form of ball joint. I use both types regularly. Whichever you choose, look into getting one with a quick-release plate. You screw it into the camera bottom and then lock the plate onto the tripod head. Latching and unlatching the quick-release plate is far easier than screwing and unscrewing the entire camera.

TIP

If you don't have a tripod handy, use a fence, a rock, a vehicle, the ground, or another item to stabilize your camera. You can also try kneeling to stabilize the camera. You may find that resting your elbow on your knee is comfortable in this position.

Tripod

I use a tripod all the time. It's good for ya. When taking macros or close-ups in the studio, formal portraits, or landscape shots, nothing works better at securing and supporting the weight of the camera. As you can see from Figure 2-12, the small porcelain cat isn't going anywhere, but using the tripod makes setting up the shot and focusing very precisely far easier.

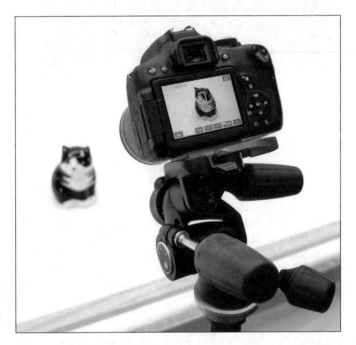

FIGURE 2-12:
Tripods provide fantastic support for cameras.

Cheap tripods, however, are affordable, but very disappointing. When it comes to flimsy tripods, the saying is true: You get what you pay for. If you want something that will be stable and last for more than two days, get a sturdy, professional tripod. It's worth it!

TIP

Aside from providing rock-solid stability, using a tripod frees your hands and allows you to concentrate more on camera setup and framing than on supporting the camera and taking a steady shot. You won't grow as tired, either.

Monopod

Monopods have a single leg that telescopes in and out to the height you want to work at. Professional photographers use monopods all the time. They stand, sit, or kneel on the sidelines at sporting events and use the monopod to support the weight of their camera. If using bulky, heavy lenses, you need all the support you can get. Telephoto lenses often mount right to the monopod, as shown in Figure 2-13.

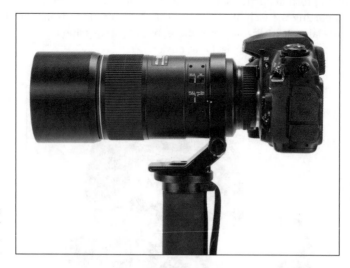

FIGURE 2-13: Monopods offer stability, support, and mobility.

REMEMBER

Walking around with a monopod is much easier than lugging around a tripod. They're faster to set up and tear down. Setting the exact height you need with one leg is easier than fiddling around with three. The trade-off for this convenience, however, is stability and safety. Monopods aren't as stable as tripods, and if you forget they don't have three legs and let go, well, you're in for a nasty surprise.

Handling an Articulated Monitor

Having an *adjustable,* also called *articulated,* monitor on the back of the camera lets you view and shoot from a number of positions. Although the style may vary, the point is that you can position an articulated monitor where you want it. Using an articulated monitor isn't difficult. Your main concerns should be:

WARNING

» Don't whack the monitor against anything. It's easy to forget that the monitor extends a ways from the camera.

>> Don't overstress the monitor by cranking it around like the rearview mirror on a '57 Chevy.

The articulated monitor shown in Figure 2-14 is a good example of the type that comes completely out of the camera's back. This monitor comes stowed but can flip out and then tilt, swivel, or rotate. Pull the monitor out from the back of the camera using your thumb or finger as a lever. Then you can rotate the monitor. You can position the monitor in the camera so that it acts normally. Rather than flipping *out* (intentional humor alert), some articulated monitors flip up or tilt.

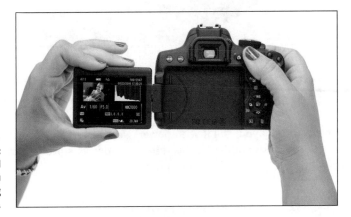

FIGURE 2-14: Articulated monitors give you a lot of viewing options.

Using a Touchscreen

Touchscreens bring the same type of gestures to dSLRs that you're used to using on your smartphone or tablet. Depending on the camera and what you're trying to do, you may tap (see Figure 2-15), touch, swipe, drag, pinch, or expand using one or more fingers. Touchscreens are fun and save you a lot of time and trouble hunting through menus, choosing settings, or reviewing photos. Some cameras even let you use the touchscreen to focus and trigger the shutter. Their one downside is when you accidentally change a camera setting with your nose without realizing it. Always be on the lookout for incidental contact with your touchscreen.

Using a touchscreen becomes more difficult when working in dusty or wet weather, or in the winter when you have gloves or mittens on. You should be ready to revert to traditional controls when necessary.

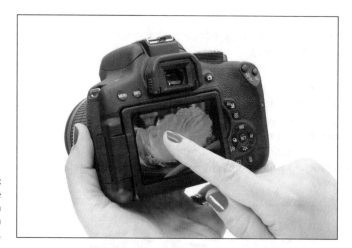

FIGURE 2-15:
Use the
touchscreen
as you would a
smartphone.

Changing Batteries

Batteries supply your dSLR with power. Never take that for granted. It's a good idea to have a second battery as a backup. Always store batteries in a cool, dry place, and charge them before you need them.

Checking battery power

Your camera has battery status indicators all over it. You should see one in the viewfinder, on the top LCD panel (if your camera has one), and on the back monitor.

You may also be able to look in your camera's menu for a more detailed estimate of remaining power. Look for a menu option related to the battery, as shown on the left image in Figure 2-16. When you select it, the battery information is shown, as illustrated on the right of Figure 2-16. In this case, you learn how much charge is left and how well the battery is expected to recharge.

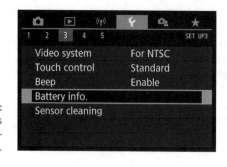
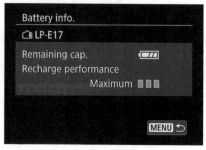

FIGURE 2-16:
This camera gives
you useful bat-
tery info.

Inserting a battery

Here's how to insert a battery into your dSLR:

1. **Turn off the camera.**

2. **Release the catch on the battery compartment cover.**

The catch is on the bottom of the camera, as shown on the left in Figure 2-17. If the cover is spring loaded, it will pop open. Some cameras have an unlock knob that you have to twist to unlock the cover.

Some cameras put their memory cards in the same overall compartment as the battery. They go in different slots so that you can't mix them up. The only danger is dropping the memory card into an empty battery compartment. If that happens, just turn the camera over and shake the card into your hand.

3. **Orient the battery and insert it into the battery compartment.**

WARNING

New batteries ship with a plastic cover that protects the contacts and keeps the battery from shorting out. Remove this cover before trying to put it in the camera.

Batteries go in contacts first. Many batteries have an arrow that tells you which way they should be inserted. Gently nudge any locking levers (shown in the center of Figure 2-17) out of the way. I use the corner of the battery to nudge with.

4. **Locks the battery in place.**

Make sure the locking lever locks the battery in place, as shown on the right in Figure 2-17. If your camera doesn't have a lever, press the battery in and use your finger to keep it from falling out as you close the cover.

5. **Close the battery compartment cover; it should snap in place.**

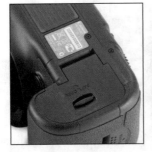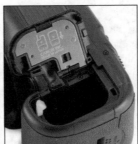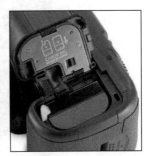

FIGURE 2-17: Be sure to move the locking lever out of the way as you insert the battery.

Removing a battery

Here's how to remove a battery:

1. **Turn the camera off.**

2. **Release the catch on the battery compartment cover.**

   The cover should pop open.

3. **If necessary, press the battery lock lever until it releases the battery.**

   The battery will spring up a bit, as shown in Figure 2-18. Pay attention to how you have the camera oriented, because some batteries aren't secured by a lock lever.

4. **Take the battery out of the camera.**

   You can pull it with your fingers or hold the camera so that it falls out.

5. **If you want, put another battery in the camera.**

6. **Close the battery compartment door.**

TIP

Most manufacturers recommend that you take batteries out of the camera if you aren't going to be using them. Likewise, they don't recommend leaving batteries in the charger after they have been fully charged. Keep your batteries safely tucked away in your camera bag and recharge them shortly before you plan on using them.

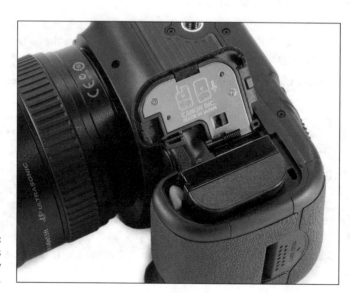

FIGURE 2-18:
A spring pushes up the battery a bit.

Inserting and Removing Memory Cards

Treat your memory cards as though they hold the most precious cargo. They do! Here are some general tips for handling memory cards:

>> **Don't expose memory cards to extreme weather.** That makes sense. Don't use them to scrape frost off your car windows in the winter or leave them out on the picnic table in the middle of summer. Keep them in the camera, in a protective case, or stored in a card wallet.

>> **Normal magnetism is fine.** Contrary to what you may believe, flash drives (which memory cards are a subset of) aren't affected by normal magnetic fields. Notice that I said *normal* magnetic field: If you run the card through an X-ray or MRI machine (the one in your basement?), you may be in for trouble.

>> **Take a load off.** Memory cards aren't indestructible. Although it may take a lot of force to do so, they can be crushed. Try not to sit on them, step on them, drive over them, or rest heavy objects on them.

>> **Don't lose them.** Keep memory cards in the camera. Store extras in a protective case or card wallet. Don't scatter them all over your desk or in your vehicle.

Inserting a memory card

To insert a compatible memory card into your dSLR, follow these steps:

1. **Turn off the camera.**

   Most manufacturers strongly suggest that the camera be powered down before swapping memory cards.

2. **Open the card cover.**

   Depending on your camera model, you may have to operate a card cover release latch. Other covers pull out and swing open, as shown in Figure 2-19.

3. **Orient and align the card properly.**

   SD cards have a notched corner. You can use this to orient the card the correct way every time. For other cards, try to remember which way the label faces. Your camera may have an illustration on the inside of the card cover that shows you the proper orientation of the card.

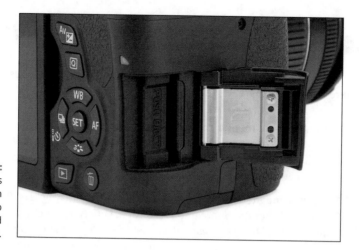

4. **Insert the card into the slot and press until it's securely in place.**

An eject button may pop up, indicating that the card is in position. When inserting Compact Flash cards, be careful not to bend the pins inside your camera or card reader. Gently align the card in the slot and seat it properly on the pins before pressing further to secure it in place.

5. **Close the card cover.**

6. **Turn on the camera.**

7. **If you like, test the card.**

Take a test shot and confirm that the photo was stored and can be viewed.

Removing a memory card

To remove the card, follow these steps:

1. **Turn off the camera.**

2. **Open the card cover.**

3. **Eject the card.**

Depending on your camera model, press an eject button once to make the card pop up. This is how Compact Flash cards work. Or, gently press the card so that it releases and pops up, as shown in Figure 2-20. SD and Memory Stick cards work this way.

4. **Grab and fully remove the card.**

5. **Insert another card, if you want, and then close the cover.**

- *Don't* use a canned-air spray blower. Don't use a blower brush, either. Use a blower that you squeeze with your hand.

- *Don't* dally. The more you have the camera open, the more dust can get back in.

8. **Put down the blower and put the camera back together.**

9. **Turn off the camera.**

10. **Turn the camera back on and check to make sure it's working.**

Take a few test shots. Stop down to a small aperture and take a photo of the sky or your ceiling. Can you see any dust spots? If you do, you can repeat this series of steps and hope another round of cleaning works better, try swabbing the image sensor yourself (see the next section), or send in the camera for maintenance.

Swabbing or brushing the image sensor

If your camera needs a serious cleaning inside, send it to an authorized service center. You'll appreciate having your dSLR cleaned by someone trained and practiced in it. It's not the end of the world to pay for a bit of maintenance. You may want to schedule yearly cleanings, or have it looked at before important trips, holidays, occasions, or other very special events.

WARNING

If you can't wait and need to clean the sensor yourself, look in your manual for the proper procedures, if possible. *Don't open your camera and touch anything inside it unless you're sure of yourself and willing to take the risk.* However, many people swab their sensors, and do it successfully. Look for more information on the Internet or visit your local camera shop if you want to try this.

Protecting Your Camera

Take reasonable steps to protect your camera, lenses, and accessories from damage. If you've ever dropped your phone and cracked the glass, you know what I'm talking about.

Using a camera strap

Using a strap is an important step toward safeguarding your camera. My straps have saved me and my cameras a number of times. You will feel a tug when you drop your camera, but it won't crash to the ground and ruin your day. You'll find a strap in the box your camera came in. You can also buy third-party straps. The more comfortable your strap is, the more likely you'll be to use it for long periods of time. Straps come in many styles and with different features. If you're looking for something more adventurous, BlackRapid (www.blackrapid.com) makes some unique straps.

TIP

As an additional safety precaution, put the strap over your neck before mounting or removing your camera from a tripod. I learned this lesson the day I triggered the tripod release lever without having a good grip on the camera. Because of its heavy lens, the camera took a nosedive off the tripod, and I was barely able to catch it.

Carrying a camera bag

Camera bags protect your gear and make carrying it around easier. I have several bags, and I pack the one that matches my needs for the day. Look for these characteristics when deciding on a bag:

>> **Type:** Conventional carry bags, often called shoulder bags, are like small luggage. They have a shoulder strap and a handle. Most people put them down when shooting. Large conventional camera bags make great base camps to work out of. Smaller conventional bags hold less gear but are easier to carry. Sling bags tend to be smaller and slip over your shoulder. They are meant to be worn more than the larger bags, and they swing around from back to front when you need access to your gear. Backpacks have two shoulder straps and are comfortable to use.

>> **Size:** Most bags let you carry a dSLR and a few lenses. If you need more space, get a bigger bag. If you need less, look for a smaller bag.

>> **Padding:** Bags with more padding protect your gear better.

>> **Strap support:** Look for a bag with a wide, padded, comfortable strap if you're going to be wearing it a lot.

TIP

Be sensible when packing your bag. My experience is that bags are easier to use and more practical if you focus on packing the essentials. Most often, you won't need to take everything with you on every excursion.

Buying extra lens and camera caps

Always protect your camera and lens with the proper caps. Front and rear lens caps go on lenses. Body caps go on the camera body in place of a lens. Consider buying extra caps as backups in case you misplace any. I have a number of extra rear lens and camera body caps (see Figure 2-25). As long as the lens mount is the same, rear lens caps are interchangeable. Likewise, cameras that have the same lens mount can share body caps.

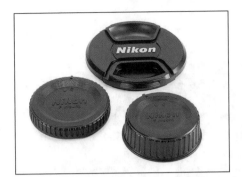

FIGURE 2-25:
Keep extra body
and lens caps in
different camera
bags.

Buying multiple front lens caps isn't as practical as for other lenses. Lenses with different front filter sizes require differently sized front lens caps. If you use large filters and step-up rings to match lenses with the filters, you should buy several front lens caps the same size as your standardized filters. In my case, that's 77mm. When the step-up ring is screwed into the lens, it requires the larger lens cap, not the original.

Armoring your camera

You can buy silicon armor to provide extra protection for your dSLR, as shown in Figure 2-26. It's inexpensive and shields the camera from occasional bumps, dings, and scrapes. Everything that needs to be exposed — the lens mount, built-in flash, shutter button, dial, and so forth — is exposed, yet most of the camera is covered, including the buttons on the back. There's even a plastic cover to protect the back monitor. For a wide range of cases, check out easyCover (easycover.eu).

Dealing with adverse weather

It's not always sunny and 72 degrees outside with no chance of rain. If you want to shoot in bad weather, protect yourself and your camera. Here are some suggestions for being out in different conditions:

>> **Dust:** If you're working in extremely dusty conditions, try putting a rain cover around your camera. That will help keep the dust out. Don't remove your lens in a dust storm. Be wary of scratching lenses and monitors if they are covered with dust and you decide to clean. To avoid scratching your lens, use a blower or soft brush to clean the glass when around dust. Don't use a microfiber cloth or the carbon end of a lens pen.

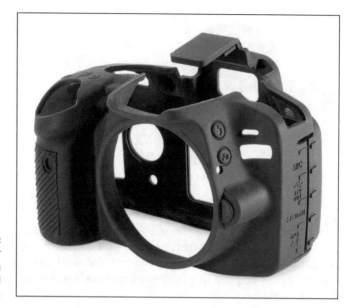

FIGURE 2-26:
Body armor gives the camera additional protection.

» **Heat:** Don't leave your camera lying around in the sun, which is hot and can melt your gear. Not only that, monitors don't like heat and can become discolored. Be prepared to let your camera adjust to the heat and humidity when going outside from an air-conditioned interior. The lens will fog up if you don't let it sit outside with the lens cap on until it warms up. You can also place your camera in a non–air-conditioned room to adjust before leaving.

» **Wet or humid weather:** Rain equals water, and water is bad for your camera. If it's a slow sprinkle, the threat isn't that bad. Monitor the situation and keep your camera wiped dry when it gets too wet. If it's raining heavily, try to find shelter that you can shoot from, as I did in Figure 2-27. If you must go out in the rain, put a rain cover on your camera. You can find inexpensive rain covers online. You can also make your own from plastic bags and duct tape.

Try to keep lens changes to a minimum in wet weather. If you must, seek cover as I did in Figure 2-27 or point the camera away from the spray.

High humidity is a threat to the electronics in your camera. Take shelter in a dry, air-conditioned location as often as you can to keep your camera from picking up too much moisture.

» **Cold:** Working in the cold makes everything more difficult. Plastic and metal get extremely cold and uncomfortable to touch. You can't wear mittens the size of boxing gloves and easily press buttons or turn dials. Thin gloves can be slippery or ineffective against the cold.

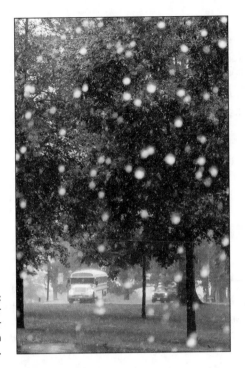

FIGURE 2-27:
Take shelter
or protect your
camera from
heavy rain.

If you do a lot of cold-weather shooting, check out special gloves designed with silicon "grippies" that make holding the camera easier. Some have finger caps that come off, exposing one or more fingertips to operate the camera with. Some are fingerless.

Always give your lenses and camera time to adapt to the cold. If you don't, the lenses will fog up and you'll be forced to wait anyway. Set the bag outside to adapt while you stay warm inside.

WARNING

When you're working in the cold, plastics become more brittle. Be careful not to drop your camera or lens. That's always good advice, of course! In addition, your batteries don't last as long as normal when it's very cold.

>> **Snow:** Snow is easier on the camera than it is on you. You will have to deal with cold temperatures, moisture on the camera from melting snow, possibly high winds and low visibility, different depths of snow, and slippery footing. Keep your camera and lens wiped dry as often as you can, and be careful. Lens hoods can help protect the lens from blowing snow. Despite the difficulties, shooting in a raging snowstorm (see Figure 2-28) can be very rewarding and yield beautiful photos.

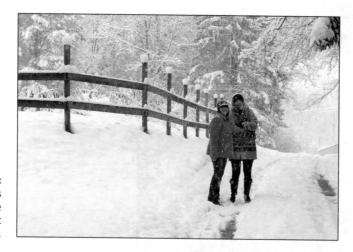

» **Underwater:** Buy a special underwater housing that's certified for use with your camera. They vary greatly in capability and price, so shop around. Some are little more than sturdy plastic bags with room for lenses and access for your fingers. Others look like they were invented by Jacques Cousteau.

Make sure to take care of yourself, too. Wear clothing suited to the weather and don't forget about footwear. One of my favorite accessories is the pair of sturdy waterproof boots shown in Figure 2-29. I take them with me whenever I expect to be trudging through mud, in and around rivers and lakes, and even in the snow.

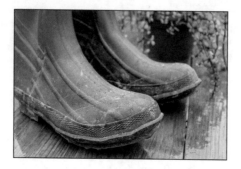

Chapter **3**

Learning about Lenses

Prepare yourself for an action-packed chapter on lenses. You start by learning how to decode lens names, which are loaded with helpful identifying information. You also see how lenses are organized into different categories and complete a course on lens anatomy. The chapter finishes with practical information on working with and cleaning lenses. Sounds like a winning combination.

Keep in mind that this chapter aims to offer an overview on lenses to get you started. My focus is on introducing you to various bits of technical and handling information. Book 2, which covers shooting with different types of lenses, helps you concentrate on the practical applications of each lens in action without stumbling over the technobabble of their names and features.

Identifying and Naming Lenses

All dSLR lenses share a few basic characteristics, which, like cameras, are listed with the name. I want to help you crack the code so that you can have an easier time understanding what you're looking at. Consider two examples. The name Canon EF-S 18-55mm f/3.5-5.6 IS STM, shown in Figure 3-1, tells you a lot about it: who makes it; the mount; focal length; aperture information; and more. By the same token, the name of Nikon's AF-S DX NIKKOR 35mm f/1.8G lens, shown in Figures 3-2 and 3-3, shows just the right information to help you know what it is and what it might be good for.

Image Stabilization

Maximum apertures

Mount   Focal lengths

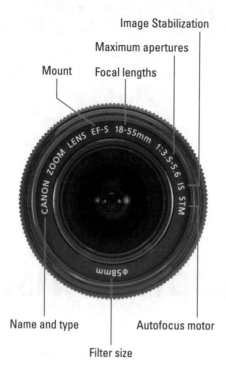

FIGURE 3-1:
Many lenses print
information on
the front.

Name and type

Autofocus motor

Filter size

REMEMBER

Quite often, lens information is printed on the front of the lens (refer to Figure 3-1). However, some lenses are devoid of any markings on the front, as shown in Figure 3-2. In that case, you need to look for identifying markings and information on the side, as you can see in Figure 3-3.

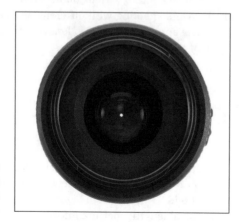

FIGURE 3-2:
If the lens has
nothing shown
on the front . . .

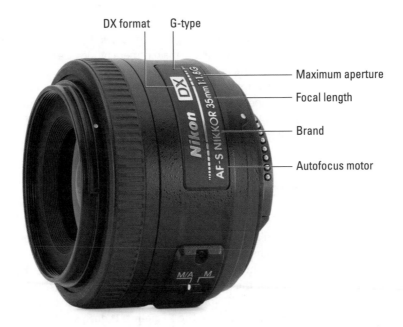

DX format   G-type

Maximum aperture

Focal length

Brand

Autofocus motor

Brand name

Lenses list the brand at or near the beginning of the lens name. In some cases, it's the same as the camera. Here is a list of the names of popular lens manufacturers that you might see:

» Canon lenses use the Canon name.

» Nikon lenses use the NIKKOR brand name. It can be a bit confusing until you know a bit about Nikon's history. The name NIKKOR is composed of two elements. First, Nikko is an abbreviation of Nippon Kougaku, which means Japan Optical. That was the original Nikon company name. In addition, it ends with the letter R, which was originally used to designate lenses in the product line. NIKKOR, therefore, means Nikon lens.

» Sony creates its own lenses, but also use the Zeiss brand. Older Minolta A-mount lenses are compatible with Sony A-mount cameras because Minolta created the A-mount that Sony adopted (like the old Remington razor commercial, they liked it so much they bought the company).

» Pentax lenses are named Pentax.

» Olympus E-system Four Thirds dSLRs use Zuiko lenses. Its Micro Four Thirds cameras use M.Zuiko lenses.

Learning about Lenses

>> Third-party lenses such as Sigma, Tamron, and Tokina all make dSLR lenses that are compatible with the main camera brands. Zeiss makes some manual focus lenses compatible with Canon and Nikon cameras, including the Milvus line. Zeiss has many high-quality lenses with features for both still photographers and cinematographers who use dSLR or mirrorless bodies. There are many other brands out there if you look around: Samyang, Rokinon, Vivitar, Irix, Meike, Yongnuo, and more.

Lens mount

The lens mount is where the lens attaches and locks on to the camera. There is no standardized lens mount specification. Each camera manufacturer creates its own, which means that they are incompatible with each other. I cover lens mounts by manufacturer in Book 1, Chapter 1, so I don't duplicate that information here except to say that the term *lens mount* is not always present in the lens name. For example, the AF-S DX NIKKOR 35mm f/1.8G lens does not mention the mount because all Nikon dSLRs use the F-mount. It does say DX, but don't confuse that designation with the mount; it relates to sensor size. NIKKOR Z lenses are designed to fit Nikon's mirrorless cameras that use the Z mount. The name of the Canon EF-S 18-55mm lens indicates that it is an EF-S lens and has the EF lens mount but is not compatible with full-frame bodies. Canon's RF line of lenses, which work with Canon's mirrorless cameras, are named after the RF mount. Sony's E and FE series of lenses are compatible with its E-mount mirrorless cameras.

Focal length

Focal length is the distance between the optical center of the lens and the image sensor. It is expressed in millimeters, such as 85mm. Zoom lenses zoom in and out, so they have a focal length range, such as 18-55mm. Prime lenses, on the other hand, have a fixed focal length. You can't zoom in or out with a prime lens, so it will have a single focal length, such as 50mm.A lens's focal length plays an important role in your photos' appearance. Because of how lenses work, shorter focal lengths show a wider field of view than longer focal lengths do. Lenses with shorter focal lengths are called wide-angle lenses. Lenses with longer focal lengths have a narrower field of view and are called telephoto lenses. What they show is magnified.

The specific angle of view that you see from a lens depends on your camera's sensor size. As I discuss in Book 1, Chapter 1, smaller sensors appear to crop scenes compared to larger sensors. This means that you see a different angle of view when using a lens with the same focal length. Go back and have another look at Figure 1-9 in Book 1, Chapter 1 to see the difference.

When you're out taking photos, the angle of view doesn't really matter. Zoom in and out to take the photos you want. I bring the angle-of-view concept up to let you know that when discussing lenses with particular focal lengths, you need to know what type of camera a person is referring to. When someone raves that 85mm lenses are perfect portrait lenses on a full-frame camera, realize that you would get the same photos at 50mm on a cropped-frame camera. To convert a cropped-frame focal length to its 35mm equivalent focal length, multiply the focal length of the lens by the crop factor of the camera. To find out what would lens would take the same photos on your camera, divide the equivalent focal length by your crop camera's factor. For example, if you are interested in replicating the look and feel of classic 50mm film photography on your Canon APS-C camera with a crop factor of 1.6x, divide the focal length of the full-frame 50mm lens by 1.6 to get 31.25mm. That's the focal length that you should be shooting at.

Aperture

Camera lenses have an adjustable aperture — an opening — in their center to allow light to pass into the camera body. The relative size of the aperture is expressed as a number called an *f-number* or *f-stop.* It is not a direct measurement but rather a ratio of the focal length of the lens to the diameter of the aperture. F-numbers are written with the letter f, and then a forward slash, and then the value, like this: f/8 or f/5.6. Sometimes the aperture is written with a capital *F* and without the slash: F2.8. The tricky thing for new photographers to remember is that larger f-numbers let in less light than smaller ones. For example, f/8 lets in less light than f/5.6 does.

Lenses like the Canon EF-S 18-55mm f/3.5-5.6 list a range of apertures. These are the maximum apertures possible at each of the focal length limits. In this case, the first aperture, f/3.5, is the largest aperture possible when the lens is zoomed out to 18mm. The second aperture, f/5.6, is the largest aperture possible when the lens is zoomed in to 55mm.

Some lenses are listed with a single aperture, like the NIKKOR 50mm f/1.4G. The f-number shown is the largest aperture that the lens can use, whether it is a prime lens or a zoom lens. You have to look into the specification to find the minimum aperture. All prime lenses list a single aperture. Some high-quality zoom lenses feature a constant aperture, which means that the f-stop doesn't change, regardless of how much you zoom. For example, many professionals own a Canon 70-200mm f/2.8 lens.

Knowing the largest aperture that a lens is capable of is important because it gives you an indication of how well the lens performs. Lenses that let in a lot of light give you more flexibility as a photographer.

Image stabilization

Some camera manufacturers feature lens-mounted image stabilization whereas others implement it within the camera body. In the latter case, you will not see image stabilization listed as part of the lens name or present anywhere physically on the lens. In the former case, you can rest assured that companies proudly announce the fact as part of their lens naming scheme. Many wide-angle, prime, some mid-range focal-length zoom lenses, and less expensive telephoto lenses do not normally have image stabilization.

Nikon uses the term Vibration Reduction, abbreviated as VR. Canon calls its feature Image Stabilization, abbreviated as IS. Depending on the lens, you may be able to select specific IS modes, from 1 to 3. Each is optimized to counter a particular type of movement. You will not see VR or IS on any Nikon or Canon lens that does not have image stabilization.

Third-party lens manufacturers may or may not have image stabilization technology. Sigma lenses with image stabilization are labeled OS, for Optical Stabilization. Tamron calls its stabilization technology Vibration Compensation (VC). Tokina lenses equipped with a Vibration Correction Module (VCM) are stabilized.

When companies say their image stabilization features reduce shake and vibration by a number of stops, you can lower the shutter speed by that many stops and still take a sharp photo. Of course, it doesn't always work as well as advertised, and there is a limit to how slowly you can shoot without a tripod or other support even if you have image stabilization engaged. The effectiveness also depends on what type and how much movement is encountered. Do not expect great results if you are doing jumping jacks.

TECHNICAL STUFF

An old-school rule of thumb suggests not setting the shutter speed slower than the inverse of your 35mm-equivalent focal length when shooting handheld. That works out to using a minimum shutter speed of 1/80 second with a 50mm lens on a Canon APS-C camera that has a crop factor of 1.6. If you use 1/80 second as your unaided minimum shutter speed and then engage image stabilization whose effectiveness is up to two stops, you can theoretically slow the shutter speed to 1/20 second without blurring. Not bad.

Other identifiers

A number of other lens identifiers may make it into the name. A few of them are:

>> **Quality:** Canon L-series lenses are their highest quality product. Sony designates its high-end lens series as G Master.

>> **Type:** Nikon identifies the type of lens by a letter that immediately follows the aperture of the lens. For example, the 50mm f/1.4G lens is type G. The latest is E-type, which has a different type of interior aperture mechanism than prior lenses (electromagnetic instead of mechanical), enabling smooth and constant control over the aperture by the camera. Its G-type lenses were the first to do away with a manual aperture control ring. You have to set the aperture from the camera, not on the lens. Older D-type lenses have a combination of new (autofocus) and old (most have a manual aperture ring) technologies and are still very popular.

>> **Autofocus motor:** Canon uses two autofocus motor technologies: USM and STM. Nikon lenses also have two types of autofocus motors: AF-S (Auto Focus—Silent Wave) and AF-P (Auto Focus—Pulse). Consumer-level Nikon camera bodies do not have internal focus motors and require AF-S or AF-P (as opposed to simply AF) lenses for autofocus to function. Pentax lens motors are designated DC or SDM.

>> **Glass:** Some companies put additional identifiers in the lens name to showcase their glass quality or coatings. Nikon, for example, uses ED to indicate Extra-low Dispersion glass, which resists chromatic aberrations. Pentax lenses can have special HD or SP coatings.

>> **Sensor size compatibility:** Nikon labels lenses designed to work best with cropped-frame dSLRs with DX. DX lenses can be used on FX camera bodies in crop mode. Canon uses the EF-S mount identifier similarly, except that EF-S lenses are not compatible with full-frame cameras. Sony DT lenses can be used with cropped and full-frame cameras (you will get a cropped photo in that case, however).

>> **Macro:** Some lenses are identified by the term *macro.* This means that they are designed to get in close to focus and reproduce what they capture nearer to actual size than other lenses. Nikon names its macro lenses *micro.*

I don't have room to put every combination of identifier from all manufacturers. Take the knowledge you've gained from this small section to help you research more lens terminology on your own.

Other lens characteristics

If you look at the supporting product page for a lens or read the manual, you'll run across other specifications that describe even more characteristics. You may be interested in knowing these facts about the lens:

>> **Filter diameter:** Identifies the diameter, in millimeters, of the screw-in filter compatible with the lens.

>> **Minimum focusing distance:** The closest distance the lens can focus at.

>> **Minimum aperture:** The smallest aperture you can set the lens to. You'll often find lenses that can shrink their aperture to f/16, f/22, or even f/32. Knowing the maximum aperture is typically far more important. However, minimum aperture gives you an indication of how the lens will perform in some situations, like on the surface of the sun where the lighting is really intense.

>> **Construction details:** Information about the number of optical elements in the lens, which are often arranged into groups.

>> **Angle of view/field of view:** Angle of view measures, in degrees, the width of your view through the lens, either horizontally, vertically, or diagonally. Field of view describes the size of the area captured at a known distance. If you shine a flashlight against a wall, the angle of view tells you how wide or narrow the beam is. The field of view is how much wall you can light, which changes if you move forward or back. Angle of view is irrespective of distance.

Older lenses

Older lenses may have different markings than you're used to. The lens in Figure 3-4, for example, has markings on the front that help identify the lens. The side, shown in Figure 3-5, has no identifying information. The colorful scales and numbers show the focal distance, depth of field, and aperture. Be prepared to do some extra research to make sure that any lenses you look at are compatible with your camera body or any you plan to purchase. Although this lens was manufactured in 1981 or so, it still works on many Nikon dSLRs.

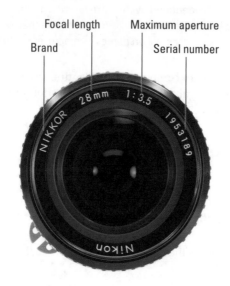

FIGURE 3-4: You may have to research old lenses for more information.

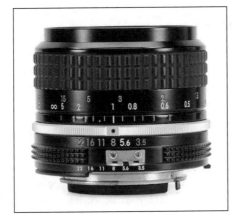

Categorizing Lenses

This section explains and summarizes many of the most-used digital SLR lens categories in use today. It's pretty helpful to get to know how manufacturers categorize their lenses and how photographers use them.

In Table 3-1, I have organized lenses into general categories based on their focal. Notice that different sensor sizes may cause a lens to be placed in a different category. There are many types of zoom and prime lenses, ranging from those that specialize in wide angles, to general purpose, to telephoto.

TABLE 3-1 **Rough Focal Length Categories**

Category	Full-frame	APS-C	Four Thirds / Micro Four Thirds
Ultra wide-angle	20mm and below	15mm and below	10mm and below
Wide-angle	20–40mm	15–25mm	10–20mm
Normal	40–60mm	25–40mm	20–30mm
Near/medium telephoto	60–200mm	40–135mm	30–100mm
Telephoto	200–300mm	135–200mm	100–150mm
Super telephoto	300mm and up	200mm and up	150mm and over

Some lenses cross category boundaries. For example, the Canon EF-S 18-135mm f/3.5-5.6 IS USM lens is able to shoot wide-angle through normal and all the way into medium telephoto focal lengths.

Normal lenses

Lenses with focal length values approximately the same as the diagonal measurement of the image sensor are considered *normal* lenses. They are called normal because they cover the same basic field of view as the human eye. Most kit lenses cover the entire normal focal length range of the camera they are bundled with.

For full-frame cameras, 50mm lenses are the gold standard. A history and tradition of fantastic photography is built around these lenses. If you're using a zoom lens, anywhere between 40–60mm puts you in the normal range. For cameras with cropped-frame sensors, what appears normal depends on the crop factor. For crop factors of 1.5x and 1.6x, set your zoom lens between about 25mm and 40mm. If you want to use a prime lens, 35mm puts you very close to that classic normal lens look. Figure 3-6 shows a nice portrait taken with a cropped-frame dSLR at 35mm — right in the middle of the normal range. For Four Thirds and Micro Four Thirds cameras with crop factors of 2.0x, zoom lenses between 20mm and 30mm fit into this category. If you want a normal Four Thirds prime lens, look for something around 25mm.

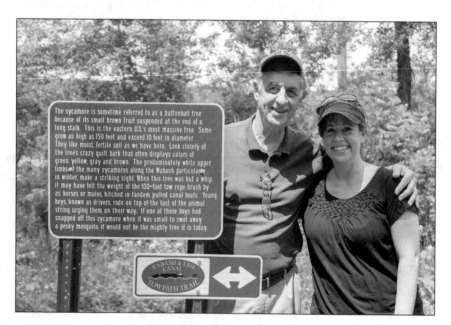

FIGURE 3-6: Normal focal lengths produce classic photos.

Wide-angle lenses

Focal-length values that are less than the diagonal measurement of the image sensor are considered *wide-angle.* Wide-angle lenses have impressive angles of view and can capture large amounts of scenery. They are, however, prone to distortion. Most kit lenses have the ability to shoot wide-angle shots.

For full-frame cameras, wide-angle territory covers everything between 20 and 40mm. I took the shot in Figure 3-7 using a full-frame camera with 28-105mm lens set to 28mm. Although not extreme, the focal length is still wide enough to capture the river quite nicely. For APS-C sensors, wide-angle lenses are between 15mm and 25mm. You would want to use a 24mm lens to take this photo. Four Thirds and Micro Four Third lenses are considered wide-angle between 10 and 20mm.

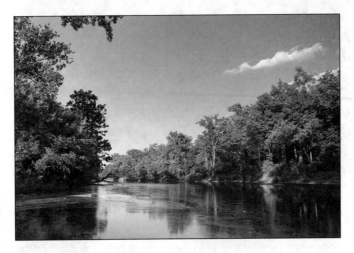

FIGURE 3-7: Wide-angles capture scenic vistas.

Some lenses are considered ultra wide-angle lenses. These lenses are incredibly fun to use, and capture sweeping landscapes and interiors of all sizes beautifully. Their focal lengths are below 20mm for full-frame, below 15 mm for APS-C cameras, and below 10mm for Four Thirds. For more on shooting with wide-angle lenses, turn to Book 2, Chapter 2.

Telephoto lenses

Lenses with focal length values greater than the diagonal measurement of the image sensor are considered *telephoto* lenses. Dedicated telephoto lenses abound, and most everyday kit lenses can reach into telephoto range when they are fully zoomed in.

For full-frame cameras, focal lengths greater than 60mm or so are considered telephoto. I took the photo shown in Figure 3-8 using a full-frame camera. The focal length is 73mm — ideal for portraits. For APS-C cameras, telephoto focal lengths start at approximately 40mm. Four Thirds and Micro Four Thirds cameras begin the telephoto range around 30mm. Initially, the telephoto range is called *near* or *medium* telephoto. As you continue to move into longer focal lengths, the category changes to *telephoto*, and then *super-telephoto* (have a glance back to Table 3-1 to see the focal lengths of these categories). Turn to Book 2, Chapter 4 to learn more about telephoto lenses.

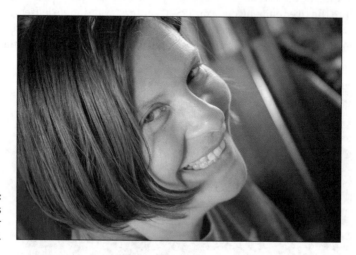

FIGURE 3-8:
Near telephotos are great for portraits.

Prime lenses

A *prime* lens (see Figure 3-9) has a fixed focal length. You can't zoom in or out with prime lenses. When you compose your shots, you have to move closer or farther away to zoom in and out. Its magnification level is fixed from the day you buy it until your grandkids sell it on eBay.

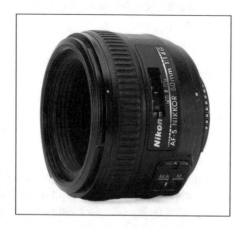

FIGURE 3-9:
Prime lenses do not zoom in or out.

Prime lenses specialize. Everything is optimized for the lens to produce the best photos at its focal length. The downside to prime lenses is the major reason that zoom lenses are so popular: People get tired of being limited to a single focal length and the time it takes to swap lenses when they want to change it.

Prime lenses come in a wide variety of focal lengths. There are wide-angle primes, normal primes, portrait primes in the near telephoto range, and all kinds of telephoto and super-telephoto prime lenses. When shopping for prime lenses, look for lenses with the focal lengths that you find yourself using the most. For example, you might like shooting portraits at 50mm or landscapes at 28mm. Remember to look for focal lengths appropriate to your camera's crop factor.

General-purpose zoom lenses

General-purpose zoom lenses (see Figure 3-10), also called *standard zoom* lenses, excel in versatility. Most kit lenses sold are in this category. They include wide-angle, normal, and near-telephoto focal lengths. It's hard to go wrong with general-purpose zoom lenses.

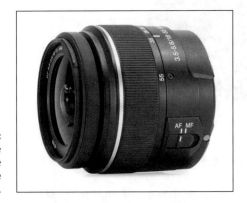

FIGURE 3-10: General-purpose zoom lenses are versatile and take good photos.

Wide-angle zoom lenses

A *wide-angle zoom* lens zooms in and out, just as general-purpose zoom lenses do, but with a focal-length range that's limited to wide-angle territory. This zooming capability gives them a versatility that a wide-angle prime lens won't have. Being able to zoom in and out when you're capturing a landscape or a tight interior is a welcome feature because you're often limited in how you can move in relation to the scene. Ultra wide-angle zoom lenses (see Figure 3-11) give you expanded wide-angle coverage. Wide-angle zoom lenses really are great at what they do and fun to use. I heartily recommend them.

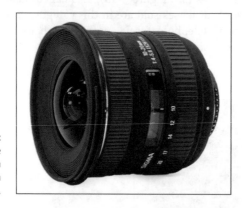

FIGURE 3-11:
A wide-angle zoom lens is an excellent addition to your bag.

Telephoto zoom lenses

Typical *telephoto zoom* lenses operate over a huge range of telephoto focal lengths. There is a lot of variety among telephoto zooms, both in the starting and ending focal lengths. You'll find some that specialize in the near–telephoto range, some that extend into telephoto and super–telephoto focal lengths, and more.

Specialty lenses

Other specialty lenses offer creative and artistic uses:

>> **Cinema lenses,** also known as Cine lenses, are specialized lenses optimized to shoot movies. In contrast to still photographers, who largely use autofocus, professional

filmmakers and videographers primarily focus manually. This approach requires lenses wih large focus rings and more precise aperture controls.

>> **Macro** lenses specialize in capturing extreme close-up photos of objects. Although they don't generally magnify, macro lenses appear to do so because the subjects look so much larger than normal. Macro lenses achieve this look because they have a *reproduction ratio* (the size of an object on the sensor compared to the actual size) as close to 1:1 as possible. Most macro lenses are primes.

>> **Fisheye** lenses capture scenes with an angle of view approaching 180-degrees. The photos are characterized by extreme barrel distortion, which makes the center of the photo bulge, often to the point where the entire photo turns into a circle.

>> **Tilt-shift** lenses (see Figure 3-12) can change the orientation of the focal plane by tilting. The effect of angling the focal plane is to completely discombobulate what should be in focus compared to a normal lens. Objects can look surreal and toylike. These lenses can also move the imaging circle of the lens that hits the camera's image sensor by shifting, thereby allowing you to move the subject's location within the photo without moving the camera. The shift effect is useful when photographing subjects that can easily distort if you have to point the camera up or down to capture them.

>> **Pinhole** lenses don't actually have a lens. They have a small hole in them, about the size of a pinhole (thus the name). You have no way to zoom in and out, and you cannot focus. Basically, they are a plastic body cover with a pinhole in it. It's pretty easy to make one yourself if you want to try it out. Expect longer exposure times or higher ISO speeds because of the small aperture. Pinhole lenses create soft, dreamy photos.

>> **Creative lenses** break the mold of most traditional lens types. Here are a few popular types:

- **Lensbaby** lenses were originally based around a mechanism that resembled a bellows. Later, the Composer and Composer Pro were released, which were also manual focus but were made using a swivel ball mechanism. The Composer Pro mounts directly to the camera's lens mount and holds different interchangeable optics with varying properties. You can angle the lens in different ways, which moves the focal plane somewhat as a tilt-shift lens does. Optics range from the Sweet 35 to pinhole, plastic, and double-glass. The effects are endless. Lensbaby also produces stand-alone lenses like the Velvet 85 and Twist 60. They are super creative and fun to play with.

- **Holga** cameras are cheap plastic film cameras that have a large following. They create very distinctive photos with dark corners and a soft focus. You can join the fun by mounting a plastic Holga dSLR lens on your camera. Very cool. I love mine.

- **Diana+** are similar to Holga lenses but have much longer effective focal lengths. For example, the Diana+ fisheye lens acts like a standard lens on a dSLR. Diana+ lenses are meant for dreamy and artistic photos.

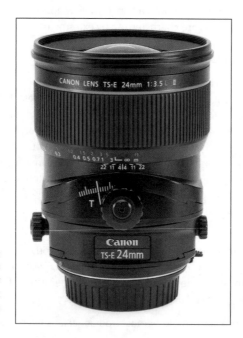

FIGURE 3-12: Tilt-shift lenses are specialty lenses that capture unique photos.

LOVING LENSES

You might have noticed that I have praised every type of lens I have described. That's because I love them all. Each serves a purpose. Your challenge as a photographer (well, one of many) is to find the lens that suits *your* purpose, whether that's shooting artistic shots, portraits, landscapes, or fast-moving action.

Looking at Lens Anatomy

Knowing what the different parts and pieces on lenses are is as important as knowing what all the buttons, dials, and displays on your camera body are for. Depending on the lens you have, it might have these features (see Figures 3-13, 3-14, 3-15, and 3-16 for reference):

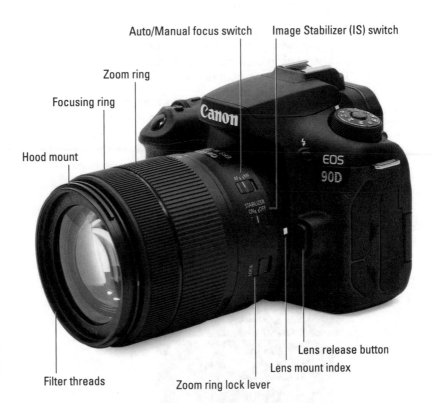

Auto/Manual focus switch

Image Stabilizer (IS) switch

Zoom ring

Focusing ring

Hood mount

Lens release button

Lens mount index

Filter threads

Zoom ring lock lever

FIGURE 3-13: This kit lens has a number of features to learn.

>> **Hood mount:** Many lenses come with a detachable lens hood, which usually rotates on with a quarter- or half-turn. Lens hoods block stray light from entering the lens and can protect your lens if you bump it against something or drop the camera.

>> **Filter threads:** Most lenses mount screw-in filters at the front. Filter size is measured in millimeters. On some lenses (those with very large front diameters, for instance), filters go toward the rear and are dropped in with special trays.

>> **Focus mode switch:** Lets you switch between manual and auto focus. Some telephoto lenses let you choose a distance region. Not all lenses have this switch.

>> **Zoom ring:** On zoom lenses, the zoom ring changes the focal length, which lets you zoom in and out. Depending on the lens, the zoom ring may be larger than the focus ring. Some lenses do not turn when they zoom in and out, but rather push or pull.

>> **Focusing ring:** Called a focus ring by Nikon and others. Use this ring to focus manually. In the days when manual focus was the only option, focus rings were often larger than zoom rings. Their importance is generally diminished now, so they've become much smaller on lenses that autofocus.

>> **Vibration reduction (VR) or image stabilization (IS) switch:** This switch turns on the lens's internal vibration reduction or image-stabilization feature. When your camera is mounted on a tripod and you are not panning or moving it, you should turn off this feature. Check your lens manual for details. Some Nikon lenses, for example, have a special tripod mode that changes what type of movement the lens will counteract.

>> **Focal-length scale:** Zoom lenses show you what your lens's focal length is, as shown in Figure 3-14. Line up the number with the focal length index line.

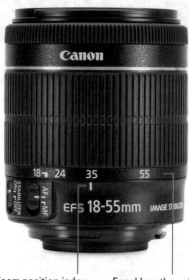

FIGURE 3-14: The focal-length scale is on top of the lens.

Zoom position index   Focal length scale

>> **Distance or depth-of-field scale:** The scale (see Figure 3-15) shows you the *focal plane distance* (the distance that the lens is focused at, measured from the camera sensor) and sometimes the depth of field. Though this feature is handy at times, it's becoming much less prominent on new lenses.

Distance scale

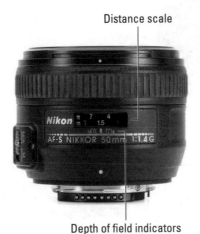

Depth of field indicators

FIGURE 3-15: Some lenses give distance and depth-of-field information.

>> **Lock switch:** Some lenses let you lock in the current focal length. This prevents *focal length creep* when you're pointing the camera down. Some cameras let you lock in the focus, as opposed to the focal length.

>> **Mount:** The rear of the lens is the mount, which locks into the camera. Keep the rear cover on lenses when not in use.

>> **Lens mount index:** The side or rear of the lens usually has a dot. Match it to the corresponding mark on the camera mount before inserting it into the camera.

>> **CPU contacts:** These little gizmos send computerized data to the camera from the lens. See Figure 3-16.

CPU contacts are critical to modern lenses. Don't bend them, break them, or otherwise mess with them. Keep them covered.

WARNING

>> **Aperture ring:** Older lenses as well as some new or specialized lenses have an aperture ring on the lens. Newer, computerized lenses forego it — you have to set the aperture in-camera.

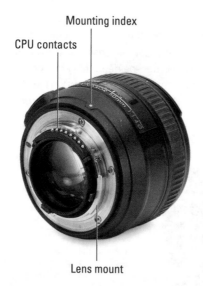

CPU contacts

Mounting index

Lens mount

FIGURE 3-16:
Modern lenses and dSLRs communicate through these contacts.

Working with Lenses

The skills you use when handling lenses are just as important as those you use when handling the camera body. This section covers how to grip your lenses; mount and remove your lenses; zoom in and out; switch from auto to manual focus; manually focus; and activate image stabilization. When you treat your lenses well, they will give you a lifetime of service.

WARNING

Lenses are round and they like to roll. Take care not to lay them on their side next to a table edge. Some lenses are tall and can be knocked over easily. Please secure your flailing arms, loose elbows, cats, kids, flying squirrels, and other forms of clumsiness when you set lenses down. Place your unattached lenses in their cases, your camera bag, or other suitable storage container to secure them.

Getting a grip

This section prepares you to mount and remove lenses by suggesting two different types of grips. I've written the material from the perspective of removing a lens, which is the more perilous task. To use these grips when attaching lenses, put your hands in the same positions. The difference is that when you grab the lens with your right hand, it's not attached to the camera. Your right hand will move it into position while your left hand (and possibly body) steady the camera.

Grip 1

Refer to Figure 3-17 to see one of the recommended grips and follow these steps to execute it:

1. **Hold the camera's left side with your left hand.**

    Press its right side in to your body for additional support.

2. **Put your left thumb on top of the cameras (in this case, on the mode dial) and stretch your left pinky underneath the camera for additional grip.**

    The camera will be facing to your right. Use your left index finger to press the lens-release button. If the lens-release button is on the side of the shutter button (Pentax cameras), use your right index finger or knuckle.

3. **Use an overhand grip on the lens the way you would put your hand on a railing.**

    The C formed by your right index finger and thumb grips the lens from the top and faces the camera body.

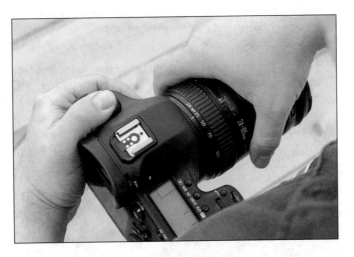

FIGURE 3-17:
Grip 1 uses your body to help support the camera.

Grip 2

Refer to Figure 3-18 to see the second recommended grip. This grip is similar to Grip 1 in that the camera faces to the right. However, rather than use your body for support, your repositioned left hand does all the heavy lifting. This grip does not work as well with cameras that have their lens-release buttons on the

Learning about Lenses

shutter-button side of the camera, such as Pentax dSLRs. I explain how you should change the grip as I go along.

1. **Angle the camera and grip it in your left hand.**

The main point of initial contact is the skin between the thumb and index finger. Your left palm extends down the camera back while your left thumb wraps over the top of the camera. In this case, the base of my left thumb covers the LCD panel.

Pentax users should place their left thumb on the back of the camera, toward the top, rather than wrap it around. This gives you the reach you'll need later. If you have large hands, you might be able to put your thumb on top of the camera.

2. **Firmly grip the camera with your left thumb.**

This is where you get most of the strength of this grip.

3. **Reach down with the fingers on your left hand to the back of the camera and grab the bottom.**

Your left index finger rests on the back monitor. Use it to stabilize things. You should be able to hold the entire weight of the camera with this hand. (It feels like you're shaking hands with the camera, using your left hand.)

If using a Pentax camera, you should wrap your left fingers farther under the camera than shown. You need to be able to reach the lens-release button with the middle finger on your left hand. Grip the camera with the ring and pinky fingers on your left hand. The strength of your grip comes from the base of the left palm and those two fingers.

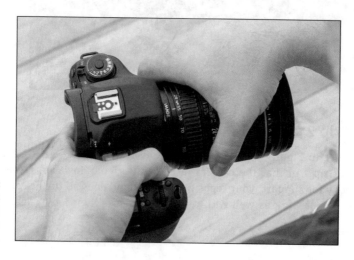

FIGURE 3-18: Grip 2 requires your left hand to support the camera.

4. **Put your right hand on top of the lens.**

   Grip the lens with your right index finger near the lens collar (the part of the lens that's nearest the camera body). Your right thumb should be on the side of the lens nearest you.

5. **Use the knuckle on your right index finger to press the lens-release button when you're removing a lens.**

   The last part sounds dodgy until you do it. Then it feels totally natural. If you're using a Pentax camera, use the middle finger on your left hand to reach underneath the camera toward the front.

Tips and pointers

Here are some things to keep in mind when using these grips:

>> If you don't feel like you can hold the camera and remove or attach lenses without dropping something, mount the camera on a tripod or set it down. You have no reason to feel embarrassed.

>> Try angling the front of the camera down a bit. Although it may feel awkward at first, this position helps prevent dust and other debris from getting into the camera.

>> Practice so that you can attach and remove lenses without angling the camera up to see what you're doing. After some experience, you should be able to attach and remove lenses while blindfolded.

>> Your grip doesn't have to be as steady when changing lenses on smaller cameras. You can sort of wing it. However, heavy cameras and lenses offer more of a challenge.

>> If the camera is mounted on a tripod, most of the handholding and camera-supporting descriptions in this section are moot. The camera should be well supported by the tripod. Hold tightly to the lens, however.

>> If you're using a lens-mounted support (monopod or other), turn the camera instead of the lens to remove it.

Mounting a lens

Although mounting lenses isn't difficult, it can be a little frightening until you get used to it. I remember being nervous about the camera's insides being open to the world while I made a lens swap. Don't be. Unless you're in a dust storm or outside in the rain with no cover when changing lenses, the camera will survive. Just don't drop the lens. (No pressure.)

The key is to be quick without rushing and to be firm without being harsh. Got it?

Here's how to attach a lens to a digital SLR camera:

1. **Turn off the camera.**

   If you forget (I do all the time), it isn't the end of the world. Ideally, though, the power is off.

2. **Remove the camera body cap or lens, if one is attached.**

   Most body caps twist off. Some have a locking function. Put away the cap or lens, if necessary. See the next section for how-to steps on removing lenses.

3. **Quickly remove the rear lens cap from the lens.**

   Place the cap on a table, in your camera bag, or in your pocket for safekeeping.

   I take the rear lens cap off most lenses with my right thumb and index finger while palming the lens in the same hand. If I can do it (my hands aren't huge), you can. Caveat: I don't palm heavy or incredibly expensive lenses, just the normal variety, and I don't hold them over a cliff or sea of boiling lava when I do this in case I drop something.

4. **Get your grip on.**

   In other words, grip the camera and lens using one of the hand grips described in the "Getting a grip" section, earlier in this chapter.

5. **Line up the mounting index on the lens with the one on the camera body, if it exists.**

   The Canon EOS 90D is shown in Figure 3-19. Canon APS-C cameras can mount two types of EF lenses. EF lenses use the round, red index and EF-S lenses use the square, white index.

6. **Insert the lens onto the mount.**

   You feel the lens and the camera fit together if they're properly lined up.

7. **Rotate the lens in the proper direction until it locks and clicks in place.**

   You should hear a click or feel it lock. Don't mess with the lens-release button as you mount the lens.

   Nikon lenses rotate toward the shutter release button to lock. Others lenses rotate toward the opposite side, which feels more natural to me because I've said "righty-tighty, lefty-loosey" all my life.

8. **When you're ready, turn the camera on and remove the lens cap from the lens.**

   Check and set switches on the lens, such as autofocus or vibration reduction. You're ready to shoot.

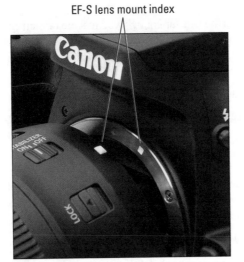

EF-S lens mount index

FIGURE 3-19:
Carefully line up the index marks.

Removing a lens

Taking a lens off is pretty easy. If you're feeling nervous, practice over a soft bed or couch. Follow these steps to remove a lens:

1. **Turn off the camera.**

2. **Get your grip on.**

   In other words, grip the camera and lens using one of the methods suggested in "Getting a grip," earlier in the chapter. Make sure that you have a good hold on both camera and lens.

   If you like, set the camera on a table for support. As you become more comfortable with changing lenses, you'll be able to manage the camera and lens in a variety of situations, such as when using a tripod or a strap. To limit the amount of dust that might make it into your camera, don't set or point the camera upwards without a lens mounted.

3. **Press and hold the lens-release button.**

   Make sure to continue holding the lens as you press the release button so that it doesn't accidentally fall out. I press the button with my left index finger or the knuckle of my right index finger, which is connected to the hand that is holding the lens.

4. **Turn the lens until it releases from the mount.**

   After the lens turns a bit, you don't need to hold the lens-release button. Nikon lenses turn away from the shutter release button when you remove them. Other types turn toward the shutter release button.

When you've turned the lens far enough, you feel the tension ease and the lens float free within the mount. You might hear the lens come up against the mount stops. The mounting index will line up between the lens and the camera body.

5. **Pull the lens straight away from the camera body.**

   If you angle the lens as you take it out, you might damage the sensitive contacts on the rear of the lens, the collar, or the mount.

6. **Secure the lens.**

   Put the rear lens cap on quickly and set the lens in a safe place. If that spot is in your camera bag, you're done with it. Otherwise, make sure to pack it away safely when you take care of the camera body.

7. **Replace the body cap or attach another lens.**

   Don't leave the camera open to the elements. Always replace the body cap or mount another lens on the body right away.

Zooming in and out

Use the zoom ring on the lens to zoom in or out. Most lenses have their zoom ring closer to the base of the lens, which is shown in Figure 3-20. Some zoom rings are about as large as the lens. Typically, you'll turn the zoom ring toward the shutter release button to zoom out and turn it away from the shutter release button to zoom in. Many lenses actually extend (see Figure 3-21) and retract as you zoom them. Others move internally.

Focal lengths are often printed on the lens's zoom ring. Read your current focal length by noting the number (extrapolate if you're between printed numbers) lined up with the zoom position index.

I'm holding the camera in Figure 3-21 with my left hand on the zoom ring. Unless you're manually focusing, keep your hand here so that you can zoom in and out quickly if using a zoom lens. This position works well for looking through the viewfinder and using autofocus.

If you're manually focusing, zoom in or out first and then move your hand to the focus ring, as shown in the next section.

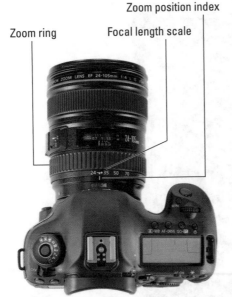

Zoom position index

Zoom ring   Focal length scale

FIGURE 3-20:
Zoom lenses have
a focal length
scale on top.

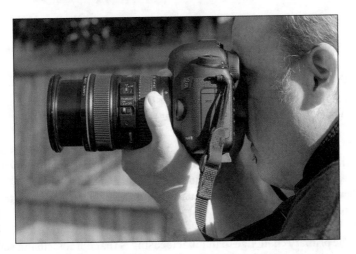

FIGURE 3-21:
Zooming in using
my left hand.

Switching from auto to manual focus

To change to manual focus, switch the focus mode switch on your lens to MF, as
shown in Figure 3-22. Some cameras have a second switch on the camera body.
That enables the camera to support lenses without a focus mode switch.

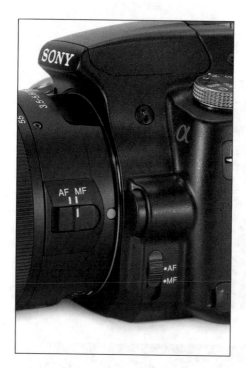

FIGURE 3-22:
Switch to MF
to take total
focusing control.

Manually focusing

Despite how powerful modern AF systems are, there are situations when you need to step in and manually focus to get the best photo.

Mechanically, focusing is pretty simple. Turn the focus ring one way or the other until your subject is in focus. Your camera may have a manual focus–confirmation feature, which gives you an audible or visual signal when the AF point over your subject comes into focus. Manually select the AF point you want to use beforehand for best results.

The primary challenge to manual focusing is that dSLR focusing screens are not all that helpful. Old SLRs were designed with viewfinder focusing screen optimized for manual focus. My older Nikon FE 2, for example, has three manual-focus aids that help me see when the subject is in focus: a split-image rangefinder, a micro-prism collar, and a matte field. In addition, manually focusing can be difficult when the light is dim.

Manually focusing changes how you hold and support the camera because your fingers have to control the focus ring. I'm holding the camera horizontally in Figure 3-23. My right hand is supporting the weight of the camera while the fingers of my left hand focus and assist in weight relief. In Figure 3-24, I am holding the camera vertically. The fingers of my right hand stiffen and hook around the front of the grip. The camera can almost hang off them. The left hand performs the same focusing task.

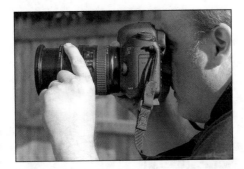

FIGURE 3-23: Manually focus in horizontal hold.

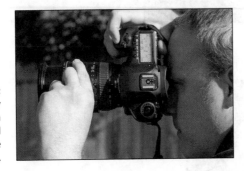

FIGURE 3-24: Manually focusing in vertical hold takes more practice.

I recommend zooming in and checking your focus using the camera's Live View feature and monitor when you're using a tripod. A magnified view makes it easy to see when things are in good focus, as shown in Figure 3-25. If your camera has a feature called Focus Peaking, enable it to have the camera show edges that are in focus. They will be highlighted on the monitor, which makes manually focusing easier.

Activating lens-based image stabilization

To turn on lens-based image stabilization, set the appropriate switch on your lens to On. See Figure 3-26.

Some lenses may have more than one IS mode. Some Canon telephoto lenses, for example, have several different types. Mode 1 is normal. Mode 2 enables you to pan and follow a subject without the IS system trying to counter the sweeping motion of the camera. Mode 3 engages only when you have the shutter button pressed fully to take a shot. Hybrid IS (available on a Canon macro lens) corrects for the type of lateral shifts experienced in macro photography instead of rotational movements from camera shake.

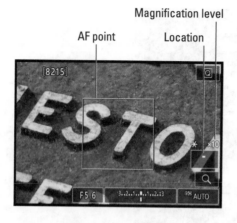

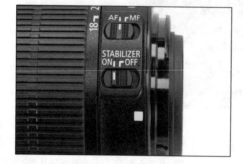

FIGURE 3-25: This shot is in excellent focus thanks to magnifying the Live View.

FIGURE 3-26: Engage the stabilizer!

Cleaning Lenses

Despite your best efforts, your lenses are going to get smudged and dirty with use. Don't beat yourself up over it. It happens all the time to everyone. Make cleaning your lenses part of your routine, just like charging your camera's battery.

REMEMBER

You should become comfortable cleaning lenses whether or not they are attached to the camera. You will rarely need to clean the rear lens element (it's normally covered by a cap or the camera), but you should check it occasionally. Make a habit of checking front and rear lens caps as well as the camera body cap for dust and debris. To clean a lens, follow these steps:

1. **Very gently, blow or dust the lens surface clean, as shown in Figure 3-27.**

   The idea here is to remove anything that might scratch the lens when you clean the surface. You can use a soft-bristled lens-cleaning brush or a blower. Do not use canned air because the propellant can shoot out of the can and damage the lens or camera.

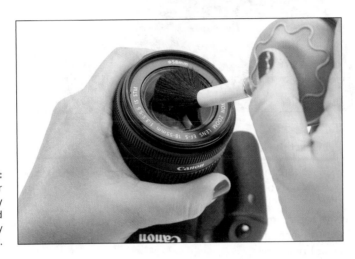

FIGURE 3-27: Brushing or blowing gently removes grit and other scratchy things.

2. **If needed, apply lens-cleaning solution to your preferred wipe or cloth.**

   Don't overdo it. A little goes a long way, and you can always reapply and continue cleaning. Avoid spraying the solution on the lens. You don't want fluid seeping into spots where you can't remove it. Some lens-cleaning pads come pre-moistened. If you're using a microfiber lens or glasses cleaning cloth, you may not need to use a solution — but it should be moist. Lightly dampen the cloth with water before you clean.

WARNING

   Lens manufacturers recommend against using paint thinner, benzene, or organic solvents when cleaning. Be wary of using other potent chemicals on lenses with coatings.

3. **Clean the lens with a clean wipe, pad, or other lens-cleaning cloth, as shown in Figure 3-28.**

   Some recommend cleaning from the center out. Others recommend wiping from the outside in, using a circular motion. If the lens is badly smudged and has oil from your fingers, you may need to clean it two or three times. Be patient and don't overdo it. The oil will come off.

   You can buy cleaning pens that typically have a brush on one end and a rubbery cleaning tip that wipes the surface of the lens on the other. LensPen (www.lenspen.com) has a number of handy products that work well.

Learning about Lenses

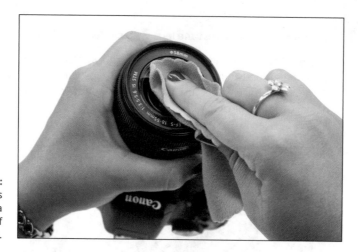

FIGURE 3-28:
Cleaning lenses
should be a
regular part of
your routine.

4. **Inspect the lens.**

   Make sure that the lens is clean and dry. Then get back to shooting or put the
   cover back on.

TIP

Always carry a microfiber lens-cleaning cloth with you when you're out shooting.
Use it to touch up the front of your lens if you need to. If you see dust or debris,
blow or brush first.

Chapter **4**

Exploring Menus and Camera Settings

Don't let the fact that digital SLRs are powerful electronic devices loaded with features freak you out too much. So are cars, HDTVs, smartphones, gaming systems, tablets, and laptops. Even refrigerators, washers, dryers, and doorbells have gotten into the act. People have grown used to it. This isn't 1984, when people couldn't set the timer on their VCRs.

But, like everything else, you have to communicate with your digital SLR. This chapter walks you through basic options of how to set it up and get going. You'll use a series of menus to tell it who you are, set the time, format memory cards, set the image quality, and accomplish a whole host of other tasks.

Understanding How Menus Are Organized

Camera manufacturers organize dSLR menus into convenient categories. The goal is to make it easier for you to find things. A large portion of dSLRs sold today share a handful of common menu groups:

> » **Shooting:** Shooting menus are devoted to common photo settings such as Image Quality, White Balance, Noise Reduction, Color Space, ISO, and so forth.

Live View and Movie menus may be located with or at the end of the Shooting menu because they pertain to recording as opposed to playing back or setup.

>> **Live View:** Live View shooting involves using the camera back instead of the viewfinder. The camera will have menu options and settings unique to Live View shooting. They include features like focusing methods, options to configure the display, a metering timer, and so forth. Some cameras do not have a Live View menu, instead offering a single Shooting menu. If that's the case, you may see only Live View menu choices when you enter your camera's Live View mode.

>> **Movie:** Some cameras have a Movie menu that groups all the different movie options together. Other cameras put the movie options in the Shooting menu, but you see them only when you switch to the movie mode.

>> **Playback:** Playback menus house options that relate to image and movie playback. You'll find things like Protect Images, Rotate, Erase, and Slide Show. Sometimes retouching options are located in the Playback menu. Other cameras have a specific Retouching menu.

>> **Setup:** Setup menus include options such as Language, Help, Battery Information, Sensor Cleaning, Copyright, and more. You'll use some features only once. Others, such as Format Card, you'll use many times.

>> **Custom:** This group includes custom menus that you create, custom camera settings, and other functions.

Although common, these categories are not definitive. You may see other menu names in different cameras. Sony cameras, for example, have a few unique menus, such as Memory Card Tool and Clock Setup. You may also see Camera Settings and Wireless menus.

Finally, you may see menus and options change based on the shooting mode you've chosen. For example, Canon doesn't display advanced options when the camera is set to a Basic Zone mode. Canon cameras also change the Shooting menus when you're in Movie mode.

The features I describe in the following sections are common to most digital SLRs. You'll find major concepts grouped into separate headings, and a plethora of menu displays to illustrate the points. If you can't find a corresponding option in your camera's menu hierarchy, have a look at your manual's table of contents or index to locate it.

Opening and Using the Menu

Before getting to details about digging through specific menu choices and options to set up and configure your camera, you should familiarize yourself with the basics of accessing and navigating your camera's menu. It's pretty simple and won't take long.

Typically, here's how you get to the menu and make changes:

1. **Press the Menu button.**

Most cameras position the Menu button on the far left side of the camera, as shown on a Canon T8i in Figure 4-1. The Menu button is normally next to or just above the monitor. The Menu button is labeled. Use your left thumb to press it.

You might see the Menu button placed on the right side of the monitor. When on the right, press it with your right thumb.

Menu button

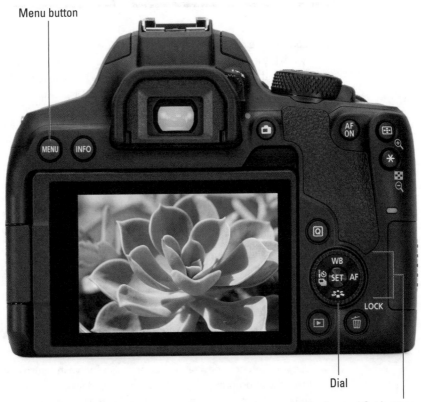

FIGURE 4-1:
This camera's Menu button is very conveniently placed.

Dial

Navigation and Set buttons

Exploring Menus and Camera Settings

Your camera's menu will appear on the back monitor or in the electronic viewfinder. It will display until the camera turns the monitor off to save power or you press a button not related to menu navigation or selection, such as the shutter button.

Figure 4-2 shows the menu of a Canon dSLR in the Guided display mode. All the menu items are available, but the camera shows additional screens to help you find what you're looking for. Because I am acting as your guide throughout this book, I've turned this and other types of guides off.

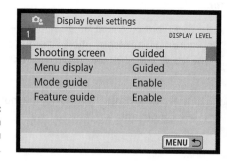
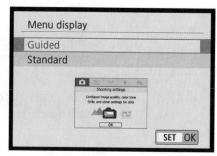

FIGURE 4-2: You may see a simplified menu display.

Contrast the menu in Guided display mode with the one shown in Figure 4-3, which is the standard Canon menu. Standard menus use color-coded tabs or icons so that you can tell at a glance what section you're in. If the menu doesn't appear, you may have to press your camera's Display or Info button to turn the monitor on.

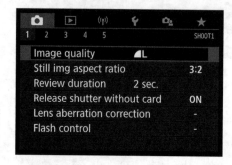

FIGURE 4-3: This is how the standard Canon menu looks.

2. **Navigate to the menu or tab that contains the option you want and highlight an option.**

   Use your camera's navigation buttons (also shown in Figure 4-1) or controller. Press the appropriate button to navigate up, down, left, or right in menus and settings. If using a touchscreen, simply tap the tab and menu you want to use. I've highlighted the Still Image Aspect Ratio option in the left image of Figure 4-4.

It is located in Shooting Menu 1. Note that the current setting is shown next to the option name.

REMEMBER

Not all navigation controllers look identical. Some cameras have separate arrow keys. Many cameras use a round dial that you can press in any of the four directions. Other cameras have a controller that acts like a little joystick. You may also be able to navigate your menu system by spinning a control dial (a.k.a. *command dial*). Navigation controllers are also called by different names: *Arrow keys, multiselector, multi-controller, four-way controller, quick control dial, arrow pad,* and *cross keys* are other examples.

You may need to turn other dials or press other buttons to get around and make selections. Check your camera's manual to see whether this is the case. For example, some Canon models use the main dial or the Quick Control button to move between tabs in the menu system.

3. **Press the Set or OK button to open the settings.**

After you navigate to the menu you want to use, activate it. Think of it as clicking your mouse. To choose an option, press your camera's Set (Canon) or OK button (Nikon). Some cameras call it the Enter or Control button. Touchscreen users can simply tap the menu option they want to use.

Choose the setting you want. In this case, four options are available: 3:2; 4:3; 16:9; and 1:1.

TIP

To cancel an operation and go back a step, you can press the Menu button. You may also be able to press the shutter release button halfway to kick yourself out of the menu system. Touchscreen users often have a return arrow you can tap.

4. **Highlight the specific setting you want to use, as shown on the right in Figure 4-4.**

The current setting (3:2) is shown in blue. The setting I have scrolled to (16:9) is highlighted. Your camera may indicate active settings and choices differently. Some cameras place checks or bullets next to the currently selected option to show that it is enabled, while others outline the current option in a different color.

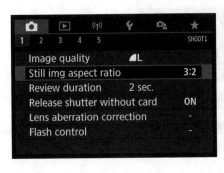
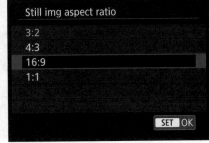

FIGURE 4-4:
Select an option you want to change, press OK, then choose a setting.

5. **Press Set or OK to change it.**

6. **Press the Menu button to exit.**

REMEMBER

I used a Canon camera to illustrate these steps. Compare it to the other menus from different cameras sprinkled throughout the chapter.

Setting Up Your Camera

When you first turn on your camera, it prompts you to set the date, time, and language. When you finish that task, you should take care of a few other things to help you get started on the right foot.

Date and time

Set the date and time correctly so that all your photos will have the proper date and time imprinted in their *metadata* (data stored in the file but not shown in the photo). Some cameras show the date and time when turned on. Set the time zone, too, and remember to enable daylight saving time, if applicable. You often see a snazzy map. Sometimes you simply choose your zone from a list. In Figure 4-5, I'm setting the proper date and time, plus the time zone I am in.

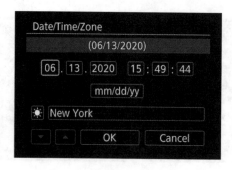

FIGURE 4-5:
Setting the date, time, and time zone.

TIP

Remember to reset the time zone if you travel, and check it on any cameras you may rent.

Language

Specify your language so that you can read all the menus and screens. The day is coming when you'll be able to turn on your dSLR and ask Siri, Cortana, Google, or Alexa to open the menu and format the memory card — just like a smartphone or tablet.

Feature guides and expanded help

If you're a seasoned photographer and don't need your camera to continually explain features or give you photography hints, turn the Feature Guide (Canon), Guide Mode (Nikon), In-Camera Guide (Sony), or Guide Display (Pentax) off. If you need a bit of assistance as you operate your camera, leave that option enabled. You can always turn it off when you're comfortable with the camera.

Review time

This feature specifies the number of seconds a photo appears on the LCD monitor immediately after you shoot. If you find yourself pressing the Playback button every time you take a photo to look at it — whether it's to check focus, brightness, or cuteness — lengthen the review time. Give yourself more than a second or two, as shown in Figure 4-6. On the other hand, if you find yourself continuously pressing the shutter button halfway to get back to taking photos, either reduce the review time or turn it off. You can always press the Playback button to review specific photos.

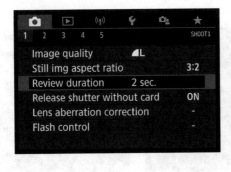
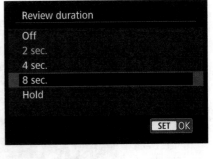

FIGURE 4-6: Setting Auto Review to 8 seconds.

Auto power off

Most dSLRs automatically turn off and save batteries after a period of inactivity. Although some cameras have a "one size fits all" setting, others allow you to customize the time. Figure 4-7 shows four different options on an inexpensive Nikon dSLR.

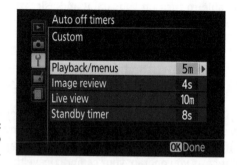

Sound

Most cameras give you audio feedback in the form of beeps and boops. You can turn them off, if you like. Touchscreen cameras may beep when you touch them. You can often disable this while keeping other sounds on.

Touchscreen settings

Cameras with touchscreens typically have options that enable you to alter their sensitivity or turn them off entirely. Canon has a Touch Control menu in Setup Menu 3 of the Canon EOS Rebel T8i (see Figure 4-8), for example, that has three options: Standard, Sensitive, and Disable. Set it to your liking.

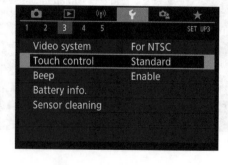 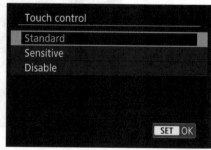

No card

This option, which might be named Release Shutter without Card, determines whether you can take photos if no memory card is in the camera. I recommend setting this option to off to prevent you from taking photos without a card in the camera, even if your camera warns you about the fact. You don't want to accidentally take what you think is a great photo only to realize after the moment has passed that you forgot to put a card back in the camera. The only time I allow the camera to take a photo without a card is when I am configuring something and don't want to store the photos. For example, my Fotodiox lens mount adapter requires that I take several shots with different camera settings to program it. I don't want to delete 50 photos from my card when I'm done, so I temporarily enable this feature.

Setting Typical Shooting Options

Your camera's basic still and movie recording settings control how your digital SLR shoots and saves photos and movies, as well as other photo- and exposure-related options. If you're in an advanced mode, you'll have to set (or change) these settings yourself.

Image size and quality

When you're holding a dSLR/dSLT/mirrorless camera, you've got a modern-day marvel in your hands. It can take magnificently clear, compelling photos in several different sizes, aspect ratios, and qualities. Figure 4-9 shows the Quality option of the T8i from Canon. Note that this camera shows you the megapixel count and pixel dimensions of the current setting.

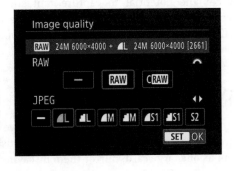

FIGURE 4-9: Image Quality combines several options in one place.

REMEMBER

This is one of the more important options you can set on your camera. Image quality is composed of two elements: file type and size/quality. Here are my suggestions for setting the file type:

» **Choose JPEG** if you want to use a final product right out of the camera and don't want to mess with storing or processing Raw photos. This option is ideal if you use JPEGs on your computer, email them, text them, or put them online. You can't upload Raw files to Flickr, Facebook, your blog, or your web page. Don't even think about tweeting them.

» **Choose Raw or Raw + JPEG** if you want creative control over your photos and look forward to processing them yourself. You will have the flexibility of making multiple edits throughout the process. For you, saving storage space and transferring photos faster aren't as important as having the flexibility, quality, and creative control that you get with Raw files. Although I use up more space on my memory card and computer, I always use Raw + JPEG. I use the JPEGs as previews and edit the Raw photos to create my final product.

Follow these guidelines when setting the size and quality:

» **Larger is almost always better,** especially if you plan to print your photos. This idea applies to JPEGs, which will almost always have several size options, and Raw photos, which can sometimes be saved in different sizes. Reduce size if you genuinely don't need a larger photo. At times, you may need to compromise to be able to store more photos on a memory card.

» **Higher quality is almost always better,** especially if you expect to edit or print your photos. This idea applies to JPEGs mostly, which normally have three compression options. They are sometimes noted by stars but may be shown by value or as a smooth or stepped arc.

In the end, choose the settings that work best for you and your situation. Every image-quality option has the potential to capture fantastic photos. Larger, higher-quality files, especially Raw images, give you the greatest editing and print options. Smaller files and JPEGs may be perfectly fine for you. Book 5, Chapter 2 has more information on image-quality settings.

Using multiple memory cards

If your camera uses multiple memory cards, you should have an option that enables you to configure how they are used. You may be able to use them sequentially, which treats them as one large card, mirror them by saving the exact same data to both cards, or save Raw files to one and JPEGs to the other. Figure 4-10 shows the Memory Card Options menu for the Pentax K-1 Mark II.

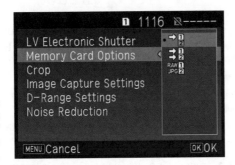

FIGURE 4-10: Set storage preferences if using multiple memory cards.

ISO settings

Typically, you can not only set the ISO speed (the camera's sensitivity to light) but also limit the camera's Auto ISO to minimum and maximum values. Some cameras enable you to control valid ISO settings even when shooting manually. Disable Auto ISO if you want to set the ISO manually in advanced shooting modes. You don't have a choice when using automatic modes. I cover ISO more fully in Book 3, Chapter 4.

Picture control or creative style

This option specifies how the camera processes JPEGs from the image data. You normally have Standard, Portrait, Landscape, Vivid, Neutral, and Monochrome choices. Depending on the camera, you may have more or fewer choices. This setting doesn't affect Raw photos. Figure 4-11 shows some of the options available from a Nikon camera.

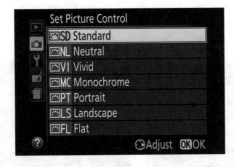

FIGURE 4-11: Choose an option to control how JPEGs are processed by the camera.

WARNING

If you aren't saving raw exposures, *be careful:* When a picture style is applied to the raw data by the camera and saved as a JPEG, you can't change it afterward. Test the settings you like with copies of photos — not the ones you want to keep.

Exploring Menus and Camera Settings

Color space

Specify the color space assigned to JPEGs file. Choose from two color space options:

TIP

>> **sRGB** defines a smaller color space but is the de facto standard. It is so ubiquitous that devices with no color management capabilities assume that colors are defined in sRGB and reproduce sRGB photos perfectly. I recommend assigning this color space to your photos.

>> **Adobe RGB** defines a larger color space than sRGB but is less widely used. The danger is that you may be viewing or editing colors on your system that other people can't display or print. If you work in an environment that's tightly color managed, you may be able to take advantage of Adobe RGB's greater color range.

Raw images *don't have* a color space; one is assigned by the raw processor when you convert it to TIFF or JPEG format. Turn to Book 5, Chapter 3 for more information on managing color spaces.

Highlight and shadow options

These options, also called brightness and contrast or dynamic range options, try to protect you from blowing out highlights and losing details in shadows. It's not a bad deal, but not a free lunch, either. You may lose detail in certain tonal ranges, depending on what the camera has to do to enhance or protect shadows or highlights. You can do the same thing yourself, and enjoy total control over the process, when you process raw exposures and, to a limited degree, edit JPEGs. Canon options include Auto Lighting Optimizer and Highlight Tone Priority (both shown in Figure 4-12). Nikon uses Active D-Lighting. Sony uses the term D-Range Optimizer. Pentax has D-Range settings that you can alter.

FIGURE 4-12:
These options help preserve detail in bright or dark areas of photos.

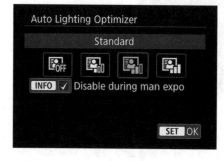
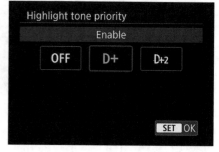

Noise reduction

You can often toggle two types of noise reduction: long shutter speed and high ISO (both shown in Figure 4-13). The camera automatically processes the photo when you take it according to the type of noise-reduction settings you've chosen. This processing takes a bit of time, so it may reduce your shooting speed. You may also lose some detail in your photos. However, if you want cleaner-looking photos right out of the camera, these options are incredibly useful. With the exception of Long Exposure Noise Reduction, noise reduction is not normally applied to raw files.

FIGURE 4-13: Set noise-reduction options to keep noise under control.

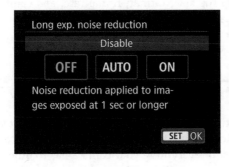
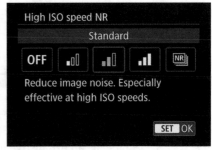

Aspect ratio

Set the aspect ratio you want your photos saved in. Standard 35mm-type photos have a 3:2 aspect ratio. Four Thirds cameras shoot with a 4:3 aspect ratio. You should also be able to select widescreen (16:9) and square (1:1) ratios. When shooting JPEG-only, the camera saves only the cropped photo and discards any additional data. When shooting Raw photos, cropping information is typically stored in the file for you to use in your processing software. Unless you're certain of what you want, I suggest shooting 3:2 photos in Raw and cropping your shots in the camera or using software later. That way, you can decide yourself what to keep and what to cut.

Red-eye reduction

Enable your camera's Red-Eye Reduction option if you're photographing people or animals and using a flash. Otherwise, leave it off. Red-eye reduction is often located in a Shooting menu as a separate option, but some cameras consider this a flash option.

Exploring Menus and Camera Settings

Flash options

Some cameras have very few flash options. You may be able to choose between automatic and manual. If you choose the latter, you can set the flash strength. Other cameras enable you to set up wireless flash, use high-speed sync, and many other advanced flash options. You can find more information on using your camera's flash in Book 4, Chapters 2 and 3.

Movie options

You can typically set up the size, format, frame rate, and compression type for movies from a Movie menu.

Making Other Choices

Read through these sections and complete these setup options at your leisure. I've included important or interesting features that you'll benefit from. This is by no means an exhaustive list of everything your camera has to offer. See the manual for specific details on these and other options.

Display settings

Configure what information you want displayed in the viewfinder or on the monitor. You'll find options like these in a Shooting or Setup menu:

>> **Grid:** This option (shown in Figure 4-14) displays a grid in the viewfinder or on the monitor. In some cases, you may be able to customize the grid by having more or fewer lines. Typical values are 3x3 or 6x4. You may even be able to show diagonal lines.

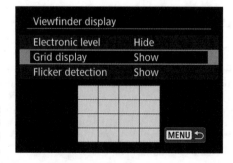

FIGURE 4-14:
Grid lines help you frame a scene.

TIP

Keep your camera's grid turned on to help level the scene through the viewfinder or on the monitor. You'll be able to frame a better shot.

>> **Electronic level:** Turn on the electronic level or virtual horizon to level your camera. Figure 4-15 shows the setting in the camera menu. The icon in the lower left indicates that the level will be shown in the viewfinder when shooting.

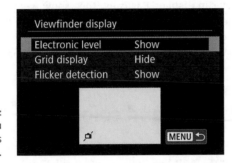

FIGURE 4-15: Levels help you keep things straight.

>> **Warnings and alerts:** You may be able to display warnings in the viewfinder, such as when there are flickering lights or when the shutter speed is too slow and might result in a blurry photo.

When shooting in Live View, you may have more display options to configure:

>> **Shooting information:** When you're using Live View, you can toggle between a little or a lot of information shown on the monitor, as shown in Figure 4-16. Press your Info or Display button to cycle through these displays.

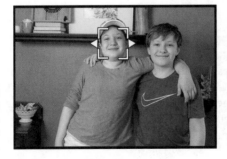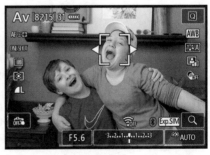

FIGURE 4-16: You can toggle the display to show very little or a lot.

Exploring Menus and Camera Settings

>> **Histogram:** Decide whether you want to see a live histogram displayed. A histogram is a graph that reveals the distribution of brightness in the scene. This helps you determine the overall balance between bright areas and dark regions, and whether you are in danger of under- or overexposing the photo. RGB histograms show color-channel information instead of an overall brightness.

Electronic viewfinders outperform optical viewfinders in terms of the amount and type of information they can display. Basically, they show what the monitor displays on the back of the camera. You may be able to adjust the brightness of the viewfinder, change its color temperature, display shooting information graphically, show all shooting information, show none, and even display a histogram in an electronic viewfinder.

Display brightness and color

You may be able to dim or brighten your monitor. Dim the beast if you're taking photos at night or somewhere in low light, where a super-bright monitor might be distracting. Lowering the brightness of the monitor also slows battery drain. Figure 4-17 shows the Display Brightness option on a Canon camera.

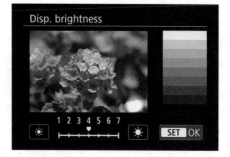

FIGURE 4-17: Brighten the monitor when you're in strong light.

Filenaming and numbering

This setting determines how the camera names your files. The camera counts every photo you take, from 0001 to 9999, and puts the number to a preset base filename. You can sometimes change to a different base name and change the camera's behavior when it starts over on the renumbering. Figure 4-18 shows a few simple file numbering options.

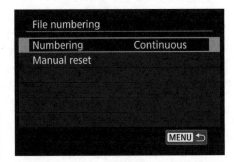

File and folder structure

Some cameras let you change the way folders are named on the memory card from a standard form (sequential numbering) to a date form (based on the date you take the first photo in the folder).

Auto Rotate (camera orientation)

The Auto Rotate setting records the camera's orientation when you take the picture and stores the information in the EXIF information. When you review the photo or open it in *smart software* (photo management or editing software that looks at the orientation information in the file to correctly display it), the picture is automatically rotated to its correct orientation. The Auto Rotate option prevents you from having to turn the camera every time you review a portrait-oriented photo. It makes the photo look smaller, though.

Copyright

Enter your name or organization in your camera's Copyright information, if possible. This information gets embedded into your photos and helps to secure your rights. The left image in Figure 4-19 shows the Copyright Information menu in the Canon T8i. I've entered my name on the right.

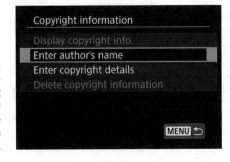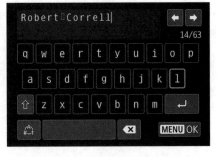

Exploring Menus and
Camera Settings

Wi-Fi connectivity

New dSLRs, dSLTs, and mirrorless cameras are ready to connect to networks and other devices right out of the box. That's a wonderful thing! Have the right password handy to access your network, if necessary. Some cameras have an Airplane mode that turns off wireless features. Use it just as you would on your mobile phone.

Video mode or system

You may need to change the video mode (a.k.a. system) to play back movies when your camera is connected to a TV. You have two video standards to choose from: NTSC and PAL. NTSC stands for National Television System Committee. This standard is used in North and Central America and several countries in South America and Asia (South Korea, Japan, and the Philippines, to name three). PAL stands for Phase Alternating Line and is used in Europe, Russia, China, Australia, much of Africa, the Middle East, and India. Changing this setting may also change the available movie frame rates on your camera.

Controlling Playback

Your camera should have an entire menu with a whole host of options devoted to playing back photos and movies. It's an important aspect of using your camera.

TIP

Cameras with touchscreen controls make playback a breeze. Instead of mashing buttons to scroll through photos, you can swipe as you would using your phone.

Protect Images

Use the Protect Images option if you review your photos and want to keep yourself from accidentally deleting them. Beware: They aren't protected from reformatting. Some cameras may not have this menu. If that is the case, you can protect images during playback.

Rotate

You can rotate photos during photo playback if you like. Simply select the Rotate option from your Playback menu, choose a photo, and then rotate the image. This is helpful if you don't have Auto Rotate (which is typically in the Setup menu) on or the camera gets the orientation wrong.

Erase/Delete

WARNING

You can erase or delete one or more photos. Be careful! You can typically erase photos as you review them on the back of the camera by pressing the Erase or Delete button. You can also erase them by first selecting the Erase or Delete menu option, as shown on the left in Figure 4-20, and then selecting a method to tag them. In this case, I can individually select and erase images from a playback screen, select a range of images, or erase all the images in a folder, or on the card.

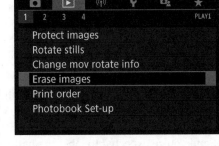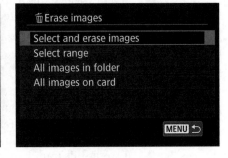

FIGURE 4-20: Delete multiple photos using the menu.

Print order

Identify exposures to print, and the order you want them printed, on a compatible PictBridge printer and many photo-finishing kiosks by setting the *digital print order format (DPOF)* options. Depending on your camera, you can imprint each photo with the shutter speed, aperture, file number, and date the photo was taken.

Slide show

Set up and display an automatic slide show of your photos or movies. Figure 4-21 shows the slide show settings on a consumer-level dSLR from Nikon.

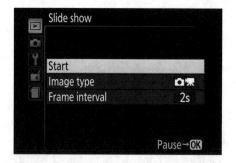

Retouch

Some cameras let you retouch photos. You'll enjoy being able to quickly produce finished photos in-camera. This is a great option if you don't like using your computer or you're on location and need to touch up a photo right away. You can find those settings on the Retouch menu.

Keeping Everything Running Smoothly

Several menu items help you keep your camera running smoothly. Check out these options and incorporate the ones you like into your basic maintenance routine.

Showing battery information

Your camera should have a place in the menu system for you to check the status of your battery. I encourage you to do so regularly, and I explain how in Book 1, Chapter 2. Some cameras also enable you to *register* each battery with the camera. For example, the Canon 90D assigns a serial number to each battery you register. It stores this information, and you're expected to label the battery. You can track their performance by serial number from the camera battery menu.

Formatting memory cards

This option (often listed simply as Format) erases all data on the memory card. Keep these memory card tips in mind:

TIP

>> Some cameras toss only the file structure and don't reinitialize the card. If that's the case with yours, you may be able to rescue lost files before you overwrite them. Other cameras give you the option of performing a low-level format if you want, as shown in Figure 4-22. This deeper level of formatting may improve performance on cards that seem sluggish.

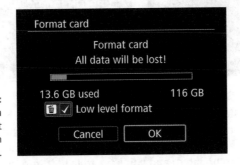

FIGURE 4-22:
Choose a low-level format to keep cards in tip-top shape.

>> To protect your privacy, be sure to reformat your card as aggressively as possible if you ever sell it or give it away. If you're totally paranoid, destroy the card.

>> I always format my cards in the camera I'm going to use them in. This produces a clean slate, created by the system that will store my photos. I also reformat the card immediately after transferring photos and putting it back in the camera. This prevents the "Have I saved these or not?" dilemma.

Cleaning the image sensor

As explained in Book 1, Chapter 2, you can have the camera automatically clean the image sensor by shaking it to knock the dust off. This menu option may be called Sensor Cleaning or Clean Image Sensor.

Creating a dust reference photo

Depending on the camera, you may have the option of taking a dust reference photo. The menu option may be named Image Dust Off Reference Photo, Dust

Delete Data (see the left image in Figure 4-23), or something similar. The right image in Figure 4-23 shows the screen you see after taking the reference photo. Here's how it works: You take a photo of a light, featureless object as a reference photo. The camera appends information to that photo that locates the little dust bunnies that are still stuck to the image sensor. Later, you can use the photo processing software that comes with your camera to automatically remove dust spots.

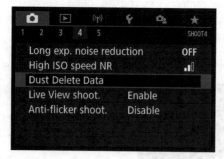 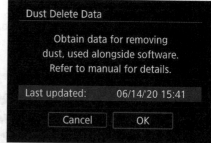

FIGURE 4-23:
Creating a dust reference photo for software to use later.

REMEMBER

Some people debate the effectiveness of creating a dust reference photo if the image sensor is constantly cleaning itself every time you turn the camera on and off. Also, this technique requires more of you than just taking photos. You have to keep the reference photo updated, and you have to load it into the provided software and apply it to your photos for it to work. Although these requirements may sound discouraging, your mileage may vary. Give it a shot and see what you think.

Resetting the camera

Being able to automatically change all options (or a good percentage of them — see your manual for details) to their factory default settings is helpful. It helps you restore the standard camera setup if you change a setting and can't later recall its original values. This option frees you to be wildly creative and experiment with your camera. The menu for resetting is shown on the left in Figure 4-24. You typically get a warning, shown on the right, asking whether you really want to reset the camera. If you made a mistake, cancel the operation.

Updating the firmware

Firmware is what runs your camera. The cool thing about digital cameras is that manufacturers update firmware to smooth out bugs or introduce new features. Canon initially released the EOS 90D without the ability to shoot 4K movies at 24fps. After a public outcry, the company changed its mind and added that feature as part of a firmware update. Visit the manufacturer's website to find out the latest version for your camera. Look in the support area, download center, or on a page devoted to your camera and then check that against what your camera shows. Update if necessary. Updating involves either putting the firmware file(s) on your camera's memory card or connecting your camera to your computer. Figure 4-25 shows that the firmware on this Pentax K-1 Mark II is version 1.02.

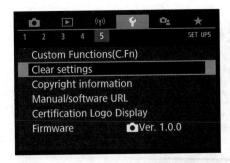

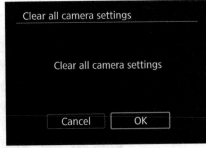

FIGURE 4-24:
Clear camera settings to reset the camera.

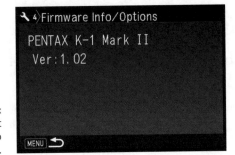

FIGURE 4-25:
Make sure that firmware is up to date.

WARNING

Please read all applicable instructions before starting. Be careful when updating your camera's firmware. Do so with a full battery. If something goes wrong, you may have to take your camera to be serviced to revive it.

Exploring Advanced Options

Digital SLRs often have a number of advanced options. They aren't always necessary but are available if you need them. That's one thing that makes dSLR photography so rewarding: The camera grows with you. I've chosen to highlight a number of different advanced options from different cameras in this section to give you an idea of what's possible. Please refer to your camera's manual for a complete list of your camera's features and how to use them.

Exploring Menus and Camera Settings

Using custom functions and settings

Some cameras place many of their most esoteric options into a group called Custom Functions (Canon) or Custom Settings (Nikon and Pentax). Each setting is typically numbered and may be grouped into categories. Figure 4-26 shows the first Custom Settings menu on the Pentax K-1 Mark II.

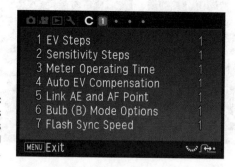

FIGURE 4-26: Custom settings and functions are advanced options.

Creating custom shooting profiles

More advanced cameras let you create, save, and load different shooting profiles with different settings. For example, you may have one ready for portraits and another for casual photography with your general-purpose zoom lens. The Canon EOS 90D has two Custom Shooting Modes. The menu where this feature is located is shown on the left in Figure 4-27, and the available options are shown on the right.

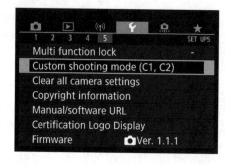 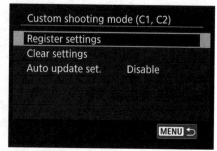

FIGURE 4-27: Customize the camera by saving your settings into a special mode.

Tweaking autofocus settings

More advanced cameras have a plethora of autofocus menu choices. This is one thing that separates professional cameras from amateur models. For example, you can fine-tune focus on more advanced cameras. You might need this option

5. **Attach an external flash, if necessary, and turn it on.**

   You may also rely on your camera's built-in flash, if it has one.

6. **Attach the remote shutter release, if desired.**

   Keep the cord out of the way, unless it's a wireless remote. In that case, you just need to get it out and have it handy.

7. **Turn on your camera.**

   Quickly make sure that everything is powered on and working properly. If you haven't already, inspect for damage.

Setting Up Your Camera

Now that you've unpacked and made everything attached and ready, it's time to set up your camera to take the shots you want. I can't suggest every possible setting that you might need in every possible circumstance, but I've tried to list the major options and settings that you should pay attention to.

Performing an initial checkup

First, perform an initial checkup. Quickly check these items:

- » **Battery level:** Note the battery level to make sure you didn't accidentally load a bad battery. Replace it, if necessary.

- » **Exposures remaining:** Check to see whether you're starting out with an empty memory card (as you should be). If not, note how many shots you can take before running out of space. You can continue using it, of course, or swap it for an empty card. If you are certain that you've downloaded the photos already, you can format it.

- » **Knobs and buttons:** Make sure that all knobs and switches are set where you want them.

- » **Lens:** Configure the lens. Set switches such as auto or manual focus and image stabilization to your preference.

TIP

Although this step may not sound necessary, I used to get tripped up all the time by leaving certain settings on the camera and forgetting to change them later. I would have the drive mode set to a timer, for example, and then want to take an action shot. Ten seconds later, the shutter would fire! Now that my kids are into photography, I also have to deal with their settings. It's always a good idea to quickly check the camera's settings before you start shooting.

Preparing for still photography

Although digital SLRs and SLTs enjoy robust movie-making modes, this chapter is mostly about shooting still photos. If necessary, turn your capture mode switch to still photos. Some cameras integrate this function into the power switch (see Figure 5-4). In that case, make sure you've powered on using the correct mode. If your camera has a Movie mode on the Mode dial (see Figure 5-1), you just need to set a still photo shooting mode, which is described in the next section. Some cameras use a switch on the back of the camera to change from still photography to Live View and Movie mode. In those cases, the switch can be in either position to shoot still photos. Just don't press the Start/Stop button or you'll start recording a movie.

Choosing a shooting mode

It's time to decide on a shooting mode. What you decide affects how much control you can exert over the camera, and to what purpose. There isn't a wrong choice here. Some people prefer to let the camera handle most of the work. Others prefer exercising more creative control. Decide on the mode you want to use based on your subject, creative goals, camera, experience, location, and environment. Table 5-1 summarizes typical shooting modes, most of which are directly on the Mode dial. You may need to press and hold an unlock button in the center of the Mode dial to turn the dial and change modes. Note that not all cameras have all the same shooting modes.

TABLE 5-1   **Typical Shooting Modes**

Name	Description
Auto	The typical Auto mode is basically point-and-shoot. You have very little input over the settings the camera uses. More advanced Auto modes detect the type of lighting or scene and configure the camera appropriately. You may be able to change the Drive mode and control the flash.
Flash Off	This mode gives you a quick way to disable the flash from the Mode dial and still take advantage of the camera automatically handling the other settings.
Guided/Creative Auto/ Creative Assist	In these modes, you give the camera information about what you're shooting, whether you want sharp or blurred backgrounds, and whether to use the flash. It handles everything else.
Scenes	Scenes allow you to identify the specific scene you're shooting, enabling the camera to choose the best settings for that scene. Typical scenes are Portrait, Action, Close-up, and Landscape. Many cameras have even more creative scenes, such as Food, Candlelight, Night Portrait, and more.
Specialty modes	Specialty modes enable you to shoot panoramas, HDR, time-lapse shots, and more. They are unique to specific cameras or brands.

Name	Description
Filters and Effects	The camera processes shots according to the filter or effect you choose. Some cameras place them conveniently on the Mode dial. You typically have little to no control over other camera settings.
Programmed Autoexposure (P)	Also called Programmed Auto, this mode bridges the gap between the basic automatic modes that give you no control over the camera and advanced modes that enable you to change settings. In this mode, you need not worry about setting the aperture or shutter speed but can configure anything else you like.
Aperture-Priority Autoexposure (A or Av)	In Aperture-Priority mode, you set the aperture you want to use (larger for more light and blurred backgrounds; smaller for less light and sharper backgrounds). The camera figures out the other settings needed to reach the best exposure. Unlike basic modes, you have total access to all other camera settings.
Shutter-Priority Autoexposure (S or Tv)	In Shutter-Priority mode, you set the shutter speed you want to use (faster for action, slower for more light and still subjects). The camera figures out the other settings needed to reach the best exposure. Unlike basic modes, you have total access to all other camera settings.
Manual (M)	Manual mode is just that. You're in charge of everything, especially exposure. The biggest difference between aperture-priority and shutter-priority modes is that after you meter the scene, you must adjust both controls to get the exposure you're after.
Bulb (B)	Bulb mode is a manual mode that enables you to keep the shutter open as long as you hold the shutter button down.

This decision affects the rest of the checklist. If you choose a more automated mode, you don't have to do certain tasks, such as set the exposure controls. On the other hand, if you're more inclined to shoot manually, you'll be *required* to adjust those settings.

REMEMBER

You don't need to worry about setting the correct exposure yourself unless you're in manual or Bulb mode. The camera does it for you. When in an autoexposure mode, the camera may not be able to set the exposure properly to take a good photo. If this happens, it will try to get your attention by beeping or flashing the shutter speed or f-stop display. You may have to change a setting or use the flash.

Automatic modes

Automatic shooting modes are fantastic helpers. The camera takes most of the technical load off your shoulders and lets you concentrate on composing the shot. Whether you're more experienced or just beginning, I encourage you to try your camera's automatic modes, including scenes. Most automatic modes are right on the camera's Mode dial, as shown in Figure 5-1. Simply dial one in and start shooting.

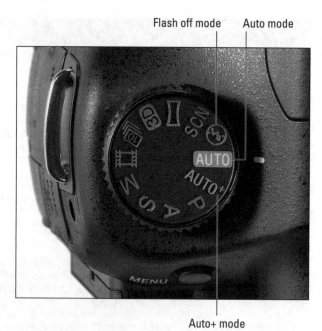

Flash off mode   Auto mode

Auto+ mode

FIGURE 5-1:
Automatic mode
symbols are often
a different color.

Here's a rundown of the types of automatic modes you might come across:

>> **Auto:** This mode (see Figure 5-2) probably needs the least explanation. You point the camera. You press and hold the shutter button halfway to focus and then press the shutter button down fully to take the photo. The camera does the rest. Simple.

Several cameras have advanced Auto modes that are smarter than basic Auto. Sony calls it Intelligent Auto, formerly Auto+. Most Canon cameras have a Scene Intelligent Auto mode. The camera senses the shooting conditions, not simply the exposure, and chooses the best settings for you to take the photo.

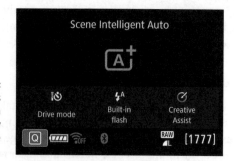

FIGURE 5-2:
Auto mode allows
you to focus on
photography
instead of the
camera.

>> **Flash Off:** This mode is Auto without the flash. It may even be called Auto (Flash Off) on your camera. Use it when you want to be in Auto mode but want to keep the flash from firing. See Figure 5-3.

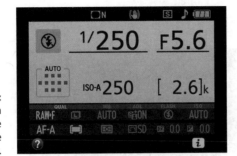

FIGURE 5-3:
Flash Off is an automatic mode that prevents the flash from firing.

Ego is the number-one reason people bypass Auto modes in favor of something more complicated. That's a shame, because no matter how smart or technically driven you are, it can be fun to just take pictures. Using Auto is also a great way to become comfortable with your camera and get used to being a photographer.

Guided creativity modes

This section features modes that share an important feature: They actively help guide your creativity. You don't have to do a lot of camera wrangling when using these modes. These modes are often located on the Mode dial (see Figure 5-4), but you may have to make several selections or choices before you can start shooting.

GUIDED/CREATIVE AUTO/CREATIVE ASSIST

These modes are automatic but give you several options for how the photos should turn out. Some consumer-level Nikon cameras have a Guide mode that walks you through a series of situations (similar to scenes) or goals (soft backgrounds and the like) to get to the right camera setup; this mode is highly interactive — not hands-off like a standard Auto mode at all. Canon's equivalent is the Creative Auto mode. It's less interactive than Nikon's Guide mode but has some of the same goal-driven choices. Canon also has a Creative Assist mode, which lets you choose the type of photo you want to take.

SCENES

Although Auto modes are great, they have a drawback that can be irritating at times: The camera doesn't know what you're photographing. You could be taking a photo of a running child or a potted plant, and the camera may not be able to tell the difference. Scenes are different. You remove the guesswork from the camera by telling it what you're shooting.

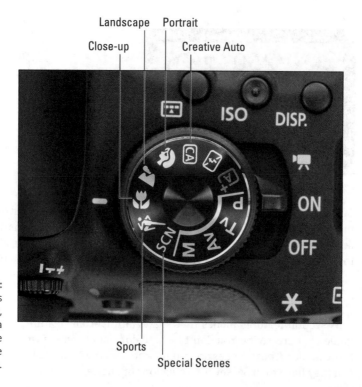

Many cameras represent scenes on the Mode dial with small symbols. You may need to refer to your camera manual to decode them the first few times. Other cameras include a few scenes on the Mode dial itself, plus a Scene mode on the Mode dial to access more scenes. Yet others may just have a Scene mode on the dial instead of individual scenes. Select this mode using the dial and then choose a specific scene from the camera display.

Here's a list of some typical scenes your camera may have:

>> **Portrait:** Use when you want to take a nice solo or group portrait. The lens is set so that the background will be nicely blurred, as shown in Figure 5-5. Skin tones are natural.

>> **Landscape:** This scene captures scenery in vivid colors and with a large depth of field.

>> **Macro/Close-up:** Use this mode to capture close-ups.

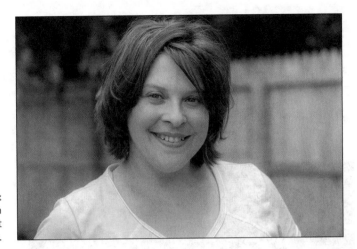

FIGURE 5-5:
Portraits often have soft backgrounds.

>> **Sports/Action:** Optimized to photograph moving subjects with a fast shutter speed, as shown in Figure 5-6. You can also use this scene when *you're* moving in order to reduce camera shake by implementing a fast shutter speed.

>> **Child:** A cross between action and portrait. Use when photographing children.

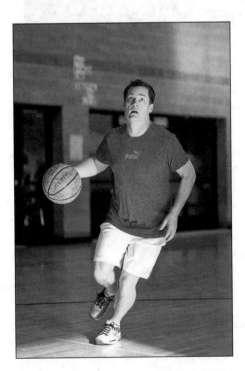

FIGURE 5-6:
The object here is to capture action without blurring.

>> **Sunset:** You got it. This scene is ideal when photographing sunsets. It brings out the red, orange, and yellow colors well.

>> **Night View/Scene:** Think landscape at night with city lights, as shown in Figure 5-7. Some cameras recommend using a tripod with this scene.

>> **Handheld Night/Twilight:** Shoot at night without a tripod.

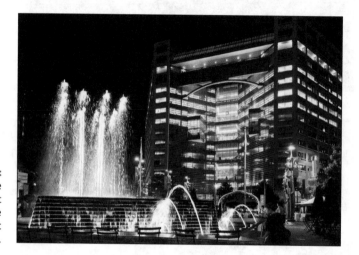

FIGURE 5-7:
This mode doesn't attempt to brighten the background at night.

>> **Night Portrait:** Shoot portraits in the dark. The idea is to allow the overall scene to remain darker than normal but still expose the subject properly. The flash may fire.

>> **Candle:** Shoot scenes lit by candlelight, as shown in Figure 5-8.

>> **Food:** For all you "foodies" out there, this mode creates a special scene to help you photograph those tasty treats you're proud of making.

>> **Others:** You may run across more scenes ranging from Blue Sky, Forest, Pet, Kids, and Surf & Snow.

SPECIALTY MODES

Some cameras have a few specialty modes that deserve consideration:

>> **Sweep Panorama:** Sony has a Sweep Panorama mode that handles everything. All you do is point, shoot, and pan — no computer required. I positively love this mode. A finished photo is shown in Figure 5-9. Sony also has a special 3D Sweep Panorama mode, which saves the panorama in two files: a

standard JPEG and a 3-D data file. Nikon introduced the Easy Panorama mode on the D3300 but removed it from the D3500.

Panoramas are saved as JPEGs, not as Raw files. Individual frames from the panorama aren't saved, either.

REMEMBER

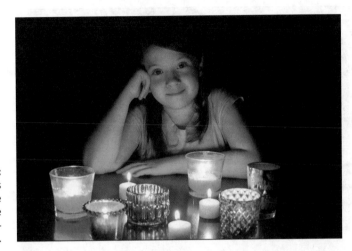

FIGURE 5-8: Special modes like this enable you to capture subjects in different settings.

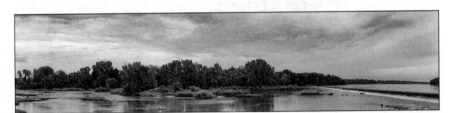

FIGURE 5-9: Automatic panoramas are fun photography.

>> **Continuous Advance Priority AE:** This Sony-only mode sets the camera to rattle off photos as fast as possible by locking the aperture open. This removes the delay from resetting it between shots. The camera also determines the shutter speed. It's great for sports but also for when someone's opening a present or blowing out the candles. Photograph pets or children as they play.

>> **HDR/Dynamic Range:** HDR, or *high dynamic range,* modes (sometimes located with scenes) are designed to capture multiple exposures (normally three) with a higher dynamic range than a single frame and then automatically process them into a single finished image. Book 5, Chapter 6 has more information on shooting HDR images.

>> **Multiple exposures:** Shooting multiple exposures is a creative challenge. The fun part is experimenting with different scenes to come up with two or more that look good together. Figure 5-10 is an example of a dual exposure shot of an abacus and math flash cards.

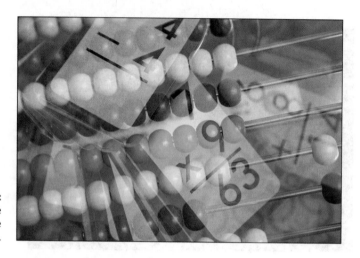

FIGURE 5-10: Creative use of multiple exposures.

FILTERS AND EFFECTS

Your camera may have a special filter or effect mode. Some even have these modes right on the Mode dial. For example, the Canon 90D has a special Creative Filter mode, which enables you to shoot photos with the filter effect applied. There are many different types of filters. To name a few: Soft focus, Fisheye, Toy camera, Miniature, HDR, Water painting, and so forth.

I strongly encourage you to play around with creative filters and effects. This is fun and creative photography. You can also shoot photos normally and apply special effects later, either using the camera or special photo-editing software.

Classic autoexposure modes

Three classic autoexposure modes are shown on a Mode dial in Figure 5-11. They evaluate the exposure automatically but allow you to control everything else (metering mode, autofocus options, white balance, drive, and so on).

Shutter-priority mode

Aperture-priority mode

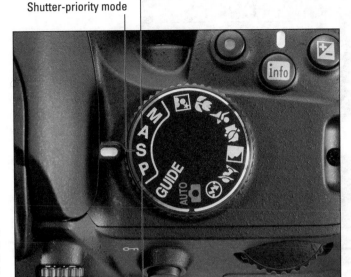

FIGURE 5-11: These autoexposure modes unlock more camera options for you to use.

Programmed autoexposure mode

The modes are

>> **Program Auto (P):** Also known as Programmed Auto, Program AE (for autoexposure), or programmed autoexposure. Program Auto is basically an advanced Auto mode. The camera is set on automatic exposure and selects an aperture and shutter speed combination that it thinks is best. You control all other settings. It's great for snapshots.

Most cameras have modes called either Program Shift or Flexible Program mode. This mode let you choose a combination of shutter speed and aperture that you want to use. Use this mode if you have a particular aperture or shutter speed you want to achieve a certain depth of field (for aperture) or to freeze action (for shutter speed). You have more creative input this way. Figure 5-12 shows a camera display in Program Auto mode.

>> **Aperture-priority (A or Av, which stands for Aperture value):** Also known as aperture-priority auto or aperture-priority AE. In aperture-priority mode, you set the aperture and the camera determines the shutter speed needed to reach the proper exposure. This mode is good when you want to control the depth of field. Use it for portraits, landscapes, and close-ups. Aside from exposure, you control all the other settings. Figure 5-13 shows a camera display in aperture-priority mode.

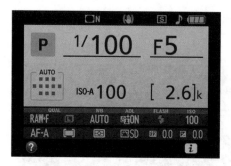

FIGURE 5-12:
Programmed
auto screen with
typical options.

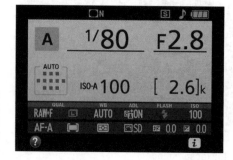

FIGURE 5-13:
Settings you
might see in
aperture-priority
mode.

>> **Shutter-priority (S or Tv, which stands for Time value):** Also known as shutter-priority auto or shutter-priority AE. This mode works the same as aperture priority, only you set the shutter speed instead of the aperture. It's best used when you need control over the shutter speeds. Use it for sports, action, and when you are moving. Aside from exposure, you control all the other settings yourself. Figure 5-14 shows a camera display in shutter-priority mode.

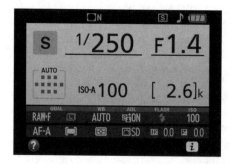

FIGURE 5-14:
A shutter-priority
shooting screen.

Manual mode

Switch to manual mode when you want full control over exposure. Although "manual mode" sounds intimidating, you can exercise as much or as little control as you want in other areas. I recommend using manual mode when aperture- or shutter-priority modes aren't able to capture photos with the exposure you want. You also benefit from manual mode when you want the exact same settings for every photo in a session. There are two manual modes, which are shown on a Mode dial in Figure 5-15:

>> **Manual (M):** You control all camera settings, including the exposure controls. Auto ISO may not be available in manual mode. Manual mode is shown on a camera display in Figure 5-16.

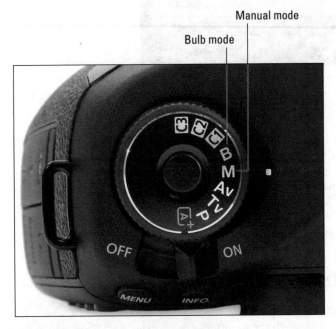

FIGURE 5-15:
Manual is always
M; Bulb (B) may
or may not be on
the dial.

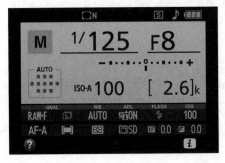

FIGURE 5-16:
In manual mode
you can play
around with
custom
exposures
without
the camera
interfering.

>> **Bulb (B):** Bulb mode is a special type of manual mode. You select an ISO and aperture normally, but the shutter is untimed. When you press the shutter button, the shutter opens, and when you release the button, the shutter closes. This mode is great for long exposures and fireworks. If your Mode dial doesn't have a B setting, try entering manual mode and lengthening the shutter speed until it reads B (Bulb). A camera in Bulb shooting mode is shown in Figure 5-17.

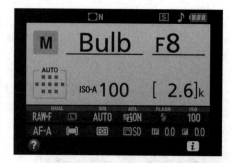

FIGURE 5-17:
In Bulb mode the shutter duration is up to you.

Setting the image quality

Set Image Quality after you have decided on a shooting mode. Some shooting modes limit your choices. The Image Quality option is located on a Shooting menu for most cameras. Your camera will have a number of options. I prefer to have the camera record Large/Fine JPEGs and Raw images simultaneously because it gives me a high-quality JPEG right out of the camera. I can process the Raw version later at my leisure. You may not need the largest, highest-quality images. Book 1, Chapter 4 has more details.

Choosing a viewing mode

Digital SLRs, SLTs, and mirrorless cameras offer two ways for you to view your scene: through the viewfinder or by using Live View, which displays a preview on the back of the camera. Which one you choose depends on the situation at hand and your personal preferences.

Viewfinder

The viewfinder is a great way to compose and take photos, as shown in Figure 5-18. I like it for most situations because I feel that I can concentrate on the scene better instead of being distracted by everything else going on. Some dSLRs have large, bright viewfinders that make looking through them a joyful experience.

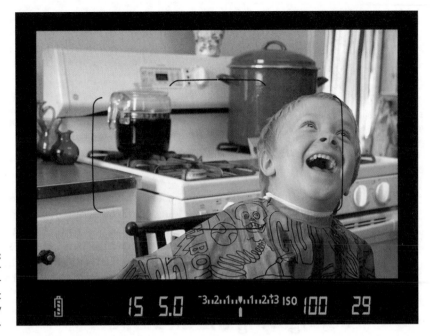

FIGURE 5-18:
Use your viewfinder for the classic photography experience.

You will see a number of exposure settings as well as autofocus points and possibly metering aids. You may be able to turn on grid lines and other indicators (a level, for example) that will help you line things up in the viewfinder. Use everything at your disposal if you need to.

REMEMBER

I hold the camera steadier when I use the viewfinder because I'm able to support it better, which helps me take sharper photos.

Live View

If you prefer to compose shots using the monitor, switch to your camera's Live View mode, as shown in Figure 5-19. To make this choice, you may need to use the menu, press a button, or move a switch. If necessary, enable Live View from the menu. If your camera has a monitor that can flip out and rotate (called an articulated monitor), position it if you need to.

Live View works great in the studio, where you can mount your camera on a tripod and take the time to precisely compose the scene and focus. Live View, especially in tandem with an articulated monitor, makes it easier to shoot in some funky positions where the viewfinder is inconvenient. You can hold the camera over your head and shoot over obstacles, or hold the camera down low without having to lie down on the ground. Be prepared to turn up your monitor brightness when using Live View outside in bright daylight. Look in your camera's menu system (see Book 1, Chapter 4 for more information on menus) for Live View settings.

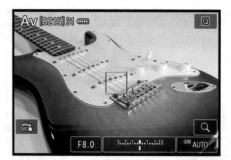

FIGURE 5-19:
Live View shooting is a very effective photography style.

TIP

When using Live View, you can zoom in when focusing (generally by pressing some sort of zoom button, depending on the camera). The magnification, which is far more than you can get through a viewfinder, makes getting the precise focus a snap. In addition, some cameras have focus helpers. Sony dSLTs, for example, have a feature called *Focus Peaking.* When on, edges in the area in focus are high-lighted with the color of your choice. It's a very nice visual indicator to have.

Configuring the display

You may want to change the information that is displayed through the viewfinder or on the monitor. As shown in Book 1, Chapter 4, you can turn on a grid, use an electronic level, and show or hide different warnings and alerts. You can also change the amount of information shown.

TIP

When you're setting up your camera using Live View and working out the expo-sure, it helps to have everything turned on in the display. However, when you're framing, turn off everything except the grid so that you can concentrate on the shot.

Setting exposure controls

If you're using one of the advanced shooting modes, you need to set the exposure controls to the values you want before shooting. Aperture and shutter speed are normally set by a dial, or graphically using a shooting information screen. ISO often has its own button, but can also be changed graphically or from a menu. Here is a quick review of the controls:

>> **Aperture:** The opening in the lens, as expressed by an f-number. I cover aperture more in Book 3, Chapter 2.

>> **Shutter speed:** How long the shutter stays open, measured in fractions of a second or seconds. For more information on shutter speed, turn to Book 3, Chapter 3.

>> **ISO:** ISO controls how sensitive the image sensor is to light. Most of the time you can leave it on Auto. If you need to set it manually, use the lowest ISO you can. You'll get less *noise* (graininess). You may need to raise the ISO if you can't open the aperture on the lens any more than it is and need a fast shutter speed. When necessary, set your camera to Auto ISO and specify a maximum ISO for your camera. I cover ISO in Book 3, Chapter 4.

For more information on exposure, turn to Book 3, Chapter 1. Here are some guidelines for each shooting mode:

>> **Program:** Setting exposure controls isn't necessary, but you may want to use your camera's Program Shift feature to choose a specific shutter speed/aperture combination.

>> **Aperture-priority:** Use large apertures (small f-numbers) to let in more light. You will be able to use faster shutter speeds, which keeps photos sharp. The background will also be pleasantly blurred. Large apertures are very effective for portraits. Use small apertures (larger f-numbers) in very bright conditions and to take photos with sharper background. This mode is very effective for landscapes and macros.

>> **Shutter-priority:** Use fast shutter speeds to capture action and to take sharp photos of other subjects. Use slower shutter speeds for creative effects like blurring falling water.

>> **Manual:** Set the aperture and shutter speed to achieve the exposure and creative side effects that you want.

>> **Bulb:** You decide how long you want to keep the shutter open when you take the photo. I use Bulb mode regularly for fireworks. Set the aperture before shooting.

Setting other parameters

Depending on the mode you're in, you may need to set a number of other parameters, some of which are outlined in this section. If you choose an automatic or guided mode, the camera does most of this for you. That's the idea, and it's why those modes are very popular. They remove a lot of the guesswork for people who don't know how to set up everything.

Flash

If you're using the camera's built-in flash and in an advanced mode, open it pressing the Flash button. For more information on setting up and using a pop-up flash, or using a flash, refer to Chapters 2 and 3 in Book 4. I'll wait for you here. If you're using an external flash, make sure it's mounted and turned on. Attach any flash modifiers, such as a diffuser. Set the flash type you want to use: Slow Sync, Red-Eye Reduction, or Rear-Curtain Sync. Use your experience as a guide, or take a few test shots and compare. Don't forget about using flash compensation or controlling the flash's output manually in certain situations.

Drive/Release modes

Set the drive/release mode (see Figure 5-20) to match the type of shooting you're doing. Some cameras have a Drive button. Others require you to set the drive from a shooting settings screen.

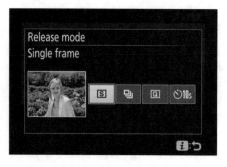

FIGURE 5-20: Set the drive/ release mode to take single, consecutive, timed, or remote shots.

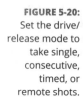

TIP

>> **Single shot:** Take one shot at a time (also known as *single-frame* shooting). Use this deliberate mode whenever you just need a single picture.

>> **Continuous (a.k.a. sequential or burst):** Continuous modes (there are two types: high-speed and low-speed) fire off exposures for as long as you hold the shutter button down or until the memory card is full. Capture speeds slow down as the camera's buffer gets filled and images wait to be stored on the memory card. How quickly this happens depends on the image size and quality, type (JPEG+Raw, or just one format), and size of the buffer. Choose low-speed when you want to capture a few shots in sequence but don't need 50. Depending on the action or the moment, you may want to switch to high-speed continuous. It's perfect for capturing fleeting moments and slices of action. Use continuous mode when you're shooting brackets.

>> **Self-timer:** Many cameras have 2 and 10 or 12-second timers. These are great if you want to take a self-portrait or if you want to minimize camera shake when using a tripod.

>> **Remote:** If using a wireless remote, set the drive to the correct mode to support it.

Focus mode

Choose a focus mode using the switch on the lens. Some cameras also have this switch on the camera body. Here are your options:

>> **Autofocus (AF):** Most people prefer using autofocus. When using autofocus, you have options of changing the AF point selection method (manual or some form of automatic) and the AF mode of operation (single versus continuous). More advanced cameras have powerful autofocus options that help you do things like track and capture action more effectively and refine the focus of lenses that may be a bit off.

>> **Manual focus (MF):** Manual focus can be effective in situations in which the camera has trouble autofocusing. I use it when photographing stars or the moon. However, it is much harder to manually focus in low light conditions because you can't see to focus. It is also difficult if you have the aperture set very wide, which can dramatically narrow the depth of field. Live View makes manually focusing easier, especially when you can magnify the view or use a focus-peaking feature. Focus peaking highlights edges that are in focus to make it easier to see areas of the scene that are in or out of focus.

AF modes

If you've decided to use autofocus, you have quite a bit of control over how the system works. Your camera has *AF modes*, sometimes called AF Operation. You can change them using your camera's menu or shooting information display. See Figure 5-21. Here are three common types of AF modes:

>> **Single focus:** The camera focuses once and beeps at you. The AF point used might light up in the viewfinder. This works well for portraits and other nonmoving subjects. Also called *one shot* or *single-servo AF.*

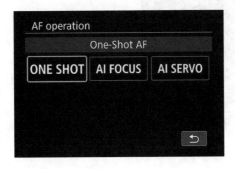

FIGURE 5-21: This mode determines whether the camera keeps autofocusing.

>> **Continuous focus:** The camera continually focuses for as long as you hold the shutter halfway down. Use this mode to track moving subjects, or if you're moving. Continuous focus is also called *AI servo* or *continuous-servo AF.*

>> **Automatic switching:** In this mode, the camera automatically switches between single focus and continuous focus as the need arises. Also called *AI focus* or *auto-servo AF.*

AF point selection methods

Another way to refine how the autofocus system works is to change how it determines what *AF points* (specific points in the camera's viewfinder it uses to focus) to use. Some cameras have an AF Point Selection button. Others require you to use a function or settings screen, as shown in Figure 5-22. There are two broad categories that define how AF points are selected:

>> **Automatic AF point selection:** You let the camera decide which points to use. Most of the time, it does a pretty good job. However, it does have a tendency to focus on the closest object, regardless of whether that's what you intend.

Automatic AF point selection may not be precise enough when you're working with extremely shallow depths of field (the area that appears in focus) or when needing to focus on one of several objects at different distances.

>> **Manual AF point selection:** You select the AF point yourself. You generally have to press an AF Point Selection button or make a menu choice to make your selection. Depending on your camera, you may be able to choose a point, a zone, a group of points, a dynamic group of points, or other AF point selection methods.

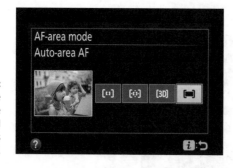

FIGURE 5-22:
You can allow the camera to decide or take control of the AF points yourself.

Live View focus modes and methods

Your camera will have different autofocus options in Live View. Newer Canon cameras, for instance, offer four Live View autofocus methods, as shown in Figure 5-23: Face Detection + Tracking; Spot AF; 1-point AF; and Zone AF. Each mode has its pros, cons, and quirks. The Nikon D3500 has four AF area modes when in Live View: Face-priority AF; Wide-area AF; Normal-area AF; and Subject-tracking AF. You can change focus modes generally from the menu or the Live View shooting display.

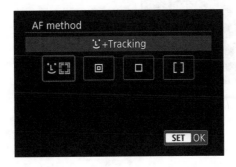

FIGURE 5-23:
Investigate your camera's Live View focusing modes.

Metering modes

Your camera has a number of metering modes that enable you to prioritize how it reacts to light in different parts of the frame. Pattern, Evaluative, Matrix, or Multi-segment metering modes evaluate the entire frame to determine how bright the scene is. Center-weighted Average uses the entire frame but gives priority to the center of the frame. Partial covers a large area in the center of the frame. Spot metering meters a small circle in the center of the frame or the selected auto-focus point (depending on the camera). Check your camera for specific metering modes. Some cameras have a Metering mode button. Others require you to access the menu or a shooting information display. I go into more metering detail in Book 3, Chapter 1.

White balance

When your camera's white balance is set correctly, you won't even notice it. Photos will look good and that's that. When the white balance is off, your shots will have an unnatural-looking color cast to them. Things that should appear white will look yellow or blue.

I advise changing the White Balance setting on your camera only if you notice that photos look overly blue or yellow, or have a distinctly odd look to them. Change the White Balance setting to match the lighting conditions of your subject. Typical presets are shown in Figure 5-24 and described in this list:

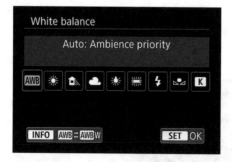

FIGURE 5-24:
You have a number of white-balance options to choose from.

REMEMBER

>> **Auto:** The camera figures out the conditions and sets a color temperature. This setting works well outdoors and when you're using a flash, but not so well indoors without a flash.

Auto isn't foolproof. The camera can get it wrong. When working with Raw files, you can reset the white balance as if nothing ever happened, without any loss of image quality. This is one of the best reasons to shoot Raw photos.

>> **Direct sun:** Use this White Balance setting whenever you're outdoors in the sunlight.

>> **Flash:** When you're using flash, choose this setting.

>> **Cloudy:** Use this setting on cloudy days.

>> **Shade:** The Shade setting is used differently from the Cloudy setting.

>> **Tungsten lights:** Use it when you're indoors, working with normal "old-fashioned" light bulbs with a tungsten filament in them.

>> **Fluorescent lighting:** You may have a few options for fluorescent lights. For example, higher-level Nikon cameras offer Sodium-Vapor Lamps, Warm-White Fluorescent, White Fluorescent, Cool-White Fluorescent, Day White Fluorescent, Daylight Fluorescent, and High-Temp Mercury-Vapor.

TECHNICAL STUFF

>> **Custom/Set temperature:** Set the color temperature based on a photo of a white object you take on location (see Figure 5-25), or manually, in (geekazoid alert) degrees Kelvin.

Some cameras have a White Balance button. Others require you to access settings from the menu or a shooting-information display.

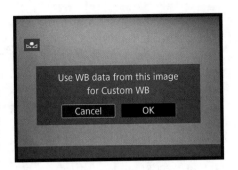

FIGURE 5-25:
The camera
evaluates the
light and sets a
custom white
balance.

REMEMBER

Don't confuse a good White Balance setting with reality. I noticed this effect when sitting in church one day. I could see the pastor in person and at the same time could see him on one of the large live video displays. In person, he had a nice, warm, golden glow on his shirt and skin. He looked great. The video, whose white balance had been set to counteract the color of the light, "balanced out" the golden glow and made him "cooler" than he actually was. It looked nice but wasn't an accurate depiction of the scene. When seen in person, I preferred the real thing. However, I would choose the corrected version to print or publish online, because people don't want to see a yellow color cast even if that's what the scene actually looked like.

Configure other parameters

Make sure to configure other features or parameters that are important for this sequence of shots. They are available from your camera's menu or a shooting information display. Here are some suggestions:

>> **Exposure helpers:** If necessary, set or change options like the Auto Lighting Optimizer or Highlight Tone Priority (Canon), D-Lighting (Nikon), Dynamic Range Optimizer (Sony), and any others.

>> **Noise reduction:** Set any noise reduction options your camera has for using long exposures or high ISO speeds.

>> **Lens corrections:** Ensure that any automatic lens distortion or chromatic aberration correction features on your camera are enabled if you desire, as shown in Figure 5-26. Note that these corrections are applied when the camera saves a JPEG photo. If you shoot Raw photos, the lens correction information will be added to the photo's metadata and applied when you convert the photo in your camera's editing software.

>> **Brackets:** Set the number of brackets and any other parameters now. You may be able to shoot either white balance brackets or auto exposure brackets (AEB). Some cameras shoot other types of brackets. For more information on brackets and HDR, see Book 5, Chapter 6.

MAXIMIZING PRODUCTIVITY

You don't have to complete a 48-point checklist before you take every photo. The process of checking settings goes pretty quickly after you get started. If your subject remains the same and the lighting is consistent, you won't have to make many changes at all.

You won't have to make many changes, that is, if things are going well. Problem solving will slow you down. Relax, focus on the problem, and then implement your solution. For instance, if you're taking action shots and the photos are a bit blurry, the problem may be that you don't have the shutter speed set fast enough. Maybe image stabilization was turned off.

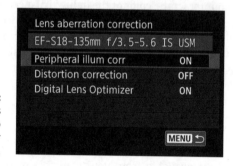

FIGURE 5-26: Enable lens corrections to create better JPEGs.

>> **Mirror Lockup or Mirror Up setting:** When this setting is enabled, the camera flips up the mirror and delays the shutter for a moment, thereby reducing vibrations and shake. You don't need this feature unless you're using a tripod or another type of support and want the most stable, shake-free shot possible. On some cameras, you'll get a mirror lockup indicated on the camera display or top LCD panel.

REMEMBER

Don't forget to revert to normal mirror operation when you finish. I've used mirror delay (and the timer, but that's another story) and forgotten about it. The next time I used the camera, my first few handheld pictures were ruined by the delay.

Taking and Reviewing Photos

Are you ready to take photos? I bet! Use these steps to get used to the process; then change things up if necessary to make them your own:

1. Confirm that the camera is ready and check shooting options.

Make sure that the lens cap is off and out of the way, the camera and any powered attachments are on, you're in a still photography mode (as opposed to movie), you've set the correct shooting mode, and the focus mode is set correctly. Nothing hurts more than not realizing that the camera was set to manual focus mode after shooting 20–30 photos.

Double-check settings for image quality (see Figure 5-27), exposure controls, color space, noise reduction, red-eye reduction, image review, creative styles, and so forth. Your specific checklist depends on your camera:

- Canon users should check Picture Style, Auto Lighting Optimizer, Creative Filters, and the like.

- Nikon users should look at Picture Control, Auto Distortion Control, Active D-Lighting, and so forth.

- Sony users should check settings like Creative Style, Picture Effect, and D-Range Optimizer.

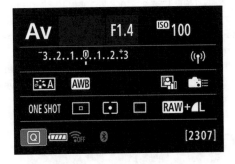

FIGURE 5-27: Check settings before you begin shooting from your camera's settings screen.

These options are dependent on the shooting mode you're in. Basic shooting modes keep you from changing certain settings.

After completing this step, you need not obsessively check these options before every photo. This step is to make sure that the camera is set up the way you want before continuing.

REMEMBER

Unless you're engaging in tripod-mounted landscape, macro, or other studio-type photography, it will take longer for you to read through the next few steps than to actually accomplish them. That's because composing, focusing, and metering can take place almost simultaneously.

2. Compose the scene.

Aim the camera at the subject. Position the subject so that it appears in the viewfinder or on the monitor. If desired, zoom in or out to alter the composition. If you're using a prime lens, you can move yourself closer to or farther away from the subject to change how the photo is composed.

When shooting certain types of shots (animals, people, or action shots), this step may take only a moment, and you may have to anticipate the action or pan the camera with your subject. When you're setting up a portrait or shooting macros in a studio, you'll spend more time perfecting the scene.

If things are totally out of focus and impossible to see, quickly press the shutter button halfway to autofocus or turn the focus ring on the lens to manually focus.

There's a tried-and-true guide to composing photos that you should know about. It's called the *Rule of Thirds*. The rule suggests that you divide the frame vertically and horizontally into thirds — like a Tic-Tac-Toe board (see Figure 5-28). The idea is to place dominant vertical or horizontal lines in the scene (like building edges, the horizon, people, and so forth) on the dividing lines. You should place important objects at the intersection of those lines or within them. You can also work along the diagonals. I set up the photo of my wife in Figure 5-28 with these principles in mind. I muted her so that you can see the grid more clearly. Note that her face is not in the center of the photo. I framed the shot so that the top horizontal grid line would run across the bridge of her nose. She dominates the central third. Everything balances out nicely without looking forced. I could have placed her on the left vertical grid line and that would have looked good too. Why not the right side? Because her shoulders are angled slightly in that direction and she would have been pointing away from the center of the photo.

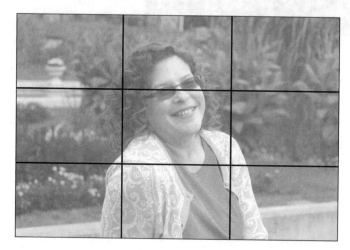

FIGURE 5-28: Visualizing a scene using the Rule of Thirds.

TIP

An advantage of using the Rule of Thirds is being able to align or balance objects in the scene against each other and the empty space. Balancing a scene involves weighing things in the frame (take size, shape, color, brightness, texture, and other factors into account) and positioning them so that most things average out. You can train your eye to see balance well enough that it becomes more of a gut feeling than a conscious act. You'll start to frame photos with balance because they "just feel right." This is especially important when taking photos of people. Never put their heads in the center of the photo. Put them more toward the top.

Do you have to use the Rule of Thirds? No. Should you? Mostly. Although there are always exceptions, humans find it more visually pleasing when things are arranged this way.

3. **Focus.**

If using autofocus, press the shutter button halfway to focus. Press it gently. Practice a bit to know what halfway feels like, and how much more pressure causes the camera to take a photo. If you're focusing manually, use the focus ring.

If you're using Live View, focus according to the procedures for your camera. That may involve moving a focusing frame over the subject you want to be in focus. If using Live View and a tripod, you can zoom in and check focus very precisely. I use this technique all the time when shooting close-ups in my studio.

Metering also occurs when you press the shutter button halfway. The camera quickly evaluates the brightness of the scene and calculates the correct exposure to produce a good photo. If desired, enter exposure correction now. If you're in manual mode, make changes to the exposure controls now. Watch the exposure index to see what affect they have on the exposure (more on this in Book 3, Chapter 1).

When you've focused and the exposure looks good, you may have time to quickly adjust your aim. You may not be able to in every situation. However, many types of photography give you plenty of time to compose the scene, focus and meter, adjust exposure settings, think about it for a while, fine-tune the focus, and then readjust the composition of the scene.

Here are some thoughts to keep in mind when focusing and metering:

- Your camera may also have an AF button that you can press to autofocus instead of using the shutter button. I use the AF button a lot when in Live View mode. This reduces the chances of accidentally taking photos when focusing. You may also be able to change button assignments.

- In low light, you may have an AF-Assist beam shine out from the camera or flash to help the camera lock onto the target. If this beam bothers you, you may be able to disable it. Other cameras use a pulse from the built-in flash to help autofocus.

- If you're using autofocus and you have a problem focusing on the subject you want, change focusing modes or focus points if necessary.

- If you're using AE lock, you'll compose the scene differently than normal. Center your subject, focus, and then press and hold the AE Lock button. While holding the AE Lock button down, recompose and take the photo.

4. **Reality check.**

   Check focus indicators, exposure settings (see Figure 5-29), and, if possible, depth of field. This may take only a fraction of a second. For example, if you see the ISO spiking and don't want a noisy photo, you may want to make changes before you take the shot. By the same token, if you're photographing people and notice that the shutter speed is so low that they will be blurred, change it.

FIGURE 5-29:
Quickly confirm
that everything
is within normal
parameters.

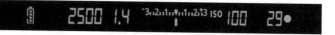

5. **Press the shutter button fully to take the photo.**

   If you released the shutter button earlier, press it halfway again to focus and meter. When focus is confirmed, press the shutter button fully to take the shot.

6. **Review the photo.**

   I like reviewing every photo unless the action is fast and furious. Then I review the first few and glance at the rest until there is a break in the action. At a minimum, you should periodically review sample shots to make sure you're not wasting your time.

   Check to see that photos are in focus, well-lit, have good color, and are framed the way you want them to be. If necessary, use the zoom in or zoom out buttons in Playback mode to look closely at the photo, and the left, right, up, or down buttons to pan. This is also a good time to look at the histogram. Figure 5-30 shows the final shot.

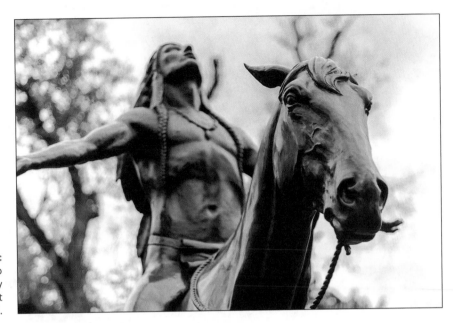

FIGURE 5-30:
Review photos to ensure that they captured what you intended.

REMEMBER

7. **Correct problems.**

    Correcting problems is an important step. If you identify problems when reviewing photos, make changes to correct them.

    You're looking to solve these general issues:

    - **Composition:** Level, even, or as planned.

    - **Exposure:** Good, with details in bright and dark areas, or as intended. Check metering mode if necessary to get a better reading of the scene.

    - **Focus:** Sharp, unless you're after a special effect.

    - **Color:** Good, with correct white balance.

    - **Subject-related:** Eyes open, looking at the camera or where you intend.

8. **Rinse and repeat.**

    Depending on what you're shooting, you may be able to quickly cycle back to Step 2 and keep at it. If you want to make dramatic changes to your setup, such as changing lenses, trying different shooting modes, or changing other major settings, return to the earlier section "Setting Up Your Camera" and reconfigure the camera.

2
Looking through Lenses

Contents at a Glance

Chapter **1**

Appreciating Standard Zoom Lenses

Standard zoom lenses are very popular lenses — and for good reason... They are incredibly versatile. You can shoot anything from wide-angle landscapes to telephoto portraits simply by twisting the zoom ring. As I show you in this chapter, there's not a lot you *can't* do with these zoom lenses!

Relatively inexpensive standard zoom lenses are often bundled with popular consumer-level camera bodies and sold as kits. As a result, these lenses are often called *kit lenses*. Standard zoom lenses are not just for cost-conscious photographers, though. Even professional photographers use zoom lenses, except theirs cost $1,000 to $2,500 instead of $250.

Embodying Versatility

Standard zoom lenses, also known as a *multipurpose zoom, zoom, normal zoom,* or *general-purpose zoom,* are designed to be versatile enough to be useful in a wide variety of circumstances. The name sort of gives that away.

Other types of zoom lenses exist as well. Some cover wide-angle or telephoto territory exclusively. Others have a wider range of focal lengths than general-purpose zoom lenses do. Standard zoom lenses, though, cover the focal length range that you need most of the time for everyday photography. In other words, the "sweet spot." They dip into wide-angle territory, fully encompass normal focal lengths, and extend into the telephoto range. This makes them very handy lenses to have.

Standard zoom lenses come in a few different price ranges. Most kit lenses are relatively inexpensive. Manufacturers try to keep costs down when bundling the camera and lens together. You can also buy mid-level zoom lenses and professional models that cost a lot more. Pro-level lenses, like that shown in Figure 1-1 (AF-S NIKKOR 24–70mm f/2.8G ED), are very expensive, but they deliver the goods. They have better optical qualities and construction than less expensive models, can stand the rigors of shooting without breaking as easily, and take outstanding photos. To see more examples of standard zoom lenses, have a look at some of the cameras and lenses shown in Book 1, Chapters 1 and 3.

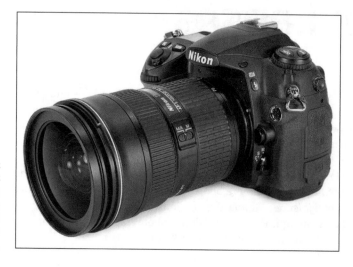

FIGURE 1-1: Zoom lenses range from inexpensive to professional models like this one.

Here are some points to consider when using a standard zoom lens:

>> **Enjoy the versatility:** Enjoy the focal lengths that standard zoom lenses specialize in, and resist the temptation to think you need something else right away. Although you won't be able to take ultra-wide-angle shots or capture the moon the same way a 400mm telephoto lens can, you can photograph a lot of cool stuff in between. That's okay!

>> **Map out an upgrade path:** If you love the focal lengths you've been using, consider purchasing a higher-quality standard zoom lens to continue your career. If you notice that you tend to use one focal length more than others, look at prime lenses close to your sweet spot. Use a program like Adobe Lightroom to see which focal lengths you typically shoot at. Each photo has the focal length it was shot at as part of its metadata. If the lens has frustrated you, you can retire it and get into lenses with more extreme wide-angle or telephoto focal lengths.

REMEMBER

In the sections that follow, I make sure to mention the brand of the camera I used for each photo, the sensor size, and the focal length the lens was set to when I took the photo. This is enough information for you to calculate the 35mm equivalent focal length for cropped-frame dSLRs on your own, should you want to. At times, I include the 35mm equivalent focal length to emphasize a point. Refer to Book 1, Chapters 1 and 3 for more information on image sensor sizes, crop factors, and 35mm equivalent focal lengths.

Taking Wide-Angle Shots

Wide-angle photography captures a greater angle of view than normal or telephoto focal lengths. Sometimes you perceive the photos as being very expansive. At other times, you hardly notice it. It all depends on the subject and how you frame the scene.

Figure 1-2 shows a farmland scene that I took using a Sony APS-C camera and a standard kit lens zoomed out to 18mm. The scene is in wide-angle territory, but not in the extreme. When shooting wide-angle landscapes, try zooming all the way out to capture as much of the scene as possible. That approach captures the full breadth. Details in the scene add depth. In this case, the corn and the clouds take up most of the frame. They also provide color and interesting details that enliven the photo. The homestead sits in the distance, intriguing and yet purposefully small. That's exactly what wide-angle shots are good for. Notice that I employed the Rule of Thirds in this shot. Typically, wide-angle landscape shots do not look as good when angled or out of balance.

TIP

You don't always need an over-the-top-ultra-mega wide-angle lens. Try taking several shots of the scene and stitching them together in software to create a panorama. See Book 5, Chapter 5 for more information on shooting and creating panoramas.

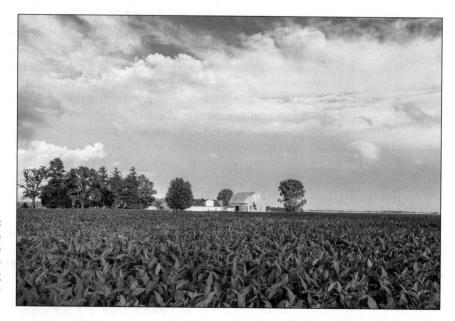

Figure 1-3 shows a very different type of wide-angle shot. I photographed these elevator doors with a standard zoom lens and Canon APS-C camera. It's a unique perspective that almost hides that fact that it's a wide-angle shot. I zoomed all the way out to see everything in the scene, and then angled the camera a bit and zoomed in until I liked what I saw. I took the photo with the lens set to 20mm.

The fact that I angled the camera adds some quirkiness to the photo. It's not meant to be a serious shot of the machinery or architecture, but rather a fun look at the red doors. Because I was using a standard zoom lens, I was able to zoom in and out as I photographed objects and scenes around the doors, even inside the elevator, without having to change lenses.

Not all wide-angle shots have to be landscapes or interiors. In Figure 1-4, I was standing behind a protective fence, photographing my youngest son, Sam, running toward home plate. I was using the same APS-C camera and lens, and even focal length (18mm) that I used in Figure 1-2. I was much closer to my main subject, however, and composed the scene differently.

This shot has a number of wonderful elements. Sam, the coaches, the other kids, the ball in the air, and the scenery all capture the essence of the action as it was happening. Although action shots look great when taken zoomed-in, some — such as this one — work as wide-angle photos.

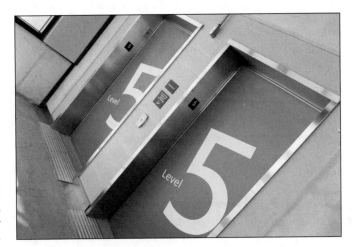

FIGURE 1-3:
Get close and zoom out to capture interior scenes in detail.

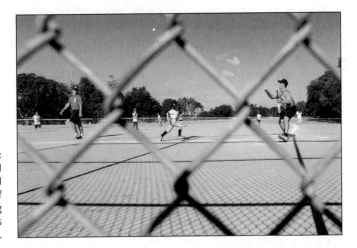

FIGURE 1-4:
Zooming in would have cropped out many of the interesting elements of this scene.

TIP

Standard zoom lenses give you the ability to tell complete stories without having to mess with stopping and starting to change lenses. You can take wide-angle supporting shots, zoom in and take normal shots of particular elements of the scene, and then zoom in further for close-ups of details.

Here are some tips to consider when shooting wide-angle shots with your standard zoom lens:

>> **Try it.** Most people like zooming in more than they appreciate zooming out. Don't fall into the trap of not using the wide-angle range of your zoom lens. Zoom out, Luke.

>> **Use smaller apertures.** Combine a wide angle of view with a deep depth of field by using an aperture of f/8 or smaller. This makes more of the photo appear to be in focus.

>> **Composition is more challenging.** The more you put in the frame, the harder it is to get everything to work well together. Pay attention to the background and edges of the frame, the alignment and balance of the scene's elements, and distractions like power poles and cables.

Working with Normal Focal Lengths

Normal focal lengths are the bread and butter of traditional photography. They are very pleasing to the eye because they look very much like what you see. I took the shot shown in Figure 1-5 from the deck of a boat house on an incredible snowy day by a lake. I walked up on the deck with the intent of photographing the water and far bank, and realized the snow on the railing would make an interesting subject. I used a Canon APS-C camera and standard zoom lens set to 33mm.

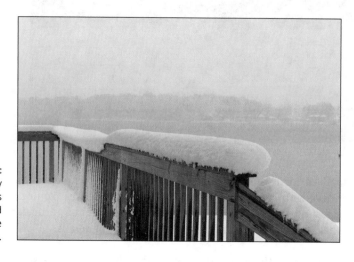

FIGURE 1-5:
Not every landscape has to be captured with a wide-angle focal length.

I'm convinced that this photo works as well as it does because the focal length is within the normal range (about 58mm in 35mm equivalent terms). Had I zoomed out, the railing would have shrunk and taken a less dominant role in the photo. The background would have become more important, which was not the point. Had I zoomed in and framed a tight shot of the railing, the bigger picture would have been lost.

Figure 1-5 was an unexpected, spur-of-the-moment shot. Having a zoom lens gave me the flexibility to quickly choose just how to frame the scene. I didn't have to move closer or farther away — I simply gave the lens a twist and took the photo.

Figure 1-6 shows an entirely different scene, shot using a Canon APS-C camera and kit lens set to 32mm. As a family, we had been out playing in the yard. I took some casual shots of everyone and then gave the camera to my wife so that she and the kids could review them. While they enjoyed the photos, I grabbed another camera and took this shot.

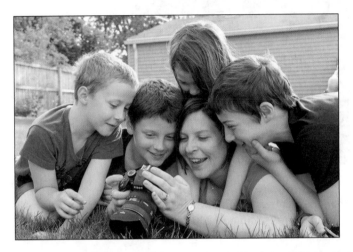

FIGURE 1-6:
Use normal focal lengths to keep people from looking distorted.

For this scene to work, I needed to select a focal length that would capture everyone in the shot (it's a group photo, after all). I zoomed out initially to see what that would look like. Too wide. I quickly zoomed in and stopped when I was satisfied with the composition. Just right. The final focal length was 32mm. That's about 51mm in 35mm equivalent terms — which is just a hair over the "mother of all normal focal lengths," 50mm. I could have zoomed in further to focus more on them, but I would have sacrificed the background in the process. It's a tough call, but I left it loose and can always crop in software if I decide to later.

When shooting portraits, zoom in to minimize an unattractive background.

Finally, I took the shot in Figure 1-7 using the Nikon APS-C camera and professional lens shown earlier in Figure 1-1. I composed the scene using a focal length of 40mm. That was close to the middle of the focal length range of the lens, and right on the edge between normal and near-telephoto focal lengths. In this case I wanted the attention focused mostly on the tree, and yet I didn't want the tree to totally obscure the lake and other scenery in the background. Given my distance to the tree, a normal focal length achieved the right effect. Zooming out would have overemphasized the background, and zooming in would have eliminated it.

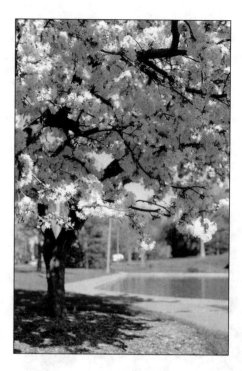

FIGURE 1-7:
Zoom in and out
to find the right
balance between
foreground and
background.

Keep these things in mind when shooting in the normal focal length range, which is around 30–35 mm on APSC cameras:

» **Everyday use:** Normal focal lengths are perfect for everyday photography.

» **Normal look:** These focal lengths produce the most normal-looking photos. Use them when you want a classic 35mm feel to your shots.

» **Less distortion:** Normal focal lengths tend to produce photos with less distortion than wide-angle focal lengths.

TIP

» **Use the vertical:** Hold the camera vertically at times to change the composition.

Zooming In

Most people want to get larger or closer shots of their subjects. I know I do, and my wife and kids are the same way. I've got great news for you: Zoom lenses are perfect for this. How much you can zoom in depends on your lens, of course.

When zooming in, consider these points:

» **Shutter speed:** The more you zoom in, the harder it is to take sharp photos. Camera shake becomes more of a problem. Make sure that image stabilization is enabled, and select a faster shutter speed if needed to keep things from getting blurry.

» **Portraits:** Taking shots of people in the near-telephoto range of your standard zoom lens can result in very effective portraits. Try these focal lengths: 50mm (cropped-frame) or 85mm (full-frame).

» **Distance matters:** Using the telephoto focal lengths of a standard zoom lens at close range will produce very tightly framed shots. When you're outside or shooting something farther away, the same focal lengths will produce very different results.

Capturing telephoto shots

Zoom in and capture your distant subjects using the telephoto focal length range of your zoom lens. Although you would think you need the biggest, baddest lens possible, you really don't. Many reasonably priced zoom lenses have maximum focal lengths from 135mm to 200mm.

Picture this: One day my family and I heard an odd sound coming from outside. We all ran out the front door (there are six of us, so that is an event in and of itself) to see what it was. Lo and behold, it was *the Goodyear Blimp!* I ran back into the house and grabbed the camera (Canon APS-C). Thankfully, the lens I was using had a maximum focal length of 135mm (that's over 200mm in 35mm equivalent terms). I zoomed in fully and captured the blimp before it flew away. See Figure 1-8.

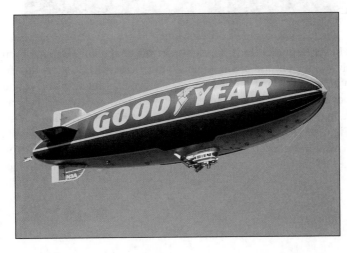

FIGURE 1-8: Zoom all the way in to capture objects at a distance.

In cases like this, having a camera with a healthy number of megapixels really helps. Although you clearly want as much zoom as you can get out of your lens, the pixel count gives you the option of cropping out extra space without compromising the photo's quality if you decide to get a large print made.

Capturing portraits

Figure 1-9 shows my three boys in costume one Halloween. I used the kit lens of a Sony APS-C camera to frame the shot how I wanted it, which came out to a focal length of 45mm. That doesn't sound like a lot, but the crop factor of 1.5x makes this the equivalent of 68mm on a full-frame camera. That puts this shot just inside the near (or medium) telephoto range. Compare this photo to the group shot in Figure 1-6. I'm standing farther back in this shot and have zoomed in more. Although the aperture in both photos is f/5.6, the background is more attractively blurred in this photo. You get that by using a longer focal length.

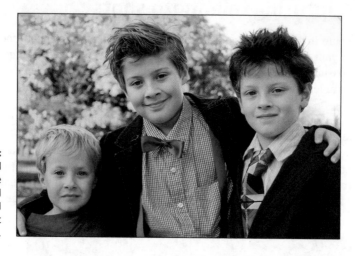

FIGURE 1-9: Longer focal lengths enable you to stand farther back and still capture great portraits.

Finally, Figure 1-10 is a casual portrait of my wife outside prepping for a family dinner on our picnic table. I shot this with a Canon full-frame dSLR using a 24-105mm lens set at 105mm. That makes this a near (or medium) telephoto portrait. Aside from marveling at just how pretty she is (natural smiles and laughter make for great photos), notice the background in this scene compared to Figures 1-6 and 1-9. This one is by far the most pleasing. Part of the reason is the lens, but it's also the fact that the focal length in this photo (105mm) is the longest. That equates to 65mm on an APS-C camera with a crop factor of 1.6x.

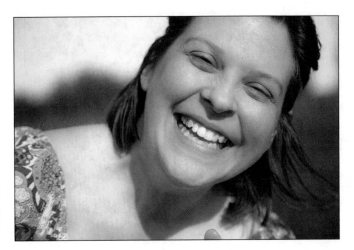

FIGURE 1-10:
Zoom in to
capture stunning
near telephoto
portraits.

REMEMBER

Near telephoto focal lengths on standard zoom lenses are quite effective at shooting group *and* individual portraits. Unlike the group shot of the boys, having a single subject enabled me to focus entirely on her. The result is a great photograph — shot with a really nice zoom lens.

Capturing close-ups

Close-up photography is another category that you can pursue very effectively with a standard zoom lens. As with telephoto shots, you zoom in to magnify the subject. The key difference between the two, however, is that you are typically closer when shooting a close-up.

Figure 1-11 is a classic close-up of a bowl full of radishes sitting on a table taken with a Canon APS-C camera and standard zoom lens. I set up this classic "foodie" shot from start to finish. I chose the subject, the lighting, the placement, the distance I stood at, and the focal length I used (55mm). I was able to get the shot I wanted without having to resort to any special equipment or a macro lens.

Portraits shot as close-ups also work well. Figure 1-12 is a fun shot of one of my kids. We were all out in the backyard one hot August day playing with water balloons, hoses, and shaving cream (we run a fun household). Jacob has on goggles to protect his eyes and is lathering himself up before his mom turns the hose on. Nothing says "close-up action-portrait" more than that!

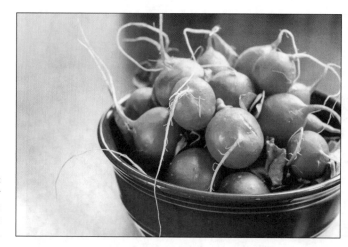

FIGURE 1-11:
Get close to your subject and then zoom in to get a nice close-up.

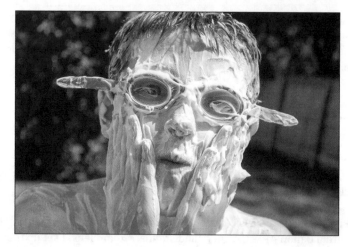

FIGURE 1-12:
Step closer and zoom in if you need to capture a nice close-up.

While he was getting ready, I moved close and zoomed in to 44mm with my Nikon APS-C dSLR. The combination of being relatively close and zooming in resulted in a wonderfully nice, tight shot of his face and pleasantly blurred background. Compare how I framed this photo to the one in Figure 1-10. Although their faces take up similar space within the frame, I was standing much closer for this photo, which meant I had to zoom in less.

REMEMBER

You want a nice, shallow depth of field in a portrait. You can get that by choosing focal lengths in the telephoto range as well as by using a wide aperture.

Finally, flowers make fantastic close-up subjects. They are beautiful, colorful, easy to find, and don't blink. They don't even blink. (I had a *Dr. Who* moment there.) Figure 1-13 is a nice close-up of a vase of flowers I shot on a table in my studio. I mounted my Canon APS-C dSLR on a tripod, composed the scene using the camera's Live View mode, and minimized camera shake even further by using a wireless remote shutter release. Taken with an inexpensive kit lens at 55mm, this close-up shot is simply gorgeous.

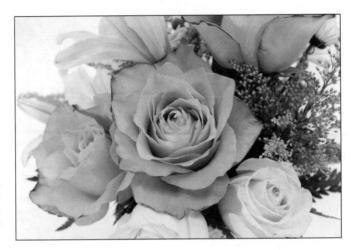

FIGURE 1-13: Shoot a close-up to capture as much detail as you can.

Chapter **2**

Enjoying Wide-Angle Lenses

When you think of wide-angle photography, sweeping landscapes and large cityscapes probably come to mind. Those are the show-stopping shots we've all seen. However, you can also capture great-looking shots of other interesting subjects using a wide-angle lens, including shots of buildings, interiors, people, and more. You can easily fall in love with this type of photography, and it offers a refreshing change of pace from stalking the cat around the house. Join me in this chapter as I walk you through how to take great wide-angle shots of a wide range (get it?) of different subjects.

Wide-Angle Whatzit

Wide-angle focal lengths are shorter than those on other types of lenses. They take photos with a wider angle of view. The long and the short of it is that focal lengths less than 25mm are considered wide-angle on cropped-frame cameras, whereas focal lengths less than 40mm are wide-angle on full-frame cameras.

You need to consider the camera as well as the lens. For example, putting a 35mm lens on a full-frame camera puts you in wide-angle territory, but not if you put the same lens on a cropped-frame camera.

Most cropped-frame kits for consumer-level APS-C cameras have zoom lenses with focal lengths from 18–55mm. That means you're equipped and able to shoot wide angles when you zoom out. Four Thirds cameras with kit lenses from 14–42mm should zoom out to at least 20mm to enjoy wide-angle photography.

If you're a full-frame user with a standard zoom lens, you probably have good wide-angle capability built into your lens. For example, the Canon EF 24–105mm f/4L IS USM lens operates well into wide-angle territory.

Aside from standard zoom lenses with wide-angle focal lengths, a number of different types of dedicated wide-angle zoom and wide-angle prime lenses are available from most lens manufacturers. You can also pick up an ultra wide-angle zoom lens, as shown in Figure 2-1. Turn to Book 1, Chapter 3 for more information on focal lengths and how wide-angles compare to everything else.

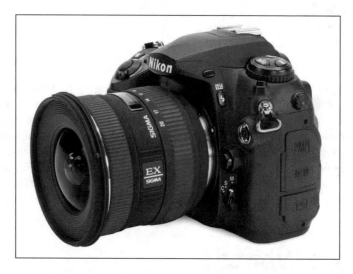

FIGURE 2-1:
Ultra wide-angle lenses capture amazing scenes.

REMEMBER

In this chapter, I mention the camera and sensor size along with the focal length of each photo. With this information, you can calculate a 35mm-equivalent focal length if you like, and compare it to your setup. Book 1, Chapters 1 and 3 have more information on how to do this and why it's sometimes necessary.

Looking at Landscapes

You can find few better tools for shooting landscapes than a digital SLR with a wide-angle lens. Throw in a tripod and a remote shutter release and you're set. The tripod lets you take longer exposures without worrying about keeping the camera steady. I recommend using a remote or setting the drive mode to a timer in these instances to minimize camera shake.

I photographed the sunset in Figure 2-2 using just those tools. The weather at the lake was ideal. It was late afternoon and the sun was well off to my right. The lighting was bright but not as harsh as during midday. The color of the sky and lake were amazing. I took this photograph with my Nikon APS-C dSLR. I set the lens to 20mm to capture a wide but still natural-looking shot.

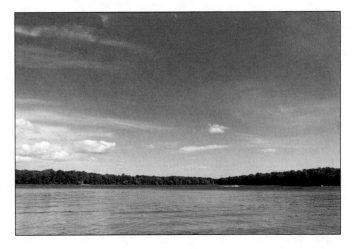

FIGURE 2-2:
A beautiful lake photographed with an ultra wide-angle lens.

Figure 2-3 shows a totally different scene, shot using the same basic wide-angle landscape technique. I used a different Nikon APS-C camera, set the lens to 11mm, mounted the camera on a tripod, and used a remote to trigger the shutter. The entire scene was well lit by the evening sun, which is to the left of the frame. The clouds add welcome texture and detail to the sky.

Keep these tips in mind when shooting wide-angle landscapes:

>> **Great shots are about great locations.** The world has many pretty places, but some of them are plagued with power poles, lines, and signs that take away from the natural beauty. I've discovered that the landscape shots that I like the best are free from these distractions. Finding these locations is not always easy, so keep an eye out. You may have to go off the beaten path to get to them.

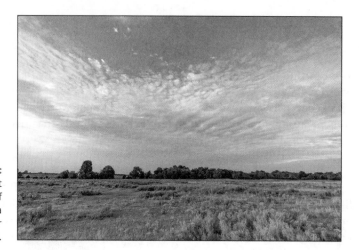

FIGURE 2-3:
The wind-swept plains of Oklahoma captured near sunset.

TIP

» **Keep the camera level.** If possible, align the camera so that the horizon is straight. Use a tripod to lock in the orientation. If you don't feel comfortable eyeballing it, use your camera's electronic level to help. Some elements of the scene may not cooperate. Tree lines are notorious for being uneven. That's okay, so long as it doesn't feel like the photo tips one way or the other. If necessary, make corrections after you've taken the photo in the camera or Photoshop.

» **Compose using the Rule of Thirds.** Remember the Rule of Thirds is even more important than usual when framing wide-angle shots, especially landscapes with the horizon. Notice that in my two examples, the horizon is situated toward the bottom third of the photo. You can compose your shots so that the land, rather than the sky, dominates. If you don't get it right on location, try straightening and cropping the photo in software.

REMEMBER

Wide-angle lenses *vignette* quite often, which means their corners are darker than their centers. You can correct this problem in software or with special in-camera lens correction options, if available. I sometimes use vignetting purposely to make the photo look interesting.

Capturing Wide-Angle Cityscapes

Wide-angle lenses also excel at capturing cities and skylines. Figure 2-4 shows one way to capture an expansive view. I took this shot from inside the top of the Gateway Arch, a 630-foot-high monument in St. Louis, Missouri. The sun is off to the left of the frame and made shooting in that direction very difficult. I chose to angle the camera to the north for this shot. Notice that this photo is an example of not strictly following the Rule of Thirds. The horizon is in the center of the frame, which is normally bad. In this case, I think it works because of the diagonal elements in the scene. Your eyes gravitate toward a point below the center of the photo and off to the right. The window frame also accentuates this line.

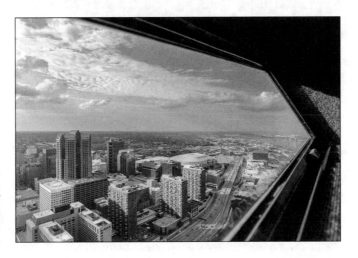

FIGURE 2-4:
You can capture large parts of cities from the right vantage point.

This photo is interesting because you can see about 30 miles (48 km) toward the distant horizon, yet the buildings in the city below are nice and detailed. The highway angling away from the Arch is a great element. The cars and trucks traveling on it are mostly dots. This is a stunning location to shoot from. I took this shot using a Nikon APS-C camera and ultra wide-angle lens set to 14mm.

Not every city has a good vantage point from which to photograph. Of those that do, not all are equally accessible. You should, however, be able to find some interesting buildings to photograph. Look at your downtown area near the city center. If that doesn't work, look at other parts, perhaps well outside. These are often photogenic. Schools, museums, memorials, and government buildings are often ideal subjects. When you find the right subject, make sure to have your wide-angle lens with you, because you'll need it.

Figure 2-5 shows a small part of downtown Detroit. I am standing on Brush Street, looking southeast toward the Renaissance Center. This street reminded me of a canyon, so I got in the middle and used the buildings on both sides to frame the far end of the street. I set the lens to 20mm and took the shot with my Sony APS-C camera. Notice that I'm a few blocks away from the subject of the photo. This is a testament to how tall the building is. In situations like this, you may have to physically move to the right distance for your shot to work.

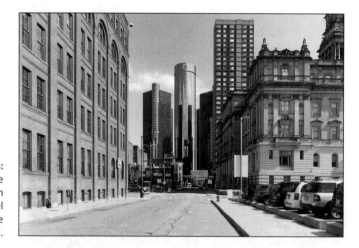

FIGURE 2-5:
This cityscape
was shot from
ground level
and has a more
immediate feel.

TIP

When you're shooting cityscapes, keep these tips in mind:

>> **Do a walkabout.** Choosing the right vantage point is probably the most challenging aspect of capturing cityscapes. In some cases, you may not be able to find a good view at all, especially if the terrain is flat and there are no surrounding hills or heights. You can often find a good spot to shoot from if the city is bordered by water on one or more sides.

>> **Watch the horizon.** A crooked horizon can be distracting unless it's a purposeful design element of the photo. Use your camera's level if possible.

>> **Check the foreground.** Pay attention to what's close to you as well as what's off in the distance.

Focusing on Single Buildings

Single buildings are often easier and more convenient to capture than a larger cityscape is. Figure 2-6 shows the former Dearborn Hyatt Regency (now Edward Hotel & Convention Center) located just across the road from the Ford Motor Company world headquarters in Dearborn, Michigan. It's a large, curved, 14-story building. I took several shots of the entire building, but then moved in close to the entrance and held the camera vertically to capture this photo. It showcases the curve of the top very nicely, along with the restaurant on top. The white car in front of the door was a matter of fortunate timing that I took advantage of. I used a Sony APS-C camera for this photo, and set the lens to 10mm.

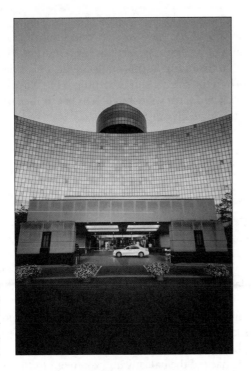

FIGURE 2-6:
Single buildings
are natural
subjects for
wide-angle
photography.

Figure 2-7 shows another close-up of a single building. This time it's the Allen County War Memorial Coliseum (named well before the original 140-character limit imposed by Twitter), located in Indiana. Originally built in 1952, this large arena was updated in 2001 when builders literally raised the roof over 40 feet. They made other extensive renovations and improvements at that time, and have since added on almost 50,000 square feet of additional conference and event space adjoining the arena. It's impressive to be in and photograph.

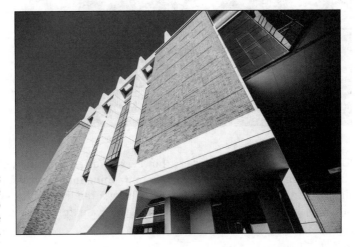

FIGURE 2-7:
Point the
camera up to
capture creative
viewpoints.

The building is so large that you have to step well back to photograph it, even using wide angles. For a more dramatic, artistic presentation, I chose to get close and point the camera up, resulting in this angled shot. This side of the Coliseum faces west, and light from the setting sun is bathing it in golden-hour goodness. I used a Sony APS-C dSLR and ultra wide-angle lens set to 10mm. This shot would be impossible without using wide-angles.

TIP

Find out as much as you can about what you're photographing. Learning about a location draws you closer to your photos and gives you stories to tell.

Photographing Interiors

Believe it or not, a wide-angle lens is indispensable when shooting indoors, whether you're in a large or small location.

I took the photo shown in Figure 2-8 from the balcony of a local church. The modern sanctuary is large and open, and ends in a stage rather than a pulpit. The room invites you to photograph it with a wide-angle lens. In fact, it really requires it. I had to move to the back of the balcony and zoom out to 10mm with my Nikon APS-C camera to fit the entire room in the frame.

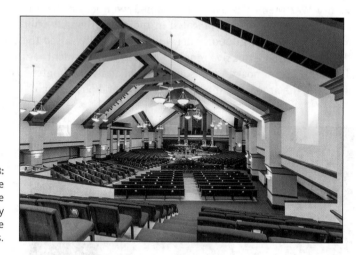

FIGURE 2-8:
Interiors, large and small, are captured nicely by wide-angle lenses.

The problem with large interiors, however, is often with the lighting. Although the scene may look fine in person, photographing interiors usually requires more light than you think, and larger rooms have a tendency to be even darker. The situation is made even more difficult if you want to use a smaller aperture to increase the depth of field (also called *stopping down*). To cope with the lighting and capture a reasonable shot, use a longer shutter speed, higher ISO, additional lighting, or a technique like HDR (high dynamic range) photography.

TIP

Wide-angle lenses can be incredibly practical. Take your digital SLR and a wide-angle lens (a zoom lens may work fine) with you when house shopping. When you review the photos, you'll see *rooms* instead of corners. That will make it easier to plan how you will furnish and decorate.

Keep these points in mind when shooting wide-angle interiors:

>> **Watch for vertical distortion.** Pointing the camera up or down will introduce vertical distortion, which is particularly unappealing in interior shots. As you compose the scene, pay attention to vertical lines. If they tip toward or away from you, you know you have a problem. Unless you have an overriding artistic purpose, keep the camera pointing straight away from you (as opposed to up or down).

>> **Use a tripod if possible.** Although you may think you don't need a tripod when shooting inside, exposure can be a real challenge. Being able to use slower shutter speeds will help you keep the ISO low, which will in turn keep noise from overwhelming an otherwise good shot.

Shooting Wide-Angle Portraits

My wife took the shot shown in Figure 2-9 of our three boys and me as we were dropping one of our kids off at summer camp. We're proudly displaying our sunglasses and having a great time hamming it up for her. She used a Canon APS-C dSLR and standard zoom lens set to 18mm. That's right in the middle of the wide-angle range for an APS-C camera. Although it doesn't contain an impressive landscape, this is nonetheless a very valuable wide-angle shot to show. You can capture artistic shots or photos of everyday life, including portraits of people, using wide angles. Simply put, this is one of my favorite photos, and it was shot spontaneously.

One key to using wide angles when photographing people is not to be too far away. Unless you're photographing a large group of people, stay close. Another important point is to makes sure the shutter speed is quick enough to capture guys who are giggling and being silly. My wife set the camera to shutter-priority mode with a shutter speed of 1/500 second. That was possible because we were outside in bright sunlight.

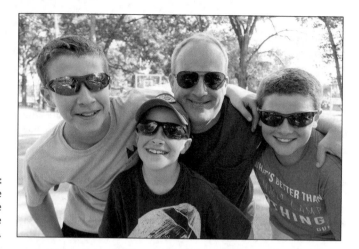

FIGURE 2-9:
Wide-angle
portraits capture
groups of people
very effectively.

Not every wide-angle shot requires a special lens, tripod, remote, or other extra gear. Keep your standard zoom lens attached and zoom out when you need to.

REMEMBER

Improving Your Wide-Angle Shots

Wide-angle photography is incredibly fun, and there are many ways to improve your photos. When you go out to take wide-angle shots, try to use wide-angle focal lengths to your advantage. You will be rewarded with special photos if you recognize and emphasize elements of the scene that cry out to be photographed with wide angles.

Frame tall objects from afar

When you're shooting a scene and want to make sure to get it all in, step back and use a wide-angle lens. Figure 2-10 is an exterior shot of the Gateway Arch. My family and I had just arrived for a visit and were walking down the trail from the now-demolished parking garage toward the Arch. I took a series of shots as we got closer. In this one, I estimate my position to be about 100 feet away. It looks closer than that in the photo, but the Arch is huge, and distances can be deceiving in wide-angle shots. The legs, for reference, are 54 feet wide at the base. The moral of the story is this: Distance can make a world of difference when shooting in wide-angle territory. I was able to capture the entire Arch with very little apparent distortion because I stood back and used an ultra wide-angle lens set to 14mm on a Nikon APS-C dSLR.

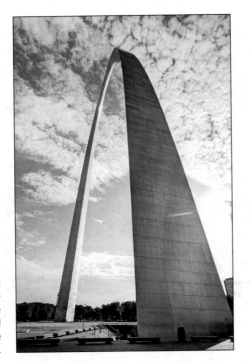

FIGURE 2-10: Scenes like this beg to be photographed with a wide-angle lens.

Pointing the camera up or down when you're working with focal lengths in the wide-angle region causes vertical distortion. At times, you have no choice. In this case, though, I moved back to photograph the Arch. That kept vertical distortion in this photo to a minimum.

TIP

Some wide-angle scenes confuse automatic focus modes. If your scene is complex and you have a specific point that you want in focus, try choosing the specific AF point or switching to manual focus.

Get up close and personal

I took the photo shown in Figure 2-11 from a low perspective, but more important, up close and personal. The camera is about 18 inches away from the front wheel of this gorgeous yellow Harley. I used a Sony APS-C dSLR and set the focal length of the lens to 10mm.

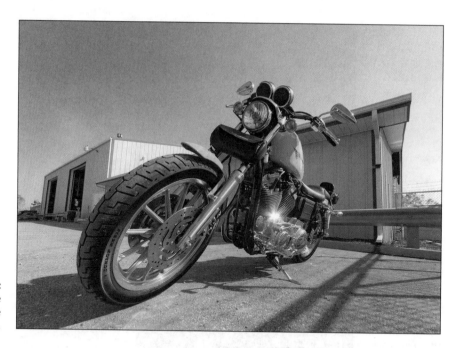

FIGURE 2-11:
You can get close
with wide-angle
lenses.

The point here is that I was able to feature the entire bike and still have room for the building and the sky by getting pretty close. In fact, I was sitting on the ground when I took this shot. The result? Everything fits without making the motorcycle seem small. In fact, it dominates the frame. This would not have been possible with another lens. I would have had to photograph a particular part of the bike or move away to fit it all in.

If you continually set your tripod to the same height, your shots will end up looking similar. Shake things up — consider using the ground for support, instead — even when you're using a wide-angle lens. Remember, you don't always need to be standing when you take a photo.

Use the vertical

Don't be afraid to switch your camera to a vertical (portrait) orientation, even when shooting wide-angle shots. The photo in Figure 2-12 is an effective example. I took this shot using a Nikon APSC-dSLR and wide-angle zoom lens set to 10mm. I didn't need to hold the camera vertically, but after taking a series of shots holding the camera normally I decided I wanted a change of pace. I therefore switched to portrait orientation (holding the camera vertically). The result is a compelling shot that enabled me to capture much more of the lake and sky than I would have otherwise.

FIGURE 2-12:
Frame some
subjects vertically
for a change of
pace.

Combine different elements into one shot

Sweeping landscapes and impressive cultural monuments aren't the only beautiful scenes out there to capture in wide angles. Figure 2-13 shows a local park. It's simple, but still very interesting. I took this shot with a Nikon APS-C dSLR and an ultra wide-angle lens set to 11mm. The scene has several elements that make it work. The colorful brick path is covered with a scattering of small leaves and is very important to the photo. It extends away and disappears as it sweeps to the right in the distance. That creates a feeling of mystery. The trees on each side add color, and the lamps, bench, and fences add interesting details. The clouds and the sky are equally important. I was able to capture all these different elements in one shot without making the photo look cramped. In fact, it feels nice and relaxed.

Emphasize height

Use wide-angle shots to emphasize height. The photo shown in Figure 2-14 is of the Cadillac Tower in Detroit, Michigan. This building is 40 stories tall and 438 feet high. Although that is almost 200 feet shorter than the Gateway Arch shown earlier, it still looks quite impressive in this shot.

Enjoying Wide-Angle Lenses

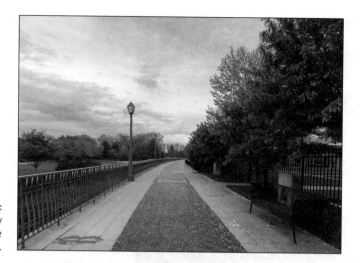

FIGURE 2-13:
Beautiful scenery
is everywhere
around you.

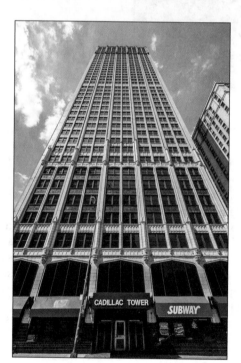

FIGURE 2-14:
Wide-angle lenses
can emphasize
height as well as
width.

I used a wide-angle lens set to 10mm and held the camera (Sony dSLR with an APS-C image sensor) vertically to fit the entire building in the photo. That's the beauty of using wide-angle lenses. You can fit in so much more than normal lenses, including very tall buildings. The reason this shot appears to have quite a bit of vertical distortion is that I had to point the camera up to get the top of the building in the scene. Although I could have stood farther away and held the camera closer to horizontal, I chose to get right next to the building and look up. I wanted to fill the frame with as much of the building as possible for artistic effect and to emphasize its height. Compare this to the Arch shown earlier (refer to Figure 2-10), where I was able to stand farther back and not point the camera up as much.

DEALING WITH DISTORTION

Depending on the subject, wide-angle lens distortion can go unnoticed. However, some scenes shot with extremely wide angles bring it to the forefront. This is particularly true of people. If distortion (including odd perspectives) bothers you, try easing up on the focal length. See whether you can find a sweet spot where the distortion is minimal. You can also try removing or minimizing it with your photo editor or Raw converter. Not all wide-angle lenses perform the same. If you have a lens with particularly bad distortion, you may consider returning it to the store for a different brand or model of wide-angle lens. For more on image processing and editing, turn to Book 5.

Chapter **3**

Capturing Macros and Close-ups

Macros and close-up photos give us a vantage point we don't normally see. Small bugs become huge. Hidden details become visible. The mundane becomes magical. You can literally see the hair on a fly's backside. These photos evoke "oohs" and "aahs" from us because they are so different and interesting to look at. I've packed this chapter with information about macro and close-up photography so that you can see it in action.

True macro photography has a technical side that I describe in this chapter, but you don't have to be a stickler for definitions to take close-ups and enjoy them. Take advantage of the tips and techniques I share to help you get started and capture amazingly cool photos. Finally, shop for accessories that will help you shoot close-ups with normal lenses. Enjoy!

Defining Macro and Close-up Photography

Technically, macro photography relies on special lenses called *macro* lenses. (Nikon calls them *micro* lenses.) Macro lenses have two defining characteristics:

» **Reproduction ratio:** Macro lenses focus objects on the sensor closer to their actual size than non-macro lenses. This is called the *reproduction ratio*. Ideally, macro lenses should have a one-to-one ratio. That means that if you're photographing a common black ant that is 3 mm long, it will be 3 mm long on the image sensor. Some macro lenses enlarge objects.

Not all macro lenses have the same reproduction ratios. When you're shopping for a macro lens, look carefully at its specifications if you want small things to be photographed as large as possible. Look at reviews to determine whether people are happy with the lens or find that it disappoints.

» **Close focusing distance:** Some macro lenses have a low minimum focusing distance, which means that you can put the camera very close to the subject and autofocus will still work. For example, the AF-S DX Micro NIKKOR 40mm f/2.8G lens can be as close as 6.4 inches and focus. The Canon EF 100mm f/2.8L Macro IS USM lens, on the other hand, has a minimum close focusing distance of a foot. Most normal lenses have close focusing distances of between one and two feet. Telephoto lens close focusing distances may be several feet.

Both of the preceding characteristics make focal length a less important measure of lens capability for macro photography than for other genres. For example, you can take great macros with a 100mm lens or a 40mm lens. This is why you can find *macro primes* (those with a fixed focal length) in a whole range of focal lengths.

Although similar to macro photography, close-up photography is a less technical pursuit. Anything you photograph from a relatively close perspective qualifies. The point of a close-up is to zoom in or get close enough to the subject to make it appear large. You can use any lens you want.

Regardless of how you take your macros and close-ups, you can always zoom in further when you process the photos in software. That's a great advantage of having a camera with a few million pixels to spare around the edges.

Shooting at Close Ranges

Macro lenses and normal lenses fitted with the right accessories can focus on objects much closer than standard zoom or prime lenses. Depending on the lens you're using, you may be able to position yourself exceptionally close to your subject.

I've done just that in Figure 3-1. This is a photo of one of my kids' toys (just like the ones I used to play with). He's the one throwing the hand grenade. I put him down on the table and snuck up on him real close to take this shot. He appears to be happy with his work, and his uniform fits him like a glove. I took this photo in a studio setting, so I had a lot of bright lights shining from several angles.

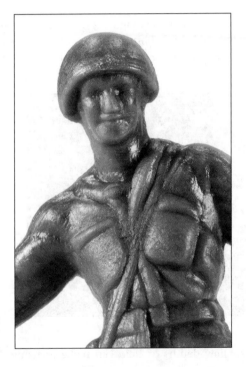

FIGURE 3-1:
Gung Ho for
macros.

TIP

Using the viewfinder can sometimes be problematic when shooting this close. If you can't see what's happening through your viewfinder, switch to Live View. You may have to increase the ISO speed to brighten the scene on the monitor. Doing so also helps if you manually focus.

Managing Depth of Field

Keep in mind that the aperture settings you use when shooting macros and some close-ups don't always produce the same results as standard photography. When you move close to your subjects, the depth of field shrinks noticeably, even when you use smaller aperture.

When shooting macros or close-ups, I often work with apertures set to f/16 or smaller. This setting increases the depth of field enough so that my subjects are reasonably sharp. The depth of field is still small, however. When it's a problem, I rely on positioning to manage depth of field. Rather than shoot at an angle, I try to flatten the composition so that as much detail as possible is on the same focal plane. The army man in Figure 3-1, shot at f/22, is a good example of this.

Of course, you can have fun either way. Figure 3-2 shows rain droplets on a leaf. Shot at f/8, the depth of field is incredibly narrow — only a few small water droplets deep. In this case, that makes the photo much more interesting.

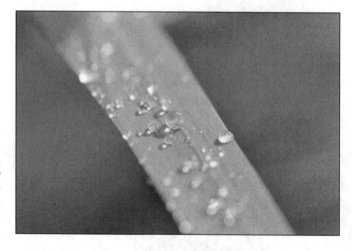

FIGURE 3-2:
This depth of field is about four water droplets from front to back.

REMEMBER

Working with very shallow depths of field can make focusing difficult. Add in camera weight and subjects that may not stay still for long, and you've got a real challenge. When that happens, relax and take a deep breath. Switch off your targeting computer and trust yourself, as Obi-Wan suggests. Focus the lens as best you can and then take your hand off the focus ring. Move the camera until the scene looks best, and take the photo.

Shooting Handheld with a Flash

You can set up a base camp and mount your camera on a tripod to shoot flowers, but if you want to shoot the bugs on them, well . . . bugs move. They flit here and there. When I set up my camera on its tripod and zero in on a flower, all the bugs chose the other flowers to land on. Hmm. If that happens to you, ditch the tripod and stalk bugs on foot with a long focal length macro lens.

Figure 3-3 illustrates a good example of a handheld shot for which everything seemed to work perfectly. The image of the fly is sharp, colorful, and in focus. If you look carefully, you can see my reflection in the fly's body segments. The brighter spots are from the external flash I used to help light the scene, which I shot in the late afternoon. I set the aperture to f/11 as a compromise between having a decent depth of field and needing more light, and I raised the ISO marginally. Even with those changes, the shutter speed was a paltry 1/60 second. Thankfully, the macro lens had vibration reduction.

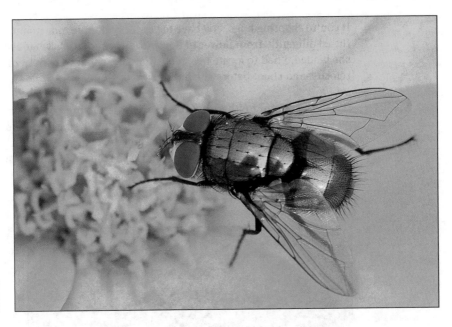

FIGURE 3-3:
So close you can
see the hairs!

The long focal length I used helped, too. I had the amazing Micro-NIKKOR 105mm f/2.8G lens mounted on an APS-C body, and in case that wasn't enough, the TC-20E III 2x teleconverter was attached. The total 35mm equivalent focal length was 315mm. This let me position myself and the lens farther away from the fly than, say, a 60mm macro. A longer macro is better for photographing skittish, stinging, or dangerous insects that are likely to fly away or attack you when you're too close.

TIP

Exposure can sometimes be a problem when you *stop down* (set a smaller aperture). If necessary, raise ISO or use a flash, if possible.

TIP

Take breaks more often when you're shooting handheld macros, especially if you're outside in the heat. The weight of the camera and macro lens will tire you out faster. Although these factors may not seem like such a big deal, remember that you're focusing on such tiny items that any camera movement can knock you out of the focal plane. Keeping elements steady is difficult, even with fast shutter speeds and vibration reduction turned on.

If you're patient in the right situation (for example, you have a bird feeder within close range that gets regular visits), you can set up your camera on a tripod and pretend that you're on safari.

Maximizing Shutter Speed

If you're shooting bugs, you have to be able to handle movement. One bee I tracked flitted diligently from flower to flower to flower. (That's what bees do.) Every time she landed, I had to locate her, reposition myself and the camera, and then frame, refocus, and shoot before she buzzed away.

If you're shooting either inanimate or slow-moving objects, tracking, framing, and focusing get easier. Figure 3-4 shows a bug that moved more deliberately. I was able to follow him for quite some time before he left. I stopped down to f/22 to maximize the depth of field and increased shutter speed to 1/400 second. These adjustments kept most of the beetle in focus and froze his movement. I increased ISO to 1600 to make up for the aperture and shutter speed.

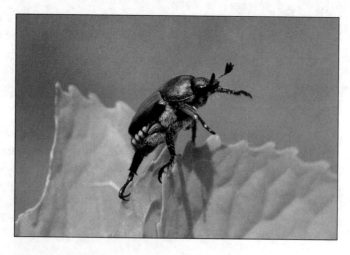

FIGURE 3-4:
Even with close-ups, you freeze movement by increasing shutter speed.

Shooting in Controlled Conditions

When you're working inside your studio (refer to wherever you shoot inside as your *studio*, whether it's your dining room table, kitchen counter, a corner of the basement, or a 20-x-20 outbuilding), you have much more control over your setup and lighting. You don't have to worry about the sun, wind, flying bugs, or a camera that grows heavier with every photo you take.

Figure 3-5 shows a close-up of my college class ring that I took with a Holga digital SLR lens and 60mm macro attachment. I perched the ring in a ring box with a black velvet interior to stabilize it for the photo. You're seeing about an inch (2.54 cm) from left to right. Interesting rings and other jewelry make great subjects for macro photography.

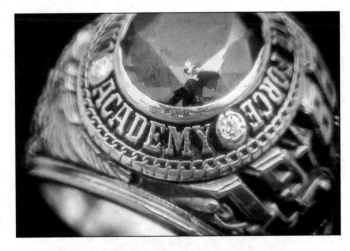

FIGURE 3-5:
Shooting in a studio enables you to design the shot you want more precisely.

REMEMBER

When you're in the studio, mount your camera on a tripod to ensure stability. Doing so also lets you make the shutter speed as slow as you need.

My preferences when shooting in-studio run like this:

>> **Continuous lighting:** I've rigged up several homemade *soft boxes* (a soft cover than diffuses light) to light the scene. I know exactly what the ISO, shutter speed, and aperture need to be before I even turn on the camera. This knowledge comes from shooting hundreds of shots in the same location with the same lighting and setup.

>> **Manual focus:** The best way to focus in a studio setting, with the camera mounted on a tripod, is to switch to your camera's Live View mode and

magnify the view. This approach enables you to very precisely focus using whatever part of the scene you wish. If you use autofocus, you should select and use a single AF point. Position it over the spot that you want to be in the area that is in focus. Quite often, I move my subject very slightly to lock in the final focus.

>> **Focus rail:** 2- and 4-way focus rails are ruler-looking devices that incorporate racks, pinions, and rails that enable you to focus very accurately. Mount your camera to the rail and focus using the rail's fine-focusing adjustment knobs. Use with a tripod for best results. 2-way rails move forward and backward. 4-way rails also move side to side, enabling you to alter the composition slightly.

Figure 3-6 shows an inexpensive 4-way rail that I picked up to experiment with. If you're on the fence and want to try it out without spending hundreds of dollars, I encourage you to take this approach to see whether you like working with it. If you do, you can always go out and buy a better model.

>> **Dusting and taping:** I always brush and blow dust off my subjects, but it's impossible to remove all traces of dust and miscellaneous fibers. Use blown air and masking tape as well. When you're shooting small subjects, you might need to remove dust by using your favorite photo editor.

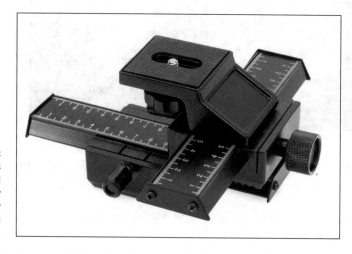

FIGURE 3-6:
Focusing rails make manual focusing very precise by slowly moving the camera.

Your other challenges are mainly lighting and depth of field. Here are some additional lighting pointers:

>> **No flash:** You can shoot macros in a studio without using a flash. The character of the lighting is different than with a flash, though, and you may struggle to find the right white balance. Try setting a custom white balance or take several test shots to get it right.

- » **Pop-up flash:** Don't even bother unless you have a very short macro lens. It's very hard to keep the lens from casting a huge shadow over everything. Pop-up flashes won't work in these cases.

- » **External flash:** Seriously consider investing in an external flash or Speedlight/Speedlite. When you mount one on your camera's hot shoe, the flash can clear the lens in most situations. You can also get a *ring light,* specifically designed to light close subjects unobtrusively.

  Ideally, you can position the flash away from the camera but stay connected using a sync or flash cord. (Wireless is even better.) From there, creatively design the photo and position the flash away from the lens. When you're working at very close ranges, it can mean the difference between lighting your subject or not.

- » **More complicated lighting setups:** The possibilities that arise from using extra gear are endless. You'll be able to patiently work your craft and *design* the shots you want. It's incredible fun and very rewarding!

Exploring Creative Alternatives

In Book 1, Chapter 1, I say that one of the reasons to embrace digital SLRs is because there are accessories for seemingly every situation. Macro and close-up photography are types of those situations.

Although you can get yourself a dedicated macro lens and enjoy macro photography like a pro, you don't need to start there. Even if you have a great macro lens, you might want to explore other options. You have many ways to pursue a passion for close-ups using different lenses and other equipment. This section is dedicated to showing you some of the possibilities.

Relaxing your angle of view

Not all macros or close-ups need to be microscopic wonders. Depending on the lens you're working with and the distance you are from your subject, you may enjoy shooting close-ups of larger subjects. Figure 3-7 is a shot of my son's Raspberry Pi, an amazing little computer packed onto a small circuit board. Although smaller than a typical computer, it's far larger than a bee, ring, and many other close-up subjects.

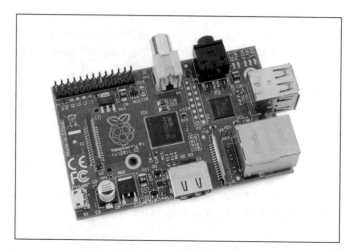

Shooting close-ups with everyday lenses

Remember, you can shoot close-ups with just about any lens you have. All you need to do is look for scenes that you want to zoom in on. Figure 3-8 is a shot I took with a very nice 50mm prime lens and inexpensive Nikon camera. I arranged the candles on a tray and set them on my bed (of all places) to take the shot. I set the aperture to f/1.4 and was pretty close to the candles, which kept the depth of field nice and shallow. The background candles are pleasantly blurred. Overall, this is an excellent illustration that proves you can shoot great close-ups with what you have on hand.

Using telephoto lenses

Although telephoto lenses excel at photographing distant objects, you can also use them to take nice-looking close-ups. Figure 3-9 is a close-up of a succulent we bought one summer to liven up our home. I was using a 300mm telephoto lens to take other photos, and on the spur of the moment decided to try some close-ups. I grabbed this plant and put it on our picnic table outside. I had to stand away from it to get the lens to focus, but the result is one of my favorite photos. The strong light enabled me to use a low ISO and quick shutter speed of 1/500 second.

TIP

Fast shutter speeds are important with lenses that have very long focal lengths because they help you shoot shake-free photos.

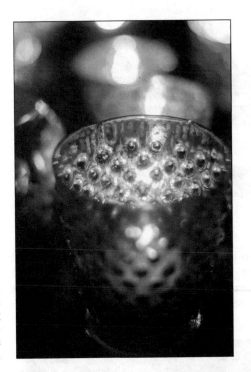

FIGURE 3-8:
Shooting
close-ups with
everyday lenses
is easy.

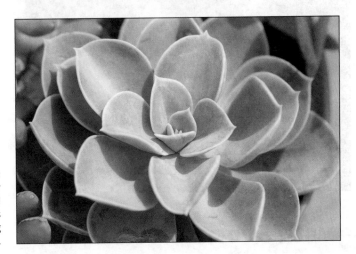

FIGURE 3-9:
A fast shutter
speed allowed
me to take this
photo with a long
focal length.

Using Holga lenses

I'm a huge fan of the Holga digital SLR lens and accessories. The Holga lens is a cheap, plastic, fixed-aperture manual focus lens developed for the popular Holga film cameras. You can customize the basic lens with macro and close-up attachments like those shown in Figure 3-10.

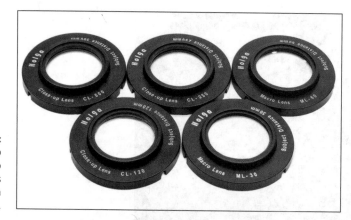

FIGURE 3-10:
Close-up and macro attachment sets for the Holga dSLR lens.

Although shooting with Holga lenses requires a lot of manual effort (focusing and calculating exposure), it's worth it. Figure 3-11 shows a stunning macro taken with the 30mm macro attachment. It really shows off the capabilities of attachments like this. I have more on Holga lenses in Book 2, Chapter 5.

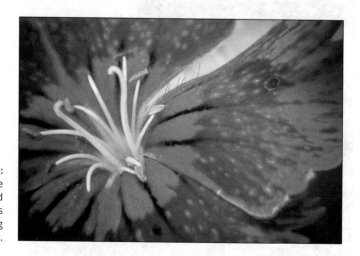

FIGURE 3-11:
Holga photos are softer compared to typical lenses but are brimming with personality.

Shooting with Special Accessories

If you don't have a macro lens, I recommend looking into some special accessories for standard lenses. They typically make shooting close-ups easy and rewarding by making a standard lenses act like a macro lens. Most of the techniques used to shoot with these accessories are the same as or similar to what you would do with a macro lens. You can use many of these accessories with your favorite macro lens for even more macro-tastic power.

Using a teleconverter

Teleconverters are tubes with optical (and sometimes electronic) elements that attach between the lens and your camera. Attach the lens to the teleconverter, and mount the combined unit to the camera. They increase the focal length of your lens — normally between 1.4 and 2 times. Figure 3-12 shows an older TC-201 2x teleconverter from Nikon.

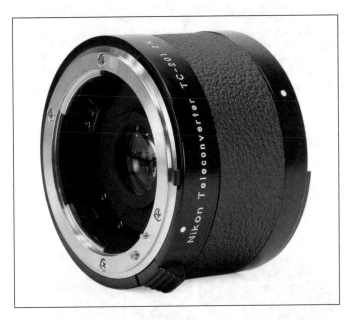

FIGURE 3-12:
Teleconverters increase the focal length of the lens.

REMEMBER

Teleconverters can be finicky. Make sure your lens and camera are compatible. Newer and better versions communicate information between the camera and lens and even autofocus. Cheaper versions may not have very good optics.

However, you can take great photos with teleconverters, especially if you're using a decent lens. Figure 3-13 shows a photo of close to a hundred BBs I took with the TC-201 2x teleconverter and vintage (1981) Zoom-NIKKOR 35-70mm f/3.5 AI-s manual focus lens on a modern APS-C camera. That adds up to 210mm of macro power.

Using extension tubes

Extension tubes are open tubes without optics that move the lens away from the focal plane in the camera, which magnifies the scene. They also reduce the minimum focusing distance. Extension tubes look something like teleconverters and attach to lenses the same way.

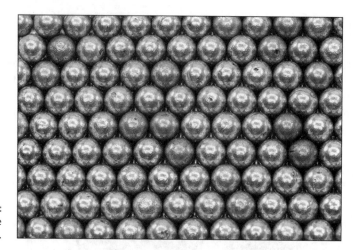

Figure 3-14 shows an inexpensive extension tube set from Zeikos. Most sets come with three different-sized tubes. This set has a 12mm, 20mm, and 36mm. You can mix and match them to create different magnification ratios.

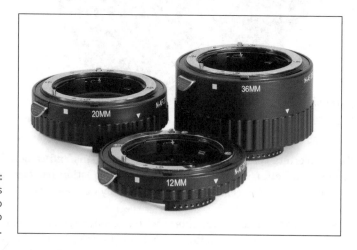

FIGURE 3-14:
Extension tubes
turn any lens into
a potential macro
lens.

Because extension tubes don't have lenses inside them, you don't have to worry about degrading the optical quality of the lens you mount them to. You may, however, experience light falloff (more distant objects quickly become darker), vignetting (photo corners are darker than the center), or light leakage (light that you don't want seeps in through the connections) when using a tube. When using an extension tube, you are also unable to focus out as far as you could without it. This situation is the opposite of how lenses normally work. Typically, you're always able to focus on infinity but can't get too close to your subject. With extension, it's the reverse.

Figure 3-15 shows a macro taken with a 50mm lens on a cropped-frame camera and extension tube. It's George Washington's face from a dollar bill.

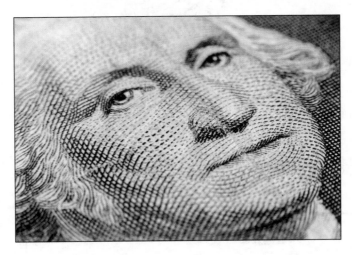

REMEMBER

One consequence of how the magnification factor is calculated (I won't bore you with the formulas) when using extension tubes is that magnification goes down as focal lengths go up. For example, an extension tube and a 35mm lens will have greater magnification than the same extension tube on a 50mm lens. Therefore, remember to use shorter lenses to get greater magnification when paired with extension tubes. The same rule applies to reversing rings, discussed in "Using reverse rings," later in this chapter.

Using diopters

If you don't want the hassle of putting extension tubes or a teleconverter between your lens and the camera, try screwing in one or more diopters on the front of the lens. Diopters are like corrective glasses that magnify the subject. They work with any lens that can accept screw-in filters. In contrast to extension tubes and some teleconverters, they don't interfere with shooting modes, autofocus, or other camera features that rely on communicating with the lens. They can be mixed and matched to increase the amount of magnification.

Figure 3-16 shows a Hoya close-up filter set. It came with three filters of different strengths: +1, +2, and +4. In this shot, one is mounted on a Nikon 18–55mm lens with the help of a *step-up ring* (an adapter that mounts a larger filter on a smaller lens). I use step-up rings a lot. They allow me to standardize all my filters to 77mm. All I need to do is get another step-up ring if I get a new lens that doesn't match what I already have.

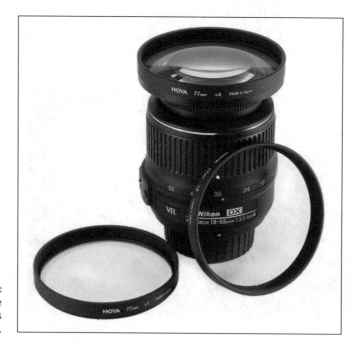

FIGURE 3-16:
Diopters are like
corrective lenses
for lenses.

REMEMBER

As you can see, a diopter *is* an optical element. The glass is very important. Take care of your diopters by always keeping them in a protective case and cleaning them regularly. Cheaper diopters will degrade your photos more than a high-quality set.

Figure 3-17 shows a nice shot of some flowers I took with a diopter attached to the standard kit lens mounted on a Canon dSLR. I zoomed in to 55mm, and the diopter took care of the rest.

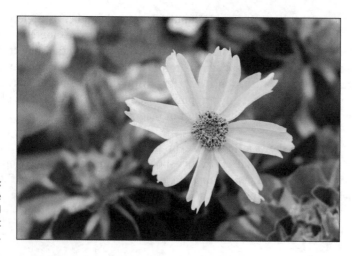

FIGURE 3-17:
Diopters are
easy to use and
produce great
close-ups.

Using reverse rings

Reverse rings are a totally cool way of having fun with macro and close-up photography. They enable you to mount a lens on your dSLR *backward.* Reversing the lens turns reality inside out. Instead of reducing objects to fit on the image sensor, the lens magnifies them in relation to its focal length. Try this experiment: Hold up a lens without a camera and look through it. You'll see an upside-down version of the scene in front of you that looks small. Now turn the lens around and look at something very close. You'll have to find the right focal distance for it to clear up. Try using a book or something with text. Much larger!

One side of the reverse ring adapter (see Figure 3-18) has very fine threads that screw onto the front of your lens just like a filter. The other side, which is a lens mount, attaches to your camera like a lens.

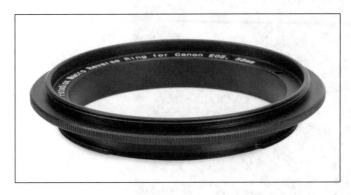

FIGURE 3-18: This 58mm reverse ring mounts lenses backward on Canon EOS cameras.

TIP

Reverse rings aren't necessarily fragile, but you can cross-thread the ring when screwing it onto your lens. If you feel it resist before it's fully screwed in, back the ring out and restart to make sure that you have it threaded correctly. As long as you handle it with the same care as a filter, you'll be fine.

REMEMBER

If you want to pick up a reverse adapter ring, match the adapter with the filter size on the lens you want to use.

Because the lens is mounted backward on the camera, the camera and lens are not able to communicate mechanically or electronically. Therefore, autofocus is not an option — you must manually focus or move either yourself or your subject. Focus rails are a great help because you don't have to mess with the lens or move anything around to get a good solid focus.

Capturing Macros and Close-ups

Lenses that do not have a manual aperture control are more difficult to use because the camera can't communicate with the lens when it's mounted backward. Because of this, older manual focus lenses with aperture rings are ideal. It's easy to change the aperture by twisting the right ring. I have a few old Nikon AI and AI-s lenses that I use all the time for this purpose. Their aperture rings make controlling exposure easier. I took the shot in Figure 3-19 using this setup: a Canon dSLR and an old Nikon 50mm manual focus lens. That's right. You can use any lens that has the same filter diameter as the reverse adapter you're using. This is exceptionally liberating. Use old NIKKOR lenses on Canon, Pentax, or Sony cameras. Pick up as many inexpensive reverse adapters as you need to mount your best lenses in reverse.

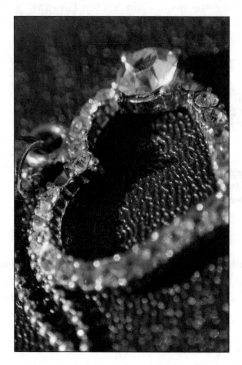

FIGURE 3-19: Reverse ring adapters are fun and totally worth trying.

Canon users have developed a unique workaround that allows you to lock in an aperture. Here's how: Mount the lens, turn the camera on, and then select aperture-priority mode. Set the aperture you want to use. Then, if your camera has one, press and hold the Depth of Field Preview button. While holding it down, press the lens-release button and carefully remove the lens — with the camera still powered up. The aperture will remain set in the lens. Yes, it's clunky. Yes, it's inconvenient. If you want to shoot with a stopped-down aperture, however, it works. I recommend experimenting and finding a favorite aperture that you want to use for most of your shots, and sticking with it. That way, you won't have to go through this process more than one or two times during a shoot.

Using a macro bellows

Macro bellows work just like extension tubes but are made of flexible material and can be extended to varying distances. One end of the bellows mounts to your camera as a lens would. You mount your lens to the far end and extend it to the distance you want. Professional-level bellows are very expensive. There are inexpensive models, however, that you can use to decide whether this is something you want to experiment with.

Chapter **4**

Reaching Out with Telephoto Lenses

Telephoto lenses are amazeballs. You can quote me on that! They enable you to photograph everything from distant objects like the moon without leaving your backyard to portraits of your loved ones at summer camp. The photos you can capture are simply stunning. You won't get the same perspective from any other type of lens.

I want to show you what's special about telephoto photography in this chapter. You'll learn what makes a telephoto lens unique and how to take advantage of its often overlooked versatility. That's right. Don't think that telephoto lenses are just for professional photographers to photograph sporting events or giraffes in the wild. They make great lenses to have with you wherever you are.

Learning the Lingo

Telephoto lenses have longer focal lengths than other types of lenses. Focal lengths 40mm and greater are considered telephoto on cropped-frame cameras, and those 60mm or greater put the lens in the telephoto range for full-frame cameras. Why those numbers? It's related to the size of the camera's image sensor, measured diagonally. If the focal length is larger than that measurement, it's called a telephoto focal length.

TIP

You need to consider the camera as well as the lens. For example, putting a 50mm lens on a cropped-frame camera puts you in telephoto territory, but not if you put the same lens on a full-frame camera.

Although most people think of large telephoto lenses, smaller lenses have telephoto focal lengths, too. There is actually a huge variety of telephoto lenses and focal lengths. Most standard zoom lenses sold with dSLRs in kits have some telephoto capability. Here's a quick summary of telephoto focal lengths:

>> **Medium (also called near) telephoto:** On full-frame dSLRs, 60–200mm is considered medium telephoto. This translates to 40–135mm on APS-C bodies and 30–100mm on Four Thirds cameras.

With certain exceptions, this is the most practical and least expensive telephoto region. It's where most people begin taking telephoto shots.

>> **Telephoto:** The telephoto range extends from 200–300mm on full-frame cameras, 135–200mm on APS-C dSLRs, and 100–150mm on Four Thirds cameras.

This focal length range is where you start taking photos that feel more like classic telephoto shots, as opposed to shooting close-ups, macros, or portraits. You can find zoom lenses that reach well into this range as well as dedicated telephoto lenses.

>> **Super telephoto:** The super telephoto range begins where the standard telephoto range ends: 300mm and up for full-frame, 200mm and up for APS-C, and 150mm and up for Four Thirds cameras. You can find some standard zoom lenses that extend into these focal lengths, but telephoto zooms and primes dominate the market. They are extreme lenses that excel at what they do.

Figure 4-1 shows the world-class Canon EF 70-200mm f/2.8L IS III USM telephoto lens mounted on a Canon APS-C camera. This lens fits squarely in the medium telephoto category when attached to a full-frame dSLR. It works well for portraits and closer telephoto work. It extends into the medium telephoto category and covers the entire telephoto category when attached to an APS-C camera. This means that subjects appear larger when the lens is mounted on an APS-C camera.

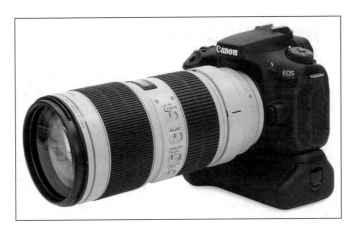

FIGURE 4-1:
An amazing
professional-level
telephoto lens
from Canon.

As you shop for lenses, remember that not all zoom lenses are considered telephoto lenses, even if they have telephoto focal lengths. For example, the HD PENTAX DA 55-300mm F4 5.8 ED WR lens is in the Standard Lens category on Ricoh's website. This lens has a tremendous range, reaching the super telephoto category when fully zoomed in. You have to look in the right category to find it. Canon's EF 28-300mm f/2.5-5.6L IS USM lens, on the other hand, is in its Telephoto Zoom category. (You have read the lens chapter in Book 1, right? It will help you decode these ridiculously long names.) Remember to take the time to look in several different categories for lenses with telephoto focal lengths, including zoom, telephoto, and prime.

REMEMBER

I make a point of mentioning the camera and sensor size along with the focal length of each photo in this chapter. This allows you to calculate the 35mm equivalent focal length for each shot and compare it to your setup. Book 1, Chapters 1 and 3 have more information if you need to brush up on the hows and whys.

RENTING LENSES

If you want to experiment with lenses with different features, focal lengths, and prices, try renting. You can also rent camera bodies. Rent something that's an upgrade or check out the competition. If you have a Nikon, for example, rent a Canon. Or, if you have a Canon, rent a Sony.

I use www.lensrentals.com for most of my rental needs. The site's employees are polite, professional, and trustworthy. Its services are timely and the list of available gear is impressive. The site offers flexible plans based on the amount of time you rent items. I recommend getting the insurance.

Using a Super Telephoto Lens

Super telephoto lenses are truly awesome. They're big, and they mean business. Use a monopod to help support it. You'll last longer and your photos will be sharper as a result. You can see a picture of the AF-S NIKKOR 300mm f/4D mounted on my monopod in Book 1, Chapter 2 (look for Figure 2-13).

With large lenses like super telephotos, the monopod will attach to the lens, not the camera body. This keeps the weight of the lens, and therefore the center of gravity of the whole setup, directly over the monopod instead of in front of it. If your monopod has a handy strap attached to it, use it. It's protection against losing an expensive lens.

REMEMBER

Hold your monopod at all times. I sometimes keep the camera strap around my neck for added protection so that if I accidentally release my grip, the strap will keep the camera and monopod from crashing to the ground.

These lenses are also expensive, which means that most people won't have one lying around the house. Don't let that stop you from looking into renting one and seeing what the fuss is about. Look at prices and be choosey. Some models can be relatively inexpensive to rent, but you will probably pay top dollar for the cream of the crop. Many super telephoto lenses are prime lenses.

Now for some photos. Figure 4-2 is a photo of a North American P-51 Mustang taxiing out to the runway at an air show my family and I attended. I used a 300mm lens on a Nikon APS-C camera, which equates to a 35mm equivalent focal length of 450mm. This is well into the super telephoto range.

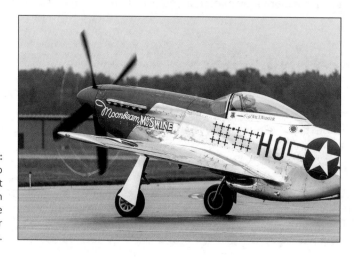

FIGURE 4-2:
Telephoto lenses bring out small details on subjects that are nearby or far away.

The beauty of using a super telephoto lens is that this photo looks as though I was standing right next to the plane with a normal lens. Details really pop out. The prop is cutting through the moist air, leaving contrails behind. You can also see the name of the plane and other markings very clearly. You can even see the screws holding the body panels on the frame of the airplane.

Figure 4-3 shows a moment after a harness race. The driver and his horse were returning to the paddock when I turned and saw them. Covered with sand, the driver has to lean to the side to see where he's going. Super telephoto lenses let you take photos from a safe vantage point that seem to put you right in the action. Although it looks as though I'm about to be run over, I was actually a good distance away with my 300mm lens and Nikon APS-C dSLR.

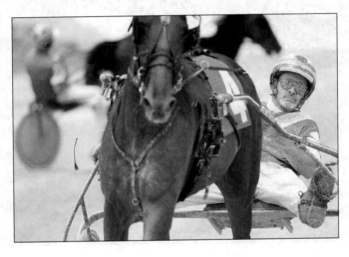

FIGURE 4-3:
This shot is a great example of how telephoto lens compression affects the background.

I quickly put the driver under my active AF point and focused on him instead of the horse, knowing that I was too close to get both in focus. Shooting with a super telephoto lens gives you shallower depths of field than similar apertures on normal or wide-angle lenses. The other elements provide context (his horse, of course, and the horse in the background) and balance the fact that he is on the right side of the frame.

One side effect of using a telephoto lens is called *telephoto lens compression*. Photos appear to lack the depth they would if taken using a wide-angle lens. Background objects are enlarged. This is how photographers take photos that make the moon look huge compared to the rest of the scene. In this case, the horse and driver in the background are far more prominent when seen through a 300mm lens than they would be with another lens. They look closer to the horse and driver in the foreground and take up more space in the photo.

Finally, to show you that telephoto lenses are indeed similar to telescopes, I present you with Figure 4-4: the moon. I took this photo using a 300mm super telephoto lens and Nikon APS-C dSLR. I also used a 2x teleconverter, which doubles the focal length. When teleconverter and crop factor are taken into account, this photo is the equivalent of a 900mm lens on a full-frame camera. Because the moon is not in full phase, more crater details stand out in relief from shadowing on the left side. Do yourself a favor and rent a lens like this to experience what it's like. Throw in the teleconverter for good measure. Simply astounding.

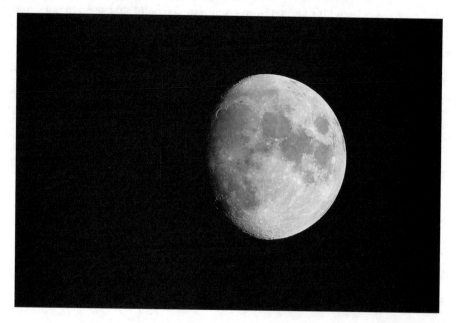

FIGURE 4-4:
The moon, shot with a 35mm equivalent focal length of 900mm.

To set the shot up, I mounted the camera and lens on my tripod in the backyard, entered aperture-priority shooting mode, and switched to spot metering. I didn't want the dark sky affecting how the camera evaluated the exposure. I played around a bit with different settings to see whether it made any difference, and settled on an ISO of 100 and aperture of f/8. The shutter speed automatically adjusted to 1/90 second. You can also use manual exposure mode for tough cases like this. Set the ISO, dial in an aperture, and then play with the shutter speed. Switch to Live View to see what the photo will look like and take some test shots to confirm your settings.

Capturing Action with Telephoto Lenses

Action shots and telephoto lenses and focal lengths just go together. Although most sports photos you'll see are taken from quite a distance, they don't have to be. Figure 4-5 is a shot of my son Sam jumping off the sidewalk of a walking bridge onto the main roadway. It's an old, decommissioned bridge over a river that is now a scenic spot for tourists and photographers, so he's in no danger.

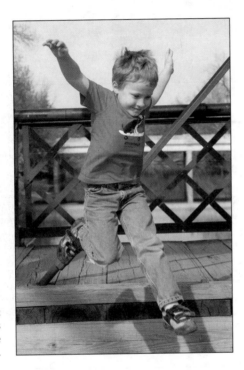

FIGURE 4-5:
Use zoom lenses to capture telephoto action.

I took this playful action shot using a nice zoom lens set to 52mm and a Nikon APS-C dSLR. 52mm? Yes. On a cropped-frame camera, that comes out to a 35mm equivalent focal length of 104mm. Even moderate telephoto focal lengths are great at capturing action, because you can stand out of the way and get a good shot. When dealing with family, friends, or strangers, it's nice to let people enjoy themselves without breathing down their necks.

Of course, super telephoto lenses also excel at action. You've probably noticed professional photographers at sporting venues photographing athletes in action. You can do that, too. For example, Figure 4-6 shows another photo I took at the horse track, this time as a harness race was under way. I used a 300mm lens on a Nikon APS-C dSLR.

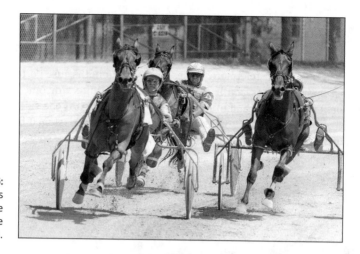

FIGURE 4-6:
Telephoto lenses
put you in the
middle of the
action.

TIP

I chose this vantage point because I was able to capture the action as the horses and drivers made the turn toward the homestretch. I was positioned off the track, behind a fence. A telephoto lens is your ticket to success at venues like this. You can stand well out of the way and still get good photos.

The lens enabled me to capture the intense look on the drivers' faces. The horses are in mid-air, solving the riddle of whether a horse leaves a foot on the ground and, if so, at what point during its gait (look up the 1878 series of photographs called *Sallie Gardner at a Gallop*).

Figure 4-7 is another shot from the rainy-day air show shown in Figure 4-2. At this time, the rain had let up and an A-10 Thunderbolt II was performing a demonstration flight. I used my trusty 300mm super telephoto lens and Nikon APS-C dSLR.

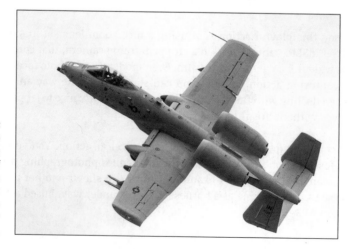

FIGURE 4-7:
Super telephoto
lenses are the
pinnacle of
telephoto
photography;
they can capture
scenes no other
lens can.

TIP

As you might expect, action shots like this require fast shutter speeds to capture the action without blurring. I took this photo with a shutter speed of 1/1000 second. You can read more about shutter speed in Book 3, Chapter 3.

If you look closely, you can see the patches on the pilot's uniform and small details on the plane. The rain makes the photo look a bit noisy but doesn't rob the photo of all its sharpness. Remember, I was standing on the ground, several hundred feet below and away from the line of flight. This kind of moment is when you want the best telephoto lens you can get your hands on. I also used a monopod for support. I also discovered that panning the camera to track fast-moving objects like jets at extreme focal lengths is challenging. Expect to take several photos of moments like this as you try to center the plane in the viewfinder and get a good focus.

Using Telephoto Lenses for Close-ups

For the most part, you'll stand at a distance from your subjects when shooting with telephoto lenses. You are not limited to that approach, however. Try standing closer to your subjects and shooting close-ups with telephoto lenses.

I took the photo shown in Figure 4-8 with this idea in mind. It's a close-up of a cactus plant set up in my studio. I shot it with a Canon full-frame camera and excellent EF 24-105mm f/4L IS USM lens set to 105mm. This is a classic close-up. It's not powerful enough to be a macro, but not far enough away to be a normal photo.

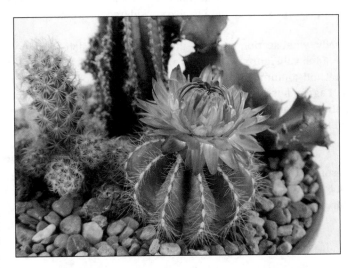

FIGURE 4-8:
Telephoto focal lengths are great for close-ups, too.

Figure 4-9 is a close-up I shot outside. The front turn-signal lens on an old, abandoned Chevy C-60 dump truck caught my attention and I decided to get in close and then zoom in for this shot. I framed it on the edge of the photo to make room for the background, which is interesting but intentionally not the focus of the photo.

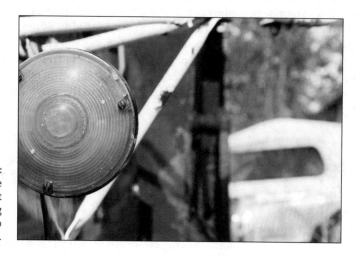

FIGURE 4-9:
Always be on the lookout for interesting subjects to zoom in on.

I used a Sony APS-C camera and standard zoom lens set to 60mm. Unlike the last photo, I didn't use a tripod and no setup was involved. I simply had to be aware of my surroundings. Bam. Telephoto close-up.

TIP

Remember, telephoto focal lengths are available even on inexpensive kit lenses. Although I love showing you shots that I took with a 300mm super telephoto lens, 60mm on an APS-C camera is also considered telephoto.

Finally, what section on close-ups would be complete without a flower? Not this one, I tell ya! Figure 4-10 shows a colorful flower that I shot using a Nikon APS-C dSLR and 300mm lens. It's ridiculous to use that sort of lens for this kind of close-up, I agree, but as I tell my kids, "I specialize in ridiculous." Notice the *bokeh* (the aesthetic quality of the unfocused area) in this photo. Good super telephoto lenses can make backgrounds look very nice.

The key to shots like this is having enough light so that the shutter speed can be reasonably fast. Shooting close-ups accentuates the importance of having a crisp photo. In this case, 1/250 second was fast enough to prevent camera shake from blurring the photo.

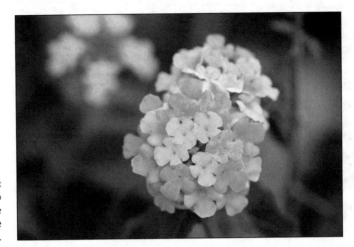

FIGURE 4-10:
Telephoto
close-ups make
for very attractive
bokehs.

You will also have to deal with narrow depths of field when shooting close-ups at very long focal lengths. You can try to use smaller apertures to increase the depth of field. You may also need to raise the ISO or try using a flash.

Capturing Portraits

Try using a standard zoom lens to capture portraits in the near-telephoto range. If you can get away with *not* lugging around a 300mm telephoto lens all the time, do so.

Figure 4-11 shows a group portrait of my kids after summer camp. I know this doesn't feel like a telephoto shot, but it is. I took it with a Canon APS-C camera and basic zoom lens set to 45mm, which is just inside the near-telephoto range.

I set up this shot by standing back and zooming in, which meant that I was in the telephoto range of this kit lens I was using. The kids are nice and sharp while the background is blurred. Everyone looks natural with no discernible distortion from the lens, which can happen when you stand too close and shoot your portraits using wide-angles. I also made sure they stood in a line. This helped me keep them all in focus, despite having a shallow depth of field due to the aperture and focal length.

Telephoto lenses and focal lengths are also very useful for individual portraits. When you're photographing a single person, you can afford to stand closer. Figure 4-12 is a playful shot of my wife, who has Easter Bunny ears on her head. I shot this using a Nikon APS-C camera and fast 50mm prime lens.

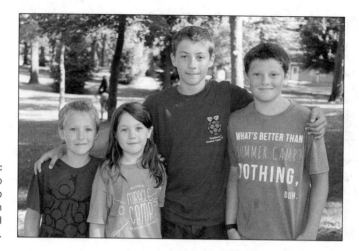

FIGURE 4-11:
Stand back to shoot group portraits with telephoto focal lengths.

Better, more expensive lenses like the AF–S NIKKOR 50mm f/1.4G I used will have more attractive *bokeh* than average kit lenses. They will also have larger maximum apertures, which helps let in a lot of light and blur the background.

Finally, I took the photo of my oldest son in Figure 4-13 using the full-frame Pentax K-1 dSLR. I set the zoom lens to 95mm. That's the longest equivalent focal length of the three photos in this section. To frame the shot, I stood back at a comfortable distance and zoomed in so that I would get him and the fence in the background.

TIP

Many photographers like using 85mm telephoto lenses on full-frame cameras for portraiture. Shooting 50mm on an APS-C camera puts you right in that ballpark. Figures 4-12 and 4-13 use focal lengths that are very close to this figure.

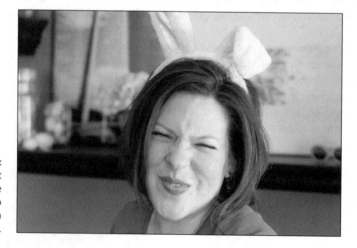

FIGURE 4-12:
A fun portrait shot in the near-telephoto focal length range.

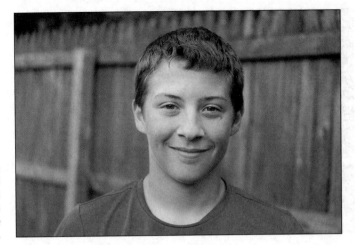

FIGURE 4-13:
Classic telephoto portraiture with a nice lens on a full-frame camera.

I would not go above 135mm on full-frame or 85mm on cropped-frame cameras for close portraits because you'll run into lens compression, and people's faces will appear flatter than they are.

Photographing Animals

People love taking photos of animals. It doesn't matter whether it's of a lion on safari, giraffes at the zoo, or your own pets. Using telephoto lenses and focal lengths will make your photos really stand out.

Figure 4-14 is a nice photo of our cat. He was looking out the window when I took this. It was very bright outside, and the natural sunlight makes this photo shine. I took it with the full-frame Pentax K-1 dSLR and nice Pentax HD D FA 28-105mm f/3.5-5.6 standard zoom lens. I zoomed in to 80mm to frame his face. Again, that is very near the ideal 85mm portraiture focal length.

Figure 4-15 is a photo of a wild kit (the technical name for a baby rabbit) we rescued. She's up on a table with a white background and some red cabbage to keep her occupied. The cabbage also looked prettier than her normal diet of timothy hay. I was using a Canon 5D Mark III full-frame dLSR with the lens set to 105mm. Although I was in my studio, I didn't use a tripod because I had to react to and track a moving wabbit.

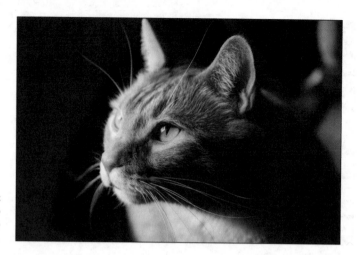

FIGURE 4-14:
Use telephoto focal lengths to photograph pets.

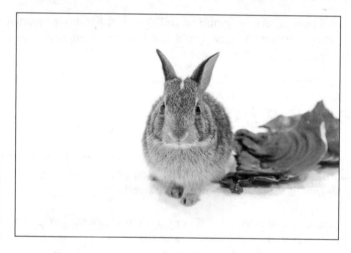

FIGURE 4-15:
Use long focal lengths to photograph animals you don't want to frighten.

Focus and aperture control are vital in shots like this. I set the aperture to f/8 to give myself more depth of field to work with, which forced me to raise the ISO to 2500 to compensate. The shutter speed was 1/60, which is on the slow side for a photo like this, but fast enough to capture brief pauses in the action. Having a good lens with image stabilization helped to keep the photo nice and sharp. Had she run around more, I would have had to set the shutter speed faster, enlarge the aperture, and increase the ISO.

Finally, having a telephoto lens is a must when photographing close-ups of dangerous animals like the crocodile in Figure 4-16. I took this photo at our local zoo using a Nikon APS-C dSLR and 300mm super telephoto lens. Although I was outside the enclosure, I was able to get this low perspective by positioning myself on a sidewalk leading downhill from the side toward the front.

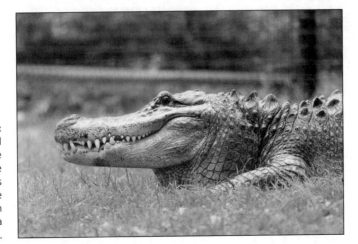

FIGURE 4-16:
Long focal
lengths enable
you to capture
dangerous
animals in the
wild or animals in
captivity from a
distance.

REMEMBER

The great thing about using a super telephoto lens is that you can be pretty far away from the action and still feel as though you're right in the middle of it. (That last sentence is brought to you by Mr. Obvious.)

Chapter **5**
Exploring Other Lenses

Before I finish the minibook on lenses, I would like to encourage you to seek out alternative designs. Even though a lens must fit your camera body, not every lens has to fit the same mold. In fact, you can have a lot of fun with creative lenses or accessories like the ones I showcase in this chapter. The wide range of different and sometimes exotic lenses that are available really sets dSLRs apart from smartphones, tablets, and other types of digital imaging devices.

Note: You may want to mount your camera on a tripod or monopod for support when using lenses with small apertures so that you can work with longer shutter speeds. The extra support also helps you compose and focus your shot. I typically use a tripod when shooting macros and close-ups with Holga lenses, when setting up detailed tilt-shift shots, when shooting long-exposure shots with a pinhole lens, and when I'm in my studio.

Fisheye Lenses

On the extreme end of the wide-angle spectrum are fisheye lenses. Just like their wide-angle relatives, they're incredibly fun to use. The (roughly) 180-degree diagonal angle of view puts a whole new twist on taking unique photos.

Fisheye lenses have been around for a long time, and they were designed with full-frame cameras in mind. This means that you *will not* get the complete, circular, fisheye effect when you mount a full-frame fisheye lens on a camera with an APS-C image sensor. It takes more oomph than many lenses have to squeeze the scene onto a smaller-sized sensor.

For example, the AF Fisheye-NIKKOR 16mm f/2.8 lens sounds nice, but it has an effective focal length of a whopping 24mm when mounted on a cropped-frame Nikon dSLR. This focal length results in a 107-degree angle of view, which is less than required for the true fisheye experience. The AF DX Fisheye-NIKKOR 10.5mm f/2.8G ED, on the other hand, was designed specifically for DX (cropped-frame) Nikon cameras and has a 180-degree angle of view. However, this lens has a catch. Nikon calls it a "frame-filling" fisheye lens, which means that you won't see the circular fisheye effect with this lens either.

You can purchase screw-in fisheye optics that, although not fisheye lenses from stem to stern, so to speak, widen the field of view so much that they achieve a fisheye or near-fisheye effect. They range in price, but all are relatively inexpensive. The Opteka HD2 0.20x AF Fisheye Lens, shown in Figure 5-1, lists for just under $40. I heartily recommend trying out this solution in lieu of buying an expensive fisheye lens. There are a few things you should be aware of, however, before you start:

>> **Screw-in optics mount to the front of existing lenses.** You must buy one that is compatible with the filter size of the lens you want to use. Some optics have multiple step-rings that enable you to mount them to different lenses. For example, the Opteka set I purchased has a native thread of 52mm and comes with three rings (one of which is shown in Figure 5-1 leaning against the main lens): 55 to 52mm, 58 to 52mm, and 67 to 52mm. I can use any lens in my camera bag that has one of these four filter sizes (52mm, 55mm, 58m, or 67mm).

>> **The effective focal length of the optic depends on the lens you attach it to.** To get the greatest fisheye effect, mount the optic on a lens with wide-angle capability.

>> **Optics are mostly for cropped-frame cameras.** If you have a full-frame camera, dedicated fisheye lenses will work well for you.

Figure 5-2 shows a picturesque lake scene I shot looking out along a pier. I was standing on the beach, and I took special care to hide that fact. With such a vast angle of view, it's harder than you might think to keep your feet and other items out of the photos. The far side of the lake shows off the curve of the lens. The pier doesn't appear to have much distortion. It does look a bit distant, however, because the wide angle appears to push it away from the camera.

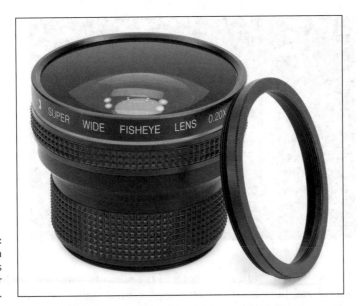

FIGURE 5-1:
This Opteka fisheye lens screws on to your existing lens.

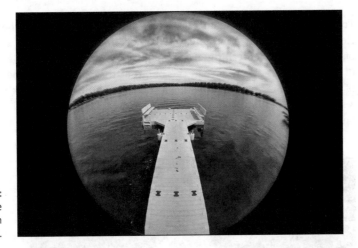

FIGURE 5-2:
Shoot unique landscapes with fisheye lenses.

Figure 5-3 shows off the circular effect of the fisheye lens. It's a shower curtain, which certainly sounds like an odd thing to photograph for a book. However, the small squares on the curtain provide a great point of reference because they illustrate what should be straight. They are 11/16 of an inch, or about 18mm square, and are arranged in relatively orderly columns and rows.

TIP

Don't lock yourself into one mode of thinking. Take your fisheye lens and photograph everything you can with it.

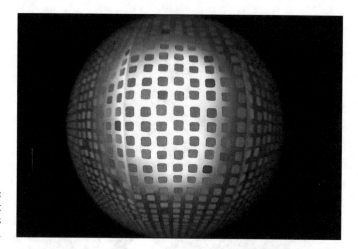

FIGURE 5-3:
Use objects that
show off the lens
distortion.

The fisheye lens causes the center of the photo to bulge out. It also bends all the vertical and horizontal lines toward a central vanishing point along each axis. Although it's not the greatest tool to take precise architectural photos, I love it.

The flower I photographed in Figure 5-4 shows what happens when you get really close to an object. It dominates the center of the scene. There's plenty of space on the sides for everything else, though, because the lens has such a wide field of view. My feet are almost in the photo at the bottom, and the bottom quarter of our neighbor's garage is visible at the top. Notice that even though I'm using a standard kit zoom lens and inexpensive screw-in optic, the flower looks sharp and very clear.

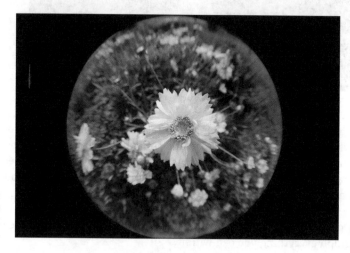

FIGURE 5-4:
Fisheye lenses
are great at
close-ups.

Although I have not shown this aspect of using a fisheye lens, another completely viable approach is to take extreme wide-angle shots with a fisheye lens and remove the distortion in software. You'll get nice photos with extreme angles of view that are impossible to take with most other lenses.

Tilt-Shift Lenses

Tilt-shift lenses are special-purpose lenses with two distinct features:

>> **They tilt.** The front of the lens swivels, or tilts, to point at an angle. This angles the focal plane so that it isn't flat anymore. The depth of field changes to a wedge shape, which gets larger as it extends farther from the camera.

>> **And shift.** The lens can also shift up or down while pointing in the same direction. Shifting the lens moves a different part of the view as seen by the lens onto the camera's image sensor to be captured during an exposure.

This view is possible because tilt-shift lenses have a larger *image circle* than normal lenses. The larger image circle means that they project a larger image of the world (you guessed it — it's circular) inside the camera. You don't see what runs off the image sensor. It's like putting a large round tablecloth on a small rectangular table and then moving it around.

Figure 5-5 shows the Canon TS-E 24mm f/3.5 II, tilted to the left but not shifted. I took all the tilt-shift photos in this section with this lens. It's an amazing, although heavy, lens that captures great photos even when not tilted or shifted.

Notice the knobs and markings on the lens. Operating a tilt-shift lens requires you to set the amount of tilt and shift you want to apply and then lock it down. If you're using a tripod or shooting in a studio, you can set up the lens very precisely using all the helpful information on the lens. Tilt-shift lenses require you to use manual focus.

REMEMBER

Manually focusing is a challenge to using this type of lens unless you are already proficient in it.

Canon also offers 17mm, 45mm, and 90mm versions. Nikon has three tilt-shift lenses at these focal lengths: 24mm, 45mm, and 85mm. Other manufacturers offer various tilt-shift lenses, such as Rokinon and Samyang. Arax also makes tilt-shift lenses in several focal lengths.

Exploring Other Lenses

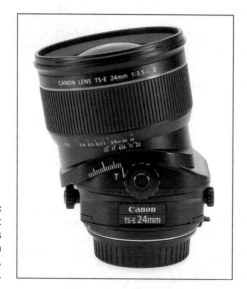

REMEMBER

Tilt-shift lenses were originally created for 35mm film cameras. The range of available focal lengths are therefore optimized for full-frame dSLR image sensors. The 45mm Canon tilt-shift lens acts like a 72mm near-telephoto lens on a Canon cropped-frame dSLR. The 24mm lens, on the other hand, sits at 38mm on a cropped-frame camera, so it feels like a normal lens. The 17mm lens would allow you to shoot wide-angle shots with an effective focal length of 27mm.

Tilt-shift lenses have long been used by photographers to photograph buildings and other scenes to eliminate perspective distortion. When you point your camera up, vertical lines in the scene converge rather than run parallel. Shifting a tilt-shift lens helps counteract this effect. Shifting the lens also enables you to shoot panoramas without ever having to move the camera.

Tilt-shift lenses have an artistic nature to them as well, which is what I want to focus on. You can create interesting depth of field effects using the tilt feature of the lens. Figure 5-6 shows a friendly game of sand volleyball under way at camp. The sun was shining nicely. A nice breeze was blowing. It was an idyllic scene. I tilted the lens so that the girl in the pink shirt was the primary focal point. You can see the sharp area of focus extending from her to the opponents on the other side of the net and into the trees.

Figure 5-7 is a totally different shot. I took this photo of the first floor elevator doors at my favorite parking garage at the university I work at. I was able to get the left door to be nicely in focus while blurring the right door by tilting the lens. The unusual depth of field plays mind games on you. You're not seeing a model or small diorama. These are full-sized elevator doors.

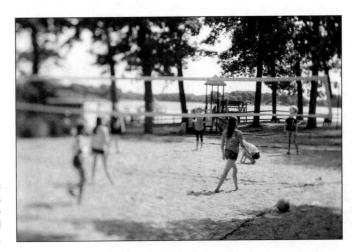

FIGURE 5-6:
Tilt-shift lenses create unique depth-of-field effects.

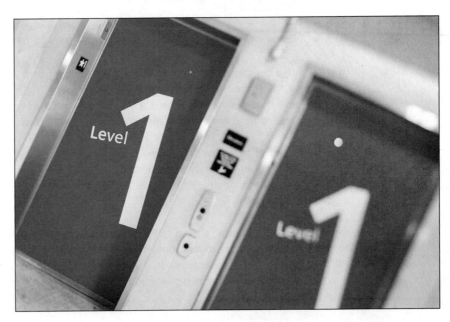

FIGURE 5-7:
This set of elevator doors looks like it's from a model.

Finally, the scene in Figure 5-8 presents another shot that looks miniaturized. This scene, shot with the same lens as my other tilt-shift shots, features the buildings across the main street in a quaint little town in Michigan. I tilted the lens, angled the camera a bit, and focused on the building on the corner. Other objects near the same distance are not in focus, whereas the sign and corner of the building I have concentrated on are. This is the effect you get when tilting the lens.

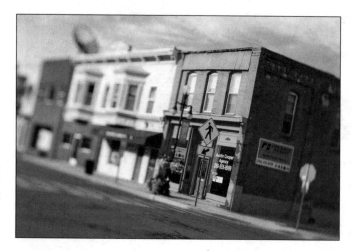

FIGURE 5-8:
Create
interesting
depth-of-field
effects even
at a distance.

Holga Lenses

In 1981, Holga began manufacturing a 120mm medium-format film camera called the Holga 120S. It was simple, inexpensive, and plastic. In fact, it was so unlike anything else that people considered it a toy camera. However, that toy camera that often leaked light took amazingly cool, analog, sometimes messy photos.

The Holga digital SLR lens is derived from the lens on the original camera. It has a focal length of approximately 60mm, a fixed aperture of f/8, and has very rudimentary manual focus. You'll have to use your camera's manual shooting mode, too.

Aside from the main lens, shown in Figure 5-9, Holga makes a remarkable number of attachments that mount onto the front of the lens. They include macro and close-up lenses, telephoto, wide-angle, fisheye, and filter accessories. There is even a pinhole lens. Pick things up à la carte or buy kits with the add-ons you want.

Although these lenses are plastic, and you have to guess at the initial exposure settings, I love playing around with them. I've taken many photos with my Holga lenses and feature several of them in this book. It's a great lens to experiment with.

TIP

Pay attention to the focus distance set on the lens. There are five different symbols, each representing different subjects and distances. Focus before you frame the shot because it's hard to turn the lens when looking through the viewfinder. I set the focus distance to match the scene I plan on shooting, take the shots I want, and change the focus distance only when I change scenes.

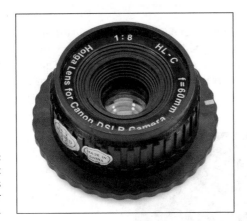

FIGURE 5-9:
The Holga plastic dSLR lens mounts directly to your camera.

Figure 5-10 is a scene from my favorite local university. I used it as a photo destination long before I began working there. I was taking photos of buildings and other things when I decided to station myself along the main walkway and photograph students coming and going. Although this shot doesn't have many people in it, the main focus of attention is a young woman in silhouette walking away from me. This is one of my favorite shots that I have taken with the basic Holga lens.

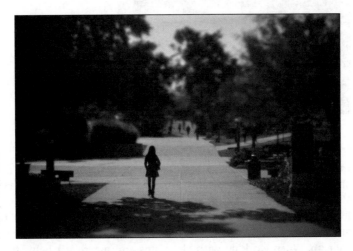

FIGURE 5-10:
I processed this Holga shot through a creative filter for additional effects.

I boosted the ISO to 800 to have a quick exposure time of 1/500 second. That guaranteed a crisp photo of moving subjects and no camera shake from me. I used an additional in-camera filter to blur portions of the scene, accentuate the color, and boost the contrast.

The bridge shown in Figure 5-11 shows a completely different scene shot with the same basic digital Holga lens. I got up early one foggy morning and was taking photos around the base of a bridge near where I live. The water level is low and the light is very subtle. I framed the scene from behind some tree branches, which adds to the moody effect.

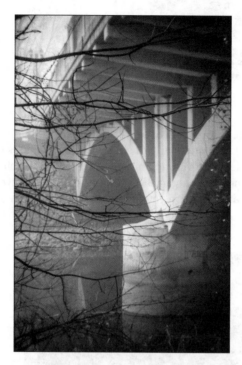

FIGURE 5-11: Holga lenses are a great change of pace from traditional lenses.

Holga lenses need a lot of light. If you're not out in bright sunlight, expect to raise the ISO. I had to raise the ISO to 6400 to take this shot, and still couldn't make the shutter speed any faster than 1/60 without underexposing the scene.

Finally, Figure 5-12 shows an example of a macro shot. I slipped the 30mm macro attachment onto the front of the basic Holga lens, and used a tripod to set this shot up. When working with close-ups and macros, it helps to frame the scene using Live View. I raised the ISO through the roof so that I could see and focus, and then switched to the viewfinder and lowered the ISO to take the shot. Of course, focusing with a Holga lens is harder than with a normal lens. In cases like this, I move the subject to focus. Try mounting your camera to a 4-way focus rail (see Book 2, Chapter 3) to move the camera very precisely. Shooting macros and close-ups with Holga lenses is incredibly fun and very rewarding.

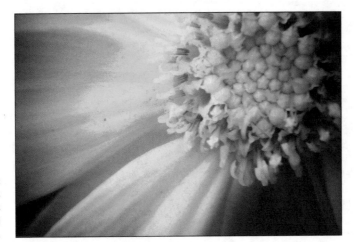

FIGURE 5-12:
Shoot macros and close-ups with additional attachments.

Lensbaby Lenses

Lensbaby (visit www.lensbaby.com) has created several unique and creative lenses and accessories for digital SLRs. The main creative lineup features the Composer Pro, shown in Figure 5-13, which is a manual focus tilt-swivel lens body that accepts removable add-ons like the Double Glass, Single Glass, and Plastic Optics. They continually come out with additional lens bodies and optics, like the Composer Pro II (an upgrade to the Composer Pro, featuring metal body), Edge 50 Optic, Sweet 35 Optic, Circular Fisheye, and Velvet 56. These aren't traditional lenses, but they aren't toys. They feel solid.

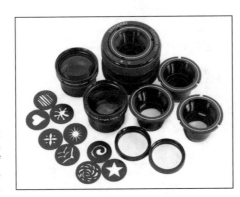

FIGURE 5-13:
Lensbaby has a wide array of creative lens products.

I shot Figure 5-14 using the Composer Pro with the Double-Glass Optic installed. Tilting the lens up and to the right a bit let me move the circle of sharp focus where I wanted it. The words in this poster of the United States Declaration of Independence that aren't in this sweet spot are blurred, which is the main effect this lens offers.

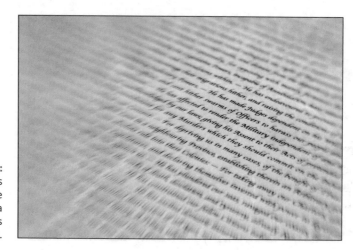

FIGURE 5-14:
This poster shows off how the lens creates a selective focus effect.

Although the newer optics feature built-in apertures, part of the charm of the older optics is that you control the aperture by manually swapping out aperture disks. This feature allows you to use creative aperture disks with cutouts for special effects. Figure 5-15 shows a star effect caused by light reflecting off several silver votive holders.

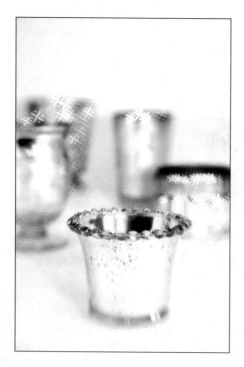

FIGURE 5-15:
Additional aperture disks create unique special effects.

Pinhole Lenses

Pinhole lenses aren't really lenses at all. They are simply covers with a small hole in them. The idea of using a hole to project an image, also called *camera obscura,* can be traced back to the beginnings of photography. Smaller holes created sharper images. Figure 5-16 shows a pinhole lens that I picked up from Lenox Laser.

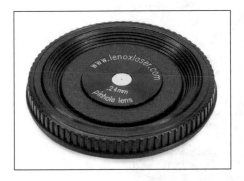

FIGURE 5-16:
This pinhole "lens" is a precision-machined body cap.

I've found an effective approach to making pinhole lenses myself. I drill a larger hole in a camera body cap and then tape a piece of aluminum foil over the hole. I carefully prick the foil in the center with a small straight pin to make the pinhole. The size of the hole matters, depending on the brand of camera you're using and the size of the image sensor. Make sure to use an extra body cap that you don't mind putting a hole in.

REMEMBER

As with other creative lenses, you will experience a pretty big difference between using a pinhole lens on a full-frame dSLR versus a cropped-frame body. Normal pinhole lenses have a wide-angle look on full-frame cameras. In some cases, they will look like telephoto shots on cropped-frame cameras. The challenges of pinhole photography are twofold. First, the aperture is so small that it's hard to see the scene in order to compose your shot. Second, you have to determine the proper exposure for each scene by trial and error. However, after you settle on an ISO and an exposure time, if the lighting is the same you can easily repeat them for follow-on shots.

Figure 5-17 shows a photo I took using a pinhole lens on a Nikon APS-C dSLR. It's soft, which is what you get with pinhole lenses. I processed the photo in Adobe Lightroom to make it look a bit older. I also left in the dark spots, which are caused by dust on the image sensor. Normally these spots are fuzzy, and you may never notice them. I think they add to the nostalgic effect in this photo. It was a bright day, so I used a shutter speed of 1.3 seconds and an ISO of 100.

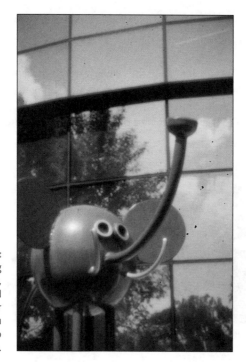

FIGURE 5-17:
When using pinhole lenses, use a tripod and longer shutter speeds if you don't want to raise the ISO.

Diana F+ Lenses

Plastic Diana cameras were introduced in the 1960s and have made a real comeback in recent years. Although the cameras themselves use film (just as Holga cameras do), you can mount the lenses on a dSLR with the right adapter. Figure 5-18 shows the Diana F+ fisheye lens mounted on a cropped-frame dSLR.

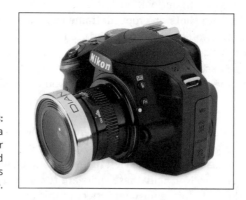

FIGURE 5-18:
Attach the Diana F+ lens adapter to your dSLR and then add the lens of your choice.

One note of advice regarding the Diana lens focal lengths: I recommend the fisheye lens as a most practical focal length for dSLRs. The Diana lenses are designed to be used on film cameras whose 120 film is much larger than a cropped-frame dSLR sensor. In fact, it's far larger than 35mm film and full-frame image sensors. You're only going to see a small portion of what the lens is capable of capturing. Longer focal lengths will create shots with a telephoto-like field of view.

I took the photo shown in Figure 5-19 with the Diana F+ 20mm Fisheye Lens attached to a Nikon APS-C dSLR with the help of the proper adapter. I used an external flash held to the side with the help of an off-camera hot shoe cord (see Book 4, Chapter 3). The result is amazing, and I hope inspires you to try out creative lenses like Diana F+ with your dSLR. I've certainly had fun!

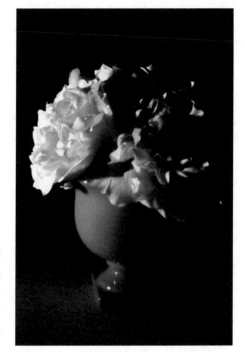

FIGURE 5-19: The Diana F+ fisheye lens has a good field of view and captures soft, dreamy scenes with a retro vibe.

Exploring Other Lenses

3

Taking Creative Control

Contents at a Glance

Chapter **1**
Making Sense of Exposure

E xposure is a funny thing. Most people leave it up to the camera and capture fantastic shots. You can also take control of things yourself. Either way, it helps to know a thing or two about exposure so that you can capture the photos and movies that you want. A little bit of knowledge will also help you troubleshoot if things don't go the way you want them to.

Even if you plan on letting the camera do most of the work for you, this is a very practical chapter for you to digest. I start by covering a few things about exposure in general, and then I move on to monitoring exposure on your camera. You also learn how to choose between different metering modes, review photos, and analyze histograms. I wrap things up by sharing some tips on troubleshooting exposure problems.

Understanding Exposure

The word *exposure* is thrown around a lot in photography. In the old days, people referred to photos themselves as exposures because you exposed film in the camera to light when you took a picture. Today, most people use terms like shots, photos, images, or even files to refer to their pictures.

Exposure is still a pretty important word in photography, even though most of us don't call our photos exposures. I want to dispense with the technical details, for the moment, and bring it down to one very important but simple point:

REMEMBER

Exposure is about taking photos and shooting movies that are as dark or as light as you want them to be.

Simple, right? Keeping that straightforward goal in mind puts the details of this chapter in context. What may be confusing at times is learning the different pieces to the exposure puzzle. Exposure involves:

>> **Monitoring and evaluating:** The camera evaluates the scene's brightness and suggests exposure settings to capture the best photo. This is called the standard exposure.

>> **Metering:** The camera needs to measure the light in the scene. This is called metering.

>> **Reviewing:** Reviewing photos and looking at their histograms helps you understand what is happening with the camera and where you may need to change settings.

>> **Troubleshooting:** There are several ways to troubleshoot. They include techniques like switching metering modes, using your camera's manual shooting mode, dialing in exposure compensation, using exposure brackets, and using AE lock.

You can take more or less control over most parts of the process.

Evaluating exposure

As you evaluate exposure, the point is to assess whether your photos and movies look the way you want them to. You have only three options. They can be underexposed, exposed just right, or overexposed. Figure 1-1 shows an example of each.

>> **Underexposed:** Unacceptably dark photos and movies are underexposed. For whatever reason, the image sensor captures too little light.

Underexposed photos and movies often have clipped shadows. These are dark areas that turn black and lose all detail.

REMEMBER

>> **Just right:** When everything comes together and to the camera captures just the right amount of light to produce a good shot, that shot has been properly exposed.

FIGURE 1-1:
These photos
illustrate the
broad range
of possible
exposures.

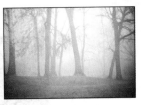

Underexposed   Good exposure   Overexposed

In general, your goal will be to capture shots that look good — not too dark and not too bright. Exceptions to this idea exist, of course, but shots normally have a "sweet spot" that produces the best photos and movies most of the time.

REMEMBER

>> **Overexposed:** Photos and movies that have been overexposed are too bright.

Overexposed photos and movies often have *clipped* or *blown highlights*. When this happens, the pixel turns pure white. There are no details at all.

The amount of light that can cause a photo or movie to be under- or overexposed can be a little or a lot. It depends on the scene and camera. If the exposure is off by a relatively small margin, you may be able to fix it using photo-editing software (see Book 5, Chapter 2 for help with this).

Controlling exposure

Your camera has several shooting modes, also called exposure modes, that determine whether you or the camera control the various exposure settings, such as the shutter speed. Figure 1-2 shows the Mode dial on a consumer-level dSLR.

REMEMBER

Autoexposure modes put the camera in charge of setting the exposure controls. The type of input you have depends on the mode you've selected. Basic autoexposure modes require no input from you. Set it and forget it.

Advanced autoexposure modes like aperture-priority or shutter-priority let you set the lens aperture or shutter speed. The camera takes care of the other controls and adjusts them for the best exposure.

You have two options if you want manual control over your camera's exposure controls: Manual (M) and Bulb (B) modes. If your Bulb mode isn't on the mode dial, enter Manual mode and lengthen the shutter speed until you see it. The camera still evaluates the scene and displays what it thinks the best exposure is, but you're responsible for setting all the controls. Although this responsibility may sound intimidating, it gives you the ability to direct the camera to do your bidding.

Making Sense of
Exposure

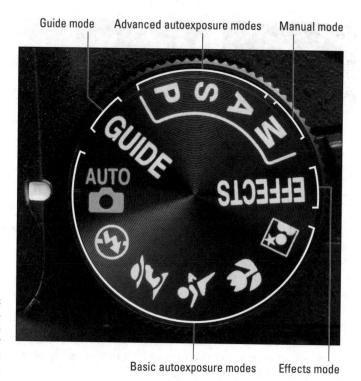

Guide mode   Advanced autoexposure modes   Manual mode

Basic autoexposure modes   Effects mode

FIGURE 1-2:
Your camera's
Mode dial is
dominated by
autoexposure
modes.

REMEMBER

Your camera is not foolproof. Even in the autoexposure modes, it sometimes gets it wrong. That's why I offer the section "Troubleshooting Exposure," at the end of this chapter.

In addition to exposure modes, your camera has three exposure controls, each with its own unique personality: the aperture of the lens; the shutter speed; and ISO speed. Each of these controls is important enough to warrant a chapter of its own here in Book 3. You can also modify the exposure by using a flash (Book 4, Chapters 2 and 3) or filters (Book 3, Chapter 5).

Comparing exposure intervals

There are two ways to describe exposure values and intervals: stops and exposure value (EV). They are different terms that basically mean the same thing. Here's what you need to know about each:

>> *Stops* are a traditional way of describing exposure intervals. They are mechanical. The term comes from how photographers changed apertures and shutter speeds on their film cameras. They would widen the aperture by a physical

stop on the lens or make the shutter speed faster by turning a knob to the next stop (see Figure 1-3). This action doubled or halved the amount of light that the film was exposed to. The term therefore made its way into the lexicon of photography as a way to double or halve light.

>> *Exposure value* is a measurement of exposure. An interval of 1 EV is synonymous with a stop. Each interval of 1 EV doubles or halves the exposure. You can change the EV by altering the camera's exposure settings (aperture, shutters speed, or ISO). For example, raising the ISO by a stop increases the EV by +1. Intervals between exposure values are most often measured in thirds and whole numbers. You can often set your camera to control exposure level increments in halves.

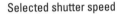
Selected shutter speed

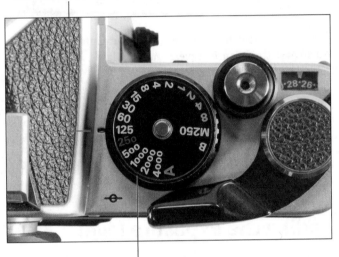

FIGURE 1-3:
Shutter speed "stops" on a film camera.

Shutter speed dial

Figure 1-4 shows the relationship between newer camera settings and stops. Each numbered division represents a stop of exposure, which is the same as on the older shutter speed dial. Each stop is divided into thirds by smaller, unnumbered marks. The difference between each stop represents 1 EV. The smaller increments are separated by 1/3 EV.

REMEMBER

There are creative and practical differences between a stop of shutter speed and aperture, but in terms of exposure, every stop is equal.

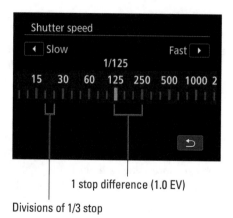

FIGURE 1-4:
This display
shows stops of
shutter speed.

1 stop difference (1.0 EV)

Divisions of 1/3 stop

Keeping an Eye on Exposure Information

Sometimes you need to keep tabs on exposure information. Thankfully, your camera displays it for you in several handy places. When you know where to look, checking becomes easy and routine.

If you don't see anything displayed, press the shutter button halfway. The camera will meter the scene and display the information in the viewfinder, on the camera back, and on the top LCD panel if the camera has one. The camera may hide detailed exposure information from you if you're in a basic or automatic shooting mode because you don't control the exposure in those shooting modes. If you want to follow along with this section, place your camera in an advanced mode.

Reading the exposure level

Your camera has an *exposure level indicator* scale (a.k.a. *exposure scale* or *exposure meter*), shown in Figure 1-5. The exposure level indicator shows exposure values relative to a center point, which is called the *standard exposure*. This is the exposure that the camera thinks will produce the best photo. It will be just right — not too dark or too light.

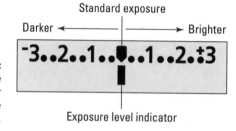

FIGURE 1-5:
The exposure
level indicator
scale shows the
exposure.

Standard exposure

Darker ← → Brighter

Exposure level indicator

The center of the scale may be labeled as 0 and is typically displayed with a slightly different mark to distinguish it from the other exposure levels. The numbers to the left and right of center tell you how many stops — or levels of exposure value (EV) — the current exposure is from 0. The size of the scale may vary, but cameras usually show a minimum of +/− 2.0 EV from the center. Some cameras have displays that read +/− 5.0 EV.

REMEMBER

In autoexposure modes, the exposure level indicator stays pegged in the middle. After all, that's the point of autoexposure. In manual mode, the exposure level indicator moves depending on your exposure settings. If you set your exposure settings so that the exposure level indicator is on 0, you'll take the standard exposure. The exception to that is when you are in manual mode and have set the camera to Auto ISO. As you make changes to shutter speed and aperture, the ISO automatically adjusts to keep the exposure at 0 EV.

TIP

After you set your exposure controls in manual mode, they don't change by themselves between shots, even if the meter displays a slightly different light level. Shooting in manual mode is an excellent way of making sure that your photos consistently use the same exposure settings, which is to your advantage when processing them the same way later.

The indicator can move left or right when you're in an autoexposure mode by a process known as exposure compensation (described later in the chapter). When you're shooting with autoexposure bracketing, each bracket's exposure is often marked with a tick mark.

Viewing exposure settings

As you set the camera up to take photos, you should track the three exposure settings: aperture, shutter speed, and ISO. Shutter speed and aperture are often paired; ISO tends to be off on its own. You can find them here:

>> **Viewfinder:** The exposure settings often appear prominently at the bottom of the viewfinder, as shown in Figure 1-6.

>> **Back monitor:** The exposure settings also appear in the various information displays, as shown in Figure 1-7. In this case, the shooting information display is along the top.

>> **LCD panel:** If your camera has a top LCD panel, you can check the exposure settings there. See Figure 1-8.

>> **Live View:** When you're using Live View, exposure data often appears at the bottom of the monitor and looks similar to what you see in the viewfinder. See Figure 1-9.

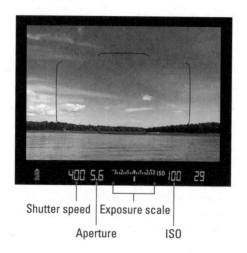

FIGURE 1-6:
The shutter speed, aperture, and ISO speed all appear in the viewfinder.

Shutter speed | Exposure scale

Aperture   ISO

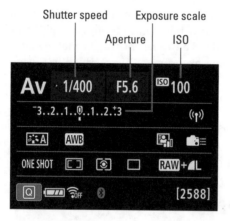

Shutter speed   Exposure scale

Aperture   ISO

FIGURE 1-7:
The shooting information display also shows the shutter speed, aperture, and ISO speed.

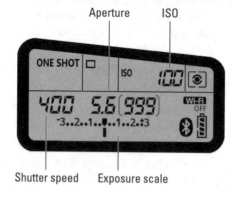

Aperture   ISO

FIGURE 1-8:
Don't forget to look at the LCD panel, if you have one.

Shutter speed   Exposure scale

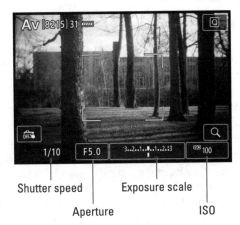

FIGURE 1-9:
Live View
displays also
show
exposure
information at
the bottom.

Shutter speed   Exposure scale

Aperture   ISO

Paying attention to warnings

REMEMBER

Your camera may have several exposure-related warnings that let you know it can't take a good photo the way the camera is currently set up. For example, you may have the shutter speed set so fast that the camera can't open the aperture wide enough to take a properly exposed photo. Typically, the setting that is the problem will blink. See Table 1-1 for a summary of problems and solutions.

TABLE 1-1   **Exposure Warnings and Their Solutions**

Setting	What's Happening	Solution
Aperture and shutter speed	If both the aperture and shutter speed values blink, the camera can't select a combination that will properly expose the image. This most often happens in program autoexposure mode.	Adjust the lighting or change the ISO setting.
Aperture only	The aperture blinks if the camera can't set the aperture to expose the image properly at the selected shutter speed. This happens in shutter-priority mode.	Change the shutter speed or ISO.
Shutter speed	The shutter speed value blinks if the camera can't select a shutter speed that will produce a good exposure at the aperture you selected. This happens in Aperture Priority mode.	Choose a different f-stop or adjust the ISO.

Measuring Light by Metering

Metering is the process of measuring how much light is in the scene you want to photograph. The amount of light helps determine what aperture, shutter speed, and ISO sensitivity you or your camera need to set in order to take a good photo.

General metering methods

There are two different ways to meter how much light is in a scene: using *reflected* or *incident* light.

Measuring reflected light means that you collect light that bounces off stuff and finds its way into your camera or *light meter* (an external accessory that measures light; jump up to Figure 1-12 to have a look at one). Cameras use this metering method exclusively. The upside to measuring reflected light is that you're able to meter distant objects. You can also meter specific objects in the scene, like a person's face. The downside to the approach is that not everything reflects the same amount of light, which can fool the metering sensor. This variation in reflected light can become a problem when photographing people of different skin colors and tones. Reflected metering can also be called spot metering.

Incident light meters work differently. Rather than sense reflected light, an incident light meter sits *in the scene* and measures how much light is falling *where the meter is.* Most incident meters have a white-colored dome or disk that bulges out from the meter's body. Ambient light passes through the dome and is measured by the meter. Cameras can't meter incident light without special attachments. The upside to this method is that, overall, it is less prone to being spoofed by objects with different reflective properties. The problem with incident light meters is that they don't take reflectivity into account. If you're photographing something very bright and reflective, an incident light meter may recommend setting the exposure too high.

REMEMBER

The long and the short of it is this: Your camera has a reasonably good reflective light meter built right in, but it's not perfect. You have to be able to switch metering modes (explained next) or manually compensate if the camera misjudges the scene. If you want an alternative metering method when shooting portraits and other studio-type shots, as well as some landscapes, consider buying a dedicated light meter.

Camera metering modes

Digital SLRs have several ways to assess how much reflected light is in the scene. They are called *metering modes.* Your camera will have three or more modes for you to choose from. They differ in how they evaluate different areas of the scene. One mode takes the entire frame into account. Other modes measure the center or very small spots. Refer to Figure 1-10 as you read the next few sections. The green areas in the viewfinder represent the areas the camera uses when metering in each mode.

FIGURE 1-10:
Metering modes
enable you to
customize how
the camera
meters.

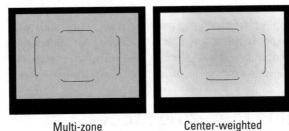

| Multi-zone | Center-weighted | Spot |

Multi-zone

When this mode is selected, the camera divides the scene into zones and evaluates the brightness of each separately. Each manufacturer has its own system for how it weighs each area and combines the information into a single overall exposure. Camera manufacturers call their multi-zone metering modes by different names: 3D color matrix metering (Nikon), evaluative metering (Canon), and multi segment metering (Pentax and Sony). You may also hear it referred to as segment or multi-pattern metering.

REMEMBER

Multi-zone is a good general-purpose metering mode and is the default for most cameras. You need not switch from it unless you're dealing with strong backlighting or want to measure light reflecting off specific objects or areas in the scene.

Center-weighted

Center-weighted mode meters the entire frame but gives more weight to elements in the center than around the edges. Though the bias varies, it's in the range of 70 percent center to 30 percent edges. Canon refers to this mode as center-weighted average metering mode.

TIP

Center-weighted metering is a good mode for portraits and other photos with relatively large subjects in the center of the frame.

Spot

Spot metering measures light in a small circle in the center of the frame and ignores everything else. This metering mode is useful if you need to measure reflected light from a specific object or point in the scene. Some cameras let you change the size of the spot circle. Canon has an extra mode, called partial metering, that covers a larger central area. Some cameras enable you to link the spot meter to the current AF point, which is very handy.

Making Sense of
Exposure

Spot metering is good when you want the camera to calculate the exposure using a very precise spot in the scene. This spot can be your main subject or an object that you don't want under or overexposed. You will often need to combine spot metering with AE lock in order to focus and meter off-center before you take the photo.

Changing metering modes

More expensive cameras have dedicated metering mode buttons, which make changing metering modes a snap. Press the button and pick a new mode, as shown in Figure 1-11. Other cameras display metering mode information in the shooting information display, where you can often change it relatively quickly. As a last resort, you can always change metering modes using the camera's menu.

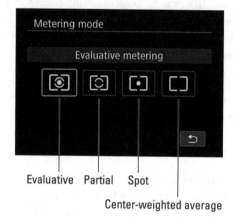

FIGURE 1-11: Learn your camera's metering mode symbols.

Metering the scene with your camera

To meter the scene with your camera, follow these steps:

1. **Frame the shot you want to take.**

2. **Press your shutter button halfway.**

   You don't have to hold the button down. The camera remembers the light measurement for a moment (this is called the *metering timer* or *AE lock time*) and suggests exposure settings based on your current shooting mode. However, most people hold it there briefly to focus before continuing to press all the way down and take the photo.

Check your camera's manual for metering options. You may be able to press a different button to meter the scene, which lets you separate metering from autofocusing. You may also be able to reprogram the metering/autoexposure function to a new button of your choice. See Book 1, Chapter 4 for more on accessing your camera's menu to take advantage of customization options.

Using an external light meter

An external *light meter* is a separate gizmo that measures the amount of light in a scene. That's all it does. It doesn't take pictures or make lattes. Figure 1-12 shows mine. More expensive light meters can measure incident light with a dome and reflected light through a spot metering lens. Some light meters measure only incident light. Although not strictly necessary, a light meter can be a valuable addition to your kit.

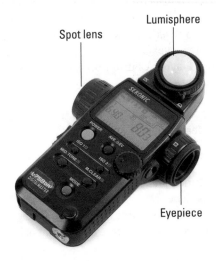

Spot lens

Lumisphere

Eyepiece

FIGURE 1-12:
This Sekonic
light meter is
ready for action.

Look up your light meter's manual for specific instructions. In the meantime, I can tell you that the general process works like this: After you set up your light meter to measure incident or reflected light, you need to enter two of the three known exposure settings you have set on the camera (ISO sensitivity, aperture, or shutter speed). Then take a reading. The meter figures out what the third exposure setting should be and shows it to you. Enter that value (aperture or shutter speed) in your camera.

Making Sense of
Exposure

Reviewing and Analyzing Your Photos

Reviewing photos is one of the most important aspects of digital photography. You've got that fancy high-res monitor on the back of your camera; use it to check whether your photos are exposed the way you want them to be.

If you don't review your shots, you won't be able to analyze the histograms and take full advantage of the troubleshooting techniques described later in this chapter.

Delving into photo playback

Photo playback involves more than you might think. It's an especially useful tool that enables you to check the exposure, color, focus, and composition of every photo you take. You have two ways to go about playback. With auto review, the camera displays the photo for a specific amount of time. You may already have auto review enabled. Turn to Book 1, Chapter 4 to find out how to customize that feature. You can also initiate playback by pressing your camera's Playback button. Figure 1-13 points out the Playback button on a typical dSLR, along with other buttons you might use during playback.

I hit the highlights in this section. You'll have to turn to your camera's manual to see how to use specific features. Pressing the Playback button allows you to do the following:

>> **Display different amounts of data.** You can change what information you see during photo playback by pressing your camera's Display or Info button. If you want a general sense of the photo, turn off everything. If you want a reminder of the settings you used, increase the amount of information, as shown in Figure 1-14.

>> **Zoom in and out.** Press your camera's Zoom button to go in and closely inspect your photos.

>> **Pan back and forth.** When you're zoomed in, use your camera's controller or cross keys to move back and forth in the photo.

>> **View indices.** You can often show small thumbnails of your photos: 4, 6, or 9 — sometimes as many as 100 — at a time.

>> **Check the histogram.** Examine the photo's histogram to check general exposure and color.

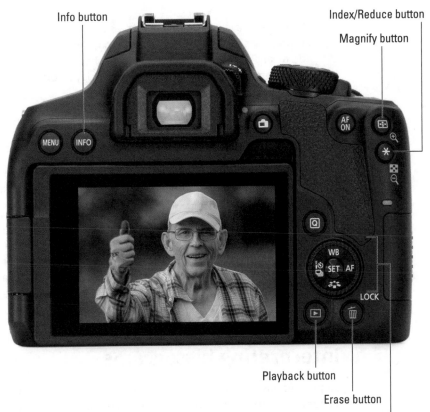

Info button

Index/Reduce button

Magnify button

Playback button

Erase button

Navigation/Selection and Set button

FIGURE 1-13:
The Playback button is somewhere on the back of your camera.

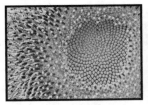
No information

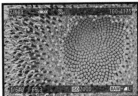
Basic information

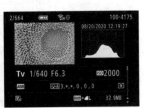
Detailed information

FIGURE 1-14:
A range of information is available during playback.

>> **Check for clipped highlights.** See whether you have clipped highlights with the Highlight Alert (Canon) or Highlights (Nikon) display during photo playback. When this feature is on, overexposed areas blink. If you see large areas blinking and that isn't your creative goal, rethink the camera's exposure and take another shot.

There is one caveat to this feature: Areas of the photo that are clipped in one or two color channels, but not all three, may not register as clipped highlights. This means they won't blink. Examine the photo's color histograms for exposure across the board. All photos have three layers of color information: red, green, and blue.

>> **Delete the bad ones.** Don't save obviously bad photos. Delete them from your camera's memory card to save space, time, and trouble. Deleting should involve pressing your camera's Delete or Erase button and confirming.

>> **Protect the good ones.** Alternatively, you can protect the photos you want to keep so that they don't accidentally get deleted. You might be able to press a specific button to protect a photo or use the menu in Playback mode.

>> **View playback on an HDTV.** If you haven't already, view playback on a large HDTV. Photos (and movies, but that's another story) look fantastic, and it's easier to spot focus, color, and exposure problems on a big-screen HDTV. Look at the terminals on the side of your camera. HDMI terminals, located on the side of your camera under a rubberized cover, enable you to connect your camera to an HDTV. Older dSLRs use analog audio/video connections.

Interpreting histograms

Simply put, *histograms* are charts. Digital SLRs display two different types of histograms: brightness and color, which is sometimes called RGB. Brightness histograms show the number of pixels in an image arranged by their brightness. Color histograms chart each color channel — red, green, and blue — separately. Live View histograms give you this information before you take the photo. You can also view the histogram of each photo during playback.

Cycle through your camera's Live View and playback displays to see the histograms. You may need to turn them on from the menu.

Brightness histograms

Brightness, sometimes called *luminance*, histograms are pretty easy to understand. As shown in Figure 1-15, they arrange pixels along the horizontal axis according to their brightness. Dark pixels appear on the left and bright pixels are plotted to the right. Pixels at the left and right edges are at the minimum or maximum level, respectively. The vertical axis shows how many pixels share that same brightness. High peaks and mounds represent large numbers of pixels. Dips and valleys show fewer pixels, and bare spots show that no pixels have that brightness. You can divide the histogram into five tonal regions. Moving from left to right, they are: very dark, dark, medium, light, and very light. Pure black is on the far left; pure white is on the far right. Some cameras put lines on the histogram to help you make sense of these general areas.

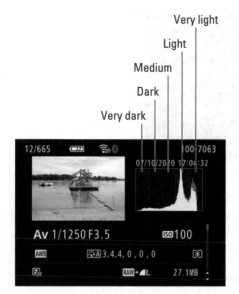

Very light
Light
Medium
Dark
Very dark

12/665

07/10/2020 17:04:32

100-7063

Av 1/1250 F3.5   ISO 100

3,4,4 , 0 , 0 , 0

RAW+ L   27.1MB

The photo shown in Figure 1-15 contains a range of brightness levels, but light and very light tones dominate. Nothing appears to have been clipped on either end.

REMEMBER

The trick with brightness histograms is to realize that they weigh the brightness of each pixel in relation to how the human eye perceives it. Information from the green color channel is the most important, followed by red and then blue. This makes them great at showing you how the tonality is distributed, but less effective at judging exposure.

Color histograms

Color histograms (see Figure 1-16) plot pixel brightness for each color channel (red, green, and blue) on a separate part of the chart. The horizontal axis plots color brightness. Bright colors are pure color — red, green, or blue, depending on the channel — whereas dark colors turn black. The vertical axis displays how many pixels are at that brightness level, just as a brightness histogram does. Peaks and mounds represent large numbers of pixels at that color brightness. Dips and valleys show fewer pixels, and bare spots show that no pixels have that brightness. The photo in Figure 1-16 has nice, strong colors with different brightness levels: dark reds from the berries, green leaves in the middle, and bright blues from the sky.

Color histograms may be displayed in black and white or in their respective color. Unlike brightness histograms, perception plays no role in how pixels are treated.

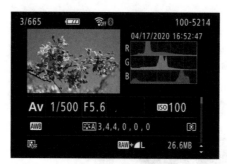

FIGURE 1-16:
Color histograms
show color
channel
brightness and
clipping.

It's easy to look at individual color channels and tell if there's clipping on either end. What can be tricky is looking at all three channels together and not overdrawing conclusions. For example, when peaks in each channel align, that's an indication of strong neutral tones, whether they are dark (blacks), medium (grays), or bright (whites). When there are strong peaks of color that don't line up, that's an indication that the photo contains distinct colors that differ in brightness. It's *not* an automatic indication of a white balance problem.

Putting it all together

Histogram shapes give you important information about your photo. Knowing how to interpret these shapes is central to effectively using a histogram.

REMEMBER

>> **Peaks and mounds** show a larger numbers of pixels. If you see a peak, the pixels are concentrated over fewer brightness levels. If you see a mound, the pixels are concentrated over a larger range of brightness levels.

>> **Dips and valleys** reveal fewer pixels at those brightness levels.

>> **Empty areas** mean that there are no pixels at that brightness.

>> **Spikes at the edges** tell you that those pixels are clipping. The chart has run out of room to display their brightness levels, whether dark or light.

Different people use different terminology to refer to clipping. Some say that details get *lost in shadows* and that highlights are *blown out.* Each can also be described as *clipped* because the chart looks cut off, or clipped, at that point.

Figures 1-17 through 1-23 are histogram displays. Compare the histograms with the photo thumbnail, as you would on your camera, to see what is going on. You don't need to zoom in 1,000 percent when evaluating histograms.

>> **Clipped shadows:** Figure 1-17 shows a scene shot from shadows in trees looking toward a lake. Some details in dark regions have been clipped and are lost. The bright areas of the sky make this a very high contrast scene, which is

always a challenge to photograph. The camera metered the scene and calculated the exposure to keep the highlights from blowing out, which can happen when using autoexposure. To brighten faces or other subjects in this situation, dial in positive exposure compensation or meter the scene differently.

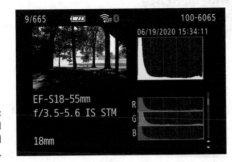

>> **Very dark tones:** The lighthearted photo in Figure 1-18 shows my wife and daughter. The photo is dominated by very dark tones from their hair and clothes. Their skin tones show up as very light reds in that color channel. Overall, the contrast is good, with tones in all regions. This is a great photo with a good exposure, even though the histogram displays mostly dark tones.

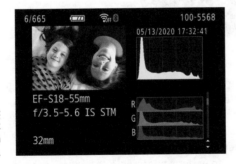

>> **Dark tones:** Figure 1-19 shows a scene I shot at a small river. I stood right at the riverbank. The water glimmers with reflected light from the sun but the rest of the scene is largely dark. There's nothing wrong with that. In this case, the histogram shows that the scene has few very bright areas. Overall, this shot has smooth brightness and color histograms.

Making Sense of Exposure

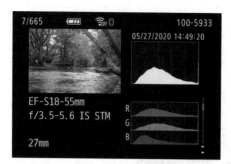

FIGURE 1-19:
The light sky and reflections keep the rest of this photo dark.

>> **Medium tones:** I took the photo in Figure 1-20 from the top of a five-story parking garage with a tilt-shift lens. Medium tones of the road dominate, followed by lighter tones from the sidewalk and the dark grass. This photo is probably a tad underexposed, as indicated by few very light tones. Tilt-shift lenses sometimes have unexpected effects on exposure.

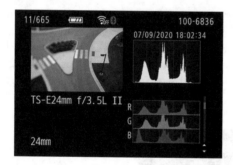

FIGURE 1-20:
This photo has a lot of tones concentrated in the middle.

>> **Light tones:** Figure 1-21 shows the same parking garage from ground level, this time with a different lens. The brightness histogram shows that the photo has a lot of bright tones, but seems to end there. If you look closely at the color histogram, you can see that the blue channel is close to being, or possibly has been, clipped. Very bright single colors can cause this type of problem in a scene. It's better to underexpose a little so that you don't blow out color highlights.

>> **Very light tones:** I set up the photo shown in Figure 1-22 in my studio. As you might expect, I was able to quickly dial in the exposure I wanted, and I achieved good overall contrast through my experience with working in the same room under identical conditions. The very bright tones of the white background show up in the brightness histogram. However, the flowers are not too dark relative to the rest of the scene. They sit very nicely in the medium-to-bright tonal region. The bump of dark blues comes from the shadows in the arrangement.

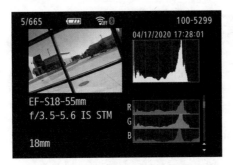

FIGURE 1-21:
Protect color
channels from
blowing out.

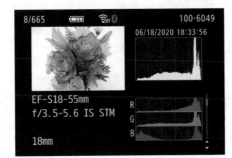

FIGURE 1-22:
Studio settings
enable you
to fine-tune
exposure.

» **Clipped highlights:** Figure 1-23 is another casual shot of my wife and daughter. Although they are well lit, the sky is blown out. This is another example of how bright skies can be so troublesome. They extend the contrast ratio of the scene beyond the camera's ability to capture. Had I accounted for the sky and lowered the exposure, they would have been too dark. Another option would have been to use a fill flash to brighten their faces with a lower exposure.

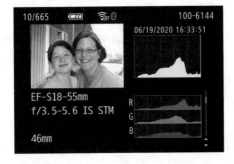

FIGURE 1-23:
Bright skies are
very hard to
control.

Making Sense of
Exposure

Troubleshooting Exposure

If everything always went as planned, you wouldn't need to read this section. The trouble is, the real world is a complicated place, and even the most sophisticated dSLR can misjudge the scene, or your intent.

After reviewing your photos and looking at their histograms, you should have a good idea as to whether they are under- or overexposed, and why. Thankfully, dSLRs are designed with plenty of tools to help you correct any trouble you might be having and nail the next shot.

Using exposure compensation

Although it may seem obvious, when you have the camera in an autoexposure shooting mode, which includes everything but manual and Bulb modes, it sets the exposure for you. To make exposure corrections in an autoexposure mode, you have to override the camera. Changing the exposure controls won't actually change the exposure, because the camera will just work around you. The way to successfully change the exposure the camera sets is to use *exposure compensation (EC).* Here's how it works:

1. **Review each photo after you take it and look to see how it's exposed.**

You don't have to get too technical about it. Does someone's face appear in shadow? Raise the exposure to brighten the face. Is the sky too bright? Lower the exposure to darken the sky.

2. **Press and hold your exposure compensation button while you dial in exposure compensation. See the left image in Figure 1-24.**

- Choose positive values, as shown in the figure, to raise the exposure and brighten the scene.

- Choose negative values to lower the exposure and darken the photo.

As shown in the right image in Figure 1-24, your camera's shooting information screen always shows how much EC you have entered.

3. **Release the EC button and take another shot.**

4. **Review the shot to see whether it's closer to what you want.**

Exposure compensation stays locked in many cameras even after you turn them off, so be careful to reset to 0 after you've taken the shot.

Your camera should allow at least two stops of both positive and negative exposure correction. Some enable you to dial in as many as five stops either way.

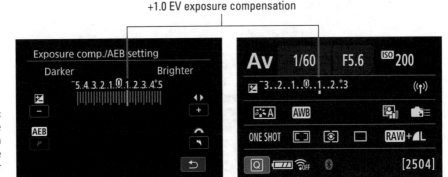

FIGURE 1-24: Exposure compensation moves the exposure up or down.

Setting the exposure manually

One of the most powerful exposure tools in your arsenal is you. Given an understanding of what you want to accomplish creatively, combined with the limitations of your equipment and the lighting on hand, you can effectively troubleshoot exposure by bypassing the camera's autoexposure modes and handling it yourself.

REMEMBER

Each photographic stop has the same effect on exposure, whether it comes from shutter speed, aperture, or ISO. You can swap one for another to get to the exposure you need.

Here are some suggested steps to setting exposure manually:

1. **Select your camera's manual shooting mode, as shown in Figure 1-25.**

2. **Decide what exposure control you want to set first.**

   Let your creative goals guide you to limit one of the three exposure controls:

   - *Aperture:* Smaller apertures are better for landscapes. This translates to larger f-numbers like f/8.0 Larger apertures are better for portraits. This translates to f-numbers like f/5.6. Read Book 3, Chapter 2 for more about aperture.

   - *Shutter speed:* When shooting normal subjects handheld, dial in a shutter speed fast enough to reduce or eliminate camera shake. Set a fast shutter speed for action and dim light. If you try another mode first and the shutter speed is too low, switch to shutter-priority mode. Set the shutter speed high enough to avoid blurring. Read Book 3, Chapter 3 for more information about shutter speed.

   - *ISO:* After the other controls are set, ISO speed will be the control you use most often to make up needed exposure. I leave mine on Auto most of the time for this reason. However, when I want to limit noise, I may set it myself or limit the maximum Auto ISO speed. For shooting still subjects from a tripod, set to lowest ISO and slow shutter speed. Read Book 3, Chapter 4 for more about ISO.

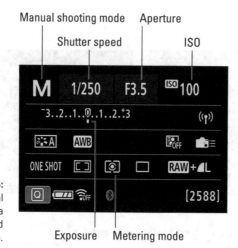

Manual shooting mode   Aperture
        Shutter speed   ISO

M   1/250   F3.5   ISO 100

¯3..2..1..0..1..2.⁺3

ONE SHOT   RAW+◢L

[2588]

FIGURE 1-25:
Setting manual
exposure for a
properly exposed
photo.

Exposure   Metering mode

3. **Set the first value.**

Typically, this will be aperture or shutter speed. Setting the aperture guarantees you the depth of field you want. The aperture I used in Figure 1-25 is a good portrait aperture. Setting the shutter speed helps you capture action or prevent yourself from taking blurry photos.

4. **Set the second exposure control.**

Quite often, you may have set the aperture first but now bring in shutter speed to guarantee a crisp photo. You may want to set the ISO sensitivity now if limiting noise is a priority and you are able to use longer shutter speeds. The fact that I set the ISO to 100 in Figure 1-25 is a sign that I set it before using the shutter speed to dial in the right exposure.

5. **Adjust the third exposure control to get the right exposure.**

This is what I call the "floating" control. It has to be able to move around so that you can set the exposure properly. The exposure scale tells you whether the camera thinks you're under- or overexposing the photo, or are right on the mark (see Figure 1-25). The shutter speed I settled on is fast enough for handheld shooting and able to capture some action. When you're troubleshooting, you may need to ignore the camera meter. If you've already taken a shot and found that it was too bright, tone down the exposure by a third, half, or whole stop. Raise the exposure if the photo was too dark.

Don't make wild changes unless the other photos were significantly off, too. Keep changes small and try to be methodical about it.

TIP

6. **Take a photo.**

7. Review it.

This is the most important step. I know you want to get back to shooting, but you can't rush this step.

- Look at the photo on your monitor and decide whether it appears too dark or too light. Be aware that your perception may be affected if you're looking at the photo in extreme conditions (bright or dim), or if you've altered the brightness level of your monitor. The histogram is helpful in these situations.

- Check the color histograms to see whether any colors are clipping.

- Zoom in, if necessary, to check details.

If everything looks good, this photo is in the bank. You may be able to use the same settings for more photos, provided that the scene and lighting don't change much.

8. Continue adjustments, if necessary.

If the photo is off, return to Step 5 and work with your floating exposure control. You may also return to Step 4 and revise the second control. If your exposure solution won't work for more drastic reasons — you can't set the right shutter speed to avoid blurring, or you're concerned about too high an ISO, go back to Step 2 and reset your priorities. You may have to live with more noise or a shallower depth of field.

Shutter speed is generally the least forgiving exposure element. It's easier to accept different depths of field or noise levels, but camera shake and motion blur caused by slow shutter speeds provide little artistic leeway.

Using AE lock

Autoexposure (AE) lock lets you handle situations in which your subject is strongly backlit and you want to offset that subject in the shot.

You'll meter and focus on one area of the scene, lock the autoexposure reading into the camera, recompose the shot, and then take the photo with the locked exposure settings. This works wonders if your subject is backlit. Simply change to spot or center-weighted metering mode and engage AE lock. Here's how:

1. Change the metering mode to spot or center-weighted metering.

Although you can use any metering mode, switching to spot or center-weighted metering is a quick way to make the camera meter where you want it to. Some cameras enable you to manually select an AF point and use that for AE lock when in certain metering modes. For example, new Canon cameras apply AE lock to the selected AF point when you set the camera to Evaluative metering mode. Read your camera's manual for specifics.

2. **Center the subject in the viewfinder, as shown in Figure 1-26.**

   Unless you are able to use a specific AF point with AE lock. See Book 1, Chapter 5 for information on selecting individual autofocus points.

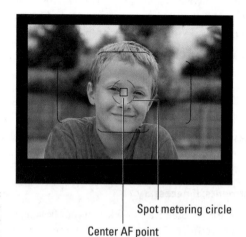

FIGURE 1-26:
Center the
subject to use
spot metering.

Spot metering circle

Center AF point

3. **Press and hold the shutter button halfway down.**

   This meters the scene and gets things in focus, unless focusing manually.

4. **Press and hold the AE Lock button, shown in Figure 1-27.**

   This locks the exposure into the camera. You may release the shutter button after the exposure is locked, but keep pressing the AE Lock button. Press the AE Lock button again if you want to update the exposure.

   Some cameras have AE lock on a timer that lasts a few seconds. If that is the case, you don't have to hold the AE Lock button down unless you want to lock that specific exposure in the camera for longer than the timer allows.

TIP

   You might feel like you have too much to do with too few fingers. Use your left hand to support the weight of the camera while your right hand presses the shutter and AE Lock buttons.

5. **Recompose the shot, as shown in Figure 1-28.**

   Remember, this is the point of AE lock. You can choose any metering point in the scene and then recompose the shot the way you want. If you have a camera that enables you to use any AF point when spot metering, you can skip this step.

   If your camera requires it, continue to hold down the AE Lock button.

AE Lock button

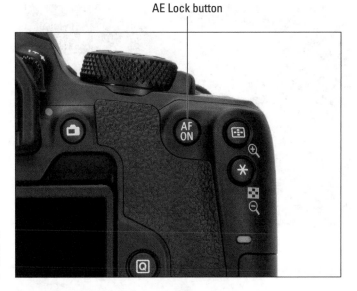

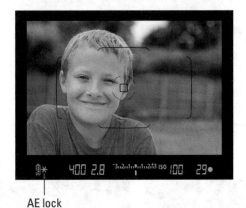

AE lock

Making Sense of Exposure

6. **Take the picture (see Figure 1-29).**

AE lock is a great way to make sure people's faces are exposed correctly when
shooting portraits. Regardless of whether it makes a large or small difference,
it forces the camera to prioritize the center of the frame when you meter. This
keeps dark and bright elements in the background from throwing the camera's
exposure off.

If you want to take more shots with these specific exposure settings, note the
shutter speed, aperture, and ISO; then switch to manual mode and dial in
those values yourself.

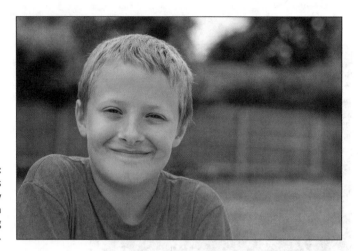

FIGURE 1-29:
AE lock is especially effective when shooting portraits.

Autoexposure bracketing (AEB)

Despite recent trends, your camera's *autoexposure bracketing (AEB)* feature isn't useful solely for *high dynamic range (HDR)* photography. If the lighting is giving the camera trouble, try turning on AEB and shooting several exposure-bracketed photos.

Set up your camera's AEB feature, as shown on the left in Figure 1-30. Tell it how far apart to set the exposure of each bracket, and how many you want to take. It may seem haphazard, but sometimes it's the best you can do. You can choose the best photo of the set. The right image in Figure 1-30 shows the brackets on the shooting information display.

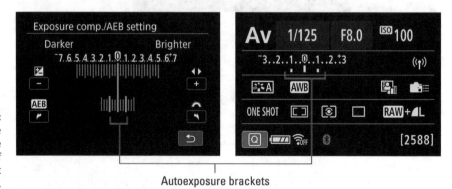

FIGURE 1-30:
Autoexposure brackets give you the option of choosing the best exposure.

Autoexposure brackets

For more information about bracketing and HDR, see Book 5, Chapter 6. The mechanics of using AEB are the same.

Using other exposure tricks

Camera makers use several other exposure tricks to help you solve exposure problems. Most have to do with overcoming a camera's limited capability to photograph very high-contrast scenes.

The names of the tricks differ from brand to brand, and not every camera in every company's lineup will have all the features. However, after reviewing them, you'll see that most of these exposure solutions are similar.

Look for these features on Canon cameras:

>> **Highlight Tone Priority** improves details in highlights by expanding the camera's dynamic range from mids to highs, thereby enabling you to capture more information in bright areas.

>> **Auto Lighting Optimizer** is a processing function that the camera uses to automatically adjust brightness and contrast. You can modify the strength.

>> **HDR mode** takes a number of shots and combines them into a single finished image.

Nikon dSLRs have these features:

>> **Active D-Lighting:** When on, this feature adjusts exposure to maximize the camera's dynamic range, protecting highlights and shadows in high-contrast scenes.

>> **HDR:** Automatically takes exposure-bracketed photos to increase the camera's dynamic range and then combines them into a single, tone-mapped image.

Sony cameras also have several tricks up their sleeve:

>> **D-Range Optimizer:** This feature is Sony's method of protecting highlights and shadows in scenes with high contrast. You can choose from several strengths.

>> **Auto HDR:** Combines AEB with auto tone mapping to provide a single-step HDR capability.

Chapter **2**

Setting the Aperture

This chapter is about the aperture of your lens. You learn what an aperture is, how it affects exposure, how to tell what a lens is capable of, and how you can set the aperture. You also learn how the size of the aperture contributes to defining the scene's *depth of field (the area in focus).*

Armed with this information, you will have an understanding of what the aperture is doing when you use your camera's automated shooting modes, and if you like, take creative control and start setting the aperture yourself.

Investigating f-numbers and Apertures

The opening in every lens that lets light into the camera is called the *aperture.* Apertures shrink and grow by means of a mechanical iris. Larger apertures let in more light. Smaller apertures let in less light. The aperture plays an important part in exposure, and it's expressed as an f-number, which I explain next.

REMEMBER

An aperture is part of the lens, not the camera body. This is one reason the lenses you choose are an important part of your overall dSLR experience.

Learning about f-numbers

Apertures are described by f-numbers. You'll see f-numbers like f/5.6, f/8, and f/16 used to identify the current aperture of a lens. F-numbers aren't direct measurements, but they do relate to the size of the aperture. They also take into account the focal length the lens is set to.

F-numbers describe the ratio between focal length and aperture diameter. Divide the current focal length of the lens by the diameter of the aperture, both measured in millimeters, to calculate the f-number. You can do the reverse as well: Calculate the physical diameter of the lens's aperture by dividing the focal length by the f-number as set on the lens or camera. For example, if the 50mm prime lens shown in Figure 2-1 is set to f/2.0, the physical aperture should be 25mm. I just measured, it and it checks out. F-numbers are also known as f-stops.

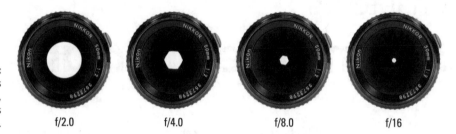

FIGURE 2-1: As f-numbers increase, aperture sizes decrease.

f/2.0   f/4.0   f/8.0   f/16

By convention, f-numbers have two digits. That's why you see f/4.0 and f/8.0 here in the book and displayed by your camera, but not f/11.0 or f/16.0. Those are displayed as f/11 and f/16. The exception to this numbering scheme involves lens names. Quite often, if you run across a lens with a single-digit whole number maximum aperture, it will be simplified. The Canon EF 100mm f/2 USM lens is one example.

Figure 2-1 illustrates how aperture size change with f-numbers. I set the same NIKKOR 50mm f/2 Ai prime lens to four different f-numbers: f/2.0 (the largest aperture shown), f/4.0, f/8.0, and f/16 (the smallest aperture shown). The fact that it is a prime lens, with a constant focal length, simplifies the situation. The only thing that changes between each photo is the f-number, which increases by two full stops each time. The focal length remains constant.

The f-number also depends on the focal length the lens is set to. To illustrate that point, I've photographed my Zoom-NIKKOR 35-70mm f/3.5 AI-s lens with the aperture set to a constant f/3.5. As Figure 2-2 shows, as the focal length increases, so does the physical size of the aperture. Remember, the f-number stayed at f/3.5 for each shot.

Lenses and apertures

Because apertures are described by f-numbers, you will see apertures listed as part of the name of the lens. The listed aperture or apertures tells you a lot about the capabilities of the lens.

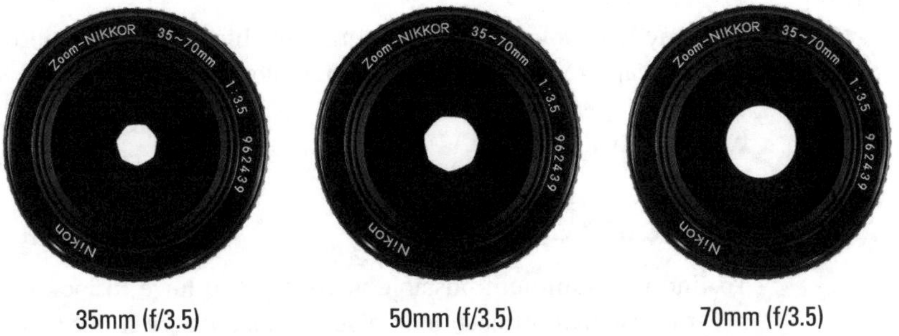

FIGURE 2-2:
Aperture size
must increase
as focal length
increases for
the f-number to
remain the same.

35mm (f/3.5)   50mm (f/3.5)   70mm (f/3.5)

Constant maximum aperture

Many lenses list a single maximum aperture in their name. This means that they have a *constant maximum aperture*, regardless of the focal length. Two types of lenses have a constant maximum aperture:

» **Prime lenses:** All prime lenses have constant maximum apertures because they never change focal length. For example, the maximum aperture of the AF-S NIKKOR 50mm f/1.4G prime lens is f/1.4.

» **Zoom lenses:** Some high-quality zoom lenses have a constant maximum aperture across their focal length range. These lenses cost more and are better than those with variable maximum apertures because you can collect the same amount of light whether you're zoomed in or out. The Canon EF 24-105mm f/4L IS USM is a good example. Although it's a zoom lens, the maximum aperture is f/4.0. It doesn't change, no matter what the focal length is.

Variable maximum aperture

Lenses with *variable maximum apertures* list two f-numbers in their name. For example, the Sigma 17-70mm F2.8-4 DC Macro HSM zoom lens sports apertures listed at f/2.8 and f/4.0. What gives? The maximum aperture changes depending on the focal length the lens is set to. You're given the two extremes: At 17mm, the maximum aperture is f/2.8. At 70mm, the maximum aperture is f/4.0.

If you plug these numbers into the f-number equation (f-number equals focal length divided by aperture diameter), you discover that the aperture diameter of this lens at 17mm and f/2.8 is approximately 6mm. The aperture diameter at 70mm and f/4.0 is 17.5mm. That's a pretty big difference! If you wanted to design this lens with a constant maximum aperture of f/2.8, it would have to be 25mm wide when zoomed to 70mm. That would make this reasonably priced lens cost a lot more!

Setting the Aperture

REMEMBER

You may look down at your camera after having set the aperture to f/3.5 and see that the camera has changed it without your permission. Here's what's happened: You've zoomed beyond the range where the lens can support your chosen aperture, so it had to adjust.

Minimum aperture

To find the minimum possible aperture, you have to look into the specification sheet or manual for each lens. You can also figure it out by attaching the lens to your camera, entering aperture-priority or Manual mode, and setting the aperture to the largest f-number possible. Common values range from f/16 to f/32.

Fast lenses

Lenses with small f-numbers in their name are known as *fast* lenses. The Canon EF 50mm f/1.2L USM is a good example of a really fast prime lens. The Canon EF 24-70mm f/2.8L II USM is a high-quality zoom lens that is also considered a fast lens. When set to the lowest f-numbers, fast lenses let in a lot of light. They excel in low-light situations, when you need to use a fast shutter speed. Some fast lenses are prized for their ability to pleasingly blur the background when their apertures are large.

Table 2-1 puts lenses into speed categories based on their maximum apertures. Table 2-1 applies to most lenses below 400mm. When you're working with super telephoto lenses at 500mm and 600mm, f/4 is considered fast. For super-duper-ooper-schmooper telephoto lenses (800mm), f/5.6 is considered fast.

TABLE 2-1   **Fast versus Slow Lens Speeds**

Speed	Maximum f-number range	Notes
Very Fast	f/1.8 and below	Professional lenses; very fast compared to all other lenses; companies often field more than one fast prime lens with different price points and slightly different maximum apertures; can be expensive; cost goes up as focal lengths increase
Fast	f/2 to f/2.8	Very expensive telephoto and zoom lenses; very good in low light; zoom lenses at this range are considered professional caliber
Medium	f/3.0 to f/4.0	Moderately expensive, but still reasonably affordable; can be used in low-light with higher ISOs and longer shutter speeds; very good outside
Normal	f/5.6 and above	Often inexpensive; come as kit lenses on consumer and some midrange dSLRs; hard to use inside without elevating ISO or using flash; fine outside; great lenses for amateurs but limited by aperture

Setting the Aperture

If you're in an automatic shooting mode, the camera sets the aperture for you. You can indirectly change the aperture only by choosing a different scene or creative mode. If you are in a more advanced shooting mode, you can chance the aperture using the appropriate camera controls and in some cases controls on the lens. The following sections explain how.

From the camera

Most modern lenses *don't* have aperture rings, which means that you have to set the aperture using the controls on the camera. Here's how:

1. **Enter a suitable shooting mode.**

Manual, aperture-priority, and Bulb are the three modes through which you can change aperture directly. You can also shift the aperture using your camera's Program Shift or Flexible Program mode.

2. **Dial in the aperture of your choice.**

Use the appropriate control for your camera. It will normally be the front or rear dial.

The camera will shows the current aperture setting on the back (as shown in Figure 2-3), in the viewfinder, and on the top LCD panel, if it has one.

You may also be able to control the aperture from a camera screen.

Some cameras have shooting modes that let you select the amount of background blur you want in the photo. Canon calls its mode Creative Auto, whereas Nikon uses a shooting mode called Guide. This is an effective way to indirectly control the camera's aperture. Selecting different scenes also affects aperture. For example, Landscape mode has a greater depth of field than Portrait mode because it sets the aperture to a smaller size.

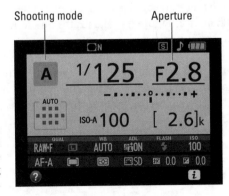

FIGURE 2-3: Set and monitor the aperture using the camera.

From the lens

Aperture rings are slowly dying out. Canon has done away with them altogether. Nikon's newer G and E (similar to G lenses but with electromagnetic versus mechanical aperture blade movement) do not have aperture rings, either. Nikon's D-series lenses, which are an interesting mix of old and new technology, still use aperture rings. Figure 2-4 shows the AF-S NIKKOR 300mm f/4D IF-ED I've used for many photos throughout this book. It's a relatively low-cost super telephoto lens that performs quite well. It also has an aperture ring, but you don't get to use it much.

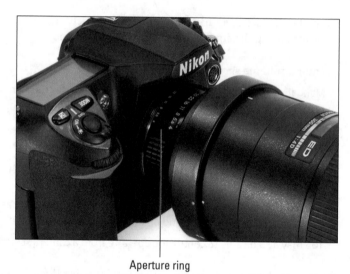

FIGURE 2-4: Notice the aperture ring on this modern Nikon lens.

Aperture ring

To use D-series lenses on new camera bodies, lock the aperture ring on the lens to its highest f-number and control the aperture from the camera.

More advanced Nikon dSLR bodies let you enter the focal length and maximum aperture of old lenses, called *non-CPU* lenses, in the camera's menu. Entering the data enables the camera to meter, recognize the aperture set by the lens, and control the flash. Book 1, Chapter 3, Figure 3-5 illustrates an old manual focus lens with an aperture ring and aperture scale.

Advanced Pentax cameras also let you mount older lenses with aperture rings. Use the Custom Function that enables you to use the aperture ring on the lens, as shown in Figure 2-5. In cases like this, you set the aperture using the aperture ring located on the lens.

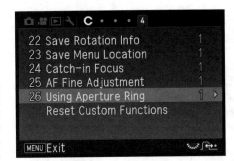

FIGURE 2-5:
You can tell some cameras that you want to use the aperture ring on older lenses.

Some specialty lenses, like certain Lensbaby optics, do not have traditional aperture rings. They require you to change the lens's aperture by swapping aperture discs with a special magnetic tool (see Figure 5-13 in Book 2, Chapter 5). It sounds clunky, but it's sort of fun.

Digging into Depth of Field

REMEMBER

The size of the aperture has a direct impact exposure by letting more or less light through the lens. The size of the aperture also has a creative side effect: Different aperture settings create different *depths of field.* Depth of field is the area of the photo that appears sharp when focused. Everything outside the depth-of-field area, whether foreground or background, looks blurred.

Figure 2-6 illustrates depth of field with a shot taken at f/1.4. The white knight in the center was the point of focus. It, and the brown pawn to the right of it, are in the center of the depth of field. The board and pieces nearer to the camera are out of focus because they're in front of the depth of field. The background, beyond the depth of field, is also out of focus.

Controlling the depth of field

One of the creative aspects of photography that makes it so interesting is that you have control over the size of the depth of field. You can, with relative ease, make it larger or smaller.

Several factors determine how large or how small the depth of field is:

TECHNICAL STUFF

>> **Circle of confusion:** The circle of confusion is a subjective value that decides, essentially, how out-of-focus something has to be before you notice it. You can ignore it.

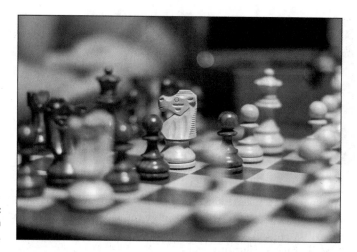

FIGURE 2-6:
A shallow depth
of field.

>> **Distance to subject:** The distance you are from your subject has an effect on the depth of field. Using the same aperture, the depth of field gets smaller as you get closer. As you focus further away, the depth of field gets larger. Some lenses have distance scales on them.

REMEMBER

>> **f-number:** Setting the aperture is where you really get into controlling the depth of field. Figure 2-7 shows two photos of the same scene taken with different apertures. I didn't move the camera, change the focal length, or change where I focused.

- Large apertures like f/1.4, shown on the left, result in shallow depths of field. Notice that the candles in the foreground and background are out of focus, and that the *bokeh* (the aesthetic nature of the blurry parts, discussed later) created by this lens is pleasing.

- Small apertures like f/11, shown on the right, result in deeper depths of field. Most of the scene is in focus.

At very close ranges, however, even small apertures create photos with shallow depths of field.

>> **Focal length:** The longer the focal length, the shallower the depth of field for a given aperture. This is why telephoto lenses produce a shallower depth of field than normal or wide-angle lenses. Telephoto lenses create wonderful bokehs, which, in turn, makes near/medium telephoto lenses very effective portraiture and wedding lenses.

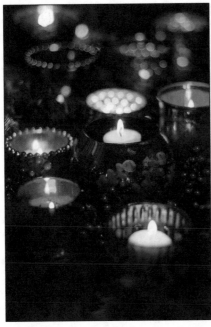
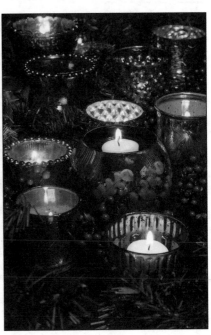

f/1.4 f/11

Previewing the depth of field

You may not realize it, but the aperture on your lens is kept wide open while you frame, meter, and focus the scene. Otherwise, it would often be too dark to see anything. When you press the shutter button to take the photo, the lens quickly changes to the aperture to what the actual setting is, which means that you don't normally see what the depth of field will be when using the viewfinder.

To correct that situation, most digital SLRs have a Depth-of-Field Preview button. When you press it, the aperture on the lens changes to the appropriate setting, enabling you to see the depth of field as it will be when you take the photo. Look for the button somewhere low on the front of the camera, either on the right or left side near the lens mount. Reach around to press it after you focus on your subject. Figure 2-8 shows the Depth-of-Field Preview button on the Canon EOS 77D. Reaching around and pressing the button feels pretty cumbersome unless you practice a bit.

TIP

Checking the depth of field is most effective when the aperture is set to a value *smaller* than the lens's maximum aperture.

Setting the Aperture

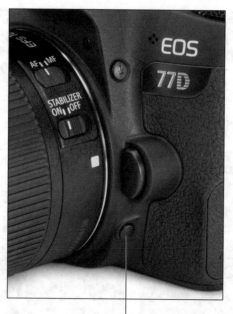

FIGURE 2-8:
The Depth-of-
Field Preview
button is often
located near the
lens mount.

Depth of field preview button

Many prime lenses have depth-of-field scales printed right on the lens, somewhere near the distance scale, which gives you a quick estimate of how large or small the depth of field will be. Many mirrorless cameras do not have a Depth-of-Field Preview button. You'll have to assign a button to this function if you want to preview the depth of field.

TECHNICAL STUFF

The scale on a full-frame compatible lens will overestimate the depth of field when mounted on a cropped-frame body by a factor equal to your camera's crop factor. To get the proper value, divide the distance given by the lens by your camera's crop factor.

Paying attention to the blurry parts

REMEMBER

The blurry area of a photo located outside the depth of field has an aesthetic quality called the *bokeh.* Not all lenses are created equal. Prized lenses take photos with smooth, beautiful bokeh. Other lenses aren't quite as spectacular.

Photos with great-looking bokeh are very attractive. Figure 2-9, shot with the AF-S NIKKOR 50mm f/1.4G, has a bokeh that looks like a painting. Lights and reflections make good bokeh, but you will see smooth, creamy bokehs even when the background is uniform. A great bokeh is a telltale sign that a photographer is using a high-quality professional lens. When it comes to bokeh, the lens really does matter.

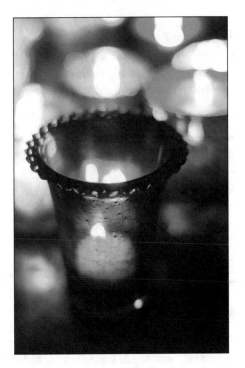

FIGURE 2-9:
Nice bokehs are
otherworldly.

Photos with deep depths of field may have no blurry parts, so bokeh is not as important. Landscape photos, for example, are often entirely in focus.

Being realistic

REMEMBER

Try not to obsess over getting the shallowest depth of field possible on the assumption that it will make your photos better. Shallow depths of field make focusing much harder. For example, when photographing people, very shallow depths of field can make getting both eyes in focus impossible.

The reverse is also true. When the aperture is very small (depending on the lens, apertures smaller than f/22), diffraction starts to become a problem. *Diffraction* happens when light waves get bent as they go around the edges of the aperture. This bending results in softness or fuzziness in areas of the photo that should be sharp.

If you're shooting at close distances (food or product shots, for example), take test shots at different f-numbers and compare sharpness. Choose the photo that best meets your depth-of-field and sharpness needs.

If a shallow depth of field is giving you fits, try this:

>> **Step back from the subject.** Don't just zoom out. Doing so doesn't increase the distance between you and what you're shooting. Actually step back.

>> **Zoom out.** If you can't step back, try zooming out.

>> **Stop down.** For example, if you're shooting at f/1.4, try f/2.8. Not many people care what aperture you use; they're interested in what your photo looks like.

If you're after a shallow depth of field, do the opposite: Step in, zoom in, and open the aperture more.

Designing with Depth of Field

The point of this section is to show you how selecting an aperture to produce a desired depth of field comes together in practice. I've chosen sample photos to show you how different apertures work with different scenes. After you've armed yourself with this information, I encourage you to go out and experiment to find your favorite settings.

I throw a lot of numbers at you in the following sections. If you need to, skip them and focus on the narrative and the photos. Come back later if you want to study the details more.

Landscapes

When shooting landscapes, you typically want as much of the scene in focus as possible. To maximize depth of field, use a small aperture like f/8 and focus on something in the distance. Doing so takes advantage of the *hyperfocal* distance, which is the focus distance where the depth of field extends to infinity.

Figure 2-10 illustrates the point. To take the photo, I used a Sony APS-C dSLT with an ultra wide-angle zoom lens set to 10mm. My aperture was set to f/8, and I focused far out into the distance. Given those parameters, the hyperfocal distance for this scene is just over 2 feet. That means that everything in this photo beyond 2 feet from the camera is in focus. It's a physical impossibility for it to be anything less. It's clear from this photo, because you can see so far into the distance. The tree line on the far side of the river is nice and sharp all the way to the point where it disappears around the bend.

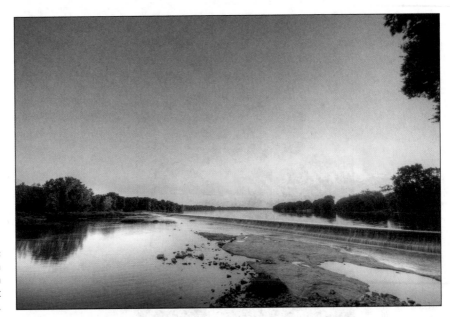

FIGURE 2-10:
Maximize depth
of field when
shooting most
landscapes.

If you want to use larger apertures, pay attention to the foreground. If you're focusing too far away, it will be out of focus. The same thing applies to longer focal lengths on telephoto lenses. To find the hyperfocal distance, check out online or printed depth-of-field calculators. I use www.dofmaster.com. You'll need to know the camera model, aperture setting, focal length you are working at, and subject distance.

Approach buildings and cityscapes as though they were landscape shots to maximize the depth of field. Use smaller apertures and wide-angle lenses if possible. If you are focusing on something in the distance, however, you can get away with using a longer focal length. I took the shot of downtown Detroit shown in Figure 2-11 with an aperture of f/8 and the lens set to 50mm. In this case, the near edge of the depth of field starts out farther away than the photo in Figure 2-10 (about 37 feet, or 11 meters), but the depth of field still extends to infinity.

Portraits

When photographing people, it is often best to try to limit the depth of field. Subjects appear more prominently if they're the only element in focus. The apertures you use to photograph them will be larger than for landscapes. Longer focal lengths and closer distance to your subject also play a role in making the depth of field smaller. As I've mentioned, though, beyond a certain point, shrinking the depth of field makes capturing a good photo impossible.

For every stop of aperture, you double or halve the size of the depth of field. That may be one of the more important sentences in this chapter.

TIP

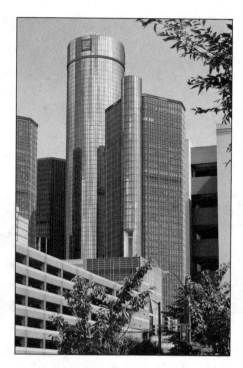

Figure 2-12 shows a group portrait of my sons and me in the kitchen. My wife had just given me a haircut and the kids were next. We were playing around, so she grabbed the camera and took this shot with a Nikon APS-C dSLR and 50mm lens. The aperture was set to f/2.8. This combination made the depth of field about a third of a foot, or 10 cm. As you can see, the background is nicely blurred.

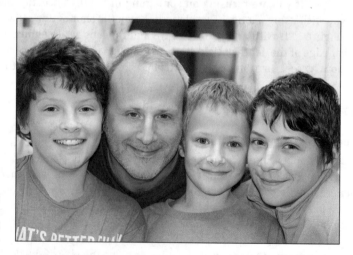

TIP

The challenge when taking group shots with a shallow depth of field is to get everyone lined up so that all of them are about the same distance from the camera. If the distance varies too much, they won't be in focus. To increase the depth of field, use a smaller aperture or step back.

You don't have to worry about lining up people when shooting individual portraits. Figure 2-13 shows a nice photo of my son Sam. I used a Canon APS-C dSLR with lens set to 42mm and an aperture of f/5.6. In this case, the depth of field is about 2 inches, or 5 cm. How can the depth of field be smaller than the last photo? I was closer to the subject.

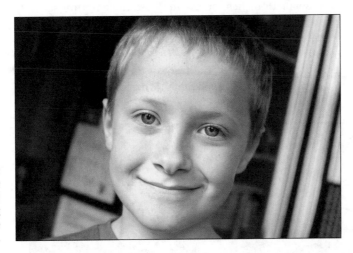

FIGURE 2-13:
Aim for a shallow depth of field when shooting portraits, but be careful.

Believe it or not, f/5.6 was the perfect aperture to use in this situation. If I had been using a better lens and been tempted to set the lens to f/2.8 or f/1.4, the smaller depth of field might have been disastrous. As it is, Sam's nose and eyes are sharp and in focus, whereas his ears are not. This is about as shallow as you want to be unless you're going for a special effect.

If you want to be meticulous with your portraits, I encourage you to calculate the depth of field you want and then reverse-engineer the aperture, focal length, and distance from the subject; that will help you achieve your goals. Base the size of the desired depth of field on things you intend to photograph:

» **A person's face:** Aim for a depth of field of a few to about 6 inches, or from 5–15 cm.

» **A person's head:** Set the depth of field to about a foot, or approximately 30 cm.

» **A group of people:** You want the depth of field to be 2 or 3 feet, or something like 60–90 cm.

Setting the Aperture

Over time, you'll know what to expect and be able to work more on the fly.

Macros and close-ups

When shooting macros and close-ups, depths of field tend to be very small. At times, this is exactly what you want. Sometimes, though, it's a struggle to increase the depth of field.

Have a look at Figure 2-14. It's a small beetle that I photographed using a Nikon APS-C camera and lens. The focal length was 105mm and my distance to the beetle was about 16 inches, or 42 cm. I had the aperture set to f/22. This created a depth of field of .4 inch, or only 1 centimeter (10 millimeters). That's right, a centimeter, even with such a small aperture. Had I used something more typical of standard photography, like f/5.8 or f/8, the depth of field would have been impossibly small. As it is, the front of the beetle and parts of the leaves are nice and sharp. The bokeh is good, and it's a great photo.

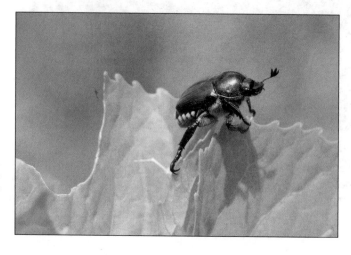

FIGURE 2-14:
Macros have very small depths of field, even when shot using small apertures.

Treat close-ups as you would portraits, even though distances are generally closer. You should use large apertures to create nice blurred backgrounds. Some shots are relatively flat whereas others have elements in the background to make them more interesting.

I set up the shot in Figure 2-15 to feature the pie, but I wanted the scene to be more than just a piece of pie. Showing a cup of coffee and the pie dish in the background creates a more interesting photo. I used a Nikon APS-C dSLR with the 50mm lens set to f/2.8 to capture the front face of the piece of pie in focus. Although everything else is blurred, you can still tell what things are.

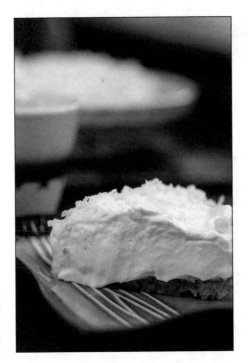

FIGURE 2-15:
Design your
close-ups with
depth of field in
mind.

As you can see, focusing on a precise point is very important when shooting macros and close-ups.

Action

Shooting action forces your hand a bit. Set the camera up for fast shutter speeds and low ISOs. Using these settings drives the aperture to open in order to expose the photo properly, which then reduces the width of the depth of field. Using a telephoto lens also gives you less depth of field. If you are struggling with a depth of field that is too small, you may be able to use a smaller aperture if the light is strong enough. If not, raise the ISO or see whether you can use a slower shutter speed.

Figure 2-16 is an example of how everything worked out. I used a Nikon APS-C dSLR and 300mm super telephoto lens to capture this scene. I set the shutter speed to 1/1000 second and ISO of 100. The aperture was f/4. Given that I was about 100 feet away, or 30 meters, the depth of field was just over 5 feet, or 1.5 meters. That was enough to capture the horse in the center and his driver sharply, along with the horse and driver to their right. Had I reduced the size of the aperture by one full stop (f/8 instead of f/4), the depth of field would have doubled. I could have offset that situation by raising the ISO to 200 or more, if I needed to. Those are the types of creative decisions you have to wrestle with.

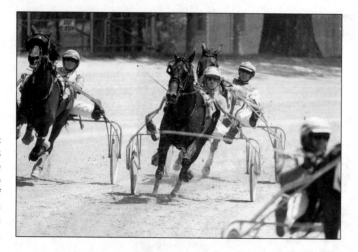

FIGURE 2-16: Action shots generally have moderate to small depths of field when shot with a telephoto lens.

Tilt-shift lenses

In contrast to standard lenses, tilt-shift lenses enable you to play with the shape and orientation of the depth of field, thereby opening a whole new world of creative possibilities.

Figure 2-17 shows a scene I took from the top of a parking garage at a local university. I tilted the lens to the left in order to skew the depth of field. The area that appears in focus does not run from side to side, as it would normally. In this case, it runs from the bottom of the photo toward the top, expanding like a wedge. Tilt-shift lenses are utterly remarkable and fun to play with. I shot this with a Canon APS-C dSLR and Canon TS-E 24mm f/3.5 II lens. See Book 2, Chapter 5 for more information about tilt-shift lenses and photos taken with them.

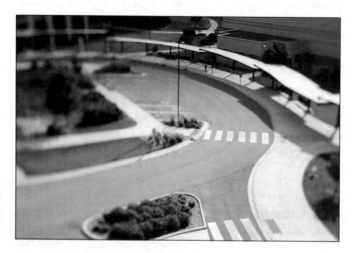

FIGURE 2-17: Tilt-shift lenses can create unique depth-of-field effects.

Chapter **3**
Choosing a Shutter Speed

I used to look down my nose at shutter speed. All I wanted to think about was aperture. Over time, though, I came to appreciate how important shutter speed is. Fast shutter speeds enable you to capture blur-free portraits and action. Slow shutter speeds may be important for exposure and creative effects.

This chapter explains how dSLR shutters work, shows you how to read shutter speed, explains how to set it, and then discusses how to combat blur caused by camera shake or subject movement. I have a section devoted to combating noise, which is a nasty side-effect caused by long exposures. I finish up with a large section with several examples of how to use shutter speed in different situations.

Decoding Shutter Speed

Shutter speed is an important setting on your camera to be familiar with. Knowing how the camera's shutter works and how shutter speed is presented will help you quickly solve problems and take better photos.

Learning about the shutter

The shutters used by dSLRs are amazing mechanical devices in the body of the camera. The shutter's purpose is to keep the image sensor hidden until you expose it to light by pressing the shutter release button. Figure 3-1 shows the shutter of a professional-level Canon full-frame dSLR. You don't normally see your camera's shutter because the mirror is in the way. Many people think of shutter speed as the length of time that the sensor as a whole is exposed. However, for technical reasons, *shutter speed* refers to how long each pixel of the sensor is exposed to light.

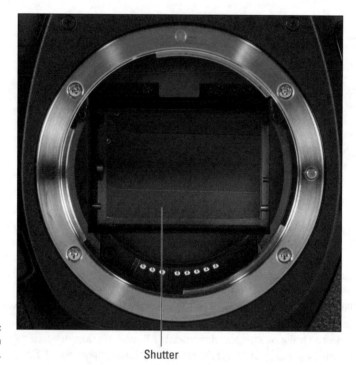

FIGURE 3-1:
The hidden
dSLR shutter.

Shutter

TECHNICAL STUFF

The shutter isn't a single door that opens and shuts. Focal plane shutters (named thusly because of their proximity to the focal plane, where the image sensor is) are made up of shutter *curtains*, or blades. The curtains act a lot like moving horizontal blinds. During an exposure, the front (also called the *first*) curtain moves down, which starts to uncover the sensor. A gap appears between it and the next curtain. At the right time, the *rear* (or second) curtain follows and covers the sensor back up. The elapsed time between when the front curtain uncovers and the rear curtain covers the same spot on the sensor is called the *shutter speed.* If you look closely at Figure 3-1, you can see the individual curtains that make up this shutter.

ELECTRONIC SHUTTERS

Not all shutters are mechanical. Compact cameras, smartphones, tablets, and some mirrorless cameras use an electronic shutter. Some dSLRs have an electronic shutter option, or a hybrid electronic option for still photography. All dSLRs use an electronic shutter when capturing movies.

Rather than rely on curtains to expose the sensor, electronic shutters either scan pixels from the top of the image sensor to the bottom (rolling shutter) or measure them all at one time (global shutter) for the duration set by the shutter speed setting. Global electronic shutters are far more complicated and expensive.

Electronic shutters have many advantages over their mechanical counterparts. They are silent, are capable of faster shutter speeds, enable you to shoot more frames per second, don't shake the camera, and will never wear out or break.

On the other hand, electronic shutters sometimes have slower flash sync speeds than mechanical shutters. Rolling electronic shutters are also prone to distortion when photographing fast-moving subjects or when panning quickly.

Some mirrorless cameras (the Sony A7R IV) and dSLRs (the Nikon D780, for example) have an electronic front curtain shutter. When enabled, the exposure is begun electronically (which is why it is called an electronic front curtain shutter) and ended mechanically by the second curtain. Using an electronic front curtain shutter speeds up shooting and reduces camera shake.

Expect to see more electronic shutters in high-end mirrorless cameras in the future. Some dSLRs may move in this direction as well, but not en masse until technical obstacles related to capturing action and other fast-moving subjects without distortion can be overcome economically.

Slow shutter speeds fully expose the entire sensor all at once. Faster shutter speeds don't. Instead, a small opening moves down the sensor, exposing a slice of it at a time. This is why the camera has a *flash sync speed*, which is the fastest speed that exposes the entire sensor at once; see Book 4, Chapter 2.

Shutter speed values are fairly standardized. Maximum speeds range from 1/4000 second (read as "one four–thousandths of a second") for consumer-level dSLRs and 1/8000 second on more advanced models. The longest timed shutter speed is normally 30 seconds.

Reading the speed

In the days of film SLRs, shutter speeds were printed on the shutter speed dial. Although somewhat cryptic, they were pretty easy to understand. You could easily see each shutter speed in relation to the others. Today, shutter speeds may appear in any one of several formats and pop up in different displays. You can also see them while you're playing back photos.

A few twists sometimes make it confusing to interpret and understand shutter speeds. The following sections translate for you.

Fractional

Shutter speeds less than a second in length are most often displayed as fractions of a second. For example, 1/30 equals 1/30 of a second. If you're scared of fractions, think of it this way: If you divide a second into 30 equal parts and set aside one of those parts, you'd have 1 out of 30 equal parts of a second, or 1/30 second, as shown in Figure 3-2.

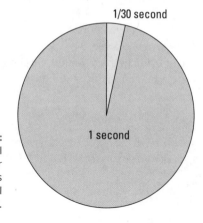

1/30 second

1 second

FIGURE 3-2:
The fractional number 1/30 second is one of 30 equal parts of a second.

To make things confusing, fractional shutter speeds often appear as a single number. The first number of a fractional shutter speed is always 1, so you can assume that it's there. You would see 1/30 displayed as 30. This shortcut often happens in viewfinders where space is at a premium. If you don't see a quotation mark (covered shortly), assume what you're seeing is a fractional shutter speed.

REMEMBER

Fractional shutter speeds are the most common shutter speed, whether they're in fractional form (1/30) or not (30).

Seconds

When you see quotation marks after a number, read the shutter speed in seconds, not as a fraction of a second. For example, 4 seconds is shown as 4". Two and a half seconds is displayed as 2.5", as shown in Figure 3-3.

Seconds indicator

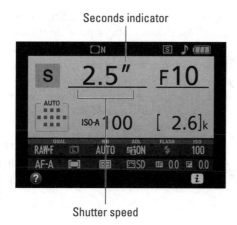

FIGURE 3-3:
The quotation mark indicates that this number is in seconds.

Shutter speed

Decimal

When some cameras get near a 1-second shutter speed, they start to flake out and go decimal on you. Remember that 0.5" means half of a second (1/2), not 1/5 of a second; see Figure 3-4.

Numerator may not be present

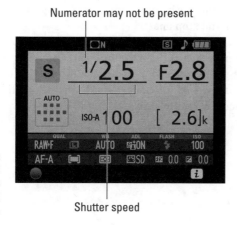

FIGURE 3-4:
This fractional speed has a decimal denominator.

Shutter speed

Seeing 1/2.5 can be confusing. Is it a fraction or a decimal? Both. It's between one-half and one-third of a second. If you divide 1 by 2.5 on a calculator, you get four-tenths of a second (0.4").

Bulb mode

There is one untimed shutter speed (or mode, depending on your camera) available to you: Bulb. It's named for the way old camera shutters worked. Photographers used a pneumatic bulb to operate the shutter, and they timed the exposure themselves. It works the same way on your dSLR, minus the actual bulb. You determine its length by pressing the shutter button as long as you want the shutter to remain open. Release the shutter button to close the shutter and end the exposure.

Do you really want to press and hold a button on your camera for 2 minutes? I don't! Use a locking remote shutter release cord, infrared remote, or wireless remote app when using Bulb. It can save your finger and help prevent camera shake.

Shutter speed and exposure

Shutter speeds have the same effect on exposure that a lens's aperture and the camera's ISO speed/sensitivity have: The difference between stops of shutter speed either doubles or halves the amount of light entering the camera.

Shutter speeds from 1 second to 1/4000 second are shown in Table 3-1. Each shutter speed is *half as long* as the one before it and *twice as long* as the one after it. This is the essence of being a full stop apart.

You'll often see shutter speeds 1/2 or 1/3 stop apart on your camera. Fractional stops give the camera greater precision and make it more likely to hit the exact exposure you need. For the sake of clarity, I did not include them in the table. You may be able to choose your preferred style of fractional stop from your camera's menu. Look for a setting called something like *EV Steps* or *Exposure Level Increments*.

TABLE 3-1

Shutter Speeds

Fractional Second	Also Shown As
1	1"
1/2	.5"
1/4	.25"
1/8	8
1/15	15
1/30	30
1/60	60
1/120	120
1/250	250
1/500	500
1/1000	1000
1/2000	2000
1/4000	4000

Setting the Shutter Speed

If you want to control the shutter speed yourself, you have to get into a shooting mode that lets you change it. Two modes are best for this task:

>> **Shutter-priority autoexposure:** The quintessential mode for the shutter speed aficionado. Set your camera to shutter-priority mode and then set the shutter speed, as shown in the left image in Figure 3-5. When the camera meters the scene, it will adjust the aperture and ISO (if you're in Auto ISO mode) to set the proper exposure. It's simple yet effective.

>> **Manual:** It's a bit harder to juggle shutter speed in Manual mode, but you can do it.

1. **Choose manual shooting mode.**

2. **Set the shutter speed based on the conditions and how fast you think it should be, as shown on the right in Figure 3-5.**

3. **Meter.**

4. **Choose an aperture and ISO that reach the right exposure.**

5. **Take a shot and review it.**

   If you see blurring, set it to a faster speed and then readjust your aperture and ISO.

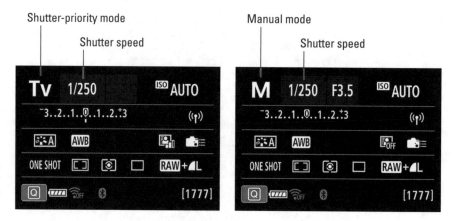

FIGURE 3-5:
Set the shutter
speed directly in
these two modes.

Combating Blur and Noise

Shutter speed is just like other exposure settings: It has an additional effect on your photos beyond exposure. In this case, shutter speeds prevent or accentuate blur. Most of the time, of course, you want to capture sharp photos, which calls for fast shutter speeds. At times, you may want longer exposures for creative effects. Long exposures can also cause photos to have elevated noise levels.

Camera shake, rattle, and roll

Camera shake, a form of blurring that affects the entire photo fairly uniformly, is caused by motion on your part. Long shutter speeds, combined with instability in your grip or stabbing the shutter button like it's the last button you'll ever press, contribute to camera shake.

The following sections explain ways to fight it.

Faster shutter speeds

In general, try to use moderately fast shutter speeds for most subjects when not using a tripod, even when you don't think you need to. Doing so helps keep photos sharp and in focus. For example, I took the photo shown in Figure 3-6 of a stationary Disc Golf basket at 1/250 second. It's not going anywhere, and I wasn't running about, but the shutter speed made sure this photo was captured crisply by the camera.

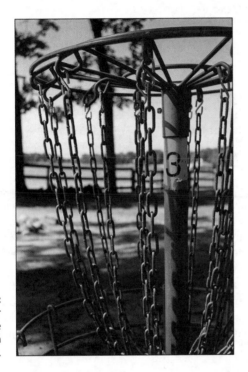

FIGURE 3-6:
Fast shutter speeds minimize handheld camera movement.

TIP

For basic handheld photography with a full-frame camera, a good rule is to set the shutter speed at least as fast as the reciprocal of the 35mm equivalent focal length you're using. In other words, put a 1 over the focal length to get the fractional shutter speed. Feel free to round that speed to a convenient number. I've taken a few common focal lengths and matched them to the closest minimum handheld shutter speeds for you in Table 3-2. Note that I have not estimated the effect of vibration reduction for this table. If you like, take the shutter speed that matches your camera and focal length from the table, and then reduce it by the number of stops your antivibration system promises.

For prime lenses, your minimum handheld shutter speed is pretty easy to figure out and remember. Zoom lenses require a bit more effort to figure out, but with practice you will easily remember. Start out by calculating the minimum shutter speeds for both extremes, and then one for a middle-ground focal length. Write them down or keep a handy note in your phone to remind you until you have them memorized.

See Book 1, Chapters 1 and 3 for more on crop factors and 35mm-equivalent focal lengths.

TABLE 3-2
Minimum Handheld Shutter Speeds

Focal Length	Full-Frame Speeds	Cropped-Frame Speeds
18mm	1/20	1/30
24mm	1/25	1/40
35mm	1/40	1/50 or 1/60
50mm	1/50	1/80
55mm	1/50 or 1/60	1/80 or 1/100
70mm	1/80	1/100 or 1/125
85mm	1/80 or 1/100	1/125 or 1/160
135mm	1/125 or 1/160	1/200 or 1/250

Sony cameras have a camera shake warning that flashes when you're in an automatic shooting mode and the camera sees that the shutter speed may be too low for a steady shot. Sony also has a SteadyShot scale, which is a series of bars that appear when the camera shakes. More bars indicate more shakery.

In some cameras, you can set a minimum shutter speed when shooting in program- and aperture-priority modes. This option is tied to Auto ISO. The camera won't let the shutter speed dip below the minimum setting you establish. Instead, it will increase the ISO to get a good exposure. For more information about ISO, including this feature, turn to Book 3, Chapter 4.

Vibration Reduction (VR) or Image Stabilization (IS)

Two features that come with your camera also help reduce camera shake: Vibration Reduction and Image Stabilization. When you turn them on, these features may let you slow your shutter speed from one to three stops or more without blurring the photo. Figure 3-7 is a close-up of a pot of African Violets that I photographed on Thanksgiving Day while we were visiting my wife's aunt.

The flowers were on a table in her living room. I took the photo in the early afternoon, but the light was not very strong. I set the aperture to f/5.0 and zoomed into 50mm. That equates to a 35mm-equivalent focal length of 80mm. The shutter speed the camera chose was 1/80, which is the minimum suggested shutter speed for that focal length when shooting handheld. I had Image Stabilization enabled, however, which helped account for any subtle movement on my part. The result is a photo that is as sharp as a tack.

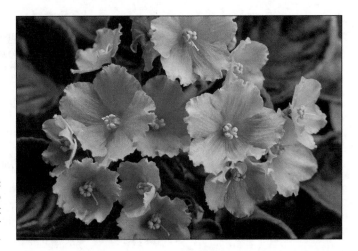

To turn on lens-based Image Stabilization, look for a switch on the side of your lens and turn it on. Enable camera-based image stabilization from the menu if the camera body has no switch or button. Book 1, Chapters 1 and 3 have more information about Image Stabilization.

Steadying the camera

You have several ways to steady the camera. Most of these are effective only when shooting long exposures with a tripod. Lens or camera-based Image Stabilization features are the exception. They should be used when shooting handheld and turned off when using a tripod. (Switch to the special tripod mode if your lens has it.) Try these techniques to steady the camera:

» **Mirror lockup:** One source of camera shake that isn't your fault is caused by the mirror. Digital SLR (not dSLTs) mirrors rotate up and out of the way to unblock the sensor. They flip back so powerfully that the camera sometimes shakes.

TIP

Use your camera's mirror lockup feature (also called *Mirror Up mode* or *Exposure Delay*) to combat this type of camera shake when using a tripod. Although it can be effective when holding the camera by hand, the delay it introduces can really throw you off. If your camera has a mirror lockup option, turn it on from the menu system; see Figure 3-8 for a Canon (left) and Pentax (right) screen.

>> **Self-timer:** Believe it or not, your camera's self-timer has other uses besides self-portraits. It's also an effective way to steady the camera. Use the timer if you don't have a remote and are using a tripod. Set this function from your camera's Drive or Release mode menu, as shown in Figure 3-9. Assuming that you're using a tripod, take your hands off the camera after you press the shutter button. The timer counts down and the camera takes the photo. Combine this technique with mirror lockup for greater effectiveness. If your camera doesn't have a mirror lockup function and you aren't using a remote, this is the most effective way to reduce camera shake when shooting with a tripod.

>> **Remote shutter release:** If your finger is causing the camera shake, increasing shutter speed won't help solve the problem. Use a wired or wireless remote and activate the shutter button without touching it. You can also switch to the self-timer and try that if you don't have a remote.

>> **Physically support the camera:** Make sure your grip is stable and that you aren't moving around when you take photos (kids are very prone to shooting on the move). Tripods steady the camera very effectively when using long shutter speeds. Monopods are more mobile and make supporting a heavy camera and lens far easier. In a pinch, you can use any kind of support that's handy: a fence, car, wall, tree, or another person. They all work.

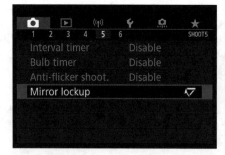

FIGURE 3-8:
Raising the mirror early lets the vibrations settle before you take the shot.

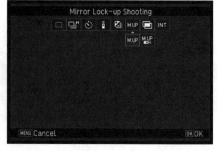

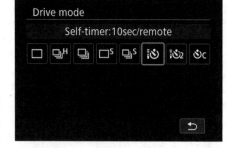

FIGURE 3-9:
Use the self-timer if you don't have a remote.

Shooting moving targets

You get *motion blur* (also called *subject blur*) when your subject is moving too fast for the shutter speed to freeze. The subject looks blurred. Unlike camera shake, this type of blur affects only the subject, not the background. Avoid this effect by choosing a faster shutter speed, if possible.

REMEMBER

You can get good shots of a fast-moving subject:

>> **Pan with that person as you shoot.** *Panning* means you follow the subject with the camera as it moves across your field of view. You wind up blurring the background instead.

>> **Move to another spot.** It's harder to capture a racehorse moving directly across your viewfinder than one traveling toward you.

>> **Try catching moving objects in moments when the action pauses.** For example, catch a tennis player at the height of her backswing, or your wife at the top of her swing (see Figure 3-10, shot with a shutter speed of 1/500 second). Every time a moving object changes direction, you can time your shot to the moment your subject's relative motion is smallest.

>> **Pay attention to your camera's autofocus (AF) modes.** Set AF to Continuous-servo (also called AI Servo AF) rather than Single. You may be able to select a specific AF point and place it on your target, or you may want to use zone AF if something is moving erratically. Regardless of which method you use, practice before it counts.

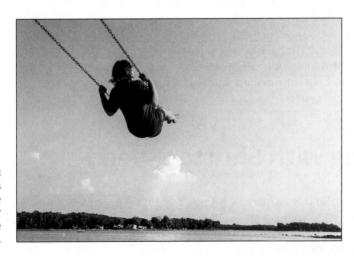

FIGURE 3-10: I captured this photo at the moment in her swing when she paused.

Focal length matters when you're shooting moving targets. The field of view is narrower and the subject is magnified greater than normal focal lengths. This tends to emphasize herky-jerkyness. Whatever's in your viewfinder can jiggle, jostle, and move much more than when you're using a normal or wide-angle lens, which causes blurring. Try a higher shutter speed.

Enabling Long Exposure Noise Reduction

Many dSLRs have noise-reduction routines that automatically kick in to clean exposures you've taken with long shutter speeds, normally a second or longer. Canon and Nikon call it the same thing: Long Exposure Noise Reduction. Pentax and other cameras call it Slow Shutter Speed NR, as shown in Figure 3-11.

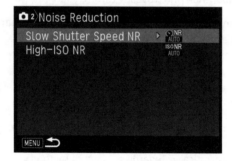

FIGURE 3-11:
Long exposure noise reduction kicks in if you're using longer shutter speeds.

REMEMBER

Noise reduction is applied to JPEGs by the camera as they are saved. If you use Raw files, you will need to reduce noise during editing, either in the camera or using a computer.

The one drawback to long exposure noise reduction is timeliness: It can delay your return to shooting. However, if you want a finished product right out of the camera, keep it turned on. Turn off long exposure noise reduction in your camera's menu system.

Designing with Shutter Speed

I finish this chapter with some interesting examples of how you can use shutter speed to your advantage. You can take all sorts of interesting photos in different conditions and of different subjects by varying it. If you're using an autoexposure mode that doesn't allow you to control shutter speed, use this information to help you troubleshoot.

REMEMBER

As you experience different conditions, you'll see how specific shutter speeds, f-numbers, and ISOs differ from scene to scene.

Shooting crisp photos

Nice, crisp photos are a hallmark of good photography. It took me a while to learn this. As I mention in the introduction, my first love was the aperture. The problem was, every time I tried to take photos at birthdays and other occasions, they would be fuzzy or downright blurry. I couldn't take a sharp photo of someone standing 6 feet away from me (about 2 meters) because I wasn't paying attention to the shutter speed.

Figure 3-12 shows how I've grown. This is a nice close-up of my son Jacob on his birthday. I set the camera to shutter-priority mode so that I could control the shutter speed, and I dialed in something reasonably fast. I took this photo at 1/125 second. Bam — crisp photo. If people are playing around, bump the shutter speed up to 1/250 or faster.

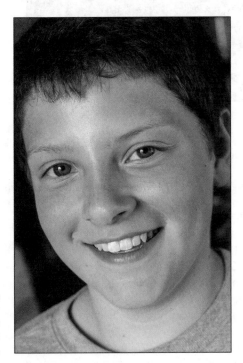

FIGURE 3-12:
Fast shutter speeds ensure nice, crisp portraits.

The challenge when shooting inside will be controlling the ISO if your aperture can't open very wide. At f/5.6, this inexpensive standard zoom lens limits my options. This shot was taken at ISO 1250.

Animal photography also requires you to pay attention to shutter speed. Figure 3-13 shows a funny photo I took of a giraffe at our zoo (you know, as opposed to our backyard). Animals have a habit of moving around, which means you should expect to use faster shutter speeds when photographing them. This will help make sure your photos are nice and sharp.

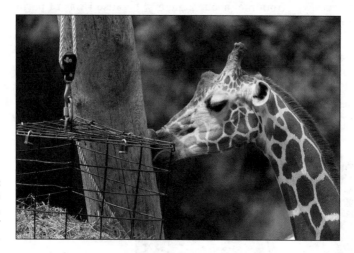

FIGURE 3-13: Photograph animals, too, with fast shutter speeds.

You should also use faster shutter speeds when the focal length of your lens is in the telephoto range. I took this shot using a 300mm telephoto lens on a Nikon APS-C camera. I used shutter-priority mode and set the shutter speed to 1/1000 second. Although that shutter speed may sound like overkill, the conditions were bright enough to support it without having to raise the ISO too much (it is 220 in this photo). The result is a nice, sharp photo.

Finally, Figure 3-14 shows another situation when you want to have a fast shutter speed: *you're* moving. I took this photo of a water trampoline by wading out into the water. I was neck-deep by the time I reached the rope and float line that separated the swimming area from the rest of the lake. My wife looked on, hoping I wouldn't trip or lose my balance and drop the unprotected camera into the water.

I was in aperture-priority mode, which sounds backward, I realize. However, the day was so bright that I didn't have to worry about switching to shutter-priority mode. I had already taken several photos and knew that the shutter speed was very fast — in this case, 1/1600 second — at the aperture I wanted to use. That's what I call fast.

Working with slow shutter speeds

Slow shutter speeds can be practically and artistically effective in other situations as well.

REMEMBER

Try shooting water, fog, or clouds with slow shutter speeds. The movement is smoothed and looks very dreamy. Although you can often shoot fast action hand-held, slow shutter speeds require a tripod or other stable support.

Figure 3-20 is a shot over our city's Dr. Martin Luther King, Jr., Memorial Bridge. I set up the camera on a tripod and framed the bridge in the scene. I wanted to catch the vehicles' taillights as they travelled over the bridge. I had to time the shot to the traffic flow and experiment with different shutter speeds. This one, at 5 seconds, is spot on.

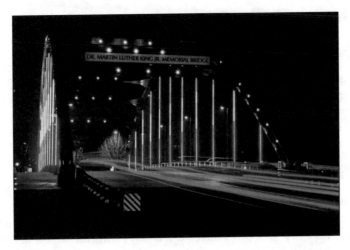

FIGURE 3-20:
Moving lights are classic subjects for slow shutter speeds.

Although slow shutter speeds normally require that you use a tripod, not all do. I took the photo in Figure 3-21 at a friend's house. He and his wife invited us over for a "3rd of July" party. We and a few dozen other people visited, played volleyball, ate hot dogs, enjoyed the apple pie and homemade ice cream, and played cards. When it got dark, we broke out the sparklers.

At times like this, you may have only a moment to set up the camera. This was not a shot I got to plan in advance. I quickly set the camera to shutter-priority mode and entered a speed of 2.5 seconds. I pointed the camera at the sparkler, pressed the shutter button, and hoped for the best.

Although my friend's patriotic tank top is slightly blurred, the effect actually contributes to the photo. The sparkler is fantastic.

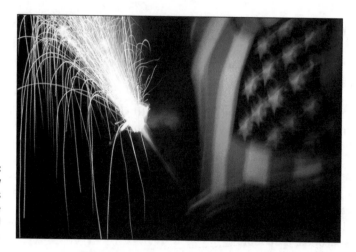

FIGURE 3-21:
Use slow shutter speeds on the spur of the moment around sparklers.

Using Bulb mode

Use your camera's Bulb mode to shoot fireworks, as shown in Figure 3-22, or lighting. All you need to do is set up your camera on a tripod and set the shutter speed or shooting mode to Bulb. It helps to have a remote. When you're ready, open the shutter and wait for the fireworks. You can capture them singly or hold the shutter open for more than one. Experiment to find your preferred method. The exposure time for this photo was 9 seconds and the aperture was f/8.0.

Shooting macros

Finally, it's time for a guest appearance by macros. You wouldn't think this subject would be in a shutter-speed chapter, but I want to point out that lighting some scenes when shooting macros can be very difficult. You'll find yourself needing to shoot with long exposure times, especially if you don't want to raise the ISO through the roof.

I took the macro in Figure 3-23 in my studio. It's an extreme close-up of a marigold. Using a tripod is important in these situations. It helps you focus and steady the camera for a longer exposure. I set the shutter speed for 1 second to capture this shot, and I used an ISO of 400.

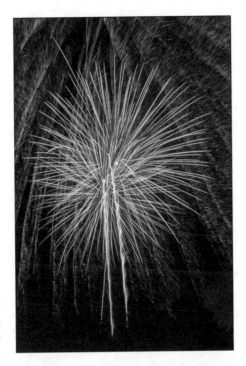

FIGURE 3-22:
Fireworks are
a great way to
enjoy shooting in
Bulb mode.

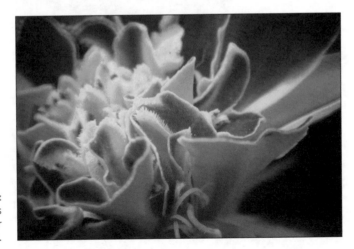

FIGURE 3-23:
Some macros
require longer
shutter speeds.

Chapter **4**

Selecting an ISO

SO sensitivity is a subject that can get lost in the mix. Controlling your camera's ISO speed doesn't offer you the same creative possibilities that you get by setting the aperture. Nor does ISO play the same role as shutter speed in capturing crisp photos. However, ISO is an important but unsung exposure control to use and keep track of.

This chapter is devoted to ISO: explaining what it is, what effect it has on exposure, and how you can set and manage it. You see some examples of photos with lower and higher ISOs, and I share some tips on keeping ISO speed and noise levels under control.

Understanding ISO

ISO is the term used to characterize the strength of the signal coming out of a camera's image sensor. ISO is sometimes called *ISO sensitivity* or *ISO speed.*

Technically, the image sensor is no more or less sensitive to light, regardless of what the ISO is set to. The ISO control allows you to crank up the "volume" of the image sensor signal. Despite this fact, some camera manufacturers and people still use the phrase *ISO sensitivity.*

In practical terms, turning up the ISO increases the exposure. Turning ISO down lowers the exposure.

A bit of history

ISO was originally a measure of *film speed* — the speed at which film in a camera reacted to light when exposed. In that context, it was often called ASA, which was short for American Standards Association.

>> *High-speed*, or *fast* film, is more sensitive to light and therefore needs less light to expose the film. It has higher ISO numbers and tends to look grainy, because it literally is. The size of light-sensitive crystals in the film have to be larger to catch the light faster.

>> *Slow* film is less sensitive to light and therefore needs more light to expose the film. It uses lower ISO numbers. Slow film is created using much smaller light-sensitive crystals and therefore has a very fine-grained, attractive look that captures small details.

Figure 4-1 shows the ISO dial on an older 35mm film camera. The numbers them-selves don't actually do anything but remind you what the ISO was for the film you loaded into the camera. The index lifts and turns so you can put the mark by the film speed. To the right is an exposure compensation index and scale. When you press the small button and turn the dial, you dial in exposure compensation, which adjusts the camera's meter. Notice that exposure compensation is meas-ured in EV even on this old film camera.

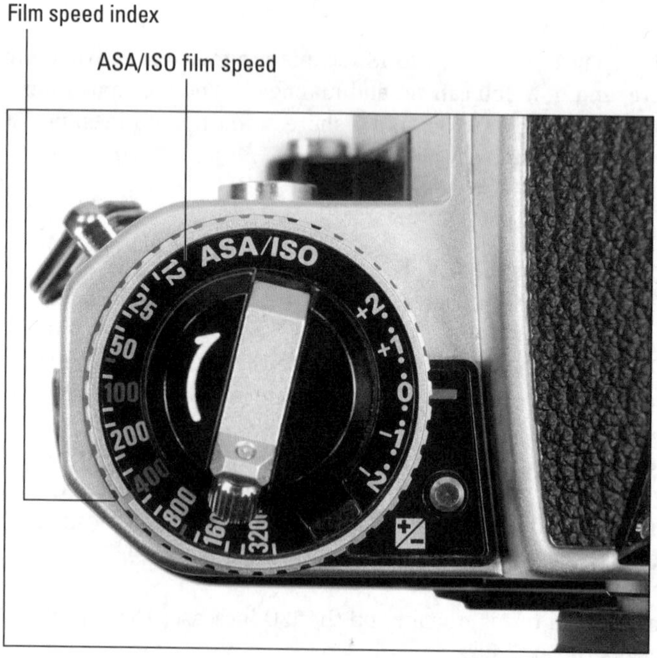

Film speed index

ASA/ISO film speed

FIGURE 4-1:
ISO on film cameras is set for the entire roll.

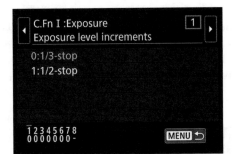

FIGURE 4-4:
Changing ISO
increments.

Generating noise with high ISOs

Being able to increase the ISO comes with a certain amount of danger to it. As you increase ISO speed for better exposure, you will eventually notice *noise* in your photos. Noise consists of small discolored artifacts in the photo. Too much noise causes the photo to look grainy when you put it onscreen or print it at larger sizes.

Figure 4-5 shows the same scene shot at low and very high ISO settings. Notice that at the low setting, the photo looks perfect. The colors are bright and the colored pencils look clean and clear. However, when the ISO is elevated, the story is much different. The colors, sharpness, and quality of this photo are all compromised.

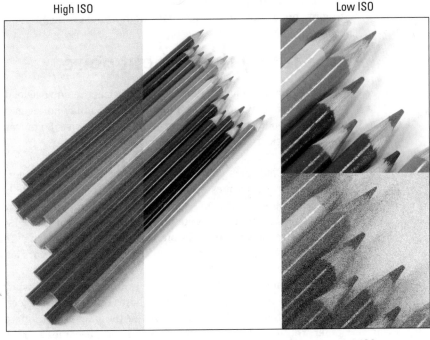

FIGURE 4-5:
High ISOs
generate much
more noise than
low ISOs.

Noise may not be obvious when you're looking at a photo on the back of the camera. However, it still takes away a photo's clarity and roughs up smooth areas of color. Notice the noise in the leaves in Figure 4-6. The naturally smooth surface of these leaves is overwhelmed with noise. It looks terribly grainy at this level of magnification.

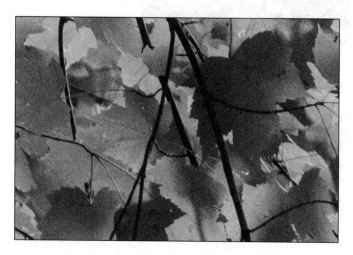

FIGURE 4-6:
You see more noise zoomed in.

Up to a certain point, you don't notice increased noise. There's an inevitable tipping point, however, where noise compromises the photo.

The funny thing about noise

Although photos have more noise as ISOs rise, the noise level doesn't affect every photo the same way. Up to a certain point, you may not even realize that noise is present in your photo. Light areas tend to hide noise. So do complicated textures. Smooth, dark areas tend to reveal noise.

REMEMBER

Don't let noise scare you. Try to keep your ISO setting under control, but know that you can sometimes ignore it. The point at which noise becomes a problem in your photos varies from camera to camera and from year to year. Consumer-level cameras tend to generate more noise starting at lower ISO levels than more expensive models do. In addition, cameras keep improving. Today's inexpensive dSLRs can operate at ISO levels only dreamed of some years ago.

TIP

Try experimenting with your camera to find the point at which noise becomes a problem for you. Shoot a number of photos of the same subject in the same lighting with different ISO speeds. Compare the photos in-camera or on your computer. You'll be able to quickly see when noise becomes a problem.

Setting ISO

ISO doesn't have a dedicated shooting mode as aperture and shutter speed do (with the exception of Pentax cameras). That means that you have to set ISO differently.

If you've set the camera to a basic shooting mode, as shown in Figure 4-7, you don't have to worry about setting the ISO yourself. You don't even have to enable Auto ISO. It's done for you. The camera automatically enables Auto ISO and won't let you set the ISO manually in these modes. That's one of the advantages of using them. You don't have to turn automatic features on individually.

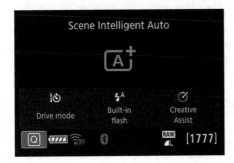

FIGURE 4-7:
ISO is set to Auto in this mode and cannot be changed.

Controlling ISO yourself

To set the ISO manually or enable Auto ISO, follow these steps:

1. **Enter an advanced shooting mode.**

   P, A, S, M, and B always work. You may be able to set the ISO manually in other modes, depending on the camera. Pentax cameras have a sensitivity-priority mode that operates like aperture-priority and shutter-priority modes except you set the ISO.

2. **Press the ISO button, as shown on the left in Figure 4-8, or equivalent.**

   This is the simplest and quickest approach to setting the ISO. An ISO display appears and you can immediately make changes to the setting.

   You can also set the ISO manually and enable Auto ISO from your camera's shooting display or menu system.

3. **Set the ISO to Auto ISO or dial in the ISO you want.**

   The image on the right in Figure 4-8 shows the ISO being set to 800. You may be able to set ISO in whole stops, half stops, or even thirds of a stop. Check your camera's menu system to see what your options are.

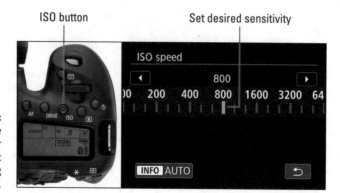

ISO button   Set desired sensitivity

FIGURE 4-8:
You can set the ISO to Auto or choose a specific sensitivity setting yourself.

TIP

If you're particular about ISO, manually control it when you can. Manual control will help you be aware of what ISO you're using and know that it isn't changing from one photo to another. This control is critical if you want all photos from a photo shoot to have the same noise characteristics.

Using Auto ISO

Using Auto ISO is very simple: Make sure it's on, as shown in Figure 4-9, and start shooting. The camera raises or lowers the ISO based on the scene and the other exposure settings. When you're concerned with getting the shot and don't mind that the ISO might rise dramatically or change from shot to shot, Auto ISO is a great solution.

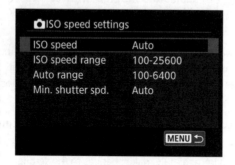

FIGURE 4-9:
ISO is set to Auto, which means that it will change automatically based on exposure needs.

Auto ISO has some oddities that you should know about:

» **Shooting modes:** Check your camera's manual to see what shooting modes have Auto ISO and whether restrictions exist. When your camera is in an Auto mode, Auto ISO is on by default; see Figure 4-8. When you're shooting in a Scene mode, you may be able to set Auto ISO or switch to manual. You should be able to use Auto ISO or you can switch to manual ISO when you enter program, aperture-priority, or shutter-priority shooting modes.

Most cameras allow you to enable Auto ISO and shoot in manual mode. However, some older dSLRs require you to set the ISO manually when you're in Manual mode.

>> **Auto ISO limits:** Most cameras limit the ISO range in Auto ISO mode. In other words, the camera's entire ISO range isn't available when you're in Auto ISO mode.

>> **Configuring Auto ISO:** Most dSLRs allow you to select new maximum and minimum Auto ISO settings. You may also be able to set a minimum shutter speed; if it hits bottom, your camera starts raising the ISO. Setting up Auto ISO is covered in an upcoming section.

>> **Display peculiarities:** In Auto ISO, some cameras round the ISO to the nearest convenient number (200 or 400, for example) when displaying the setting in the viewfinder or on the LCD screen. When you review the photo, you'll see the exact ISO.

TIP

>> **Auto ISO tip:** When shooting action (inside or out), switch to shutter-priority mode and turn on Auto ISO. This strategy puts a premium on allowing an adequate amount of light into the camera while keeping shutter speeds high enough to avoid blurring everything. If you need more ISO, switch out of Auto ISO (you may have to change shooting modes to do this) and set the ISO yourself.

Restricting Auto ISO

Take some test shots and see how much noise your camera shows at different ISOs. You may decide that you simply won't ever use photos taken at or above a certain ISO. In that case, you can restrict Auto ISO by changing its boundaries. Doing so gives you some control over an otherwise automated process.

Depending on your camera, you might be able to modify some or all of these settings:

TIP

>> **Minimum speed:** You can sometimes specify the minimum ISO. Raise this setting only when necessary. For example, you may want to limit the total range to keep the noise level relatively uniform.

>> **Maximum speed:** The highest ISO that you want the camera to use. Set this ISO to a value that reflects how much noise you're willing to work with, as shown in Figure 4-10.

>> **Minimum shutter speed:** I encourage you to use this fantastic setting. It tells the camera the minimum shutter speed you're willing to accept before it raises the ISO to keep the photo from being underexposed. The camera lowers the shutter speed below the minimum only if it can't raise ISO enough to get the necessary exposure. You can leave it on Auto in some cases, as shown on the left in Figure 4-11, or choose a specific value manually, as shown on the right.

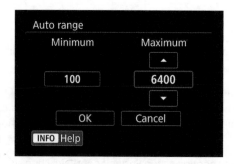

FIGURE 4-10:
Set a maximum
Auto ISO
sensitivity.

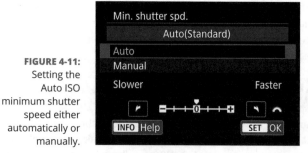
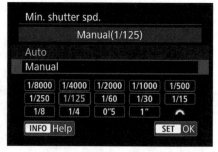

FIGURE 4-11:
Setting the
Auto ISO
minimum shutter
speed either
automatically or
manually.

Using High ISO Noise Reduction

Many dSLRs have ISO-related noise-reduction routines. Canon calls it High ISO Speed Noise Reduction; Nikon calls it High ISO NR.

Enable or disable ISO-related noise reduction in your camera's menu. Some cameras may have only one noise reduction setting. You either turn noise reduction on or leave it off. Some dSLRs enable you to configure high ISO noise reduction strength. Typical Canon settings are Standard, Low, Strong, and Disable, as shown in Figure 4-12. Nikon prefers Off, Low, Normal, and High. The curious thing about ISO noise reduction is that it's always applied, even if you tell the camera to turn it off; it's just applied minimally.

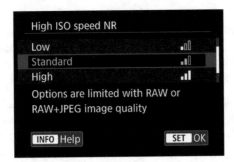

FIGURE 4-12:
Check out your
camera's high ISO
noise reduction
options.

The drawback to high ISO noise reduction is that it can delay your return to shooting.

TIP

Managing ISO

When you're shooting under normal conditions, I recommend using Auto ISO, even in advanced shooting modes. Test the exposure before getting started so that you have a sense of what ISO the camera wants to use based on the lighting and the other exposure settings. Then, once you start shooting, simply monitor the ISO each time you meter and take a photo.

You don't really have to worry about noise with new dSLRs until the ISO gets toward the upper half of the camera's ISO range. This range is around 3200–6400 or so in new consumer-level cameras and higher in professional modes. Most cameras take stunning low-ISO photos, and obsessing about it will only slow you down.

If you find the camera setting high ISOs, use these tips to get it back under control:

TIP

>> **Shutter speed:** Within reason, lower the shutter speed to let in more light. Every stop of shutter speed that you can slow down saves you a stop of ISO. For example, rather than raise ISO from 400 to 800, try lowering the shutter speed from 1/250 to 1/125 second.

>> **Aperture:** Enlarge the lens's aperture (lower the f-number) to let in more light. Opening the lens wider by an additional stop keeps the ISO a stop lower. For example, rather than raise the ISO from 200 to 400, increase the size of the aperture by changing the f-number from f/8.0 to f/5.6.

Selecting an ISO

>> **Image stabilization:** This feature helps you lower shutter speeds and prevents blurring from camera shake by one or more stops, depending on the camera and lens. For every stop you can lower the shutter speed without shaking, you save yourself a stop of ISO.

>> **Tripod or monopod:** If your subject lends itself, mount your dSLR on a tripod or monopod. Doing so eliminates camera shake and opens slower shutter speeds and lower ISOs. I rarely raise the ISO above 100 when shooting with a tripod in a studio.

>> **Flash:** Using a flash changes the game quite a bit. Raise ISO when you need to extend flash range and to brighten the background.

>> **Reflectors:** If you've ever had your photo taken professionally in-studio, you probably saw large light reflectors (that look like umbrellas or screens) pointed at you. These reflectors bounce light onto the subjects. You can use reflectors to balance light and brighten a scene. Brighter light means a lower ISO.

>> **Shoot outdoors during the day:** You can't always do this, but try taking photos outdoors in nice daylight. You won't have to raise the ISO as much, if at all.

>> **Other lighting:** If you're indoors, open the drapes and turn on the lights. All the light you can bring into the room helps lower the need to raise the ISO.

TIP

>> **Limit Auto ISO:** Set your camera's Auto ISO settings to a range you're comfortable with. If it's between ISO 100 and 400, make it so. If you're comfortable going to ISO 6400, by all means set the high end of your Auto ISO range there.

>> **Invest in fast lenses:** If you're shooting indoors a lot, ditch your slow lens and get a faster one. Faster lenses cost more, however. If you can't afford a new semi-pro or professional-level lens, look for a used lens or one from a third-party lens manufacturer such as Sigma or Tamron.

>> **Get a newer and better camera:** This step may seem dramatic, but you can often buy a brand new dSLR with improved ISO performance for less than the price of a good lens. If you're able to spend more and jump up a category (for example, from consumer-level to mid-range), you'll gain even more performance.

When getting a good exposure with your chosen shutter speed or aperture becomes a problem, use ISO to take up the slack.

In the end, if you've taken all the steps you can to keep the ISO low but you or the camera need to raise it, do so, and *don't feel guilty about it.* It makes no sense to lose the shot because you're afraid of raising the ISO. A grainy, noisy photo is much better than no photo at all.

ISO Gallery

The photos in this section illustrate certain conditions you may experience that require higher ISOs than normal. Although I list the specific ISO that I used, I want you to key in on why it was raised. Knowing the reasons will enable you to be on the lookout for elevated ISOs as you take your photos.

By and large, most of these high ISO shots look good. Remember that as you try to determine the range of ISO settings you allow and the level of noise you are willing to live with. I took most of the photos in this section with relatively inexpensive cameras and lenses. My goal is not to show you the best high ISO performance on the market, but to show you a range of photos with higher and higher ISO levels.

One final note: Although I was tempted to, I did not apply any noise reduction to the photos in this section. They are what they are. I did make corrections to the brightness, contrast, and color. Speaking of processing, you should know that dramatically increasing the brightness of a dark photo in software makes noise more apparent, as does increasing the saturation and sharpening.

Elevated ISO

Figure 4-13 is a shot of one of our family cats. He's orange, and he's big. At times, he likes napping on the back of the couch. As you can see, the door is open in the background and it's nice and sunny outside. You would think the light would be bright enough to take a nice photo with low ISO levels.

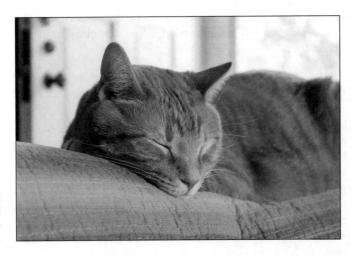

FIGURE 4-13:
Some elevated ISO shots have barely any noise.

Not necessarily. Interior shots are always more difficult. Our eyes adapt to the light and think the conditions are bright, but they aren't. There were additional factors that put pressure on the ISO. I was shooting handheld, which prevented me from setting a low shutter speed. Aside from that, the lens I used had a maximum aperture of f/5.6. The result? ISO 1600.

Figure 4-14 is another photo with moderately elevated ISO. This time, ISO 2000. Again, it's an inside shot. You can see that the room was bright and that light should not have been too much of a problem. It was. Get used to ISO rising to these levels when shooting inside.

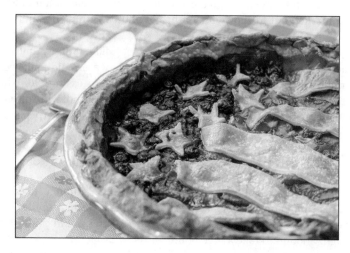

FIGURE 4-14:
Don't be afraid to let the camera increase the ISO beyond the minimum.

The good news? Neither of these photos appears to have problems with noise. If you spot any at high magnification, apply a minimal amount of noise reduction to clean it up.

High ISO levels

High ISO levels are higher than your camera's mid-range but not to the point where you've maxed out ISO. I look at ISO 3200 as the beginning point of high ISOs for some cameras.

Speaking of 3200, Figure 4-15 is a close-up of a foosball player I took in the game room at a summer camp. Foosball is a fast-paced, fun, action-packed game based on the principles of soccer (a.k.a. football). I spent hours upon hours playing foosball with my friends at college. Now I amaze my kids with my super-fast bounce shots.

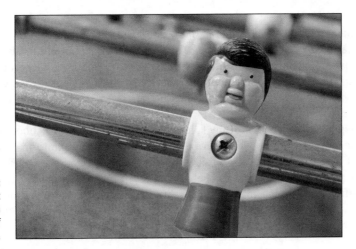

FIGURE 4-15:
Noise is evident
in the green
surface of
this photo.

You can start seeing noise in this photo. Look at the green surface of the table. It should be smooth and even-toned. It looks mottled by the noise.

Moving up to ISO 4000, Figure 4-16 is a funny photo of my son Sam putting the cat's tail up to his nose as if it were a mustache. He's wearing his camo bathrobe, but he'd grown enough by the time I took this photo that it looks like a dinner jacket.

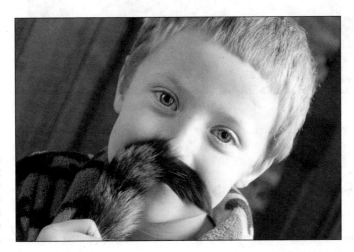

FIGURE 4-16:
This shot
requires some
noise reduction
to smooth his
skin and the
background.

This is another example of how hard it is to light interior scenes. The room seems decently lit, and you can see the light shining on the side of his face. However, even with an aperture of f/5.6 and a shutter speed of 1/80 second, the ISO had to go up to get a good exposure.

Selecting an ISO

On consumer-level cameras, ISO 4000 is getting up there. This particular model has only a few higher settings. The noise is fairly apparent in this shot. It's visible on Sam's face and robs his eyes of some sharpness. The background noise is less apparent when zoomed out but clearly mottles the photo when you look closely. With a modest amount of noise reduction, this shot will look as good as new.

Figure 4-17 is a shot of my soldering station taken at ISO 5000. I use this station to work on guitar electronics and amps. I took this photo to post on Facebook. It was a "handyman" post detailing all the stuff I had been working on that day. I grabbed my camera and set this shot up quickly. It was in the middle of the afternoon, which made it pretty bright, but whenever you shoot inside, expect ISOs to rise. The shutter speed was 1/160, which helped me capture this sharply. The aperture setting was f/5.6.

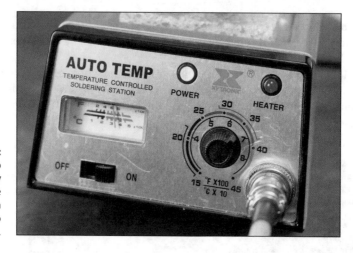

FIGURE 4-17:
This photo has barely any recognizable noise when reduced to post online.

You can't see much noise in this photo when viewed as a whole. It's more obvious in the shadows and in areas of the darker plastic.

Extreme ISO settings

Extreme ISO settings push your camera to its limits. Although they will vary between cameras, anything at or over ISO 6400 on just about anything but a professional model is extreme.

I took the photo in Figure 4-18 of my son Ben at his 16th birthday party. We hung out with friends at the music studio of a good friend of mine. Ben brought his guitar to jam and I brought one of my amps, which you can see in the background. Everyone had a blast playing games and munching on popcorn and other snacks.

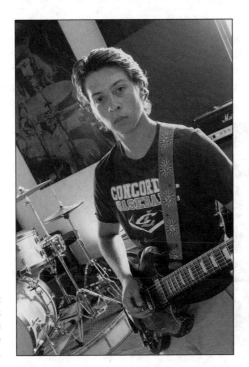

FIGURE 4-18: I processed this shot to make noise part of the artistic effect.

At ISO 6400, a noticeable amount of noise appears in the photo. It's present just about everywhere you look — especially in the artwork on the wall; on his shirt, face, and guitar; on the drum riser and the amp. Although noise can ruin some shots, it doesn't with this one. I processed the shot semi-artistically, which helps make the noise feel like part of the effect. If I wanted, I could apply noise reduction to this and it would clean up quite a bit.

I took this shot with an aperture setting of f/5.6 and a shutter speed of 1/50 second. That's about as low as I could go and still get a decently sharp photo. The focal length helped. I zoomed out to 25mm, which is the equivalent of 40mm on a full-frame 35mm camera. That meant I was within the recommended minimum shutter speed to take a reasonably sharp handheld photo.

Figure 4-19 is a nighttime shot of a bridge heading downtown. Although the bridge is lit and some other lights are present, it's still a very dark scene. I used a shutter speed of 1/60 second and an aperture of f/5.6 in manual shooting mode, making the ISO rise to 6400. As you can see, it's a pretty noisy photo!

Finally, Figure 4-20 shows a shot that I took with a professional camera set to ISO 12800. We were inside a bowling alley. This is Sam again, who had just let a ball loose down the rails and was showing off his form. I had the camera in shutter-priority mode to capture the action. The shutter speed was 1/250 second (I dared go no faster) and the aperture was f/4.

The combination of a great camera with a great lens still capturing this photo difficult without raising the ISO quite a bit. The result is noise that can be bothersome unless handled in software. Even so, the noise performance on this full-frame Canon dSLR is amazing when you compare it against cheaper cameras.

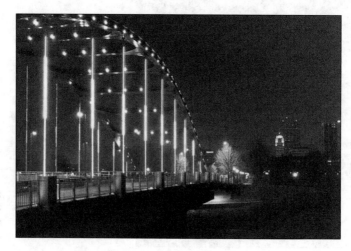

FIGURE 4-19:
Dark scenes really bring the noise out.

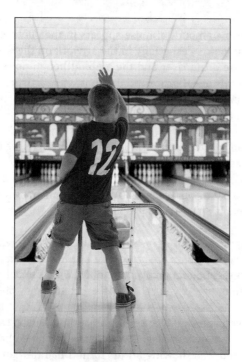

FIGURE 4-20:
Professional cameras shoot at extreme ISO levels very effectively.

Chapter **5**

Using Filters

D igital photographers have access to more advanced computer technology than ever before. That's a great thing. It has opened up creative options that everyone can use. Filters, however, are physical things. They're *real.* You can hold them in your hand. They clink musically and take up space in your camera bag. When light passes through them, something physical — not modeled, simulated, or programmed — happens to the light. I don't know about you, but that fascinates me. I want to know more.

Learning about Filters

Standing in front of a large filter display in a camera shop or going online and browsing can be highly intimidating. Questions course through your gray matter. What are these gizmos? How do they work? Should I bother? Which ones are best for me?

Looking at how filters work

Filters (sometimes called *optical* or *physical filters*) work by literally getting in the way. You stick filters on the front of or in your lens (see Figure 5-1) so that light from the outside world has to pass through on its way to the camera's image sensor — simple stuff. As light passes through a filter, it changes properties.

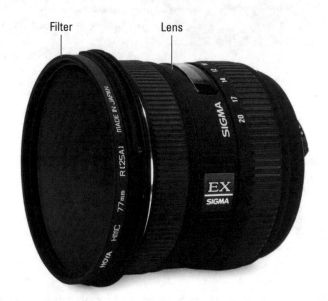

Filter   Lens

FIGURE 5-1:
Light must pass
through the filter
for it to work
its magic.

What happens to the light is different for each type of filter. Knowing what filters do will help you decide whether to invest the time and energy required to
use them. They may solve one or more problems you've been having with your
photography. Here's what filters can do:

REMEMBER

>> **Change color, tone, and contrast** by holding back certain wavelengths of
light. Filters can enhance contrast or reduce or soften contrast. When used in
black-and-white photography, color filters transform some colors into dark
tones and other colors into lighter tones in the black-and-white image.

Red filters look red because they partially block light from the other side of the
color wheel. Red light is allowed to pass through.

>> **Darken a scene** by making it harder for visible light to pass through. Neutral
Density (ND) filters specialize in reducing the amount of light that gets to the
image sensor inside your camera.

>> **Enhance color and contrast** by blocking polarized light. A polarizing filter
makes it harder for reflected light to pass through by reducing glare and
reflections from water, metal, glass, and other smooth surfaces.

>> **Reduce haze** by absorbing ultraviolet (UV) light.

>> **Create different special effects** by diffusing (softening) or diffracting (it's
complicated) light.

>> **Create other effects** by softening focus, adding mist, adding a radial zoom,
masking areas, adding lens reflections, and magnifying.

COLOR FILTERS FOR WHITE BALANCE

It's debatable whether using color filters on a dSLR for white balance is necessary. After all, you have perfectly good white balance controls on your camera. However, some people feel that correcting select light sources improves your camera's dynamic range and reduces the chance of overexposure. This has a ring of truth to it because unfiltered light does have an effect on metering and exposure, which happen before you take a shot. White balance is a processing step that happens after the fact, even when performed in the camera.

TIP

If you're familiar with software filters and effects, and with common photo-editing tasks, you can make the switch to physical filters easily. Think of the tasks you perform using software, and match that up with the physical filter that does the same thing.

Considering filter pros and cons

You don't have to go out and buy every filter at one time. Start with one or two different filters and see what you think.

TIP

Having a circular polarizer filter to block annoying reflections is a good first choice if you shoot a lot of these subjects:

>> Landscapes with water

>> Buildings with glass sides and windows

>> Portraits of people who wear glasses

If you shoot inside, or shoot mostly portraits, you'll benefit from filters that correct white balance.

Consider these benefits to using filters:

>> **Effectiveness:** *Neutral density (ND)* grads actually affect the balance of light in the scene. (*Grad* is a fancy shortening of the term *graduated,* which refers to the filter transitions from clear to shaded.) It's real and not emulated, which means that you're getting the actual effect. Someone didn't have to program it to come *reasonably close* to the real thing in software. There may, however, be quality differences between filters and brands of filters that affect how well they perform.

>> **Efficiency:** Using the right filter on the scene means that you can often spend less time processing and editing your photos.

>> **Creativity:** The amount of creativity you can express with filters is staggeringly large. It's like having a Hollywood special effects division supporting your photo shoot.

>> **Protection:** Many use clear or UV filters to protect lenses. It's cheaper to replace a scratched, cracked, or broken filter than it is a lens. Not only that, if you break a filter, you can toss it in the trash and keep shooting immediately. Not so if you scratch your lens.

And consider these challenges:

>> **Quality:** Many question the benefit of putting a $20 (or even a $100 filter) in front of a $1,500 lens. Think about it.

>> **Compromise:** Some question whether it's worth potentially degrading a photo by making light pass through more stuff to get to the camera's image sensor when you can perform most filter-like adjustments in software.

>> **Convenience:** You have to carry filters around, and they take up space in your camera bag. Software filters are much lighter by comparison. After all, they're just 1s and 0s.

WARNING

>> **Fragility:** In contrast to their software counterparts, optical filters can get scratched or broken. I've picked up a variety of filter cases to safeguard my investment; you can see them in Figure 5-2. All offer reasonable amounts of protection, just in a different package. Some filters come with soft cases. Others are shipped in hard plastic cases. In my experience, it's harder to fit more than a few hard plastic cases in your camera bag and get at them with any ease.

>> **Cleanliness:** Filters can get smudged and dirty, as shown in Figure 5-3. This issue might weigh on you and make you not want the extra hassle. I totally understand.

>> **Cost:** Filters cost money, which always seems to be in short supply. You're limited in the number of filters you can buy, the number of lenses you can support with filters, and the number of times you can replace or upgrade them. With programs like Adobe Photoshop, software filters work on every photo in your collection, whether you took it today or five years ago.

>> **Interoperability:** Different lens sizes need different filters. Software filters don't.

>> **Time:** Setting up and swapping out filters takes time and effort. Don't underestimate this aspect. To use filters, you must want to.

>> **The X factor:** When you're using a real filter, you have one chance to get it right. In software, you can try a lot of different filters and effects with the same photo until you're happy with the result.

Now that I've shared 342 reasons why filters can be a pain, I hope you're still willing to try them!

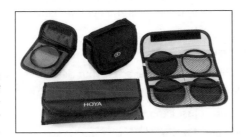

FIGURE 5-2:
Buy the type of case that fits your needs and your camera bag.

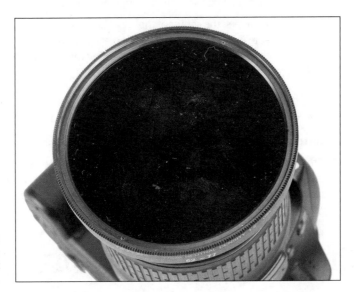

FIGURE 5-3:
The one photo I didn't dust for you.

Using filters with dSLRs

Using filters is easy. You may spend a few moments getting set up and deciding what filter you want to use, but you'll soon start taking shots. When you get the hang of it, you get pretty fast with filters.

REMEMBER

Clean your filters at home before heading out on your shoot.

Here's the process I follow when using filters:

1. **Evaluate the scene and choose a filter.**

   Decide whether you want to control exposure, color, or use a filter to achieve a special effect.

   REMEMBER

   For best results, limit the number of filters you use. Most people agree that using more than two or three filters at the same time degrades image quality. Every pane of glass, resin, or polyester is another layer between your expensive lens and the image sensor.

2. **Slide or screw in the filter.**

   Depending on your filter system, either screw your clean filter into the end of your lens or slide it in the holder. You can find more details in the next section.

3. **Compose, meter, and adjust exposure.**

   Your filter's documentation might give specific metering instructions. Experiment and take test shots to fine-tune the exposure.

   For graduated filters, the center of the scene should be properly exposed, even with the filter in place. If you're using spot metering, you may see better results from pre-metering the scene and then mounting the filter. Be prepared to review your photos and adjust, if necessary.

4. **Take the photo and review the photo.**

   Check exposure, color, glare, and whether the filter has the desired effect.

5. **Correct and start over or stay on course.**

   If the photo looks good, you're good to go. If not, try to figure out what's causing the problem. Is the filter on the lens correctly? Is this filter right for this scene? Reexamine your starting assumptions, if need be, and question whether you need *this* or *any* filter.

Taking Shape with Filter Systems

Filters come in two main flavors:

» Circular filters screw into the lens.

» Rectangular filters slide into a frame mounted on the lens.

I describe these types of filters in detail in this section.

Circular (screw-in)

Circular filters are quite popular and easy to work with. Figure 5-4 shows a small collection of Hoya 77mm black-and-white filters. When you think about it, a *screw-in* filter *has* to be circular. Have you ever tried to turn a square or triangular screw?

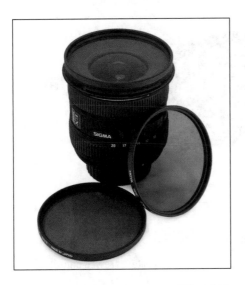

FIGURE 5-4: Circular filters screw into the front of the lens.

Circular filters have three main characteristics:

>> **They are round.** This circular piece of glass (some filters are made from other materials) is mounted in a frame. Higher-quality filters use metal frames that are quite sturdy.

WARNING

>> **They screw in.** Circular filters screw into the front end of dSLR lenses. Don't incorrectly thread a filter when you're mounting it. You might ruin the filter or, worse, damage the threads on your lens. Take your time and, if necessary, back out the filter by turning it counterclockwise until you feel it correct itself. Then get back on track.

Getting filters on isn't as much of a problem as getting them off. Handle tough filters with a filter wrench, shown in Figure 5-5. This wrench has saved me a lot of frustration.

WARNING

>> **They have a specific size.** Filters are sized by their diameter (the distance across, going through the center), which is measured in millimeters. This is important: *You must match your filter size with your lens.* Many lenses have their filter size printed on the front or top. If it's not in either of those places, check your manual.

Using Filters

CHAPTER 5 **Using Filters**   343

If you want to use filters on multiple lenses that require different filter sizes, buy a single, large filter size and use step-up rings to fit the filter to the lens. You'll buy a step-up ring for each differently sized lens, but only one size filter. I have four step-up ring sizes (52–77mm, 55–77mm, 58–77mm, and 62–77mm) that let me fit one filter size (77mm) on several lenses, as shown in Figure 5-6.

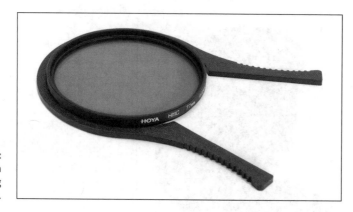

FIGURE 5-5:
This filter wrench makes removing filters a snap.

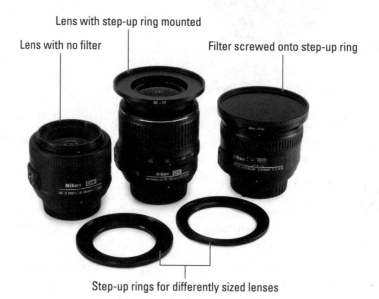

Lens with step-up ring mounted

Lens with no filter

Filter screwed onto step-up ring

FIGURE 5-6:
Step-up rings reduce the number of filters you have to buy for multiple lens sizes.

Step-up rings for differently sized lenses

Rectangular frame slide-in

The other main filter type relies on a frame mounted to the lens that enables rect-angular filters to slide in and out. The advantage of this system is similar to that provided by step-up rings. You buy the frame and enough adapters to mount it on your lenses, but you need only one set of filters. As long as you have the right adapter ring, you can use the same filters on lenses of many different sizes.

Figure 5-7 shows a filter from Cokin's Creative Filter System (www.cokin.com) attached to a 50mm lens, along with an extra adapter and filter. Rectangular filter systems have these main parts:

>> **Adapter ring:** This piece screws into the filter ring on your lens and has fit-tings to slide on the filter holder and make a secure attachment. Simply buy the correct adapter for each of your lenses and you're ready to rock. Read the manual to make sure this type of filter system works with the lenses you want to use it with. Most normal dSLR lenses work fine. You may have to buy a dif-ferent system for wide-angle lenses.

>> **Filter holder:** This element holds one or more filters. The holder slides onto the adapter and snaps securely in place. Filters slide into the holder rather than screw onto the lens, which makes changing them extremely easy. It also makes the filters compatible with many different lenses. Notice in Figure 5-7 that there's room for three filters in this particular adapter.

>> **Rectangular filter:** The reason for the entire setup is the filter. It's larger than a screw-in filter and is rectangular. Most rectangular filters don't have frames around them, so be careful when handling them. You can buy filter wallets, sleeves, and boxes for storage.

REMEMBER

All in all, the rectangular system is ingenious if you have several lenses that take different filter sizes. Having a rectangular filter holder makes a robust filter library more cost effective. However, the size of the mount with filters is bigger and bulkier than the traditional circular screw-in variety.

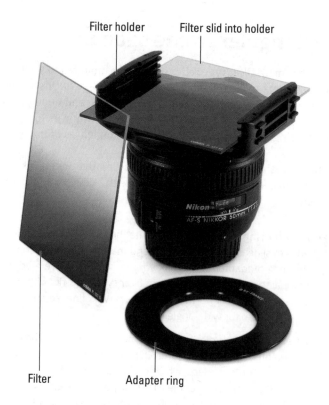

Filter holder   Filter slid into holder

FIGURE 5-7:
Rectangular
filters slide into a
holder mounted
to an adapter
that screws onto
the lens.

Filter   Adapter ring

Using Filters for Different Purposes

This section has information on several different filter types. Browse through them to see what you might want to try. Think about the photos you normally shoot as you consider whether a filter type is right for you.

TIP

The sheer number of filters and filter types can be overwhelming, and getting this straight in your mind can take some time. I summarize many of the problems that filters help solve in Table 5-1. Have fun experimenting with different brands, makes, models, and strengths!

Protective

A *protective filter* is clear, high-quality glass that protects the lens. You can leave it on your lens all the time. As long as the filter is clean, the photo shouldn't be affected. The filter essentially serves as a clear lens cover.

TABLE 5-1

Problem Solving with Filter Types

To Do This	Try These Filters	Notes
Protect your lens	Clear or UV filter	UV filters also cut haze.
Control exposure	ND filter	Available in different strengths.
Balance exposure	ND grad or color grad	Use ND grad for a neutral effect, or a color grad to emphasize certain colors.
Reduce glare or reflections	Circular polarizer	Rotate to dial in desired effectiveness.
Reduce haze	UV filter	Can also keep on the lens to protect it.
Enhance color	Color or color grad	Effect depends on the color of the filter.
Correct color	Warming, cooling, balancing, or color compensating	Use to adjust white balance or correct tints.
Tone black-and-white photos	Black-and-white filters	Special colored filters that affect how colors are translated into black-and-white tones. Common colors include red, green, yellow, blue, and orange.
Alter contrast	Contrast or other filters	Many filters affect contrast. There are also contrast-specific filters.
Special effects	Fog, haze, stars, mask, close up, mist, diffusion, and more	Experiment with many different types of filters for a range of special effects.

REMEMBER

If you put a clear protective filter in place, you don't have to constantly clean your lens. You clean the filter instead, which keeps the lens (and its irreplaceable coating) from accidentally being scratched.

Circular polarizer

Polarized filters act like a good pair of polarized sunglasses: They filter out distracting reflections and glare. The details of how this type of filter works and why are somewhat technical. All you need to know is that polarized filters block *reflected* light (which can even happen in the sky) while allowing natural light to pass through them.

TIP

You have to rotate the front of the polarizing filter so that it rejects the reflections you want.

Figure 5-8 shows two photos. I took them looking down at the water in a slow-moving river. The image on the left shows the photo I took without a polarizing filter. The blue sky is reflected in the water. The image on the right shows the photo I took with a circular polarizer filter. The effect is to block the

Using Filters

reflections of the sky, which enables you to see details beneath the surface of the water. I find the difference between the two shots amazing.

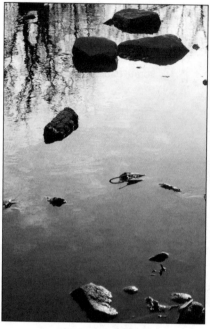 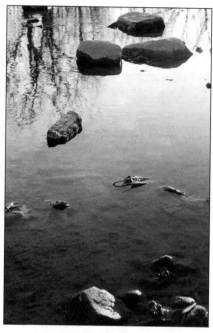

FIGURE 5-8:
Without polarizer: The blue sky reflects off the surface of the water. With polarizer: Details visible beneath the surface.

Without polarizer   With polarizer

TECHNICAL STUFF

For complex and technical reasons having to do with beam splitters and the nature of linear versus circular or non-polarized light, digital SLR metering and autofocus sensors are compatible with circular polarizer filters, not linear polarizers.

Ultraviolet (UV)

Sunglasses with ultraviolet (UV) protection are better for your eyes because they block a lot of haze. If exposed to too much UV radiation for too long, you can damage your eyes. Ditto for UV filters: They block UV light, which causes blue haze when you're shooting around water, into the air, or into the distance. (Think of the phrase *purple mountains majesty* in the hymn *America the Beautiful*.) UV filters appear clear. That's because you can't see ultraviolet light.

There's some debate as to whether digital cameras need UV filters because most manufacturers build UV and IR protection into their image sensors. In addition, many lenses are coated to reject UV wavelengths. There's no doubt that UV filters work at blocking UV light, but if the lens and the camera can do as good a job, you may not need the filter. Frankly, I took several shots hoping to illustrate how amazing these filters were for this chapter, and I couldn't tell any difference between using a standard UV filter and not. Some people recommend using UV filters as clear lens protectors, just in case.

Neutral density (ND)

Neutral density (ND) filters darken the scene by blocking light. ND filters come in different strengths, called densities. The density tells you how may exposure stops of light they block. For example, an ND filter with a density of 1.2 blocks 4 EV of light. That means that an aperture of f/1.4 acts like f/5.6 or a shutter speed of 1/60 acts like 1/1000 second. ND filters are, in essence, a negative exposure control. They are very helpful in at least two situations.

First, they enable you to use large apertures in bright light. For example, if you're outside during the day and want to take a flash photo, your camera's flash sync speed limits how fast you can set the shutter speed. If you're already at ISO 100 and want a wide-open aperture for creative reasons, you're stuck unless you have an ND filter to tone down the lighting. I took the photo of my wife shown in Figure 5-9 to illustrate the worse-case scenario. I used an aperture of f/2.8 to blur the fence behind her. I also used the camera's built-in flash for fill light because the sun was partly behind her. The ISO was at 100 and the flash sync speed limited the shutter speed to 1/200 second. Remember, the flash sync speed is the fastest shutter speed you can use with the built-in flash — you can't set it any faster to reduce exposure. The result? Massive overexposure.

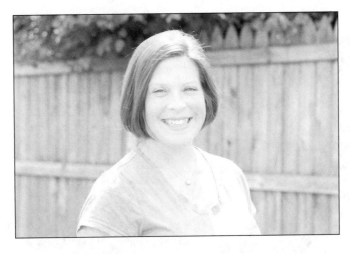

FIGURE 5-9:
Using a wide
aperture
and flash
overexposed
the scene.

I took another shot, shown in Figure 5-10, with a 0.9 density ND filter screwed onto the lens. The difference between the two shots is stunning. This photo is perfectly exposed. The filter blocked enough light so that the shutter speed could come down to 1/160 second. I kept the aperture at f/2.8 and the ISO at 100 and still used the flash. If you want to take creative portraits with fill flash and wide apertures, and don't have high-speed sync available, use an ND filter.

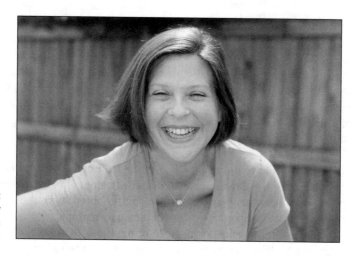

FIGURE 5-10: She obviously approves of the filter.

The second reason to use ND filters is that they help you set long exposure times. For example, you may want a long exposure that emphasizes moving water, as shown in Figure 5-11. In this case, the ISO was as low as I could set it, the aperture was already stopped down quite a bit, and I couldn't shorten the shutter speed because I wanted the water to blur. The thing that saved me was my ND filter.

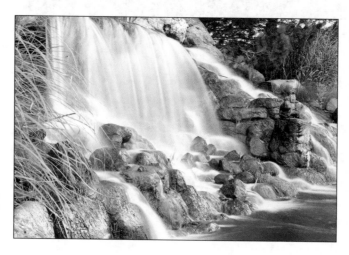

FIGURE 5-11: Use ND filters for long exposures in bright daylight.

ND graduated

ND graduated (or *grad*) filters resemble cool-looking aviator sunglasses with a gradient. As you can see from Figure 5-12, they're darker at the top to tone down light from the sky, and they're clear toward the bottom. You can reverse the effect if needed.

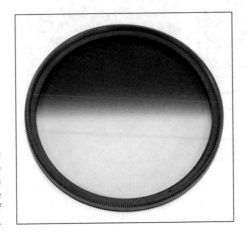

FIGURE 5-12: ND grads are useful in controlling the exposure of bright skies.

TIP

With an ND grad filter, you can set longer exposure times for the land without blowing highlights out in the sky.

Figure 5-13 shows part of a late afternoon scene looking out across a river. I shot the photo on the left without a filter and the one on the right with a 0.6 density ND grad. I processed each photo the same. There is not a huge difference, but if you look closely at the water and the bushes, they are brighter in the photo on the right. The filter blocked enough light from the sky to enable the camera to bring up the exposure for the darker areas of the scene. Details are lost in the bushes in the photo on the left, and the reflections of the sky in the water are less clear. You can tell that these are two different photos and not just a trick using software because the clouds moved between photos.

Color filter

Color filters change the color of a scene. I include *cooling* (making things look bluer) and *warming* filters (making a scene look more golden) in this color category. Think of them as white balance correction on the front end of your lens.

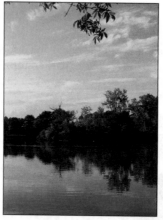
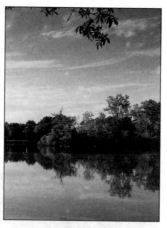

FIGURE 5-13:
ND grad
filters even
the exposure
between sky
and foreground,
which increases
the level of detail.

Without ND grad filter

With ND grad filter

Color grad filter

A color grad filter combines elements of both color and ND grad filters. Imagine an ND grad filter that isn't gray, but in color. Tiffen makes color grads designed to add color to normal or washed-out shots. Many work at sunrise or sunset, but you can also use them to create special color effects.

Other filters

TIP

A ton of filter types are available, in addition to the ones I describe earlier. If you catch the filter bug, visit a store in person or online and check them out. Download a brochure to see before-and-after photos for each type of filter.

In-camera filters

Most dSLRs offer in-camera processing options that mimic optical filters or *software filters* (some are computerized imitations of photo filters, others are more creative special effects) and retouching techniques that you might do in programs like Adobe Photoshop. Look for special shooting modes that enable you to capture photos with filters applied, or look in the Playback menu for retouching filters and effects.

Black-and-white filters

Black-and-white filters enhance contrast and emphasize certain tones by blocking or limiting specific colors. They come in several different colors. Red is popular for increasing contrast in landscapes, yellow for balancing contrast between reds and yellows, and green for shooting outdoor monochrome portraits.

The left image in Figure 5-14 shows the monochrome image of a scene I shot without a filter. I took the photo on the right in Figure 5-14 using the red filter. I processed the photos the same. It's clear that the photo on the right has added contrast and detail in the sky and water.

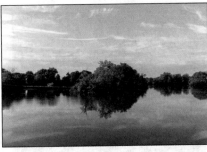
No filter

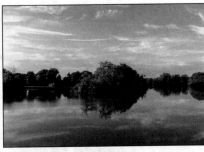
Red (25A) filter

FIGURE 5-14: The photo on the right, shot with a filter, has additional contrast and detail.

TIP

Set your camera to shoot monochrome images when shooting with black-and-white filters. The camera spits out a black-and-white JPEG, so you don't have to do anything else.

Infrared filters

I've got good news and bad news for you. First, the good news: *Infrared (IR)* filters turn your photos into surreal works of art by blocking everything except infrared wavelengths, which are invisible to the naked eye. The bad news is that dSLRs filter out infrared light by varying degrees, which makes it hard to capture infrared images, even with an IR filter.

TIP

If you're curious about IR photography, you can experiment by mounting your camera on a tripod on a bright, sunny day, composing the shot, and then attaching an IR filter (the Hoya R72 is a good IR filter). You'll have to use long exposure times and raise the ISO. You'll also have to edit the resulting shot to make it look cool.

As an alternative, the folks at Life Pixel Infrared (www.lifepixel.com) can convert your camera so it can shoot IR photos without the filter. They take your camera apart and replace the IR-blocking filter that covers the sensor.

Creative filters: Stars, mist, or haze

Use these filters to exercise your creativity. The sky is the limit. Figure 5-15 shows a photo I took with a Hoya Star-Six filter. The filter is engraved with lines. When light strikes the lines, it produces six-sided stars. I took this shot at night looking out at a well-lit bridge. The filter has transformed the lights on the bridge, the distant buildings, and the water reflections.

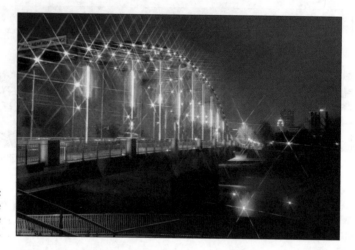

FIGURE 5-15: Star effects are very cool; use them wisely.

4

Lighting the Scene

Contents at a Glance

Chapter **1**

Working with Ambient Light

Working with ambient light means using the light that is available to you rather than your camera's flash. I love working this way, whether inside or out. It's a very natural feeling. However, not all ambient light is the same. Some conditions are more challenging to work in than others.

I invite you to learn this lesson with me as you read about photos I've taken at different times of the day, in different weather, inside and out. Finish by examining photos shot during different conditions, including indirect light, hazy days, and high-contrast scenes.

Working in Natural Light

The time you choose to go out and photograph people and other scenes plays an important role in how your photos turn out. That might sound obvious, but there's a secret to it: Light changes during the day, and it's not all equally good. I started taking much better photos when I realized that some times of the day were better than others to take photos. Knowing when the light is best enables you to plan your trips more effectively and capture the photos you want.

Shooting during the morning golden hour

I drive by the bridge shown in Figure 1-1 just about every day. Most of the time, it looks unremarkable. However, when I see it on the way to church on Sunday morning, it looks stunning. The light from the rising sun gently illuminates it from the side instead of glaring down from the top. Think about that for a minute. Objects that are normally lit from above during the day and shaded on one side or another are often beautifully and unconventionally lit during the morning or evening.

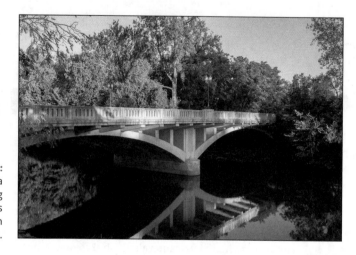

FIGURE 1-1:
Sunlight on a clear morning illuminates scenes from the side.

REMEMBER

Mornings are often clear and calm. The day is just starting and the light feels fresh. The hour or so after sunrise and before sunset is called the golden hour because of the great light.

Notice the still water of the river. It's so quiet that the bridge, sky, and foliage cast amazing reflections. You get two scenes for the price of one. Not all mornings are like this, of course. Some will be blustery, wintery, stormy, hot, muggy, or rainy. However, when it is calm, this is the type of photo that is waiting to be captured.

One note of caution when shooting in the morning. When the sun starts to come up, pay attention to the contrast levels in the scene. If you notice that your shots have lost details in areas of deep shadow or that highlights are blowing out, use exposure compensation or manual shooting mode to preserve them as much as possible. Bring out the details you've saved later in software.

Fighting with the light at noon

As I looked through my catalog of photos, I realized that I don't have that great a selection of photos taken around noon. The reason is that it's the worst time of day to photograph people, nature, and buildings.

The sun is very intense and casts harsh shadows. Because of these factors, I don't often take photos of people at noon. They squint and the photos look horrible because half their faces are in deep shadows while the other half of their faces look too bright.

REMEMBER

You're not a bad photographer if you can't take perfect shots at noon. That's just the way it is. Unless you work with a tremendous amount of portable diffusers and other gear to soften the light, it's just not worth it.

So what I have for you is a nice shot overlooking the lake at our favorite summer camp, shown in Figure 1-2. The fact that the clouds in the sky add some interest and diffuse the sunlight a bit, and that shadows aren't visually distracting, help make this photo a keeper. The highlights in the clouds were on the edge of being too bright, however, so I had to work to save details using Lightroom and Photoshop.

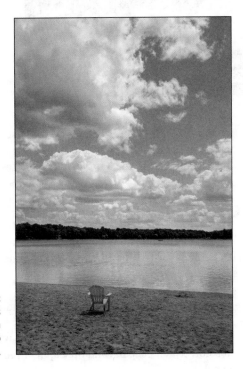

FIGURE 1-2:
Midday lighting is harsh and often difficult to photograph well.

Working with Ambient Light

Going out in the early evening

Early evening is a good time to photograph things. The harsh afternoon sun has passed and been replaced by more forgiving light. It's still bright, but not normally overpowering unless you look right at it.

While you're waiting for the golden hour (visit www.golden-hour.com to find out when golden hour starts and ends each day; there's also an app), look for interesting subjects and scenes. Many will be large and scenic, but don't overlook the small things. The petunias in Figure 1-3 are a good example. I took this photo at a park near where we live while testing a new camera. The shutter speed was very fast because of the bright light: 1/2000 second.

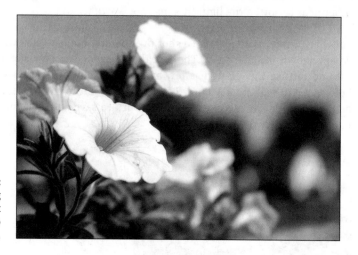

FIGURE 1-3: Early evening light is bright without being too harsh.

You can see that the flowers are well lit and the colors in the scene are nice and vibrant. This isn't just about me or my skill; it's the time of day I chose to photograph it. Time of day makes a huge difference in how your photos look.

Enjoying the evening golden hour

Don't fret. If you slept through the morning golden hour, you get another shot at it in the evening. This is my favorite time to photograph landscapes and many other outdoor subjects.

TIP

If the weather is decent, go out tonight before the sun sets and look at the sky. Take note of how the light softens and things are lit from the side, not the top. If the sky has clouds, they may be beautifully colored. On special days, the entire sky glows a gorgeous golden color, which deepens and may appear red or purple as the sun sets. It really is magical.

I took the photo in Figure 1-4 looking southwest as the sun was close to setting. It's off to the right of the photo. The Oklahoma pasture is well lit, but gently so. The clouds are bright and colorful in the distance. It's a great example of how the light appears during this time of the day.

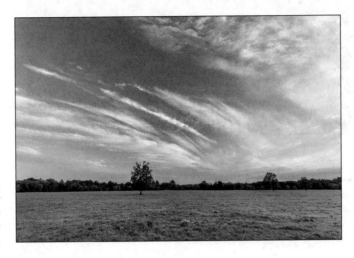

FIGURE 1-4:
The golden hour is a stunning time to be out with your camera.

Photographing the sunset

Sunsets are a special treat. If you've been shooting during the golden hour, don't pack up and leave until you've photographed the setting sun. The challenge is finding the right location. I particularly enjoy photographing rivers that run east-west because they form a natural avenue that points toward the setting sun, as shown in Figure 1-5.

In this case, I set up my tripod on some rocks in the river. I used a Sony APS-C dSLR and an ultra wide-angle zoom lens set to 10mm to capture as much of the surrounding scenery as possible.

I also included the sun in the shot. That is optional. I love the flares and the interaction between the sun and the lens, but you may not. When shooting toward the sun, you may want to use an ND grad or graduated filter to dim the light a bit. I stopped the aperture down to f/22 for this shot. I set the ISO on scenes like this to 100. The shutter speed was 1/80 second.

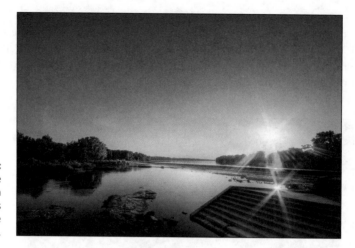

Capturing twilight

The time after the sun sets and before it gets completely dark is called twilight, or sometimes dusk (technically the darkest part of twilight). You can capture some amazing shots during this time.

Figure 1-6 shows a scene I took looking west about a half hour after the sun set. This photo features the last little bit of glow on the distant horizon. The lake both doubles the effect of the golden light and mirrors the cloudless, deep-blue sky. I shot this using a tripod and had the shutter speed set to 1/5 second.

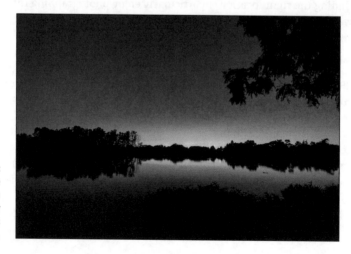

FIGURE 1-6:
Light from the
setting sun
beautifully
illuminates
twilight scenes.

Nerd Alert: The time was a minute into the phase called nautical twilight. The light is very dim, but still able to cause the foreground to be in silhouette.

Shooting at night

Going out at night to take photos is actually pretty fun. You can take interesting photos of objects that are lit by sources other than the sun. City, street, and building lights are all great helpers. I took the photo in Figure 1-7 in Detroit. It's the 40-story tall Cadillac tower downtown, right by Campus Martius Park. This area is filled with sights and attractions such as Woodward Fountain, lots of cool buildings, restaurants, and much more.

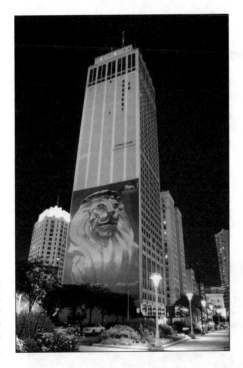

FIGURE 1-7: Skies are dark at night but this building and the foreground are well lit.

Despite the darkness, the building and street are well lit. I took this handheld shot using the camera's Night View scene mode. The camera automatically chose an aperture of f/3.5 and ISO 1600. The mode recommends using a tripod because the shutter speed in this mode is slower than normal. In this case, it was 1/4 second. That's on the super-low side and hard to keep steady. However, I didn't have a tripod with me, so I just held the camera as steady as possible.

If you don't want to use an automatic exposure mode or scene, switch to Manual exposure mode and dial in settings that you and your camera can handle. First, open up your aperture and then set a reasonable handheld shutter speed. Raise the ISO to get the exposure you want. Take some test shots and adjust accordingly.

Dealing with Weather

Although sunny days with cloudless blue skies are great to be out in, they offer little variety when photographed. Different weather conditions can spice up your shots. Study the photos in this section to see examples of photos taken in different types of weather.

Capturing clouds

As a rule, I try to go out on partly cloudy days when photographing landscapes. These types of clouds are amazing. They liven up the sky with interesting details. During the golden hour and at sunset, they turn into the most beautiful things you've ever seen. Light reflects off their sides and, as the sun sets, it shines up to illuminate them from below.

Figure 1-8 shows one of those times when everything seemed to work out just right. I was at a place that offered a scenic look toward the setting sun. Rivers and lakes seem made for photos like this. I had my tripod set up and was ready for this exact moment. The clouds were stunning and the light was profound.

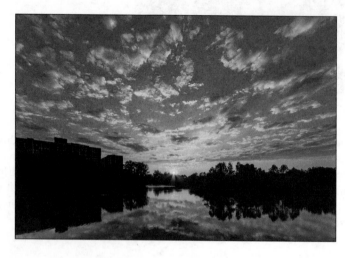

FIGURE 1-8:
Clouds make skies much more interesting, especially during the golden hour and at sunset.

Do yourself a favor. When clouds are out, get your camera ready.

Working in the snow

Shooting in the snow is completely different from running around in shorts and a t-shirt in the summer, taking pictures of the lake. It's cold, windy, possibly wet, and can be hard to walk around. It can even be dangerous. Make sure to bundle up with the appropriate protective gear for yourself and your camera. See Book 1, Chapter 2 for some pointers on dealing with bad weather. If you're alone, tell people where you're going and when you expect to be back. Make sure your phone is charged and you have service if you need to make an emergency call. Can you tell I'm a dad?

Despite the caveats to being out in the weather, snow is magical. You'll get stunning photos in the winter that aren't possible to capture at any other time of the year. The scene in Figure 1-9 is of a path leading off into the trees. To the left is a fenced-in area. In the summer, this particular location doesn't seem that special. In the winter, with the trees and fence covered in snow, it's marvelous. Lighting is diffused and gentle when the sky is cloudy or snowy. Some elements of the scene blend together, but contrasting features stand out more.

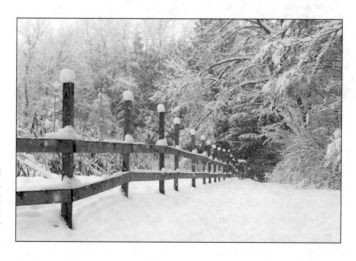

FIGURE 1-9:
Snow reduces overall contrast but can reveal details normally hidden.

Be careful not to boost contrast too high when processing snowy scenes. I toned it down here so that the dark areas of the trees didn't make the photo look too aggressive.

Working with Ambient Light

Using fog

Fog is wonderful to shoot in, the same way snowy days and some cloudy conditions are. Fog blocks direct sunlight and replaces it with a diffuse glow of its own. It's a chance for you to enjoy shooting in low-contrast conditions.

Figure 1-10 is a case in point. I was up early one Saturday morning, and my son looked out the window and commented on the weather. He wasn't excited about it, but I was like, "FOG!!!" I gathered up my gear and drove to a river fairly close to our house. I unpacked and then walked in and around the river, enjoying the conditions. This shot shows off the fog quite nicely. The nearby trees are relatively clear but the fog blankets the background. It's lovely.

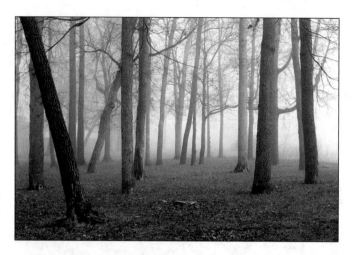

FIGURE 1-10: Fog acts like a giant diffuser on the sun.

SHOOTING MOVIES

Ambient lighting looks basically the same whether you are shooting movies or still photos. Harsh light will produce movies that have too much contrast and suffer from unsightly shadows. Soft light that is diffused will look better. You will have to pay attention to how light in your scene changes over time, however, or your clips won't match and you will have to work harder in post-processing. The other area in which shooting movies is different relates to shutter speed. You can use relatively slow shutter speeds compared to still photography without having to worry about blur. This approach helps in low light but can be a challenge in bright light. Use ND filters if the light is very bright and your scenes are overexposed.

Shooting Inside

Ambient light indoors is much dimmer than it is outside. As a result, your camera may struggle with exposure. The shutter speed might be too slow, your lens might not be able to open up as wide as you want, or the ISO may want to go through the roof. Although getting a better camera and lens are options, I want to show you how to work with what you have. It's still possible to take some amazing shots.

Photographing in large interior spaces

Large interior spaces are a breeze to shoot in if you are able to set your camera up on a tripod. Using a tripod lets you keep the ISO down and lengthen the shutter speed to capture the amount of light that you need to make the room appear bright.

I took the photo in Figure 1-11 with my tripod set up very low — just below eye level for a person sitting down. I set the aperture to f/8 to have a good depth of field. I wanted a noise-free photo, so I manually set the ISO to 100. I needed a full second to take this shot.

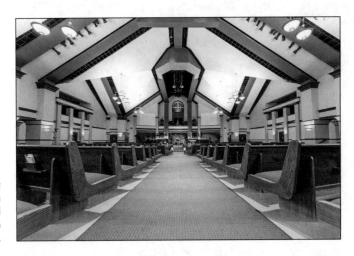

FIGURE 1-11: Natural light from the sides helped me photograph this large space.

Here's the rub: The room looked bright enough to photograph in. I had windows on either side of me, which provided much of the ambient light in the room. The chandeliers added more, with the wall sconces giving some mood lighting. Spotlights on the stage completed the setup. That's a decent amount of light in the right places for a room like this, and exposing the scene at ISO 100 and f/8 still took a second.

TIP

You won't be able to photograph people easily if you have to use long exposures. If necessary, raise the ISO or open the aperture wider.

Photographing in living spaces

Unlike large commercial or public spaces, most living spaces have windows close at hand. If possible, open blinds or curtains of nearby windows and let as much natural light in as possible. If your lens is fast enough, open the aperture wide. Expect a higher ISO than when shooting outside.

I took the whimsical close-up photo shown in Figure 1-12 of my wife's and daughter's hands one day after they painted their nails together. Their hands are on the floor and the windows are open. I did not use the flash, just the natural light. I set the aperture to f/4 and used a shutter speed of 1/60 second. That's slow, but not impossible. I made sure that vibration reduction was enabled on the lens. The ISO rose to 560, which is still low enough not to make noise a problem. Overall, this is a nice, natural shot.

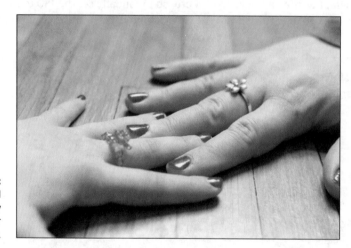

FIGURE 1-12: I used natural light exclusively for this interior shot.

REMEMBER

Depending on the color of the room and furnishings, you may need to tweak white balance to render colors accurately. Use the same techniques when shooting portraits inside. You should be ready to switch to shutter-priority mode and use faster shutter speeds if you want to photograph people without blurring.

Using stage lighting

Photographing performers on stage is fun but can be challenging. Normally, the auditorium or venue is dark. The performers are lit by stage lighting, which can vary quite a bit. If they are under bright spotlights, you might be able to shoot nice, crisp photos with fast shutter speeds and low ISOs.

If the lighting isn't cooperating, the dark conditions will push your camera to the limit. I took the photo in Figure 1-13 with a standard zoom lens. The largest aperture possible was f/5.6. I set the shutter speed to 1/125 second (I wish it were faster), which pushed the ISO to 1600. That is getting into noisy territory for the camera I was using. In the end, this photo is balanced on a knife edge. A bit slower or a bit noisier and it would not work.

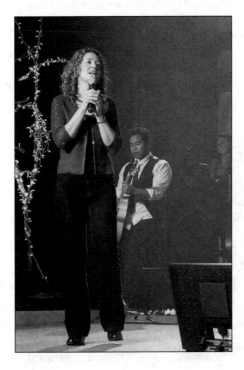

FIGURE 1-13: Stage lighting brightly illuminates performers but leaves the background dark.

Processing shots like this can be tricky. You can't always rely on automatic routines. Adobe Lightroom, for example, thinks this photo is seriously underexposed. It wants to brighten the background, which ruins the photo.

Being Creative in Different Situations

Use this section to give you some ideas of how to take advantage of (or deal with) other, different lighting situations. Seek out conditions that are to your advantage and avoid, or prepare for, those that aren't.

Working with indirect light

Indirect light is a pleasure to work with. This light is available on cloudy or overcast days and often in the morning and evening. It's ideal for portraits, actually, because the light evenly illuminates faces and does not cause harsh shadows.

Figure 1-14 is a photo of my son Jacob. He's smiling as he looks off in the distance, undoubtedly happy that he was not being blinded by the light. Your subjects will thank you for this. It's hard for them to constantly try to keep their eyes open while being blinded by the sun. In addition, uniform lighting on people's faces makes processing the photo much easier. Shadows are very difficult to remove without making people look unnatural. You may be able to alleviate some of the harsh contrast, but not all.

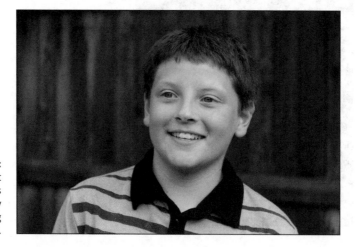

FIGURE 1-14:
Indirect light outside produces incredibly natural-looking portraits.

Capturing reflections

Reflections make for great artistic possibilities. When possible, capture them in water or on other reflective surfaces. Although I've noted them throughout this chapter, the photo in Figure 1-15 is a special one.

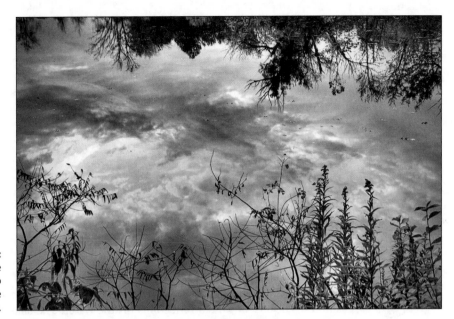

FIGURE 1-15:
Be on the lookout to capture reflections.

The photo is made mostly of reflections. The only things that aren't are the plants in the foreground and the leaves on the surface of the water. I took this photo during the evening golden hour in mid-October. Although I was out shooting landscapes, I decided to feature the reflections in this shot. I zoomed in to 29mm on my Canon APS-C dSLR, which put the lens close to the middle of the normal focal length range. I was able to hold the camera steady for a shot at 1/40 second. The ISO was 160.

REMEMBER

Unless you live close to the equator, golden hour times and their durations change throughout the year, so don't get fixated on a specific time to be out. Use an app or service like www.golden-hour.com to get local sunrise, sunset, or golden hour times. Weather.com is also great because you can check the weather after looking at the times for sunrise and sunset.

Dealing with glare and haze

Although I love photographing water, it's prone to glare throughout the afternoon and into the early evening. When photographing objects in the distance, you may also have to combat haze.

Figure 1-16 shows a scene that illustrates both problems. It's a shot of Detroit that I took from Belle Isle, which sits in the middle of Detroit River just to the east of the downtown area. I had to face west to capture this photo, toward the direction of the sun, which is just above the frame. It was late afternoon, so the sun was still pretty high.

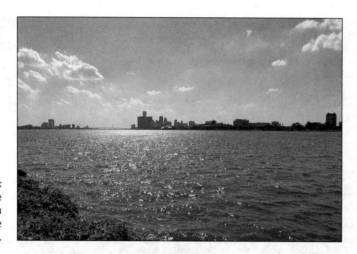

FIGURE 1-16:
Use all the techniques you can to fight glare and haze.

TIP

From a technical perspective, you combat reflective glare by using a circular polarizing filter on your lens. Rotate the front part of the filter to find the best position to cut out unwanted reflections off the water. The skies and clouds will also look better.

You can try using a UV or Haze filter to cut through the haze. Although UV filters work, the results may not be discernible. This is because digital SLRs and coated lenses are already pretty resistant to UV light. I had a Sigma DG UV filter on the lens for this shot.

You can also try to process the haze out of the photo using Adobe Lightroom or another application. Lightroom, as well as Adobe Camera Raw, has a Dehaze setting that works well.

Shooting high-contrast scenes

High-contrast scenes are normally anathema to digital cameras. It's exceedingly hard if not impossible to capture a scene's deepest darks and the brightest brights in one photo if the contrast is out of control. This is why HDR (High Dynamic Range; see Book 5, Chapter 6) photography is one popular way of dealing with high-contrast scenes.

Rather than fight it, you can take artistic advantage of a scene with too much contrast. The tunnel shown in Figure 1-17 goes underneath a road at our favorite summer camp. My wife and one of my sons are at the far end. I thought this would make a great photo, and it does. In this case, the high contrast between the dark sides and the light at the end of the tunnel (yes, I actually got to say it!) makes the scene work.

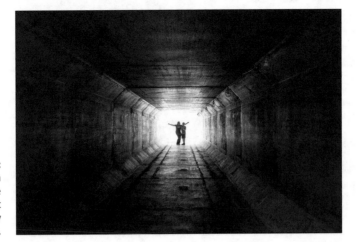

TIP

If you're after a creative shot like this, you may have to wrestle with your camera to make it happen. Try using exposure compensation to get the right light, or use your camera's manual mode. You can also switch metering modes from multi-zone or pattern to spot or center-weighted to get the camera to meter the scene the way you want it.

Photographing low contrast scenes

Technically, scenes with low contrast are relatively easy to photograph. You don't risk blowing out highlights or losing details in shadows. If you look at the histogram, the brightness will appear clumped together. I took the photo in Figure 1-18 during a snowstorm. The sky is overcast and gray, and the shore in the foreground is covered with snow. The dark surface of the lake and the floating platform in the water add contrast. It helps to have something of contrast to keep the scene from looking too desolate.

REMEMBER

When processing this type of photo, leave the overall contrast where it is or reduce it. I think we have a modern tendency to overemphasize contrast.

The Shadow knows!

Use shadows in scenes when possible. They break scenes up and can add interest. Use your judgment, of course. Shadows can also distract and take attention away from where you want it.

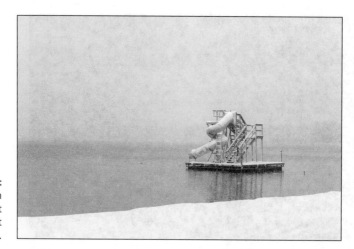

Figure 1-19 shows a scene where shadows are effective. I took this photo inside a pedestrian bridge that connects the main campus at a local university to a student housing area, which is located on the other side of a busy road. I used my digital Holga lens.

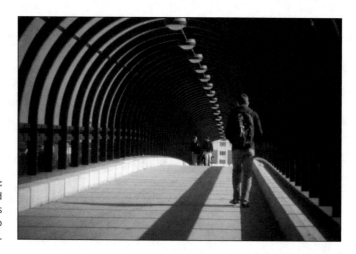

The walkway surface is a fairly dull-looking concrete. The shadows cast by the supports in the bridge tie in with the structure itself, making the scene of students walking to and fro even more interesting.

Chapter **2**

Exploring Basic Flash Photography

This chapter is devoted to demystifying the built-in flash that most digital SLRs have on top of the camera. Photography gets much more enjoyable if you know when and how to control your camera's flash. You'll be able to take photos in more situations with it than without it. For example, flash comes to the rescue when the lighting is dim and your camera is struggling with the exposure. It's also a great way to make sure people's faces are well lit, even in good lighting.

I show you how to use the flash, how to tweak the settings, and how to prevent it from firing when the camera is in an automatic shooting mode. You learn how and when to activate it yourself when you're using an advanced shooting mode. I also cover tips on how to effectively use the built-in flash and introduce you to more advanced flash techniques.

Finding the Flash

All but the most expensive digital SLRs have a built-in flash on top of the camera. It is normally retracted and locked in place. When raised, it flips up a few inches above the camera, as shown in Figure 2-1.

Built-in flash   Lift to raise

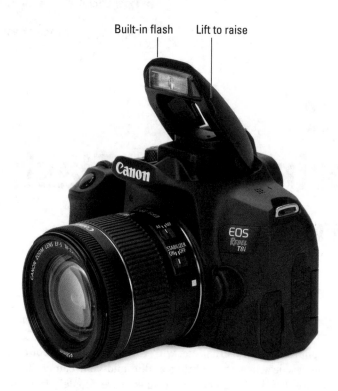

FIGURE 2-1:
The pop-up flash extends above the camera, ready for action.

If you have the camera set to an automatic shooting mode, the flash may pop up automatically when needed. This is true on most consumer-level cameras. If you're using an advanced shooting mode, press the flash button to raise it. You may need to lift the flash yourself if your camera doesn't have a flash button. You can read more on the specifics of how this happens next.

I have two important points to make before continuing.

>> **Whether you activate the flash automatically or manually, the strength of the flash is determined automatically.** The only time it isn't is when you change the flash mode from automatic to manual strength, if possible, or dial in flash exposure compensation. Those are the two situations in which you have some control over the strength of the flash.

>> **Using the pop-up flash limits the maximum shutter speed your camera can use.** This speed is called the *sync speed* or *flash sync speed*. It's related to how camera shutters work. The image sensor can be completely exposed at some point during the exposure only if the shutter speed is set at or below the flash sync speed. This limitation can be a real inconvenience.

Professional-level cameras rarely have a built-in flash because professional photographers almost always rely on other lighting techniques. They use external flash units, which I cover in the next chapter, or they shoot in a studio with remote strobes and other bright, continuous lighting units.

Using the Flash Automatically

Using a digital SLR's built-in flash automatically is pretty easy. The key to automatic flash is selecting the right shooting mode.

Setting a flash-friendly shooting mode

Most automatic shooting modes, including scenes like Portrait, automatically raise (pop up) and fire the built-in flash when the camera needs more light to take the photo. It can be a bit of a surprise if you're not expecting it.

The left image in Figure 2-2 shows a Canon camera in Scene Intelligent Auto mode. Note the automatic flash symbol. It shows that the flash is available in this mode. There are exceptions, however. The right image in Figure 2-2 shows the Landscape scene in the same camera. There is no flash icon, and flash is unavailable in this mode. Here are the types of scenes that won't fire the flash: landscapes, some sports and action modes, night scenes, many HDR scenes, and some of the more esoteric scenes like candlelight and food. Check your camera's manual for details.

FIGURE 2-2: The built-in flash is not available in all automatic modes and scenes.

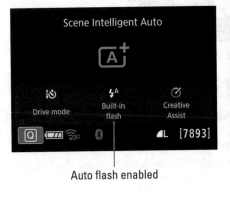

Auto flash enabled

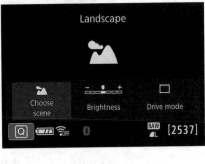

No flash

When you're finished shooting, remember to lower the built-in flash back into its stowed position.

Preventing the built-in flash from firing

Some automatic shooting modes give you the ability to turn off the flash if you don't want it to fire. On the other hand, preventing the flash from firing may be as simple as not raising it if you have a camera that doesn't pop it up for you. Look for details related to the shooting mode you've set in your camera's manual or shooting information display.

Some automatic modes don't let you disable the flash. If the camera thinks you need it but you don't want it, choose a shooting mode in which you can disable the flash.

If your camera has a Flash Off mode, shown in Figure 2-3, consider using it to prevent the flash from firing. Flash Off is simply the camera's Auto mode, but without the flash. In this case, Nikon calls the mode Auto (Flash Off). You can customize some automatic modes to prevent or force the flash. I cover that in the next section.

Auto (flash off) mode

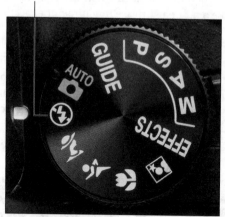

FIGURE 2-3:
Flash Off or Auto (Flash Off) mode is an automatic mode that disables the flash.

Customizing automatic flash settings

Many automatic shooting modes allow you to control whether the flash fires automatically, is forced to fire, or is prevented from firing. Figure 2-4 shows how to change the automatic flash setting in the Portrait scene using a Canon dSLR. I've activated the setting in the left image, which shows the flash currently set to Auto, and have changed that to force the built-in flash to fire in the right image. Note that this camera doesn't have a Flash Off option. With this camera, you simply don't raise the flash, even if the camera suggests that the flash is needed.

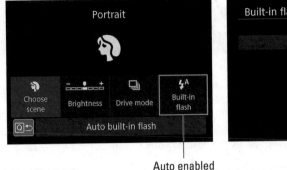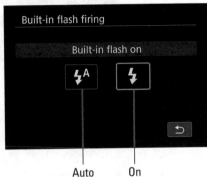

FIGURE 2-4:
Forcing the built-in flash to fire in an automatic shooting mode.

Canon users can make changes through the Quick Control screen. Nikon users can use the Information display. You can leave the flash on Auto, set it to Auto plus Red-Eye Reduction, or turn it off. Sony users push the Function button to see shooting functions. Check your camera manual for specifics.

Manually Activating the Built-in Flash

When you're in an advanced shooting mode, it's up to you to pop the flash when you need it. This section gives you some pointers on knowing how and when to do so.

Using the built-in flash

Using your camera's pop-up flash is technically quite easy. Follow these steps:

1. **Choose a shooting mode that allows you to control the flash.**

   Most often this includes programmed autoexposure, aperture-priority, shutter-priority, and manual shooting modes. Cameras tend to disable the flash button if you're in an automatic mode, which doesn't allow you to control the flash when taking a photo.

2. **Check that the flash is enabled.**

   Check your camera's Flash Control menu to make sure that flash is enabled (see the left image in Figure 2-5). If not, do so, as shown in the right image.

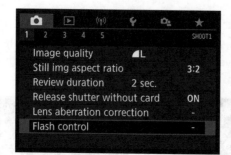

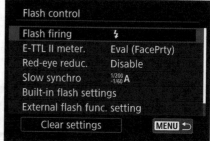

FIGURE 2-5:
The flash is
enabled and
ready.

WARNING

3. Clear the flash.

Remove anything attached to the camera's hot shoe, which is the mounting point on top of the camera for flashes and other accessories. Make sure there's enough space for the flash to pop up without hitting anything.

4. Raise the built-in flash.

You may have a flash button located on the front of the camera. Press it to raise the flash.

Other cameras, like the one shown in Figure 2-1, require that you raise it yourself. Gently lift the flash until it springs up and remains open on its own.

5. Press the shutter button halfway to meter and confirm that flash is ready.

TECHNICAL STUFF

The camera may fire off a few pre-shot pulses to help set the exposure. This is part of *TTL (through the lens)* flash metering. Makers call their latest version of TTL flash by different names. Canon uses E-TTL and E-TTL II. Nikon uses i-TTL. Sony uses ADI (Advanced Distance Integration). Pentax use P-TTL.

Wait for the sign that the flash is ready. Figure 2-6 shows one through a Canon viewfinder. Yours may be different. In this case, a small flash symbol appears next to the battery status.

6. Take and review your photos.

Your flash should fire and light up your subject or the scene. If you need to, don't be embarrassed to ask your subjects whether the flash fired. You're on the other side of the camera from them and it can be hard to tell sometimes.

7. If necessary, adjust the strength of the flash for follow-up shots using flash compensation, as explained later.

8. Lower the built-in flash when done.

Lowering the flash saves power and protects it from accidentally getting banged around.

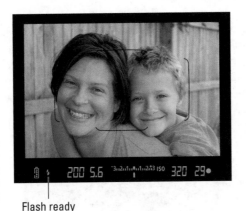

FIGURE 2-6:
The viewfinder gives you information on the status of the flash.

Flash ready

Knowing when to use flash

If you don't know whether to pop the flash, consider these scenarios:

>> **You need more light.** Most of the time, this happens indoors, where the lighting rarely compares to the natural light of the sun. Figure 2-7 shows a photo I took of my son Ben as he sat on the couch watching his sister open presents on her birthday. I was some distance away using a near-telephoto lens and flash. The flash performed perfectly, providing just the right amount of light.

>> **The subject is backlit.** Backlighting refers to situations in which the background, quite often the sky or a window, is very bright. This backlighting fools the camera. It overcompensates for the bright background by lowering the exposure, which leaves your subject in the dark. To correct this problem, use the flash, as I did for the photo in Figure 2-8. Even a low-powered burst can light your subject and save the photo. This technique is called *fill flash*. You could switch to spot metering, but that won't add any light to the scene — you'll end up with skies that are too bright.

TIP

Try flash outdoors, even when your subject is not backlit. It seems strange, but fill flash brings faces out of shadow. Watch your exposure, though. You may have to use high-speed sync (covered in the next chapter) to limit the exposure.

>> **The subject is in shadow.** Often, the lighting in the scene is decent, but it doesn't illuminate the subject well enough from the direction of the camera. I lit the scene in Figure 2-9 primarily from the window to the back right. Without the flash, the pie as well as the mug would have been too dark. This technique is also called *fill flash* because you don't necessarily need the flash but use it to create a better photo.

» **You want better light.** The flash is a nice, clean, pure burst of light that can look very good compared to some interior lighting. If you're in a room with yellows or reds (see Figure 2-10), your photos may have a strong color cast if you don't use a flash. A flash can clear up unwanted color tones. In this case, the color of the wood paneling behind my wife threatens to overpower the scene. Using the flash kept her from looking too warm.

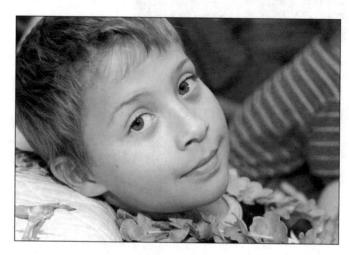

FIGURE 2-7: Interior photos often need flash.

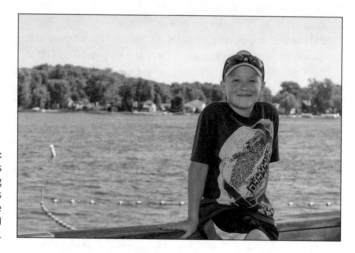

FIGURE 2-8: The flash helps even lighting differences between the background and subject.

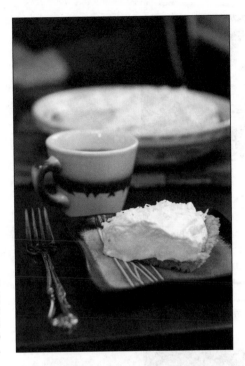

FIGURE 2-9:
Fill flash
brightens the
foreground and
makes the photo
look much better.

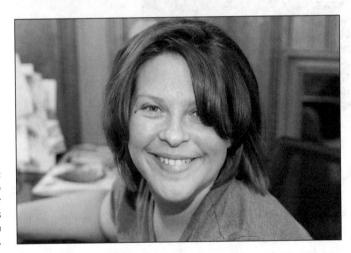

FIGURE 2-10:
Use the flash to
compensate for
strong yellows
and browns in
the scene.

REMEMBER

At times, the camera might suggest using flash when it senses low light levels, as shown in Figure 2-11. Pay attention to the cues in your viewfinder or on the back of the camera. Depending on the model you're using, the shutter speed, aperture, or ISO may flash, indicating that the camera is having trouble with the current exposure settings.

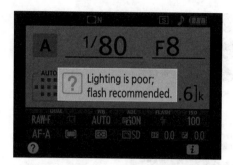

Disabling the built-in flash

You can disable your camera's flash from the menu when in an advanced exposure mode. Look for your camera's built-in flash options and set it to Disable, as shown in Figure 2-12. Although setting it to Disable might seem odd, you may want to pop the flash to help the camera focus using the AF-assist beam but not want it to fire for the exposure. Disabling it will prevent the flash from firing when raised without interfering with the operation of the AF-assist beam.

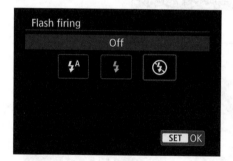

Tips on Using the Built-in Flash

Here's a list of things that will help make your flash photos better:

>> **Don't get too close.** Using a flash can mean harsh lighting if you're too close to your subject. Don't get right up into someone's business, as I did for the photo in Figure 2-13. Back off a bit.

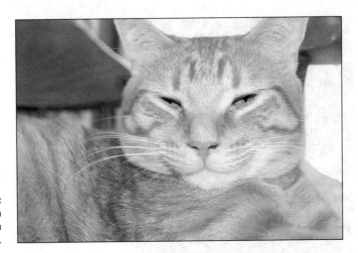

FIGURE 2-13:
Sneaking up on a
sleeping kitty with
a blinding flash.

» **Separate subjects from background.** A flash is a powerful burst of light. If subjects stand too close to a wall (or a fancy photography background), they'll cast distracting and unflattering shadows. Figure 2-14 shows an example. To correct it, move your subjects away from the background, use a light diffuser (softens the light the way a lampshade does; see Book 4, Chapter 3), or use an off-camera flash and angle it so that the shadow is hidden.

» **Use slow sync to brighten a dark background.** When the flash lights someone, often the camera thinks that the overall exposure is bright. It compensates by underexposing the background, which leaves it dark. If you don't mind the effect, it can work — and even hide a messy or unappealing background. However, to keep the background from being too dark, dial in negative flash compensation or use slow sync (an advanced option discussed later).

» **Work with your subjects.** At a certain age, all my kids became experts at flash blocking. Whenever I approached them with my camera and flash, they would throw an arm over their eyes. Work with your subjects to try to prevent flash reactivity. Some people are scared of the flash and cringe or close their eyes when they think it's going to go off. If you can, try to surprise them without scaring them, or reduce the flash intensity.

» **Avoid lens shadows.** Pop-up flashes aren't tall enough to shoot over large or long lenses and lens hoods. The lens casts an ugly shadow that ruins the photo. Know which lenses you can use with your pop-up flash and which focal lengths are safe to use with your zoom lenses.

» **Use flash compensation.** This simple solution is effective for solving many flash problems. I wholeheartedly recommend using flash compensation!

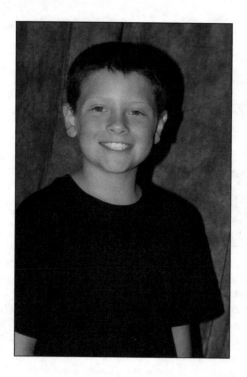

FIGURE 2-14:
Notice the strong shadow cast on the background.

>> **Consider an external (hot shoe) flash.** Buying an external flash unit (Canon calls them Speedlites; Nikon has Speedlights) that mounts in your camera's hot shoe is the next step into the larger world of flash photography and lighting. Using an external flash opens a number of creative possibilities, such as off-camera and wireless flash. You can also more easily direct, diffuse, and bounce light from external units. Most camera makers offer two or three external flash units in a range of prices and capabilities. External flash is covered in Book 4, Chapter 3.

>> **Practice.** Knowledge, combined with practical experience, is an unbeatable combination. Keep working with your flash to become an expert in using it.

REMEMBER

You don't have to become the end-all, be-all Master of Flash. You just have to know how to work your gear to create the photos you want. Start practicing in the situations you shoot most often.

Getting Fancy with the Flash

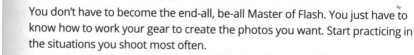

Quite often, your built-in flash just works. You can leave it on Auto most of the time and not worry about it. However, some techniques and settings will help you get more out of your flash and overcome problems when they arise. This section covers a few additional techniques and lists some more advanced options.

Enabling red-eye reduction

When you use the flash, ending up with photos of people who look like they have red, glowing eyes is not uncommon. Red-eye is caused by the pupils in the eye not closing fast enough in response to the flash, which allows light to reflect off the back of the interior surface of the eye. It's a problem mostly among people with light-colored eyes.

The effect can be very distracting and takes away from an otherwise good shot. Although you can try to remove red eyes in software, preventing it from happening is faster and easier.

Red-eye reduction causes the camera to emit a series of pulses from the built-in flash or Red-Eye Reduction Lamp, should it have one. These pulses cause the pupil to contract before you take the photo. Enable red-eye reduction from the camera's menu system (see Book 1, Chapter 4) or in the camera's flash settings, as shown in Figure 2-15.

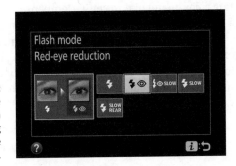

FIGURE 2-15:
Enable red-eye reduction when photographing people using the flash.

Canon dSLRs have a scale that appears in the viewfinder when the red-eye reduction feature is enabled, the flash is up, and you press the shutter button halfway to meter and focus. As you hold the shutter button halfway down, the scale shrinks and soon disappears. Red-eye reduction is most effective if you wait until this countdown process completes before taking the photo.

REMEMBER

I have one caveat that you should be aware of before enabling red-eye reduction. The pre-flashes delay the process of taking a photo, sometimes by several seconds. Don't count on being able to capture fast-paced action or catching people in natural, unposed shots when using this feature. If your subjects aren't aware of what's happening, they will often think that you've taken the photo when the pre-flashes fire, and then they start talking or blinking when you take the actual photo.

Using flash compensation

Flash compensation is a quick and easy way to adjust the strength of the flash without controlling it manually. In fact, it's the only way you can adjust the flash when your camera doesn't have a manual flash mode.

REMEMBER

If there's a flash technique that you should look into, flash compensation is it. Knowing how to manage flash compensation will help you take better flash photos reliably.

When you take a flash photo, review it before taking more shots. Note whether your subject is too dark or too bright. Compensate based on these factors:

>> **Dark subject:** Raise flash compensation or move closer.

>> **Bright subject:** Lower flash compensation or move farther away.

Check your camera manual for precise flash compensation details. You may be able to press a button or rotate a command dial to set it. Compensation is measured in stops of EV. With Canon cameras, you can also use the Quick Control screen. Press the Quick Control button and highlight Flash Exposure Compensation. After you press Set, the Flash Exposure Compensation screen appears, as shown in the left image in Figure 2-16. In this case, I have toned down the flash by 1.0 EV. After you set it, you should see an indicator on your LCD monitor, as shown on the right in Figure 2-16, or in the viewfinder.

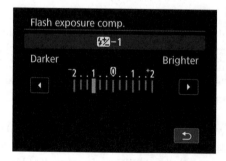
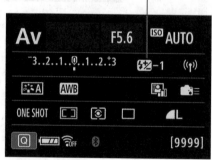

FIGURE 2-16: Negative numbers reduce the flash strength; positive numbers increase it.

TIP

Always look for telltale signs like the indicator shown in Figure 2-16 to remind you that you've made exposure adjustments. When you move on to another subject or different lighting, reset it.

Using FE Lock

Use Flash Exposure Lock (FE lock; sometimes called FV Lock) as you would Auto-exposure Lock (AE Lock). Meter the subject centered in the viewfinder, press the FE Lock button, and then recompose. The flash strength and overall exposure is locked until you release the button — even after taking multiple shots.

Controlling the flash strength manually

Setting the flash to manual mode lets you control the flash intensity yourself. Not all cameras have this feature. Through-the-lens (TTL) metering (and variations thereof) that takes the flash into account is disabled. In other words, you've switched off the targeting computer and are relying exclusively on the Force. Here's a quick guide:

1. **Switch to built-in flash control.**

To set the flash strength yourself, you must switch the flash from its normal, through-the-lens mode of operation to manual using the camera's menu, as shown in Figure 2-17. Depending on the camera, look for this feature in the built-in flash settings or in the shooting menu.

FIGURE 2-17:
Change to manual flash to set the flash strength yourself.

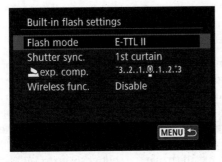
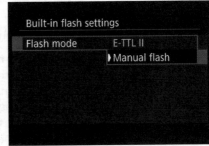

2. **Set the flash strength.**

Full power is considered normal (see the left image in Figure 2-18), and you *reduce it* to the level you desire (see the right image in Figure 2-18). Reduced flash strength is measured as a fraction of full power, and you reduce the power in steps.

TIP

If you're not comfortable using the flash manually, stay in automated TTL flash metering mode and use distance and flash compensation to tweak the flash.

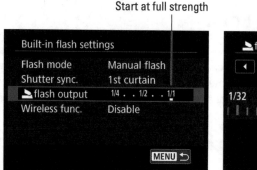

FIGURE 2-18:
Setting flash strength manually reduces the power from full strength.

Unlocking more advanced features

Depending on your camera, the built-in flash may have many more features available to it. You may hardly ever need them, but here is a list of more advanced flash options worth knowing about:

» **TTL Metering** meters through the lens. You may be able to change the TTL metering method. For example, Canon cameras have three settings: Evaluative (Face Priority); plain old Evaluative; and Average (see Figure 2-19). Evaluative (Face Priority) is optimized to make people look good. Evaluative tries to get the closest object exposure correct, even if that means that the background is underexposed. Average accounts for the entire scene and generally fires a stronger flash.

» **Slow Synchro (formerly flash sync in AV mode)** is a feature on Canon dSLRs. It gives you some control over the flash sync speed when you have the camera set to aperture-priority or Program AE mode. As shown in Figure 2-20, there are three settings. In each case, the maximum shutter speed is limited by the camera's flash sync speed. Each setting restricts the slowest shutter speed in a different way. The first allows shutter speeds up to 30 seconds. The second setting limits the minimum shutter speed to 1/60 second, which helps keep your handheld shots from being blurry. The third setting fixes the shutter speed when using the flash in aperture-priority mode to 1/200 second. This is the best way to reduce or prevent subject blur or fuzziness due to camera shake.

>> **Slow-sync flash** (see Figure 2-21) is a Nikon option that slows the shutter speed and fires the flash at the end of the exposure. The result is a brighter background. Slow-sync flash works well indoors if you're shooting casual shots or portraits with still subjects. You can also take some great shots with movement in the background and a clear subject.

TIP

Pay attention to shutter speed and blur. If you don't want blur, switch out of slow-sync flash or use a tripod.

>> **Rear-curtain sync (or second curtain)** flashes just before the exposure ends, as opposed to when it begins (normal, front curtain, or first curtain). You can shoot some creative scenes using rear-curtain flash and moving vehicles or people with lights. The lights move through the scene and the flash freezes things to finish the shot. I'm setting this option in Figure 2-22.

TECHNICAL STUFF

>> **Wireless (or Commander)** lets you take flash photos with external flash units that don't have to be hard-wired to the camera (see Book 4, Chapter 3). The wireless setting uses infrared or radio signals to activate one or more external flashes. When acting as the *commander,* the camera's internal flash fires a low-powered pulse to set off one or more external flashes. Figure 2-23 shows several options available on a mid-range Canon camera that enable the built-in flash to control one or more external Speedlite flashes. Not all cameras can be a wireless master.

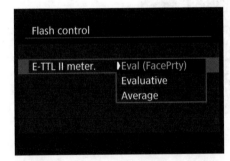

FIGURE 2-19: Canon dSLRs offer three flash metering options.

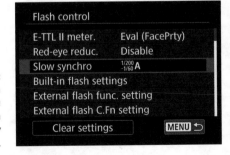

FIGURE 2-20: This Canon option gives you control over flash sync speed in Av and P modes.

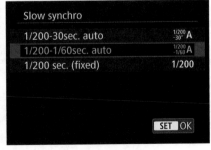

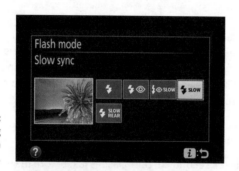

FIGURE 2-21:
Enabling
slow-sync flash
on a Nikon dSLR.

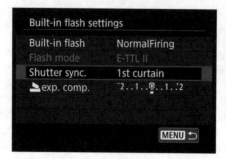

FIGURE 2-22:
The difference
between these
options is when
the flash fires.

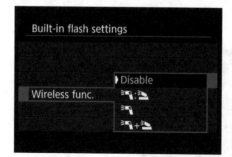

FIGURE 2-23:
The built-in
flash can often
wirelessly trigger
external units.

Chapter **3**

Using an External Flash and Accessories

As good as built-in pop-up flashes are, they have some limitations. They're attached to your camera and shoot directly ahead at a constant angle. You can't tilt or swivel them. Longer lenses sometimes get in the way and cast shadows. An *external flash* mounts to the top of your camera and solves these problems along with adding other impressive features. In doing so, an external flash opens a world of other creative lighting possibilities.

Although the built-in flash is certainly better than nothing, if you're interested in upping your game and using an external flash, this chapter is for you. I show you what an external flash looks like, what the parts are, and how to attach and remove it from your camera. I discuss various accessories and then finish with a number of different techniques that will make your flash photos better. If I hadn't written this chapter, I would be reading it!

Getting to Know External Flash Units

Companies like Canon, Nikon, Sony, and others generally offer at least one small external flash that provides basic features in an inexpensive package. These models may not offer bounce or tilt functionality, do not have many external controls, and do not have a display. They do, however, move the flash up and off the camera, and can be mounted on stands and used off-camera with longer flash cords that connect the hot shoe to the flash (see the later section, "Handling an External Flash").

Aside from showing you the basic Nikon external flash in Figure 3-1, I don't cover this type in detail in this chapter. It's one of the few simple models that has a tilting head that can bounce light off of ceilings or walls.

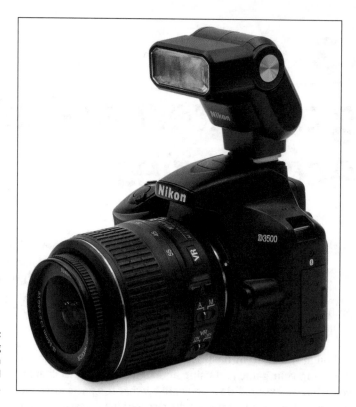

FIGURE 3-1:
This nice-looking flash from Nikon is a basic external model that tilts.

Companies like Canon and Nikon often have two or more styles of large external flashes that have additional features compared to their smaller counterparts, come with external controls and displays, and tilt and swivel. Typically, one of these models is a midrange unit listed at a moderate price (although still pretty expensive, if you ask me). The other is the company's top-of-the-line external flash. The flagship model typically looks quite a bit like the midrange model but has extra functions and features meant for professionals.

WHAT'S IN A NAME?

Different companies call external flashes by different names. I use the general term *external flash* or *flash* unless I'm referring to a specific flash name. You might run across some of these names:

- Canon: Speedlite
- Nikon: Speedlight
- Olympus: Flash
- Pentax: Electronic Flash Unit
- Sony: Flash, flash unit, external flash

Although most external flashes are pretty similar, some flashes, such as ring flashes, look very different. A ring flash is a specialized type of flash unit designed to mount on your camera and shoot around the lens. These flashes are well suited to macro, close-up, and portrait photography.

Looking at the front

Although I use a Canon flash in this section, most flashes in this category look very similar and offer comparable features. The front of the flash (see Figure 3-2) contains all the elements needed to light the scene. It may also contain different helpers.

» **Flash head:** The part that holds the flash. All but the most basic models rotate up and swivel from side to side. Most lock in place; you set them free with the release button. Some snap into place or move under resistance.

Not all flashes bounce or swivel. Some heads (entry-level models, normally) sit on top of the body and point straight ahead.

» **Flash:** Here comes the light. Pay attention to where it's pointing. Small differences in positioning can make big differences in photos.

Snap or push diffusers like the Sto-Fen Omni-Bounce directly on the end of the flash. Other accessories, such as small soft boxes, also fit over the end of the head. Some accessories rely on hook-and-loop fasteners. Wrap the loop around the head and fix it securely to itself. The piece with the hook part attaches to it.

>> **Built-in wide panel:** A built-in wide panel is a handy aspect of many external flashes. The panel slides out and drops over the flash, directing the light from the flash to cover a wider area. Most flashes have these panels, but some aren't built in. If that's the case, the flash case should have a place to store the panel. Snap it on the flash head to use it. Pop it off when you're done.

Flip the wide panel down when you're using a wide-angle lens. When you pull the panel out, the flash should automatically set itself to that focal length. If not, set the proper zoom on the flash. When you finish, lift the adapter and slide it back in.

>> **Body:** Here are the guts — the controls, batteries, connections, and mounting foot.

>> **Mounting foot:** This is a metal or plastic plate that slides into the camera's hot shoe. The mounting foot is one of the more critical parts of an external flash. Make sure that the foot is clean and not bent. Most cameras use a standard *hot shoe,* a metal guide that sits on top of the camera. Sony has a different type of connection than the other manufacturers, and although it is not compatible with them, it serves the same purpose.

Beneath the foot are the electrical contacts that connect the camera to the flash.

- Don't try to place a flash unit on an incompatible camera. You can short out the flash or the camera.

- When mounting the flash on an external light stand with a shoe adapter (as opposed to using a mini stand that has built-in protection), protect the contacts from touching metal by covering them with a bit of electrical tape. When finished, make sure no residue from the tape is left on the contacts. If you're concerned about leaving residue, use a piece of paper or other slim, non-conductive barrier.

>> **AF-assist beam/illuminator:** This feature helps the camera autofocus when the lighting is too dim for the camera's normal autofocus sensor to work. You can usually set boundaries for this feature in the camera's menu.

When the flash is mounted *off-camera* (it's wired to the camera, but not connected directly to the hot shoe), AF-assist doesn't work unless you're using a cord that supports the feature.

>> **Wireless sensor:** The sensor that detects signals from the camera that tell it what to do and when. Pay attention to the direction the sensor faces and be sure not to block it.

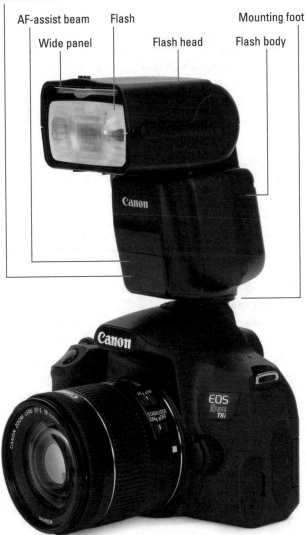

Wireless sensor

AF-assist beam   Flash   Mounting foot

Wide panel   Flash head   Flash body

Canon

Canon

EOS
REBEL
T8i

CANON ZOOM LENS EF-S 18-55mm

STABILIZER
ON | OFF

ø58mm

FIGURE 3-2:
Midrange flash
has power to tilt,
swivel, and more.

From the back and sides

You'll see a lot more of the flash sides and back. The back (shown in Figure 3-3) is where you control the unit.

» **Lock-release button:** Press this button to unlock the flash head and change the bounce or swivel angles. The button pops back out when you release it, locking the head in that position. Depending on the brand of flash you have, bounce may be called tilt and swivel may be called rotate.

If your unit has a locking button, *don't force the head* — you might break it.

>> **Bounce angle index:** Raised marks on the head show you the flash's bounce angle (the angle the flash is pointing at when not looking straight up; see ahead to "Bouncing and diffusing," in this chapter). Knowing the angle helps you duplicate setups.

>> **Swivel-angle index:** A swivel index that shows how far from center you've swiveled the flash head. The index is hidden beneath the flash head in Figure 3-2.

When holding the camera vertically, swivel the flash to bounce light off the ceiling. If holding the camera horizontally, you may find it helpful to swivel the flash and bounce light off a reflector or neutral-colored wall.

>> **Battery cover:** A plastic piece covers the area where you insert batteries. To open the battery compartment, press the cover and slide it toward the bottom of the unit to release the catch. The cover (which can fit tightly) reveals the batteries. Be sure to slide down the cover completely and exert the force necessary to open it.

>> **Battery compartment:** Put your batteries here. Four AA batteries seem to be the standard for larger flash units. Smaller, entry-level models may need only two.

Make sure you point your batteries the right way. Sometimes the orientation marks are inside the compartment instead of the door, which makes it tougher to see them. You should also remove the batteries from your flash when you're not going to use it for a while.

>> **Ready light:** Your flash may have a ready light on it. This tells you that it's ready to fire. The camera may blink the light or turn it a different color to relay more information about the status of the flash. Check your camera manual for details.

>> **Lock:** You may use a locking lever or ring to secure the flash on top of the hot shoe. Turn or slide the lever one way to lock the flash. Turn or slide it the other way to release the flash. A flash may also click into place.

>> **Controls:** Most flashes have several buttons and controls on the backs. Use them to control the flash.

>> **LCD panel:** Most midrange and above flashes have large LCD screens. They show you all the details of how your flash is set up and which mode you're in so that you can glance at the flash and see what's going on.

>> **Other indicators:** The back of the flash always seems to have room for another light or indicator.

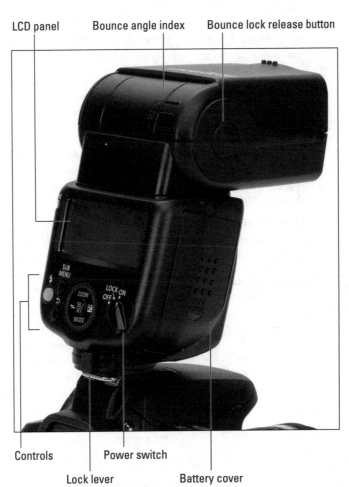

LCD panel   Bounce angle index   Bounce lock release button

FIGURE 3-3:
The rear of the flash unit has important features and controls.

Controls   Power switch

Lock lever   Battery cover

Accessorizing your external flash

Some flashes come with extras such as a diffuser and a couple of gels that you can use right out of the box. You can also find flash bundles that have many more helpful products as part of a large package.

Here are some accessories that you can use to modify your external flash:

>> **Diffusers:** A flash diffuser softens the light emitted by the flash, (ideally) getting rid of harsh shadows on your subjects. Diffusers come in a couple of varieties:

- **Hard plastic:** You can see mine in Figure 3-4. It's just a little plastic cover, but it works. If you buy it separately from your flash, make sure to buy one that's compatible with your flash unit. This one conveniently came with the flash and is technically called a Bounce Adapter by Canon. Push it onto the head so that it fits securely and doesn't fall off the first time you take a step.

Check to see whether the brand you like comes in different colors. Sto-Fen also has diffusers in green (for fluorescent lighting) and gold (to warm subjects).

- **Soft box:** Fits on the flash head. Assembly is often required. The box slips over the end of the flash and extends some distance in front. I don't normally use it when the flash is mounted on the camera, because the box dips down a little. Mounted on a stand or sitting on a table, it's ideal.

- **Other creative diffusers:** Look for other creative diffusers and accessories online or at your favorite camera shop. There are many diffusers and accessories, including collapsible panels and diffuser socks.

>> **Bounce accessories:** Although you can find several types and brands of flash bouncers, LumiQuest (`www.lumiquest.com`) has a wide selection. It has products that will bounce, reflect, and diffuse light from your flash, all at the same time. They attach to the front of your flash with the help of a hook-and-loop strap, which you aim upward (your flash must be able to point up). Light from the flash hits the surface of the bouncer and is reflected toward the subject. In the process, it's softened. The downside to this type of setup is that you have to ensure enough headroom to use it, and there's the danger of coming across like a superflash freak.

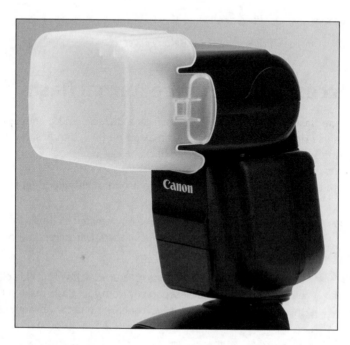

FIGURE 3-4:
You can't get any easier than this type of flash diffuser.

REMEMBER

>> **Mini stand:** Some flashes come with a mini stand (see Figure 3-5), also known as a *flash stand* or *Speedlight stand*. You can mount the flash on this small, plastic stand. If your flash doesn't come with one, you may be able to buy one.

The stand is useful for taking the flash off-camera (if it can go wireless) and putting it on a table or the floor. Plus, its light stand socket underneath gives you an easy way to mount the flash on a larger light stand.

>> **Wide-angle adapter:** Buy this adapter if your flash has no built-in adapter. It helps spread the light from the flash out to cover the additional angle of view that wide-angle lenses capture.

>> **Colored gel or filter:** Look for colored gel filters to add ambiance to a scene or use them for color correction.

>> **Adapter, bracket, cord, coupler:** The number of ways you can connect your flash to other gear is dizzying. Look for all these pieces of equipment to get connected. Check the manual that came with your flash for additional guidance.

>> **Case:** Flash cases are useful. They protect the flash and hold small accessories.

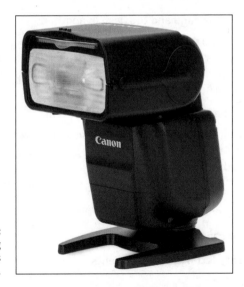

FIGURE 3-5:
Aside from being cute, mini stands are very useful.

At some point, you may want to look into studio-style lighting modifiers like umbrellas and soft boxes. By this time, you may need a background and extra lights. As your setup gets more complicated, you will need to connect everything together (wirelessly or wired).

Using an External Flash and Accessories

Handling an External Flash

This section details some of the camera-to-flash connections that you can make with your flash. There's the tried-and-true hot-shoe method, but also several other wired and wireless options for you to consider. Each has its own rationale.

Attaching it to your camera

Connecting an external flash to your camera is pretty easy. If you're not used to it, practice a few times so that you get used to handling the camera and flash at the same time. Use a camera strap or tripod for additional support.

WARNING

Don't force the flash onto a hot shoe if it seems to be sticking. Forcing could bend or break the flash foot or hot shoe on the camera. In addition, exercise care when threading items onto a stand or adapter. If the threads aren't aligned properly, things can get stuck together.

These steps can help:

1. **Turn off the flash and your camera.**

2. **Hold the camera in one hand and the flash in another.**

   Experiment until you find the most comfortable method for you. I like to hold the camera with my right hand so that I have the grip to hold onto while I work the flash with my left hand. Discerning readers will notice that the pretty hands in Figure 3-6 are not mine; they are my wife's.

3. **Bring the flash in line with the hot shoe and slide it in.**

   Line up the mounting foot with the camera's hot shoe, as shown in Figure 3-6. This process takes place mostly by feel. When you slide the flash straight onto the shoe, you should hear a click.

WARNING

4. **If you have a lock, lock down the flash.**

   Don't forget this step or the flash could slide off the camera!

5. **Turn on the camera and flash.**

6. **Make any necessary settings or adjustments.**

   You're ready to rock.

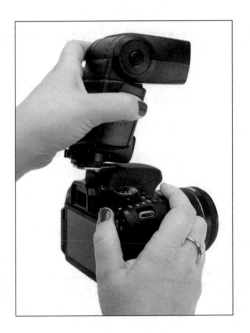

FIGURE 3-6:
Carefully align the
mounting foot
with the hot shoe
on the camera.

Removing the flash

Removing the flash from your camera is the reverse of putting it on. Follow these steps:

1. **Turn off the camera and flash.**

2. **Grip the camera with one hand.**

3. **While supporting the flash, release it.**

   This step may involve turning a ring, moving a lever, or pushing a button.

   Keep one hand on the flash at this point so that it doesn't fall. I like holding my camera pointed down a bit for this step so that the flash can't slide off on its own.

WARNING

4. **Slide the flash out of the shoe.**

   Slide it straight back so that it doesn't bind in the rails.

5. **Secure the camera, if desired.**

   You may want to put the camera down temporarily so that you aren't juggling everything at one time. If you have it secured to you with a strap, be careful of letting it swing while you put the flash away. It's easy to bump the camera into things when you're focusing on the flash.

6. **Secure the flash in its case or your camera bag.**

Tilting and swiveling the flash head

If you have a flash that can be tilted and swiveled, practice a bit before you really need it. When it becomes second nature, you'll be more likely to use this amazingly cool feature. Here's my technique:

1. **Secure the camera and flash.**

    If the flash is attached on the camera or a stand, hold and stabilize the camera or stand with your right hand.

2. **Push and hold the lock-release button with your left thumb.**

    You should grasp the flash head in the palm of your left hand, as shown in Figure 3-7, to provide the leverage you need to push the button. Use the same grip approach to position the flash head.

3. **Position the flash head.**

    Rotate the flash head upward to tilt, or turn the flash head left or right to swivel. Do not go beyond the limits of the flash or you'll crunch it. Remember, this stuff is basically plastic.

4. **Release the button.**

    You're primed and ready to bounce your flash.

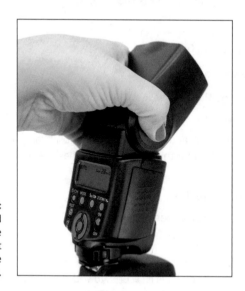

FIGURE 3-7: Make sure to hold the lock-release button as you tilt and swivel the head.

To tilt or swivel the flash when it's not mounted to anything, grip and hold the base of the flash with your left hand, then use your right hand to grasp the flash head. Your right thumb will be in the perfect position to push the lock-release button and tilt or swivel the head.

Attaching a mini stand

To mount the flash on a mini stand, follow these steps:

1. **Make sure that the flash is turned off.**

2. **Connect the mini stand to the flash.**

   - If the stand isn't attached to anything (such as a light stand), hold the flash body in your hand and slide the mini stand onto the mounting foot.

   - If the mini stand is already mounted on a light stand, slide the flash onto the stand rather than sliding the mini stand onto the flash.

3. **Lock down the flash, if you can.**

   To mount the mini stand to a light stand, screw it on.

Working the controls

This section briefly describes the common flash controls. Figure 3-8 shows the back side of a typical midrange Canon Speedlite.

Read your manual for detailed instructions for working your flash. Your flash has controls similar to these:

- **Power switch:** In this case, the flash combines a power switch with a locking mechanism that keeps you from accidentally pressing buttons or jogging the dial and changing values.

- **Mode button:** Most flash units have several shooting modes. Use the Mode button to switch among them. Read your flash manual for details.

- **Function buttons:** Pressing these buttons either turns things on or off or cycles through various settings. The settings, in millimeters, should match the focal length of your lens (or come close if they're midway). This flash has a sub-menu button that enables you to access different options.

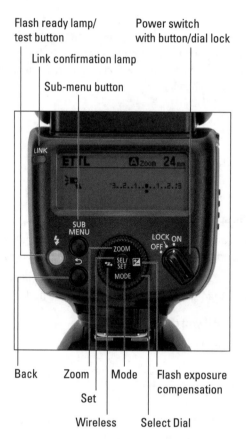

Flash ready lamp/
test button

Power switch
with button/dial lock

Link confirmation lamp

Sub-menu button

FIGURE 3-8:
These controls
are common to
most external
flash units.

Back   Zoom   Mode   Flash exposure
compensation

Set

Wireless   Select Dial

>> **Wireless button:** Puts the flash in wireless mode. Very handy.

>> **Test flash button and ready lamp:** On this model, the lamp that tells you the flash is ready and the button to test it is the same button.

>> **Select/set button:** Press the Select/Set button to choose options.

>> **Increment/decrement button or dials:** Your flash may let you increase or decrease setting values (like focal lengths) or scroll through options. If so, use the increment/decrement buttons or dials to adjust the values.

>> **Other controls:** As mentioned in an earlier section, some flashes have other controls and indicators that aren't listed here. Some work for a single purpose and some work for multiple purposes.

>> **Two-button controls:** Some flashes require you to press and hold two buttons simultaneously in order to access certain settings and information.

>> **Navigating:** Your camera manual tells you how to get around the menu. Some buttons switch options; some buttons change the value of the option you're looking at.

Configuring Your External Flash

Because each flash is different, I can't show you specifics for every option. Turn to Book 4, Chapter 2 for general information on most flash modes, and read your flash manual.

I can make some general observations about two main parts: your settings and your standings.

Look for these options in your camera or flash menu:

>> **Flash Control menu:** Some cameras group built-in and external flash settings under a single flash menu. Select the flash menu (see the left image in Figure 3-9) to view flash settings (shown on the right in Figure 3-9). If your camera uses a separate menu for the external flash, select it instead.

>> **Functions (shown on the left in Figure 3-10):** Spend a lot of time reading your camera and flash manual; standard external flash functions generally include changing the metering method, the focal length, high-speed sync, curtain synchronization, adding flash compensation, or controlling flash exposure bracketing.

>> **Custom functions (shown on the right in Figure 3-10):** Custom functions enable you to customize some features on your flash. Maybe you never could get conversions down and just have a general feeling of high-school dread when faced with the metric system; you may be able to change the distance display from meters to feet. Check into every nook and cranny for useful ways to work the way you want. You don't always have to leave things on their defaults.

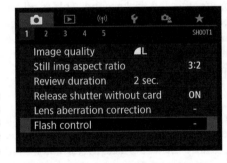
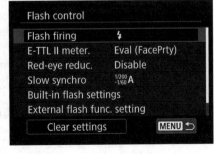

FIGURE 3-9: This camera puts all flash settings under a single menu.

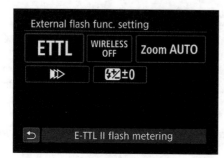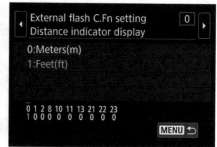

FIGURE 3-10:
Investigating normal flash functions and custom functions.

Trying Different Techniques

An *external* flash (the flash unit that you can attach to your camera, not where you mount it) is useful and a lot of fun. Although built-in flashes are capable, an external flash:

>> Offers more directional flexibility.

>> Has more power.

>> Gives you more creative freedom.

This section covers some of the techniques that are possible using *one* external flash. You can add more. The more you add, the more creative you can be.

Using high-speed sync

A flash is a useful device to have, even when you don't think you need one. Forcing the flash to fire, called *fill flash,* often makes your subjects look better and balance the brightness of the foreground and background. This is all well and good, but there are times when you run into exposure problems. If you need to use a faster shutter speed to counteract bright sunlight and wider apertures, enable your camera's high-speed sync feature (shown on the left in Figure 3-11). As shown on the right in Figure 3-11, you'll be able to use faster shutter speeds. Remember, this feature is available only when you have an external flash fitted.

High-speed sync (HSS) bypasses the camera's sync speed by pulsing the flash throughout the exposure. Figure 3-12 shows how effective this technique can be. I wanted to use a fill flash to keep my wife's face lit. Normally, that's not a problem. However, we were outside on a sunny day, and I also wanted to use a wide aperture. At 1/2000 second, the shutter speed needed to capture the shot was far faster than the flash sync speed. I was able to successfully use the settings I wanted by enabling HSS.

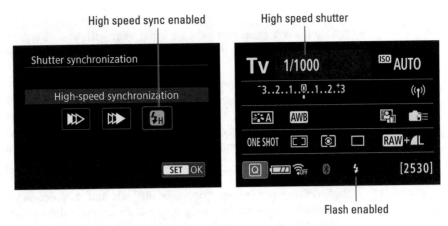

High speed sync enabled

High speed shutter

Flash enabled

FIGURE 3-11:
Enabling HSS
opens faster
shutter speeds.

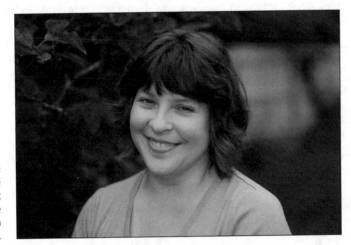

FIGURE 3-12:
HSS enabled me
to use fill light
and a wide
aperture on a
bright day.

REMEMBER

High-speed sync doesn't take you into some sort of super slow-mo, action-freezing mode. HSS lets you use fill flash outside on a bright day, or in a studio with bright lights, with a wide-open lens. This is an especially effective technique when shooting portraits.

Bouncing and diffusing

Bouncing (reflecting the flash off of a nearby surface) and *diffusing* (putting a translucent material between the flash and the subject) are two techniques you can employ to soften light from the flash. They both make shadows less prominent, reduce the chance of red-eye, and create a more natural shot.

Bouncing literally bounces light from the flash off a ceiling or other surface. Depending on how you're holding the camera, tilt or swivel the flash head so that it points at the ceiling or wall. The great thing about bouncing the flash is that you can do it even when you have no other gear with you. It's the ultimate fail-safe solution, provided you have an external flash unit with a tilt/swivel head.

Diffusing the flash requires extra equipment. Diffusers come in many shapes and sizes, including soft boxes, plastic diffusers, umbrellas, and more. Depending on what type you have, you mount it directly on the flash or between the flash and the subject. Many large diffusers require that you mount the flash off-camera and trigger it with a long cord or wirelessly. Diffusers have the same effect as lampshades. Light from the flash hits the diffuser, spreads out, and softens.

High ceilings make bouncing more difficult and may not provide enough light. If you're in this situation, switch to a diffuser and point the flash straight at the subject. You may want to consider picking up a circular diffuser. They come in different sizes. I love my large diffuser (shown in Figure 3-13) and use it all the time, even when not using the flash. I can mount it on a stand, as shown in the figure, or have someone hold it between the bright sun and my subject. It's also very useful in the studio. I hold it between continuous lighting and very reflective subjects.

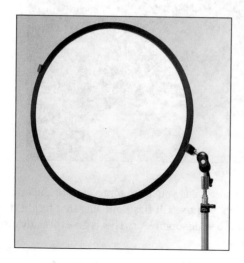

FIGURE 3-13:
This large diffuser is very practical.

Using an umbrella

Umbrellas are just what you'd expect, except they won't keep rain off your head. *Umbrellas* diffuse light from the flash even better than bouncing or using a diffuser does. The catch is that you have to set up the umbrella on a stand with the flash, as shown in Figure 3-14. That limits how portable and spontaneous you can be. However, the results are almost always fantastic.

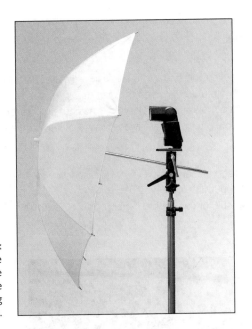

FIGURE 3-14: Umbrellas are very effective tools to have when shooting portraits.

To control your flash on a light stand with an umbrella, try enabling the wireless feature, if possible, and use your camera's built-in flash to trigger the remote external flash. You can also buy an off-camera cord that extends the range of your hot shoe or wirelessly trigger the flash. Vello (www.vellogear.com) makes a line of wireless flash triggers for different brands of flash.

Focusing light with a snoot

Have you ever watched an old *Star Trek* episode in which Captain Kirk sits in the captain's chair and his eyes are brightly lit but the rest of his face isn't? The film crew created that effect with a *snoot,* a tube on the end of the flash; it keeps the flash tightly focused on the subject. The longer the snoot, the more focused the lighting. The shorter the snoot, the more the light expands. You can even make your own snoot out of things you have on hand. In a pinch, I've used cereal boxes and tape to make snoots.

I took the photo of my son in Figure 3-15 using Gary Fong's Collapsible snoot with the PowerGrid attached. I also moved the flash off-camera to my left and back some. This meant I was closer to him than the flash was. The result is a portrait that has a lot of close-up detail, creative side lighting, interesting shadow, and a dark background. This shot would be impossible to capture with a straight-on flash.

LIGHTSPHERE

Gary Fong's Lightsphere Collapsible has a soft, collapsible diffuser that fits on the end of your external flash. It diffuses and softens your flash. You can customize the Lightsphere with different domes and gels. Gary Fong has other accessories available, including a snoot with an optional grid that divides the snoot into sections that further tighten the light beam.

Your mileage may vary, but I've been completely impressed with every aspect of this kit. A lot of ingenious people out there are devoted to making your flash photos the best they can be. If Gary Fong isn't for you, look at other products by other makers.

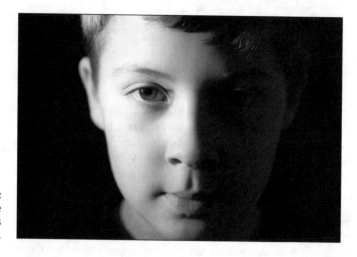

FIGURE 3-15:
Snoots are wonderful tools to use.

Using a stand

Moving the flash off the camera and using a light stand has some advantages. You can position the flash in locations that don't depend on the camera, allowing you to light the subject from different angles. You can light the subject or background, enhance or eliminate shadows, and do all sorts of other things — with one flash. A stand also enables you to move the light closer or farther away from the subject than you are. Aside from positioning, large stands enable you to use accessories like umbrellas, which attach to the stand.

TIP

Keep these points in mind when you shop for a light stand:

>> **Watch your weight.** Some stands are big and beefy. Some are flimsy. Make sure to buy a stand that's made for the weight you're going to put on it.

Although generally light, umbrellas can be large and extend out from the stand, affecting the center of gravity.

>> **Learn to adapt.** Your flash needs an adapter because its bottom is designed to attach to a hot shoe, not a tripod. A mini stand is the easiest adapter for mounting a flash to a light stand.

Elevating the flash with a bracket

I was skeptical at first about flash brackets. They make your dSLR look like an old-fashioned press camera with the flash on the side. I stuck with it and it started making sense. You can also use a setup like this to help prevent red-eye. Repositioning the flash so that it's not above the lens prevents people from looking at the flash.

TIP

Photographers who mainly hold their cameras vertically know that when you attach an external flash to the camera's hot shoe, the flash sticks out to the side, not on top. Even if you can swivel the flash, it's no longer elevated. By putting the flash on a bracket, you can position the flash so that it works more like a traditional flash on the hot shoe. I think that's a great idea.

You need a short flash cord to connect your flash to the camera. Buy one that supports the features you need to work on your flash.

Cords galore

Not all of us can go wireless. Here are options for those photographers who still need to be physically connected:

>> **Sync cord:** One solution to connecting your camera to an external flash is to wire the camera and flash together using *sync cords*. Not all flash units — nor all cameras — have sync cord sockets. Most often, you have to buy the most expensive unit a manufacturer makes to get one. Sync cords are becoming increasingly rare.

>> **Off-camera cord:** You can buy different types of cords that let you take your flash off the camera. Although technically they aren't sync cords, these cords serve the same purpose: Attach one end to the camera's hot shoe and the other end to the flash's mounting foot, as shown in Figure 3-16. Presto — they're connected. This type of cord is a workaround for not having a sync cord terminal on your flash or camera.

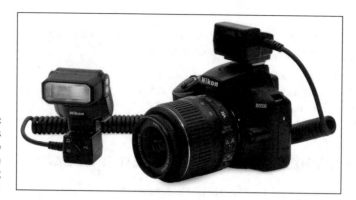

FIGURE 3-16:
Off-camera cords enable you to position the flash without going wireless.

TIP

Using a longer off-camera flash cord is useful when I want to use fast shutter speeds with my external flash unit but want to position it off-camera. Wireless setups may not support the shutter speed you need.

Going wireless

When you move your external flash off-camera (whether wired with cords or connected wirelessly via infrared, optical, or radio signals), it's called a *remote flash* or *strobe.* Unless you're telekinetic, you need a way to trigger your off-camera flash. Depending on your camera model and flash, you might be able to choose from one or more of these *remote triggering methods.* Make sure that everything's compatible; not all cameras support all methods of off-camera flash and not all external flash units can be controlled in every way.

REMEMBER

Setting up a wireless shoot is *easy* as long as your equipment is capable of wireless control. Set up the camera and flash to work wirelessly using your camera's flash menu and the controls on your flash unit. If necessary, make sure they're on the same group and channel. Within a few button presses, you'll be in business.

Wireless IR or optical pulse

Most midlevel and advanced flash units support one of two types of connectivity. Technically, they're different, but practically speaking, they act the same:

>> Wireless infrared (IR)

>> Optical pulse

REMEMBER

Check the manuals for your camera and external flash to make sure that they use the same method. Wireless IR and pulse aren't compatible with each other.

Using either system is as easy as eating cake, and you don't have to buy anything extra to get it to work.

1. **Set up your flash on a light stand or a small flash stand.**

2. **Set up your camera and flash for wireless mode.**

   Both types of wireless units can only go so far (and bend at certain angles) from the camera.

3. **Make sure that the flash and camera are on the same group and channel.**

   Remember to consult your manual for specifics on how to check and change these settings. The group and channel assignment should be visible on the back of the flash unit. You'll have to find the camera's settings in the menu.

You can also buy a dedicated wireless transmitter, as shown in Figure 3-17. This unit replaces the built-in flash as the method of communication. It has enhanced wireless features and provides triggering capability for cameras without a flash.

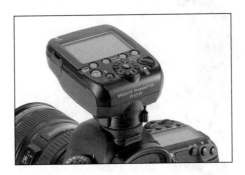

FIGURE 3-17:
This is a dedicated wireless transmitter.

If you don't want your camera's built-in flash to affect the scene, but *do* want to use the built-in flash as a wireless trigger, consider buying an IR panel. These panels block the light from the internal flash but allow the infrared signal to pass and trigger the external unit.

Wireless radio

You can try wireless radio remote flash triggers. In this case, transmitters send out radio signals that connect your camera with an external flash. Put the transmitter on your camera's hot shoe, and put the receiver on your flash unit. Third-party makers such as PocketWizard offer wireless radio. Camera manufacturers are following suit.

TIP

Radio systems can support multiple flash units as long as you have enough receivers, but the more flashes you have to control, the more expensive wireless radios can get. Radio has a longer range and better placement options (it doesn't have to be in front of the transmitter) than wireless IR does.

Wireless optical receiver

Figure 3-18 shows a strobe that is triggered by another flash. This is a wireless receiver. It relies on sensing the flash from your camera to know when to fire.

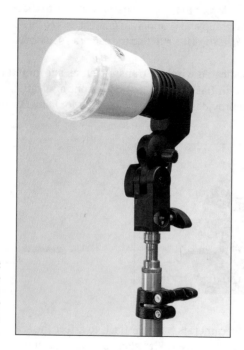

FIGURE 3-18:
This strobe responds to a flash signal or a sync cord as a receiver.

5
Managing and Processing Your Shots

Contents at a Glance

Chapter **1**

Transferring and Managing Files

File management — yikes.

You probably bought a dSLR camera to *take* pictures and movies, not to *manage* them. I know I did. I realized early on, though, that hundreds of photos quickly turn into thousands of photos and thousands multiply into tens of thousands. Photos are like rabbits, I tell ya! Movies, on the other hand, are just big slugs that take up tons of space.

Before things get out of control, start laying down the law of file management. Conveniently, that is the subject of this chapter. I show you which software to use, how to keep track of things, and how to establish a big-picture workflow.

Getting a Workflow

Workflow is an important topic in the digital SLR world. We do so much more with our photos and movies than post them on Instagram. You can do that, of course, but after you get your photos and movies out of the camera, you are able to organize, sort, rate, tag, process, edit, print, and archive them. Fun stuff? Eh. Not really, but the end product is so rewarding that it's worth the effort.

So what is *workflow?* Well, it has a few meanings. In a larger sense, it describes the process you follow as you work with your photos and movies, starting from the beginning until you're ready to archive them for long-term storage. It also means the more limited process you follow to edit and publish your shots.

That sounds simple enough. The problem is, people get all freaky-deaky about debating the details. Favorite topics include whether you should sharpen before you reduce noise or whether you should adjust brightness and contrast before you correct color. No universal workflow exists — all are based, in part, on opinion.

For the sake of getting something specific down on paper, here's a good general workflow to start with:

1. **In-camera choices.** Your workflow starts with the decisions you make when setting up the camera to take photos and movies. You may prefer working with Raw photos, for instance, instead of JPEGs. Perhaps you like setting the white balance yourself, or are shooting exposure-bracketed photos. This stuff is what this first step is about.

2. **Transfer (and import) files.** Moving photos and movies from your camera to a computer is to *transfer* them. You might say download, or even upload. It's crazy, right? In many cases, this means simultaneously *importing* them into your photo management software. I like to immediately back up my files after I transfer them to my computer.

3. **Manage.** Organize, sort, rate, geotag, filter, delete, and add keywords to your photos and movies in your management software.

4. **Fast photo processing.** Quickly develop the photos that you think are worth keeping by using a photo-processing application such as Adobe Lightroom. For example, you can make many photos look a lot better by tweaking brightness, contrast, and color, and making a few other basic adjustments. Making these tweaks doesn't take long. The idea is to spend a little time improving your photos and getting them printed or posted online. This step applies to Raw and JPEG images.

5. **Complex editing.** You can also perform more complex work using a photo editor such as Adobe Photoshop. For example, you can make targeted adjustments with masks, mash up different versions of the same shot, exercise more control over removing dust and other distractions, and much more. Some photos (especially HDR and panoramas) and movies require special software.

6. **Publish.** The entire point of the workflow is to create a finished product worth publishing. It might be a JPEG to place on your web page or Flickr photostream, or a high-quality TIFF to print. Moviemakers will normally publish a finished MP4 or MOV file. You can play them or upload to YouTube, for example, which reprocesses movies in order to stream them effectively.

7. **Archive.** Back up the original files. In addition, save any additional processing or editing you've done, either in the form of edited files or catalogs, in long-term storage.

REMEMBER

You can tailor this workflow example to suit your needs. In fact, you'll do a lot of tailoring, depending on several factors:

>> **Movies:** Do you need to change your workflow to work with movies that you've shot with your dSLR? That means more software and a substantially different editing and publishing process.

>> **Other people:** Do you have to fit into a process created by other people? Does someone else need to view or approve your work? Are you doing the approving?

>> **Time:** How much time do you have? Do you want to spend a lot of time or as little as possible per photo?

>> **Photos:** How many photos do you take? Must your workflow be able to handle tens of photos a week, or thousands?

>> **Hardware:** Do you have the camera and computer hardware to manage your workflow and run the software? Over time, of course, you will need to upgrade your system. Will you be working in an office/studio or on location? Weekend photo trips are fantastically fun. I take a laptop with me to review photos and make backup copies. If you would rather travel light, take extra memory cards. You can preview photos on a TV, should you find yourself near one (in a hotel room, perhaps), so remember to take the correct cabling with you.

>> **Software:** What applications are you using? Is everything up to date? Do you need specialty applications, such as panorama or HDR software, noise-removal plug-ins, or other creative solutions?

>> **Priorities:** In the end, deciding what to do (and what not to do) has a lot to do with your priorities. What's most important: speed, quality, compatibility, mobility, or something else?

The rest of this chapter walks you through each step.

Early Decisions

Your workflow begins with setting up your camera and taking photos and movies. The most important decisions you have to make is what format, size, and quality you want the camera to record.

For photos, you should choose Raw or Raw+JPEG if you want more control over photo processing and editing and quality is important.

If you want finished photos right out of the camera, choose JPEG. JPEGs are created from the raw image data. The camera quickly processes that data with the options you've set, such as white balance, contrast, color space, sharpness, creative filters, and so forth. The final result is compressed to make the file size smaller. Options like white balance and other photo settings are "baked in" to the final photo. You can't undo or change your mind later. You therefore need to make creative decisions concerning image size, quality, style, color, color space, orientation, and aspect ratio before you ever take the shot.

Think of it this way: Raw images are like negatives. You can develop them a hundred different ways and print them later without messing up the negative. JPEGs are like prints that you get from the camera shop or kiosk. They're done. That's nice, but a problem with the exposure or fix the color is much harder to correct. You won't get the same quality as if you were working with the original negative.

Transferring Files

Transferring photos and movies to your computer is a pretty simple process. You have several different ways to handle it, and each has its pros and cons. Some methods require additional hardware, such as a card reader.

Connecting

Before you start transferring files to your computer, you have to make a connection. This connection is usually between your camera and a computer. If you'd rather use a memory card reader, the connection is between the card reader and your computer.

Built-in Wi-Fi

New digital SLRs have built-in Wi-Fi, which allows you to wirelessly upload photos to your computer or a smart device via a dedicated app. It's really awesome, especially when you can connect directly to a smartphone to preview images and control the camera with your phone. *Upsides*: No wires, no readers, no mess.

Downsides:

>> Older cameras may not have built-in Wi-Fi.

>> You have to have a Wi-Fi access point in your home or office that you can log in to and access your computer. Getting it working the first time can be a chore. I am getting ready to pair a Canon dSLR with my computer in Figure 1-1. This is just one of several steps required to get them initially connected. After they know each other, it becomes simpler.

>> Wireless transfer uses battery power and may be slow, depending on your connection speed.

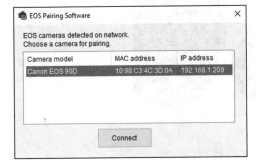

FIGURE 1-1: Pairing enables the camera to connect to the Canon software wirelessly.

When it comes to activating your camera's Wi-Fi features and making connections, bite the bullet and dig through your camera's manual for details.

TIP

Direct USB connection

Directly connecting your camera to your computer is the easiest, most straightforward method. Connect your camera using the USB terminal, which is probably on the side of your camera. *Upside:* The only thing you need, besides your camera, is the USB cable that came with the camera.

Downsides:

>> Your camera has to be on. If your battery is low and you have no backup, recharge the battery so your camera won't die in the middle of a transfer. Should the camera power off, don't panic. The files on the camera should still be there. Simply recharge the camera battery and then restart the transfer.

While the battery is charging, check the files that were transferred to make sure they are viewable. Delete anything on the computer that didn't transfer completely. If you were moving files, not simply copying them, you should check the file that was being moved for any damage by trying to view or edit it. The photos on either side of the power outage should be fine on both the camera and the computer.

WARNING

>> When you put your camera on a table and connect it to a computer (see Figure 1-2), remember that it has a cord attached. It can be snagged, tripped on, pulled, or yanked by you, your kids, your cats, or your dogs. That will ruin your day.

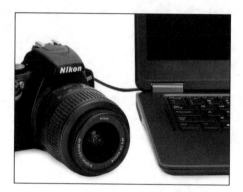

FIGURE 1-2: Secure your camera when it's connected to a computer.

External USB card reader

External USB card readers take the camera out of the transfer equation. The card reader (see Figure 1-3) plugs into your computer. You feed the memory card into it and it handles the transfer. Make sure to get a reader that's compatible with your type of memory card. I recently upgraded my SDXC memory cards to UHS-II and had to get new readers. *Upsides:* You don't have to use your camera's battery and you don't have to worry about running out of juice in the middle of the transfer. You aren't endangering your camera. Also, if the card reader goes bad or gets broken, you can replace it quickly and cheaply.

Downsides:

>> If you use more than one type of card, such as Compact Flash and SD cards, you have to either buy a card reader that can handle multiple card types or buy a card reader for each type of memory card you have.

>> External readers can litter your desktop. They also tend to fall off, forcing you to get on your hands and knees and look behind the computer to retrieve them. They can also get lost in the bottom of your camera bags.

>> If you have multiple computers to transfer files to, you must either buy more card readers or move the one you have back and forth.

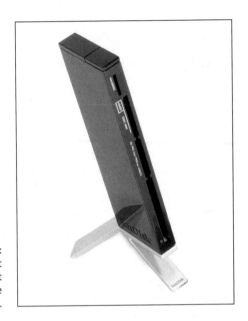

FIGURE 1-3:
Card readers that can use different card types are very helpful.

REMEMBER

Despite the few drawbacks, I prefer using external card readers. I don't have to worry about setting up Wi-Fi or camera batteries, or accidentally knocking the camera off a table. If your computer can support it, invest in a USB 3.0 or newer type of card reader. It's much faster than USB 2.0. Make sure that the connection type is compatible with one or more USB ports on your computer.

Built-in card reader

Some computers and printers have built-in card readers. New iMac desktop computers and older MacBook Air and MacBook Pro laptops have built-in SD card slots. If you own a Windows laptop, it might have come with an internal card reader. If you have a desktop PC, you can install one. *Upsides:* Built-in readers aren't as slippery as portable card readers and can't fall off your desk.

Downside: Internal card readers aren't portable, unless you're using a portable computer, and they may not support the card you need supported.

Wireless file transfer adapters

For compatible cameras that don't have built-in Wi-Fi, Canon and Nikon may have a solution for you: adapters that let you wirelessly transfer files from your camera to a computer or smart device, such as an iPhone. *Upside:* Get files off your camera when you want without tripping over cords.

Downsides:

>> You have to buy more hardware.

>> Research the adapter to make sure that it's compatible with your camera.

>> Wireless transfer sucks up lots of battery power.

Downloading

After you've decided on a connection type, you choose a download method.

Automatic download

You can use a small computer program that automatically downloads the photos to the location you choose. Some are built into your computer's operating system. Others are extra software applications that come with your camera (such as Canon EOS Utility) or part of your image editor applications (such as Adobe Bridge or Lightroom). These programs often run in the background. They're ready to bounce into action the moment they sense a camera or card reader with a memory card has been connected. The programs normally have options for where photos are saved, plus folder names and whether to erase the photos from the card when you're done. I may be in the minority, but I can't stand these automated applications.

To choose a method, you must select the program you want to handle things when you insert a memory card into an external card reader or connect your camera to the computer, as shown in Figure 1-4.

The program you choose opens the next time you connect a memory card to your computer. As Figure 1-5 shows, my choice of Adobe Bridge opens the Bridge Photo Downloader.

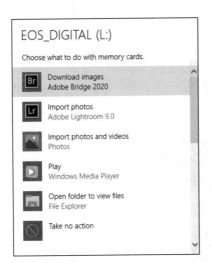

FIGURE 1-4:
Choose an
auto import
option from the
operating system.

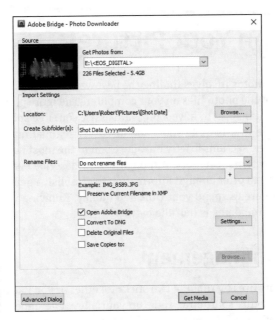

FIGURE 1-5:
Automatically
download photos
with Bridge.

Manual download

You can download photos yourself by

» Dragging the folder from the card reader to your drive and renaming it.

» Creating folders for photos using your operating system and then selecting the photos and dragging them to the appropriate folder.

I'm a hands-on kind of guy. I like to create folders and drag files myself, as shown in Figure 1-6. I organize my photos by camera and then by the date I downloaded them. I like being able to make a backup copy of the day's files and store them on an alternative drive immediately. Afterwards, I import them by folder into Lightroom.

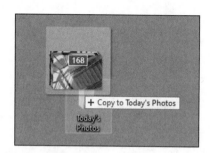

FIGURE 1-6:
I like dragging and dropping files myself.

Getting a Grip on Your Pictures

Managing your photos involves finding the best way to name, store, edit, process, and keep track of the photo files on your computer. The more photos you have, the more you'll find it helpful to have a program assist you. I've split this section into several parts. The first is quite short and discusses manual management. (Don't do it.) The next few sections briefly introduce you to the most popular applications in each basic functional category. Although I can't describe every single applications in depth, I can offer enough information to establish a general starting point as you decide where to spend your time and money. Knowing what you need and having a list of candidates is half the battle.

Manual management

If you like to start fires by rubbing two sticks together or you like to catch fish with your bare hands, this solution is right up your alley. File under R for ridiculous, cross-referenced to D for don't. Instead, put your photos in a folder somewhere and then use a good photo organizer and editor like Adobe Lightroom to keep track of them. You can create custom catalogs, tag and categorize photos, and generally do a lot more in these applications to accomplish what you want to do by renaming files.

Media-management software

There are a lot of choices here. Options range from pure media managers to applications that focus on Raw photo workflow and development. Plenty of basic photo editors have built-in basic management tools.

Adobe Bridge (see Figure 1-7) is one of the best pure media managers. It's big, credible, versatile, well supported, and backed by a powerful company. Bridge is truly a bridge. It links your photos to your other applications in a way that lets you manage thousands of photos seamlessly. You can create and manage collections, rotate photos, apply different Camera Raw settings, and more from within Bridge, but you call on other applications to complete most development and editing tasks.

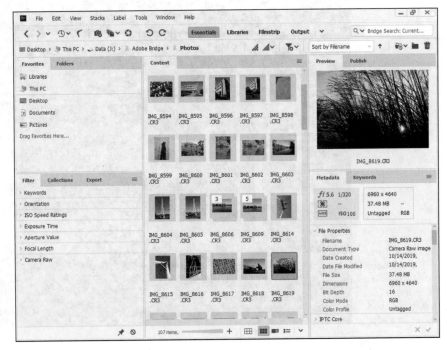

FIGURE 1-7: Bridge is a professional media manager that has a great many useful features.

TIP

You don't buy Bridge by itself. Normally, it's included with a Creative Cloud subscription. You can download it for free using the Creative Cloud app, which Adobe installs to your computer to manage your Adobe products.

Processing and managing software

This type of application focuses on photo processing and management. Photo enthusiasts can work with these applications, but they have features and capabilities that appeal to professionals, too.

Camera manufacturer software

Most camera manufacturers include free software that enables you to organize and process the photos you take with that camera. Canon calls its software Digital Photo Professional (see Figure 1-8). Nikon's free software is Capture NX-D. Sony's is Image Data Converter. Pentax ships Digital Camera Utility with its cameras.

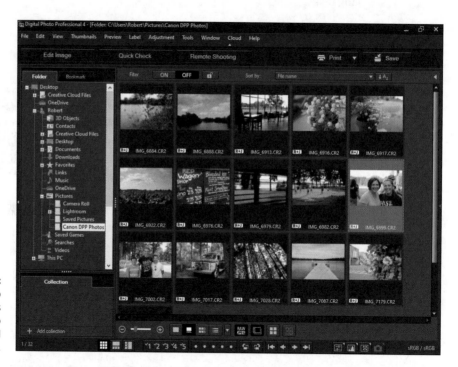

FIGURE 1-8:
Digital Photo Professional is Canon's photo management and editing app.

I have dabbled with these applications in the past. They all have their strengths and weaknesses. Their main advantage over general photo editing software is that the same people who encode data into the camera's Raw file are the people who created the software that allows you to decode it. The camera manufacturer knows more about its files and proprietary settings than anyone else. If you are dedicated to a single brand and don't plan on changing, you should consider this approach.

Adobe Photoshop Lightroom

The most popular photo management and processing application is Adobe Photoshop Lightroom, which is cloud-based, and Adobe Photoshop Lightroom Classic. Most people just say Lightroom. Lightroom is moderately priced and available by monthly subscription. It's my tool of choice.

These two versions differ in a few important ways. First, they manage your files differently. Classic keeps all your photos and movies on your computer. That's what I prefer. The cloud-based application is simply called Adobe Lightroom. A huge advantage to using a cloud is that your photos and movies are available wherever you are, as long as you have the application installed on the computer you're using. In addition, the cloud-based version is compatible with mobile devices. This makes a great choice if you're mobile and want to work on your iPhone or Android. Finally, the interface for Lightroom is simpler. It consists mostly of settings and sliders. All the figures in this book feature Lightroom Classic.

This Macintosh/Windows application is made for photographers. It has just about everything you need in order to import, manage, develop, and publish Raw and JPEG photos. Figure 1-9 shows the Library module. Look at all those cool photo-management tools! From this module, you can organize, sort, tag, rate, select, and more.

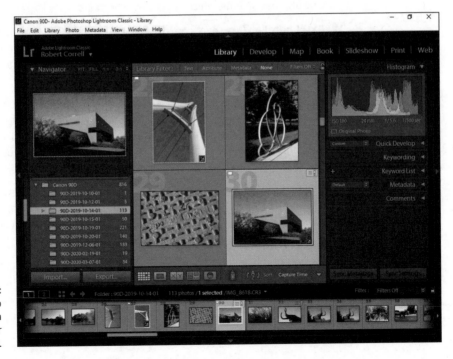

FIGURE 1-9:
Adobe Photoshop Lightroom is a fantastic tool for photographers.

In Lightroom, you can create a single massive, all-inclusive catalog or create different catalogs based on different cameras, projects, or years. When you import photos into an open catalog, they show up as thumbnails in the Library module, where you manage them. You can view, sort, filter, rate, delete, search for, compare, create, and assign keywords, quickly develop photos, and edit metadata. You can also export photos in a number of different formats. I cover the Lightroom processing features (you can use them for JPEGs or TIFFs, if you want) in more depth in Book 5, Chapter 2.

TIP

To work with layers, masks, adjustment layers, artistic filters and effects, vector shapes, 3-D support, text, frames, and other aspects unique to photo editors, you need to get a photo editor other than Lightroom. I use Photoshop for these things.

Other applications

There is a host of other products available with varying capabilities and emphasis. This list is by no means comprehensive:

>> **Capture One** (www.captureone.com/en/): Created by Phase One, Capture One is comparable to Lightroom. Import photos and then sort, rate, preview, organize, *tag* (add keywords to), develop, and publish them. Organize your photos in catalogs or work one-on-one with photos by using sessions. Capture One also has albums, which are virtual collections.

>> **DxO PhotoLab** (www.dxo.com/dxo-photolab/): DxO PhotoLab is a powerful photo editor with a suite of advanced technical tools, including noise reduction, color correction, and lens distortion removal. It also has management capabilities in the form of the PhotoLibrary.

>> **Google Photos** (www.google.com/photos/about/): Google's photo organizer (with minimal editing tools) is called Google Photos. All your files are stored online and organized in albums. You have free unlimited storage in the cloud, but only for photos up to 16 megapixels and movies up to 1080p resolution.

>> **Skylum Luminar** (www.skylum.com/luminar): Luminar is a powerful photo editor and browser. It has some great editing tools and filters, so you can be creative if you want. You can also manage your photo collection with Luminar.

>> **Apple Photos for macOS** (www.apple.com/macos/photos/): Apple Photos features photo editing and managing tools, and integrates seamlessly with the iCloud Photos. Import and organize photos, view, rate, tag, title, edit, and publish them.

Photo editors

This section lists three well-known photo editors.

Adobe Photoshop

Photoshop is the industry standard graphics editor. It has no photo-management tools. Photoshop is available by subscription from Adobe, through Creative Cloud.

I use Photoshop for things that Lightroom can't do, or does poorly. I handle all basic image processing in Lightroom and, if necessary, export the photo to Photoshop to finish it. I can remove distractions from photos, create complicated layers to isolate adjustments to certain parts of the photo (the background, for example, or a person's face), apply creative filters, and more. Figure 1-10 shows that I've created several layers to handle different edits in this photo of a waterfall. Photoshop also opens and processes Raw photos with the help of Adobe Camera Raw.

PaintShop Pro

PaintShop Pro, by Corel, is an all-in-one photo editor that feels a bit like a cross between Adobe Lightroom and Photoshop. You can manage, adjust, and edit photos using one application. PaintShop Pro supports Raw files from most cameras.

GIMP (GNU Image Manipulation Program)

GIMP is basically free Photoshop. Do you need more? Okay. The main drawback for photographers is the lack of built-in Raw support. If you need that capability and don't want to mess around with external apps or plug-ins, pass on GIMP. If you use JPEGs only and want to try an advanced image editor with plenty of other features for free, give it a try.

Transferring and
Managing Files

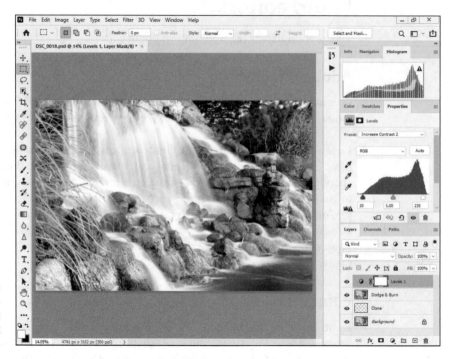

FIGURE 1-10:
Use Photoshop for more complex photo-editing tasks.

Managing Photos

Get familiar with these management tasks as you try or invest in a particular piece of software. Think about how these tasks fit into your workflow:

>> **Flagging** allows you to flag some photos as keepers and some as rejects, and you can leave the rest alone. This unflagged middle ground is always available if you want to revisit them later. I prefer to flag first, because it's faster and easier to tell whether you want to work with a photo than it is to figure out

whether it's worth 4 or 5 stars. After you flag photos, you may be able to hide photos in the interface by filtering out nonflagged photos.

>> **Rating** allows you to rate your photos from one to five stars. That's great if you need that level of discrimination. After you rate photos, you can filter your collection by the number of stars a photo has.

>> **Grouping** creates different structures to hold and organize your photos. It might be called a *library, catalog, project, album,* or *folder,* depending on the application. After it's created, you import photos into this structure, which keeps or separates one set of photos from another. That way, you don't have 10,000 pictures flopping around with no rhyme or reason.

>> **Sorting** is when you identify a criterion, such as the date or time that you took a photo, or its filename, keyword, rating, or other EXIF data; the program sorts the photos or working files by that criterion.

>> **Filtering** is similar to sorting, but weeds out photos based on the criteria you choose. You can make it so that you see only five-star photos, or those you took with a particular lens, or perhaps when the flash fired; all the rest are hidden.

>> **Face Recognition** can be a great way to organize photos. If your photo-management software supports this feature, you can use it to find photos of people, tag them with their names, and then use that information to search for or sort your collection.

>> **Keywording or tagging** is a straightforward concept. Tag every photo with descriptive keywords that help you organize, sort, find, and otherwise keep track of them. The main challenge is to be consistent in what tags to create and use.

TIP

Don't get too detailed when you're tagging.

>> **Geotagging** identifies where a photo was taken. Most often, you identify where one or more photos were taken on a map, and the coordinates are written to the photo file's *metadata* (helpful data, stored in the file, that isn't part of the photo itself; you access it by looking at the photo's info with your operating system or photo program).

>> **Stacking** different versions of the same photo on top of each other allows you to declutter the workspace.

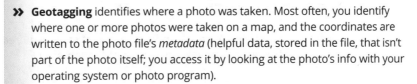

Quickly Processing the Good Ones

Photographers rarely have the time or need to process every single photo they shoot. Process good photos, not bad ones. Don't waste your time with bad shots unless you have no other choice. You can find more details on how to quickly process your photos in Book 5, Chapter 2.

Advanced Editing When Desired

Many photos look fantastic when processed using applications like Lightroom. Sometimes, however, you need more powerful editing tools. Advanced photo editors are optimized to work in layers, blend with opacity, have creative filters, use masks, and so forth.

Deciding whether you want to use a photo editor on some shots depends on finding the right balance for you. It takes extra effort, additional software, more time, and a certain amount of practice. However, you should know that many times it is very hard to perfect some photos without going this extra mile. I cover several advanced editing techniques in Book 5, Chapter 3.

Aside from the practical reasons, you can reap artistic benefits of using a photo editor in conjunction with your normal photo processor. I cover this aspect of using Photoshop in Book 5, Chapter 4.

Publishing

The process of exporting or saving your final files from your photo editor is called *publishing*. You might need to publish your work for any number of reasons: to print, upload to the Internet, send via email, or use as a new desktop background. The sky is the limit.

General considerations

Read your software manual to find out the exact steps required to export or save your work. However, consider some general thoughts:

WARNING

>> **Preserve original material.** I can't stress this advice enough. *Never* overwrite original files when saving. Your first save should always be Save As. JPEGs in particular suffer from *lossy* compression — they lose some quality every time you open, edit, and save them. If you're working with JPEGs, open, edit, and save as a *lossless* file type such as TIFF or a working format such as Adobe's PSD.

>> **Preserve working copies.** If you need to export your photo to an editor like Photoshop and create things like multiple layers, masks, and adjustment layers, do yourself a favor — save those working copies. If you *flatten* (compress all the layers into a single background layer) or delete them, you can't easily go back and change or update your work.

TIP

» **Consider quality.** When saving and exporting, you'll have several file type and bit depth options. (You can read more about that in Book 5, Chapters 2 and 3.)

- When emailing or uploading to the Internet, use JPEG.

- When printing or archiving a high-quality copy, use TIFF.

» **Enter copyright and other descriptive information in metadata.** That's what metadata is for. If you publish your photos to the web, think about adding this hidden layer of protection to your photos.

» **Add a visible copyright or watermark.** This is another way to protect your photos. Whereas copyright and descriptive metadata are invisible, a watermark, mark, or copyright on a photo is visible for all to see. In Figure 1-11, I've created a copyright watermark in Lightroom that stamps my information in the lower-right corners of photos as I export them.

» **Strip metadata, if you want.** On the other hand, you may want to strip out any metadata to protect your secrets. Not all applications remove data, but you can save *copies* of final files to a format that doesn't have metadata and then open and save those versions to your final format.

» **Resize for the web.** Unless you want your full-size photos to be posted somewhere online, such as at Flickr or SmugMug, you should resize images to make them quite a bit smaller. On the web, 24 megapixels is serious overkill. (The *pixel count* is the total number of picture elements, or dots, in a photo; in this case, 24 megapixels stands for 24 million pixels.) Some sites may reduce the size of your photos anyway.

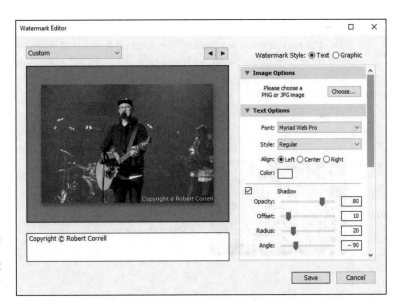

FIGURE 1-11:
Adding a copyright watermark in Lightroom.

Resizing options

TIP

Pay attention to the resizing method you choose.

For example, Photoshop has these resizing options that appear on a drop-down menu in the Image Size dialog box (shown in Figure 1-12):

» **Automatic:** Chooses the one Photoshop thinks will work best, based on the type of image you're resizing and whether you're enlarging or reducing it.

» **Preserve Details (enlargement):** This method is optimized for enlarging images. It tries to preserves details, which is a code word that tells you it also sharpens the image. (You might see the contrast go up in areas as well.) You have the ability to reduce noise, which smoothes or eliminates artifacts caused by sharpening.

» **Preserve Details 2.0:** This method uses a newer algorithm that does the same thing as the previous one, only better. Try it and see whether you can tell the difference.

» **Bicubic Smoother (enlargement):** Try this if you're enlarging an image and don't like the other methods. You will lose a bit of sharpness in details because this method smooths the final results a bit to keep them from looking jagged.

» **Bicubic Sharper (reduction):** This is probably the best method for reducing the size of an image, and it's much better than Nearest Neighbor. It produces sharpness without creating jagged edges. Still, pay attention to whether the level of sharpness suits your needs. If not, resize using Bicubic, and then come back and apply an Unsharp Mask and sharpen the image to the exact degree you want.

» **Bicubic (smooth gradients):** This method works best when you want to pre-serve smooth *gradients,* such as a blue sky that transitions from dark to light.

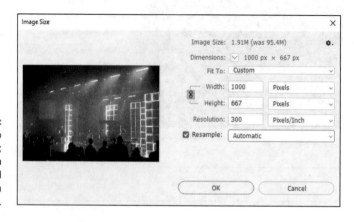

FIGURE 1-12:
Resize images to post on the web; no need for a 24 megapixel image on Facebook.

>> **Nearest Neighbor (hard edges):** Pay careful attention when you use this method. Examine the edges at 100 percent or higher magnification in the dialog box before processing to see whether things look too jagged for you.

>> **Bilinear:** This is a good method in which colors are preserved and the image is smooth. You lose a bit of sharpness, however.

TIP

To display on the web, 800 to 1,000 pixels wide is a good start. That number is large enough to see detail yet doesn't produce a huge file size. Sites like Flickr accept the original photo sizes with no problem.

Saving and exporting

You often have plenty of detailed methods with which to publish photos. Choose the one that best fits your target media requirements. Table 1-1 summarizes several typical options.

TABLE 1-1   **Publishing Options**

Name	Description
Save As	Saves the file as a new type. Type a new name and choose other file options. Use instead of Save when you want to preserve a copy of your file or create a new type.
Save for Web	Saves a new file in a web-friendly format, such as GIF, JPEG, or PNG.
Export	Saves a copy of your file as a new file type. You can often change the image size, resolution, and attach color profiles when exporting. Some applications let you export data to other programs for further editing. If using a commercial printer, check to see whether it prefers that you use this method, and what settings it suggests for your print.
Share	When set up with the proper username and password, this option saves your file online.
Print	Prints your photos on a printer connected to your computer or network.
Order Prints	Orders prints from a company. You will have to have an existing account or be ready to set one up and establish a payment method.

Figure 1-13 shows the Convert and Save dialog box from Canon's photo-editing application, Digital Photo Professional. Notice that you can change the image type, including the bit-depth, and the resolution. You can also resize it if you like, embed the color profile, and choose how much shooting information to leave in the file.

Transferring and
Managing Files

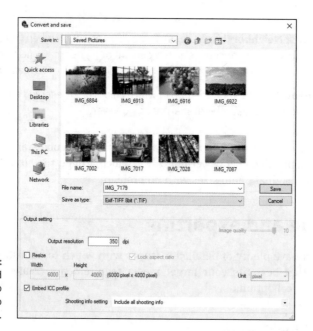

**TECHNICAL
STUFF**

On the other hand, you may be working in a professional environment where documents run through Adobe Bridge. You can publish PDF contact sheets or web galleries using the optional Adobe Output Module, which is installed separately from Bridge CC. If you use Lightroom or Photoshop, you'll likely print, export, or save archive copies from within those applications.

Archiving

Archiving preserves a copy of your photos and working files for long-term storage. In some ways, your digital photo and movie collection is easier to safeguard than photo prints and negatives. The electronic files themselves are, for all intents and purposes, indestructible — as long as you ensure the safety of the media you store them in. You don't have to worry about prints getting bent or soaked with humidity, or about boxes of them occupying an entire room.

REMEMBER

Take time to plan your backup and archive process, and diligently carry out your plans. It's not as easy as throwing a sleeve of negatives into a cardboard box and tucking them away in a closet.

Playing it safe

First, decide how you want to back up and archive your photos. You have to consider issues such as storage capacity, availability, and organization, in addition to the categories in this list:

WARNING

>> **Cost:** You want to pay as little as possible, but you have to strike a balance between being cost-effective and being simply foolish. Don't buy the cheapest (and possibly least reliable) equipment known to humankind to protect your valuable files.

>> **Capacity:** Digital photos and movies take up a lot of space. Choose a storage medium that fits your current and anticipated future workload. Table 1-2 lays out your options.

TABLE 1-2   Archival Media Pros and Cons

Media	Pros	Cons
CD-ROM/ DVD-ROM	Data can't be erased; price per gigabyte isn't bad; no moving parts to the CD/DVD itself.	Limited capacity; most camera memory cards have more space; takes up quite a bit of physical space.
Memory card or flash drive	Easy to use; doesn't occupy much space; no moving parts; relatively affordable.	More expensive per gigabyte compared to typical hard drives.
Internal hard drive	Affordable; holds lots; fast; useful for temporary backups.	Moving parts; susceptible to crashing; difficult to swap in or out; data can be accidentally erased.
External hard drive	Affordable; holds lots; portability; can be stored off site; great for long-term storage.	Moving parts; not as accessible as an internal hard drive.
Solid State Drive (SSD)	Essentially a huge flash drive; no moving parts; exceptionally fast; can be internal or external.	Price per gigabyte still higher than older spinning hard drives, questionable longevity (yes, you read that right — SSD data degrades over time as you use the drive).
Network storage	Reliable, fast, networked RAID storage increases capacity, performance, and reliability.	Requires a network, must set up and administer, can be technically demanding, can crash, sometimes stored onsite.
Online/Cloud	The ultimate in off-site storage; no additional hardware needed; can be accessed from anywhere at any time.	Time and bandwidth required for initial backup; requires computer with Internet access; requires service subscription and an account in good standing; long-term viability depends on company health; vulnerable to unauthorized access, especially if you're famous.

Transferring and Managing Files

>> **Access:** Determine whether you can easily access your backups and whether an unforeseen circumstance (like a company going out of business and never updating its software) can prevent you from protecting your work.

>> **Security:** Assess your security situation to determine how safe (physically, and from a computer networking standpoint) the files are. Put the appropriate safeguards on your home or local network, such as Internet firewalls and password protection. In addition, files can be easily damaged if you store them at home and your house burns down. If that's your only backup copy, you've lost them.

>> **The future:** Consider how easy or hard it will be to transfer archived files from one storage device to another. For example, old hard drives may require a connection that will someday be obsolete unless you occasionally update your backup technology. In the very long term, provide *thumbnails* (small pictures) or a printed index or another form of inventory that, for example, your kids or their kids can easily figure out when you're long gone.

TIP

If you have old hard drives lying around, use them as external backup drives until you can afford to invest in newer SSDs, which are now my backup media of choice. Good, terabyte-sized SSDs are under $125. Buy yourself one or more external hard disk enclosures to make the connection to your computer. I prefer toolless enclosures that connect using USB 3.0/3.1. Older hard drives will need the 3.5-inch variety, whereas newer SSDs typically come in a 2.5-inch form factor (the exception being M.2 SSDs).

Putting the plan into action

All the cool storage devices in the world are useless if you never use them. Have a plan for backing up and archiving your files. The key to making backups work is to develop a routine that matches the time and energy you're willing to invest. If the process becomes so laborious that you quit, it's worthless.

Follow these steps to walk through the type of plan I recommend, using a combination of extra *internal* (in your computer case; you'll have to install them yourself or find someone who knows how to do this) and *external* (sitting on your desktop in an enclosure of some sort) hard drives:

1. **Complete an initial photo backup.**

WARNING

Back up new photos on internal or external (preferred) hard drives when you transfer photos and movies from camera to computer. You can't afford to lose the initial transfer. These files form the basis of your collection and can't be re-created.

The mechanics of the initial backup are up to you. I simply copy and paste the photo folder to another location on an external drive. You may want to export photos from your photo-management software or use a backup program to copy a smaller bunch. This advice applies to each of the following steps.

2. **Perform a weekly internal (on your computer) backup of photo catalogs and working files.**

   Back up catalogs (which may contain the bulk of your adjustments) and any other working files to internal hard drives. If you can't afford to lose a single day's worth of productivity, consider daily backups. For a more relaxed timeline, back up catalogs, edited, and final files monthly.

3. **Perform an end-of-month external backup.**

   Back up everything to external hard drives, a file server, or a network. For a more relaxed timeline, back up quarterly or by project.

4. **Perform an annual or biannual off-site backup.**

   REMEMBER

   Create an off-site backup with all original photo files, catalogs, working, and final files. Put them in a storage barn on your property, rent a safety deposit box from a bank, or ask your grandparents to put them in their attic. Just make sure that they're physically separated from your computer and the building you're in. That way, if anything happens to your building, your photos and work files remain safe. For a more relaxed timeline, back up every few years.

The plan I suggest may not work for everyone. One alternative, keyed toward a business environment, is to treat every job as a discrete unit and back up photos, catalogs and work files according to job number. When you transfer the initial photos, back them up. When you finish the job, back up everything and tuck things away on a hard drive devoted to that client. Depending on your workload and client list, you may have one hard drive for many clients or many hard drives for one client.

Chapter **2**

Quickly Sprucing Up Shots

N ot every photo that comes out of the camera looks as good as it can. Some aren't worth saving. Many of those that are can be made better with just a little effort. Touching up photos is not that hard to do, and it will improve your photography tremendously.

If you want to learn how to quickly spruce up your photos, this practical chapter is for you. I talk about how to decide what image quality settings to choose in the camera and how that decision will affect working with your photos in software. I cover how to review and flag photos, how to get started developing them, then how to make brightness and contrast, clarity, color, and many other adjustments. The chapter concludes with a look at processing photos in the camera.

Software for Sprucing Up Photos

Whether you shoot and save Raw, JPEG, or both types of images, I recommend using an application like Adobe Photoshop Lightroom to manage and quickly touch up your photos. Lightroom excels at making this part of the process fast and painless, so it's an easy decision to feature it in this chapter. Who doesn't love easy decisions!

What Lightroom *doesn't do*, which I lament at times, is enable you to control proprietary options that manufacturers build into their Raw files. Canon's Digital Photo Professional, for example, allows you to change the strength of the Auto Lighting Optimizer setting, or disable it entirely. You can also change the Picture Style of Raw photos. These settings serve two purposes: They tell the camera how you want the final JPEG photos processed, and they are stored in the Raw image file so that you can make the same processing decisions in Digital Photo Professional. You cannot perform these actions in Lightroom.

If you don't use Lightroom, don't panic. The processing principles that I outline in this chapter, as well as most of the details, are not wholly unique to Lightroom. Experiment on your own to find the best application for you.

Deciding on an Image Quality

The decisions you make when you set up your camera to shoot have an impact on the processing process. The main issue is whether to save your photos in JPEG, Raw, or both image formats.

If you plan to do more than tweak basic brightness and contrast, I encourage you to shoot in Raw. Raw image files have the best *raw photo data* that your camera can produce. Therefore, Raw images are considered the best *source material* with which to work.

When processing, JPEGs can't be pushed as hard as Raw photos before noise becomes troublesome. In addition, camera options like white balance, noise reduction, dynamic range limitations, color, and style have already been applied to produce the JPEG. Although you can always try to fix issues later, you get the best image quality when you work with a Raw photo and run it through the sausage-making mill once.

REMEMBER

That fact doesn't mean that JPEGs are terrible. Absolutely not. From an editing or retouching perspective, though, editing a JPEG can be like trying to change the ingredients of a meatloaf after you bake it.

Benefits of Raw images

The advantages of shooting Raw images are numerous. Two of the most critical advantages follow:

>> **Control:** When processing Raw images in software, you are in control. Within certain bounds, *you,* not the camera, decide what goes into the JPEG or TIFF

when you process a Raw file using software. When you change the white balance, exposure, color profile, and many other parameters during processing, you are simply interpreting the data differently. In the end, the JPEG file is a good end product, especially for web media. When taken right out of the camera, however, all the creative decisions that go into shaping the JPEG have already been made. By the time you look at it, the original data has been thrown out.

» **Flexibility:** When you process your camera's raw exposures into JPEG files, you still have the raw data to fall back on. You can reprocess them, if the mood strikes you, whether tomorrow, next week, or five years from now.

Challenges of working with Raw photos

And now for the bad news. Working with Raw images isn't all rainbows and unicorns. It has pros and cons. If the drawbacks outweigh the benefits for you, don't be afraid to use JPEGs instead. You may choose *not* to shoot Raw photos for these practical reasons:

» **Limited compatibility:** You can't throw a Raw photo on Facebook or Instagram because they just aren't compatible with web browsers. If you want to go from your camera to the world in as few steps as possible, shoot JPEGs.

» **They take up space:** Raw files are much larger than even the highest-quality JPEG that your camera creates. JPEGs take up less space than Raw files, thereby allowing you to take many more photos than if you were shooting in Raw or Raw+JPEG formats. (Do yourself a favor, though: If you are concerned about space, go buy mo' bigger cards when possible.) Also consider how much hard drive space you're willing (and able) to use to store and work with photos.

» **Slower shooting speed:** When you're shooting Raw, the camera has to move more data from the sensor through the processor to the memory card. You'll benefit from a faster *frame rate* (how many photos you can take per second) if you shoot and store JPEGs only.

» **Impact on your time:** If you don't have the time to process Raw photos, JPEGs are your best solution. And remember, you can still edit JPEGs if you need to. Turn to the next chapter for more information.

TIP

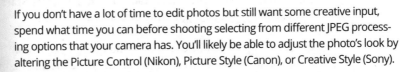

If you don't have a lot of time to edit photos but still want some creative input, spend what time you can before shooting selecting from different JPEG processing options that your camera has. You'll likely be able to adjust the photo's look by altering the Picture Control (Nikon), Picture Style (Canon), or Creative Style (Sony).

» **No need:** You may find that the JPEGs coming from your camera are just as good or better than what you can do yourself with Raw. If that's the case, use the JPEGs and don't worry about it.

Non-destructive editing

Working with raw images enables you to set whatever adjustments you would like to make without changing a single pixel of the photo. That's the nondestructive part. If you come back later and change your mind (you want to make it a little brighter, say), you can redo all your settings without affecting the original image.

For example, when you change the Exposure in Lightroom's Develop module, that setting, along with all the others, is stored in a database. What you see on your monitor is a just a preview of what will happen when the raw data is processed. The raw image isn't modified, even if you crop the photo. You can press the Reset button and undo everything whenever you want. You can also create a virtual copy of the photo to compare alternative settings. When you export the image, the settings stored in the database are used to create the new file. The original file is left unchanged.

Getting Started

Your goal should be to take the photos you shoot and quickly make them look better using your photo software. Everyone can do this. To get started, transfer the photo files to your computer and import them into your chosen application. As a reminder, I am using Lightroom to illustrate the general process. If you need help deciding on how to transfer files, turn back to Book 5, Chapter 1.

Reviewing and flagging good photos

Whether you take 10, 100, or 1,000 photos a day, *you can't worry about them all.* Focus on the good ones. That's right. Let the bad ones be bad and don't fuss over them. Spend your time making the good shots better. You'll be able to upload your prized shots to Facebook or tweet them far sooner if you work this way.

That means reviewing all the photos from a shoot with the intended purpose of identifying the best shots. That may seem backward to you. Don't start at 350 and winnow out the bad ones. That takes too much time! Start your count at 0 and work your way up by flagging the best shots.

I'm reviewing photos in the Library module of Lightroom in Figure 2-1. Except for the menu, which is off, I've got all the doodads and gizmos showing. You can show or hide each side panel, the Filmstrip on the bottom of the screen, and the Identity Plate/Module Picker at the top. If you use another application, it most likely has the same general elements that you see here.

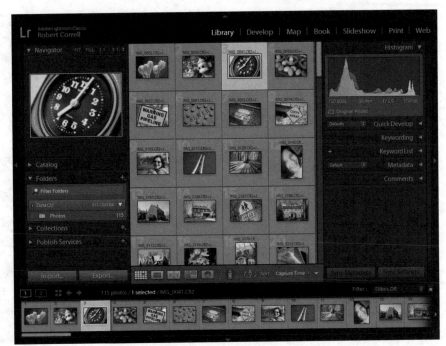

FIGURE 2-1:
Reviewing photos in Lightroom's Library.

Do yourself a favor: Don't rate your photos with stars just yet. The problem with stars is that haggling with yourself takes a tremendous amount of time and leaves you an emotional wreck. At this point, it's meaningless whether a particular photo is worth four or five stars. All you really need to decide now is whether you want to post, print, or otherwise show it off. If the answer to that is yes, it goes in the "good" pile.

With Lightroom, use the Flag as Pick feature to put photos in the good pile. Take a few seconds to look at each photo, and if the shot has "it," flag it (see Figure 2-2). With this method, you're not rejecting photos; you're simply flagging the ones you want to work with. You may end up with four, seven, or more.

After you flag the keepers, run through them again (see Figure 2-3) to and confirm each photo you've chosen. If you've flagged photos that are close to identical, chances are you don't need both. If you don't have enough, go back to the collection and add more, if possible.

TIP

Remember, pass the bad shots over and don't worry about them. Return when you have time and analyze why they weren't worth processing, however, so that you can learn from them. If you're consistently getting blurry shots, for example, you may need to change exposure modes or shutter speed.

Quickly Sprucing Up Shots

CHAPTER 2 **Quickly Sprucing Up Shots** 449

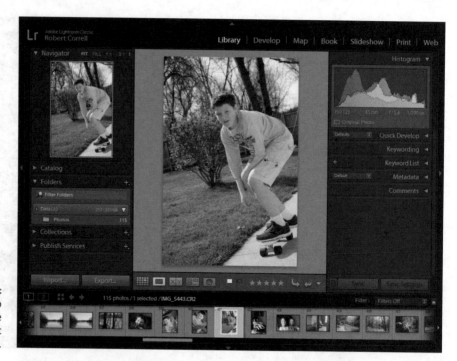

FIGURE 2-2:
Flag photos to
identify the
ones you want
to work with.

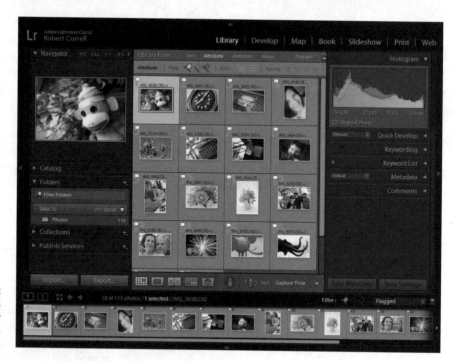

FIGURE 2-3:
Flagged photos
are identified by
a flag and can be
filtered.

Switching to the Develop module

After you choose the photos you want to work on, switch to your application's Edit window. In Lightroom, this is the Develop module, shown in Figure 2-4. The visual difference between this and the Library module is the appearance of controls on the right side of the screen. The navigation elements that were on the left have been replaced by panels suitable for image processing. I have turned off most of the additional panels and helpers that appear in the Develop module for the rest of the chapter to focus on the photo at hand and the panel I want to describe.

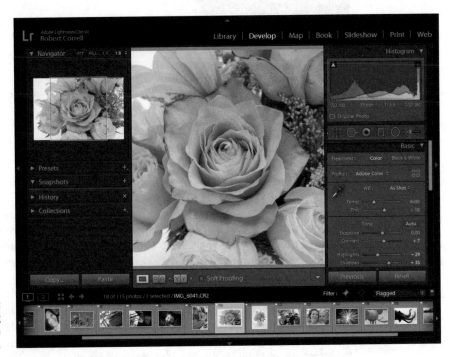

FIGURE 2-4: Developing a photo in Lightroom.

Setting the lens profile

The first thing I do is set the lens profile in the Lens Corrections panel. This feature (see Figure 2-5) automatically corrects lens distortion and vignetting caused by the specific lens that took the photo. I've found that fixing this first always gives me a better photo to start with, and keeps me from having to make adjustments to fix distortion or exposure around the edges later. If I don't like what I see, I turn it off. There are a couple catches: Lens correction data has to be available (which it is for most popular lenses) and you must be working with Raw photos (there is very little support for other formats). Open the panel and select

Quickly Sprucing Up Shots

Enable Profile Corrections. The make, model, and profile will automatically be chosen for you if you are working with a Raw image. If not, select them from the drop-down menus.

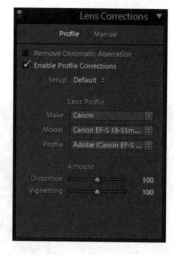

FIGURE 2-5:
Load the correct lens profile to automatically correct lens distortion and vignetting.

Testing the waters

Next, go to the Tone area of the Basic panel and click the Auto button. Lightroom evaluates the photo and makes the changes that it thinks will produce a photo with the best tonal range (from dark through bright) with as little highlight and shadow clipping as possible. If you don't like it, use Undo.

The results are sometimes great, as shown in Figure 2-6. I took this photo of my wife using the standard 18-55mm kit lens and Canon 90D dSLR. We were inside, but light from the window illuminated her nicely. Lightroom toned down the exposure and highlights, boosted the contrast slightly, and then set the white and black points based on the photo's histogram. It looks a lot better!

Of course, not every photo works as well as this one. Either way, you will learn something. You can keep the settings and be done with it, or make a mental note of them to experiment with.

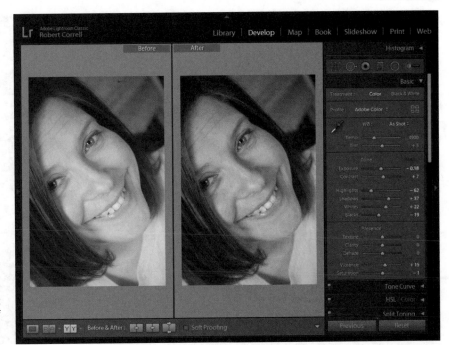

FIGURE 2-6:
Always check out the Auto button if your application has one.

Setting Brightness and Contrast

Don't be afraid to quickly tweak the brightness and contrast. It's simple and you don't have to have an advanced degree to make your photos look a lot better. If you need a quick reminder about exposure, EV, and histograms, refer to Book 3, Chapter 1.

Adjusting the exposure

Lightroom's Exposure control allows you to darken or brighten the photo. The numbers below it are f-stop equivalents, or EV. Negative numbers darken and positive numbers brighten.

Adjusting the exposure is sometimes a delicate dance. Raise or lower it until the photo looks right. Don't push exposure so hard either way that you blow out highlights or lose shadows. If you do, pull the control back. If you need to, rescue bright and dark areas of the photo with the Highlights and Shadow controls. Figure 2-7 shows a photo of my grandaunt Elouise and me taken a few years ago. I raised the exposure by 1.0 EV to brighten the photo.

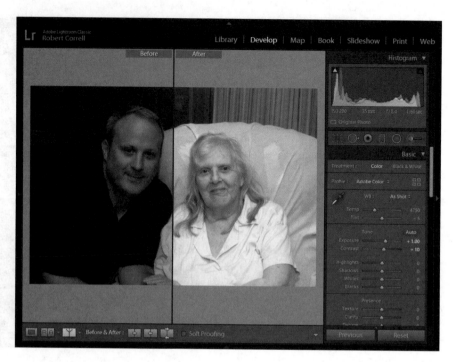

FIGURE 2-7:
Brighten or darken photos using the Exposure control.

TIP

Carefully read the documentation that comes with your software. Some brightness controls compress highlights and shadows when they reach the edges of the histogram. This squeezes them together, limiting their range but preserving some detail. Others *clip* highlights to white and shadows to black when they reach the edge of the histogram, which essentially tosses data away.

See Book 3, Chapter 1 for more information on exposure and histograms.

Improving contrast

Contrast tells you how far apart a photo's dark and bright tones are. The Histrogram panel shows this graphically. Low-contrast photos can look dull and gray because the tones are clumped closer together. High-contrast photos often have more pop because tones are spread out further.

Experiment with the Contrast control until the photo looks clear and well defined. Normally, photos with too little contrast often look dull and lifeless, as shown in Figure 2-8. They are missing a vibrancy that contrast enhances. Some may appear to have a gray sheen on them. In this case, you can see that the Before side is not as clear as when I increase the contrast. The different elements of this manhole cover, including the surface texture, all look better.

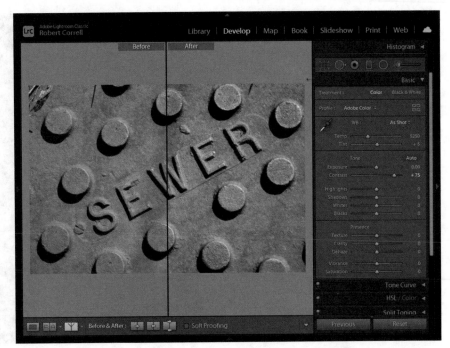

FIGURE 2-8:
This photo appears dull because it has too little contrast.

Don't overdo it. Photos with too much contrast have shadows that are too dark and highlights that are too bright, with few mid-tones to connect them.

Protecting highlights and shadows

Normally, you want bright areas in photos, but you want to keep them from becoming so bright that they are a featureless blob. Likewise, you want dark areas in your photos, but you don't want them to be featureless. I say featureless to emphasize the point. Uniform areas of white or black literally have no features, or details.

One way to protect these areas is to target them with Highlights and Shadows adjustments. This approach works best with Raw photos because they still have all the original data contained in the photo, even if you can't perceive it all onscreen. Having all the original data allows you to pull highlights back and bring shadows into a tonal range that fits into the histogram. The information was there, it was just in the wrong place.

I've done just that with the photo in Figure 2-9. I chose this shot because it's a challenging scene and shows blown highlights caused by the setting sun and overly dark shadows in the trees in the original photo. Lightroom identifies these areas in red (highlights) and blue (shadows) to make it easier to tell when things are going wrong.

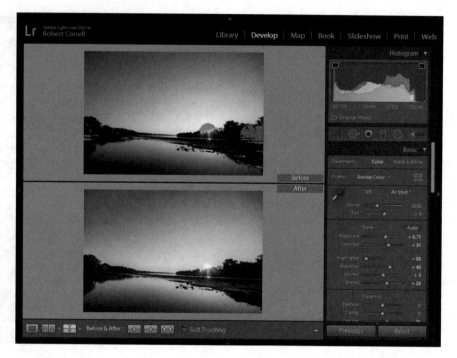

FIGURE 2-9:
Trying to keep
most highlights
and shadows
from clipping is
important.

I made several adjustments to this photo to improve the exposure and color. In the end, I lowered the Highlights setting by a whopping 95 and increased the Shadows control by 40 to keep these areas from clipping. You'll find that many elements of exposure are connected, and that you may need to come back to these controls after making further adjustments.

TIP

You don't have to eliminate all bright or dark pixels. Bring them into balance so that the photo looks good.

Setting the black and white points

Lightroom has two more important tone controls that enable you to adjust brightness and contrast: Whites and Blacks. The Whites and Blacks controls set the boundaries. That is why they are called clipping controls. In effect, you're saying "This is where white actually is — you can't get whiter" or "This is as dark as it gets — you can't get darker" when you use the controls.

The effect of sliding them left and right is to darken or lighten the photo, but don't use them for that. Instead, drag them to expand or reduce the overall tonal range of the photo so that it fits nicely within the histogram. I did that on the foggy landscape scene in Figure 2-10. Note that I didn't change the brightness or the contrast of this photo, and yet it's brighter and has more contrast. Curious, isn't it? The result was caused by the fact that white tones are now whiter and the black tones are blacker.

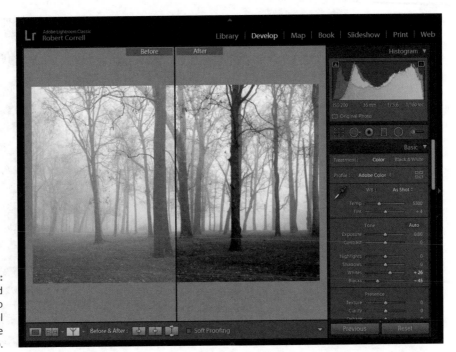

FIGURE 2-10:
Set white and
black points to
define the tonal
range of the
photo.

Working with texture, clarity, and haze

Lightroom has a few powerful controls that can help you sharpen or soften details of your photos: Texture, Clarity, and Dehaze. They are located in the Presence section of the Basic panel.

Texture softens or sharpens details found in textured areas of your photos. You can smooth out wrinkles, for example, by lowering the setting. I find this a very nice way to make people look better. You can also make details stand out more by increasing the setting.

Clarity is very similar to the Texture control. Increasing Clarity brings out details, which makes photos look sharper. Figure 2-11 shows the surface of a wooden plaque that my wife painted the word *Family* on. By increasing Clarity, the wood texture stands out much better and the text is more defined edges. By contrast, reducing Clarity makes photos look dreamy, softly focused, and misty. Be careful when increasing clarity on photos of people because too much makes them look very unattractive.

Dehaze enables you to add or subtract haze and fog from your photos. It works wonders on outside shots with blue skies and water, as shown in Figure 2-12. The blue tones are clearer and brighter. One important point: The control works in reverse. Increasing Dehaze removes haze from the photo. Decreasing Dehaze adds haze into your shot. Got that?

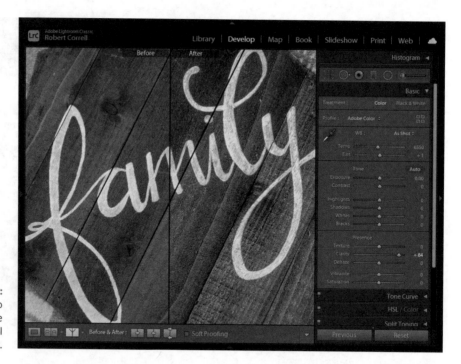

FIGURE 2-11:
Use Clarity to
emphasize
details with local
contrast.

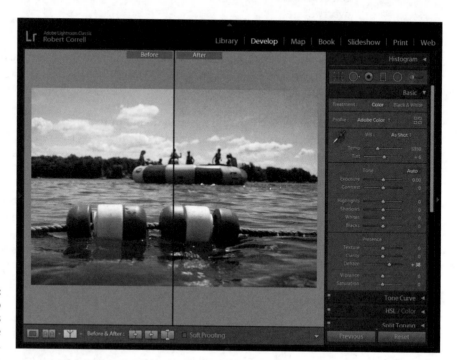

FIGURE 2-12:
Use Dehaze to
improve scenes
with lots of blue
sky and water.

Correcting and Improving Color

After making lens, brightness, contrast, highlights, shadows, texture, clarity, and haze adjustments, I move on to color. I do things in this order because color is more subjective. Getting the brightness correct is pretty fundamental, whereas some of the other adjustments are not as necessary.

Checking the white balance

Quite often, white balance is just fine. You have to worry about it only if you see something out of place. Once again, Raw photos have the advantage over JPEGs. When you set the white balance in your camera, it appends your choice to the Raw data as a suggestion. The actual data is left alone. Software uses the setting to interpret the scene and display the photo. That means you can change the white balance setting to another preset in Lightroom, or decide on a specific color temperature yourself, using the original data.

With JPEGs, however, the camera uses the in-camera white balance setting and processes the color accordingly when it saves the photo as a JPEG. Although you can reinterpret it in software, you've lost the original data. I don't mean to sound overly dramatic. It's just that you have less wiggle room when adjusting the white balance of a JPEG.

Figure 2-13 shows the White Balance Selector over an area of a One Way sign that should be white. It's not. As you can see from the detail loupe, the RGB value is imbalanced. The spot has too little red and too much blue. If the color were white or a shade of gray, the RGB values would be the same (or very close). Clicking this spot corrects the entire photo.

Adjusting color vibrancy and saturation

These simple controls boost or cut color intensity. *Vibrancy* raises or lowers the saturation of weak colors, whereas *saturation* strengthens or weakens all colors. I've used a combination of both to enhance the color of a sunset in Figure 2-14.

TIP

I like saturated photos. As I raise it, however, I'm careful to not make noise more visible or blow out highlights. Turning up *most things* while you edit runs these risks. When possible, I increase vibrancy first to see whether it does the trick. Vibrancy is more forgiving because you're not turning up all colors, just the muted ones.

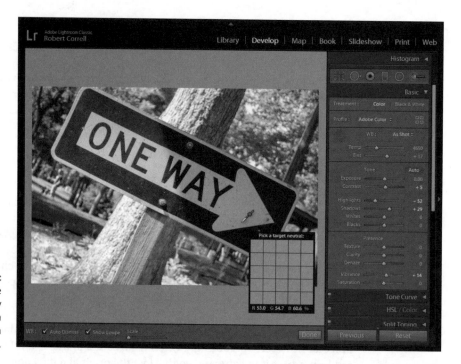

FIGURE 2-13:
Adjust white
balance by
choosing a
neutral spot in
the photo.

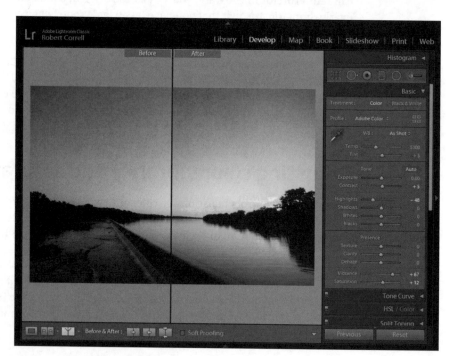

FIGURE 2-14:
Control color
strength with
vibrancy and
saturation.

Making Additional Improvements

After you get the exposure and color under control, you should begin to look at whether you need to correct sharpness, noise, or distortion. You may not need or want to apply every technique mentioned here:

>> **Sharpen:** Everybody likes sharp-looking photos. Factors such as the quality of your lens, focus, camera stability, shutter speed, and distance clearly have a large effect on how sharp a photo can be. Within those bounds, you can sharpen photos quite a bit. Figure 2-15 shows the Sharpening controls in the Detail panel of Lightroom.

TIP

If the photo has serious sharpness problems, try reshooting it with a better technique or leave it for advanced editing, where you can use more sharpening techniques. Don't oversharpen photos. Doing so makes the edges look artificial and can increase the appearance of noise.

>> **Noise reduction:** Similarly, most raw converters have some form of noise reduction. Many let you reduce noise in the Luminance channel, the photo's color channels, or both. Figure 2-15 also shows the Noise Reduction controls in Lightroom.

WARNING

Too much noise reduction removes a great deal of a photo's detail. If that happens to you, try backing off. Third-party noise reduction *plug-ins* (small add-ons that provide new or better features to the software you're using) can give you more control over noise reduction and the ability to protect or sharpen details. You can also selectively reduce noise by using layers or masks in a photo editor.

>> **Correcting perspective distortion:** Pointing the camera up makes vertical lines converge toward the top of the photo. This is called *vertical perspective distortion,* or vertical distortion. It happens most often when you photograph a building or something tall and you have to look up to get the whole structure in the shot. *Horizontal perspective distortion,* or horizontal distortion, happens when you angle the camera sideways as you take a shot. Horizontal lines run at an angle instead of being parallel to the frame or ground. Figure 2-16 shows the Transform panel in Lightroom, where you can correct any distortion.

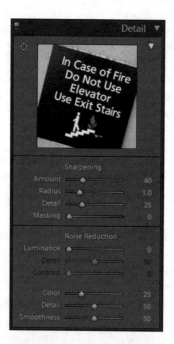

FIGURE 2-15:
Sharpen and
reduce noise
when necessary.

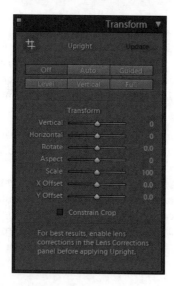

FIGURE 2-16:
Correct
perspective
distortion using
the controls
in Lightroom's
Transform panel.

My point in this chapter is to give you the basics. Remember that many other features in most photo-editing applications enable you to perfect your photos. Aside from the basic controls I've mentioned, Lightroom has many more features, controls, and options. Although having them is great, don't think that you have to use them all.

Finishing Up

When I am happy with how the photo looks at this point, I perform a few final tasks and then export it as a JPEG or TIFF.

Straightening and cropping

I prefer to straighten and crop photos last. That way, I know I have all my other adjustments in the bank and can take my time deciding whether the photo needs anything else.

When I straighten and crop, I always keep in mind that my goal is to improve the final photo. Some photos don't need to be straightened or cropped. They look fine as they are. Don't think that you have to straighten every photo that is a half-degree out of perfect. You don't. However, if the alignment causes a distraction, you should fix it.

Figure 2-17 is a shot of my wife and daughter. We were playing Uno on the picnic table, and I had my camera with me. I took this shot without thinking about the background too much. You can see an old computer case and shelf in the garage. I can improve the photo by cropping those details out, and rotate the photo a bit.

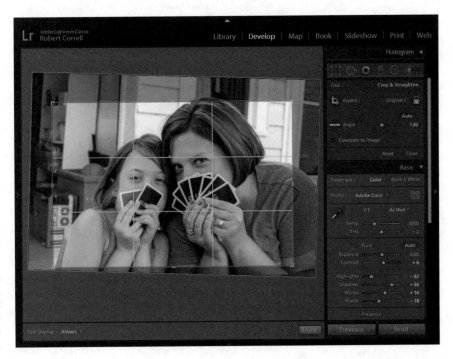

FIGURE 2-17: Rotating and cropping is about improving the final presentation of the photo.

Be aware that as you straighten photos, you lose the original corners. How much depends on how badly the shot is aligned in the first place.

Exporting images

REMEMBER

This isn't an editing task, but I want to mention it here: In Lightroom, you don't have to do anything to save or close files. After you're done developing a photo, you can select another one from the Library or another module. You can export a photo whenever you want — even in the middle of editing.

Figure 2-18 shows the Export dialog box. I've entered the settings I like to use to export a reduced-size JPEG. Aside from resizing it, I could also strip the metadata, apply a copyright, and use a watermark.

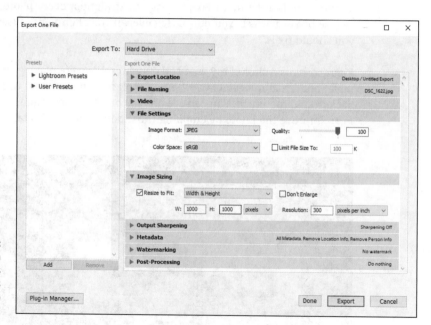

FIGURE 2-18:
Exporting a photo applies the adjustments you've made to the saved file.

Processing Photos In-Camera

Today's dSLRs come with snazzy built-in raw processing tools that you can use at the spur of the moment and with a touch of a button. This development isn't limited to a particular price point, either. For example, the professional-level Pentax K-1 Mark II and the consumer-level Canon T8i both have impressive in-camera raw image processing (sometimes called *retouching*) options.

Canon cameras enable you to change brightness, white balance, picture style, and Auto Lighting Optimizer settings; turn on high ISO speed noise reduction; set the desired JPEG image quality and color space; and correct peripheral illumination, lens distortion, and chromatic aberrations! Not bad at all.

Nikon cameras have similar options: Change the image quality, size, white balance; adjust exposure compensation; change the Picture Control settings; turn on high ISO noise reduction; change the color space; and change the D–Lighting settings.

I'm going to use the Canon EOS 90D as an example. Here's how easy it is to process Raw photos and turn them into new JPEG images:

1. **Select RAW Image Processing from Playback menu 2, as shown on the left in Figure 2-19.**

2. **Choose a photo you want to process, as shown on the right in Figure 2-19.**

   This is one of my favorite spots to take photos. It's in a parking garage on campus. I'm in the stairwell looking down from the top floor. The angles and contrast between the railing and concrete fascinate me.

3. **Select an adjustment you want to make, as shown on the left in Figure 2-20.**

4. **Make the adjustment, as shown on the right in Figure 2-20.**

   In this case, I'm decreasing the brightness by 1/3 of a stop.

5. **Save the photo, as shown in Figure 2-21.**

   After adjusting the brightness, I applied the Adobe RGB color space, converted the photo to monochrome, and applied lens correction data. I then selected Save. The camera creates a new JPEG image from the raw data, gives it a new name, and stores it on the memory card.

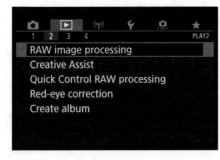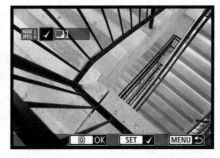

FIGURE 2-19: Selecting a Raw photo to process.

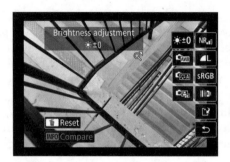
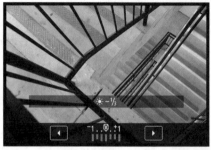

FIGURE 2-20:
Adjusting the
brightness.

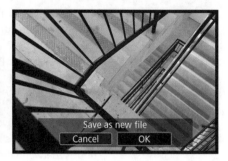

FIGURE 2-21:
Saving the image
as a new file.

Chapter **3**

Digging Deeper into Photo Editing

on't think that you have to be a total nerd to have fun editing photos in a program like Photoshop. You don't. It helps, but you don't have to go all in. Me? Oh, well, yes. I sometimes feel like King of the Nerds.

My enthusiasm springs partly from having so much fun using Photoshop. It's a real creative challenge that is very rewarding. Making photos better — even after I've gone over them using Lightroom — fills me with a down-to-earth sense of accomplishment that I thrive on.

Have fun with this chapter. In case you can't tell already, I'm urging you not to approach it too seriously. I share a few techniques that I use to make my good photos better in Photoshop. It's pretty astounding what you can do. But I don't load bad photos into Photoshop. Those shots never make it past the initial flagging phase of my operation.

Software for Editing Photos

As with the other chapters in this section, I need to make an announcement about the software featured in this chapter before getting started. I'm using Adobe Photoshop to show tips and tricks on how to edit your photos in ways that are hard or impossible in applications like Lightroom.

It wasn't a hard choice, really. Photoshop is the premier photo editor and has been for many years. Although there are competitors, Photoshop is the standard for a reason. If you have Photoshop Elements, PaintShop Pro, or another app, you'll find that most or all of the techniques I share translate with a minimum of fuss.

One final caveat: I assume that you're using Lightroom or the equivalent to perform most tasks required to get your photos into shape. Therefore, I don't cover issues like correcting exposure, contrast, and so forth in this chapter. If you want to investigate those issues, turn to Book 5, Chapter 2. There is always some crossover, of course, but I want to focus on things that are more suited to a graphics editor. Again, use these techniques to make good photos better. Don't waste your time on bad stuff.

Dealing with the Mundane Stuff

I've written this section to address some of the housekeeping chores that support the features in Photoshop that I use in this chapter.

Creating a Photoshop file

Creating a Photoshop file begins, oddly enough, in Lightroom (or your Raw processor of choice). Spruce up your best shots first. You might not even need to mess with them in Photoshop. If that's the case, export them as JPEGs and put them up for people to see.

When you want to open a photo in Photoshop, you can take one of several different paths. I typically export a full-sized 8-bit TIFF with the Adobe RGB (1998) color space from Lightroom. I then drag and drop the file onto Photoshop's workspace.

However, you have other ways of doing this. If you don't want to mess with the interim TIFF file, choose Photo ➪ Edit In ➪ Edit in Adobe Photoshop, as shown in Figure 3-1. If you've chosen a Raw file, it opens directly in Photoshop. If you have chosen a JPEG or other format, the Edit In menu has a few more options to explore.

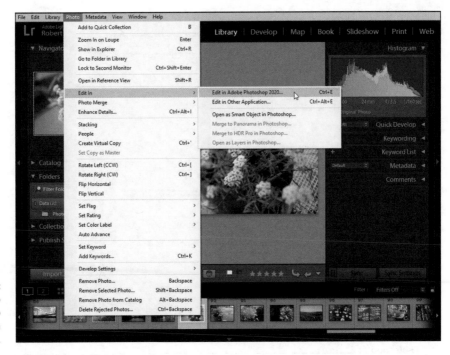

FIGURE 3-1:
Sending a photo
to Photoshop to
edit from within
Lightroom.

Choose Edit ⇨ Preferences and select the External Editing tab (see Figure 3-2) to view and change the settings Lightroom uses to send photos to Photoshop. It defaults to a compressed 16-bit TIFF at 300 dpi and with the ProPhoto RGB color space. That's a bit much. All you really need is 8 bits with the Adobe RGB (1998) color space. I prefer uncompressed TIFFs, but compressed TIFFs are smaller.

You can also export your photos in Photoshop's native file format, PSD. I prefer TIFFs because I like seeing their thumbnails on my system when I look at them in a folder, but it's really up to you.

When you get the file open in Photoshop, save it by choosing File ⇨ Save As. Change the type to Photoshop (PSD) if necessary. Choose a location and name, and that's it.

The end result is getting to a workable file in Photoshop that is ready to edit, regardless of whether you exported it out of Lightroom or sent it directly to Photoshop.

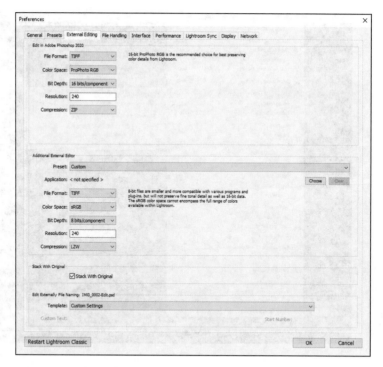

FIGURE 3-2:
Lightroom has several preferences that affect how files are sent to Photoshop.

Helpful Photoshop features

Photoshop has too many cool features to mention. However, you should be aware of a few key elements of the application that will help you edit photos. They are

>> **Panels:** The Photoshop interface is covered with panels. You can turn them on and off when needed, but you'll normally want the Tools, Properties, and Layers panels visible at all times.

>> **Tools:** Photoshop has a Tools panel on the left side of the interface. This is where you select tools like the Eraser and Marquee. Most have a keyboard shortcut. You won't need all the tools when you work with photos, but I typically need one or more of the selection tools, the Eraser, the Clone Stamp, and the Dodge and Burn tools.

After you select a tool, you can change parameters like brush size and hardness from the Options bar near the top of the screen. Then it's off to work.

>> **Keyboard shortcuts:** Photoshop is famous for its keyboard shortcuts. If you find yourself using a particular tool or feature all the time, learn the keyboard shortcut. It saves you a lot of time and hassle. My favorites are S for the Clone

Stamp tool, M for Marquee, V for the Move tool, Spacebar to switch to the Hand, and Ctrl+Alt+Shift+E/⌘+Alt+Shift+E (Win/Mac) to merge visible layers to a new layer.

» **Layers:** Layers make working with photos in Photoshop worth it. Although most other features are available in Lightroom and other photo-processing applications, layers are the realm of graphics editors. Layers allow you to stack changes on top of each other, blend them in different ways, and even organize and track your work.

» **Adjustments:** Adjustments are the tools you use to alter brightness, contrast, color, and so forth. They come in two flavors: direct, which are applied permanently to a normal layer, and adjustment layers, which are nondestructive and can be edited. I prefer the latter.

» **Masks:** Masks hide parts of layers and allow material beneath to show through. This feature makes many sophisticated editing techniques possible. You can sharpen the layer you're working on, for example, and mask out areas you don't want altered. The unsharpened photo beneath shows in the masked areas.

Coping with color management

Color management can be a tricky concept. Normal photo files have what's called a color profile. *Color profiles* help hardware like monitors and printers accurately reproduce the colors in the file to the best of their ability. That last part is key. Not every piece of hardware has the same abilities. As a result, a limited color profile was created that would work with just about anything. That profile is called sRGB.

The sRGB color profile works with everything you'll likely view, edit, or print your photos on. Although it has a smaller *gamut*, or total range of colors, it is pretty reliable. I set my camera to save JPEGs in this profile. When you save photos for use on the web, always select this profile for the final JPEG.

The Adobe RGB (1998) color profile defines a wider color space. That means that it has more colors in it. Although technically better than sRGB, it's not guaranteed to produce good colors on systems that expect sRGB. It is, however, a great profile to work in. I work with my photos in Photoshop with this profile. I also send files to the printer in Adobe RGB (1998). The last step in my process when saving a file as a JPEG is to convert the color profile from Adobe RGB (1998) to sRGB. It stinks, but it's necessary.

There are more color profiles available, but you don't really need to mess with them. Lightroom can use ProPhoto RGB, which has an even wider gamut than Adobe RGB (1998).

One quirky thing to remember before moving on: Raw exposures don't pick up a profile until you convert and export them as a TIFF or JPEG.

Saving your final images

I prefer saving my working file in Photoshop (PSD) format for safekeeping. When you want a final image to print or post, convert the color profile to sRGB if necessary, crop if desired, and then flatten the image before saving as a JPEG or TIFF. I prefer naming my final versions with "-final" appended to the name, which keeps the versions straight.

Dodging and Burning

Dodging and burning are two (dangerous-sounding!) techniques that you can use to lighten (*dodge*) or darken (*burn*) areas with a brush. I use these tools to subtly elevate brightness in areas I want you to look at, to darken areas for drama, or to balance the photo.

TIP

When dodging and burning, I create a duplicate layer of the photo to dodge and burn on. It allows me to preserve the original photo and blend with opacity if I choose to.

After duplicating the layer, select the Dodge or Burn tool, choose a brush size and hardness, and then select a range. The Range option lets you target specific tones in the image: shadows, midtones, or highlights. All you do is brush it on, as shown in Figure 3-3. In this photo, I'm brightening areas of my son's face slightly so that the tones are more even. Dodging people's faces helps make them the center of attention.

Dodging and burning work well to *emphasize* rather than correct. In other words, I dodge to brighten highlights in clouds, on water, or elsewhere to accentuate those elements. Quite often, I burn shadows (see Figure 3-4) or midtones for the opposite effect. In this case, I am burning the shadows under the bridge slightly to increase contrast.

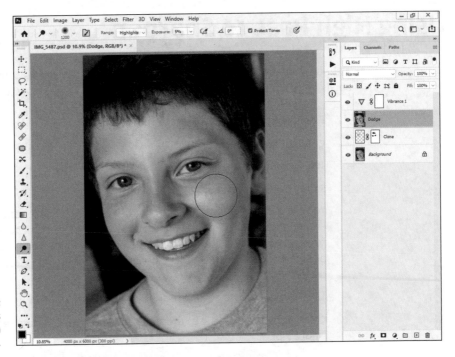

FIGURE 3-3:
Dodge faces
to brighten
them a bit.

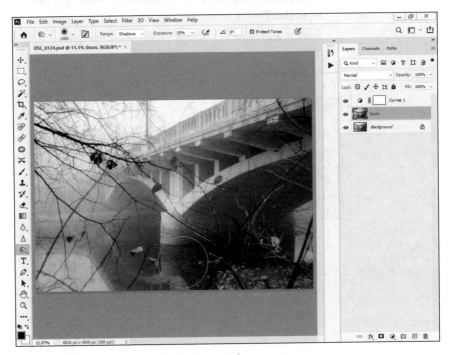

FIGURE 3-4:
Boost contrast
with a little
burning.

Using High Pass to Sharpen

Although I generally prefer light sharpening in Lightroom, sometimes a photo needs more. In that case, I use High Pass Sharpen. Here's how to do it:

1. **Duplicate the layer you want to sharpen.**

2. **Choose Filters ➪ Other ➪ High Pass.**

The High Pass dialog box opens, as shown in Figure 3-5.

3. **Select a radius, in pixels, and click OK.**

You can think of this as a strength control. I generally choose something around 2 or 5 for light sharpening, or up to 10 for more, but it does depend somewhat on the size of the image. Photos from cameras with vastly different pixel counts behave differently. Experiment with your photos to see what you prefer.

The layer will look odd. That's okay. It's working as intended.

4. **Change the Blend mode of the sharpened layer to Overlay (see Figure 3-6).**

5. **Adjust the strength further by lowering the opacity of the sharpened layer (see Figure 3-7).**

You can also mask out different areas you don't want sharpened.

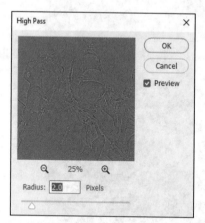

FIGURE 3-5: Increase the radius for a stronger effect.

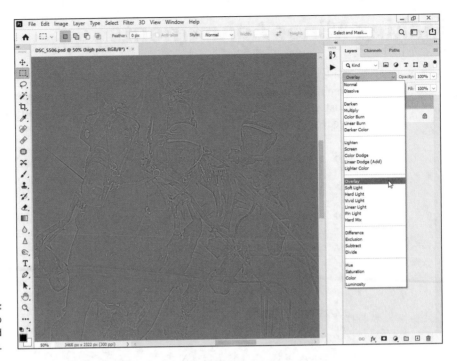

FIGURE 3-6:
Don't forget to
change the blend
mode.

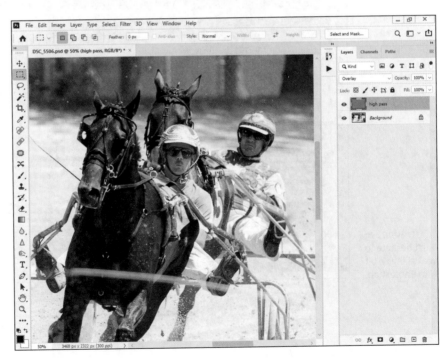

FIGURE 3-7:
The overall effect
is to sharpen the
photo.

Making Minor Adjustments

Don't be afraid to make minor adjustments to brightness, contrast, and color, even if you've worked on the photo in Lightroom before editing in Photoshop. It's most effective if you use an adjustment layer to accomplish these tasks. When needed, I prefer these:

>> **Brightness/contrast:** If the photo looks like it needs a dab of brightness or contrast, toss a Brightness/Contrast adjustment layer on top. Tweak accordingly.

>> **Levels and curves:** These are more complicated adjustments, but they are very effective at altering brightness and contrast (see Figure 3-8). Play around with the presets and experiment with the controls. They also can correct color imbalances by setting the white and black points of the photo.

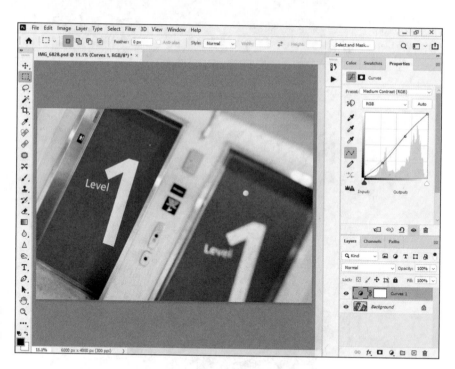

FIGURE 3-8: Don't hesitate to tweak things a bit in Photoshop.

>> **Vibrance:** Shabby or dingy colors make things look dull or prematurely aged. Give your photo a shot of color with the Vibrance/Saturation adjustment layer. Conversely, overly bright colors can be hard to look at. If that is the case, tone them down.

>> **Photo filters:** I like photo filters. They're the digital equivalent of physical filters that you put in front of your lens to filter certain types of light or ambiance. Book 3, Chapter 5 talks more about physical filters. The options in the Photo Filter dialog box are intuitive: Choose a filter type based on the description or a solid color, and then choose a density.

Applying Changes Selectively with Masks

If you don't need to sharpen an entire photo, don't. Likewise, if you need to brighten only the sky, keep your adjustments to that area and leave the rest alone. How? Masks.

Masks enable you to apply changes to selective areas of photos. I love using masks. They give you the freedom to repair, correct, or enhance specific areas of a photo without unnecessarily altering the entire thing.

I used a Levels adjustment layer on the photo of my daughter in Figure 3-9. The trick is, I used the built-in mask to apply the change to the background only. I masked her out.

Adjustment layers are created with white masks, which have no effect. To mask out areas and prevent them from being affected by the adjustment layer, select the adjustment layer mask from the Layers panel and then paint black on the canvas over the areas you want to hide using the Brush tool. Size the brush according to the area you want to paint, and don't forget to make it softer or harder to blend edges. You'll see the mask update in the panel. Press the Backslash key to toggle the mask on or off as a Rubylith overlay. In case you're wondering, Rubylith is a brand of masking film used by people in the graphic arts industry. It is so prevalent that the product name has become synonymous with masking. Rubylith masking film is actually red, although you can change the color in Photoshop.

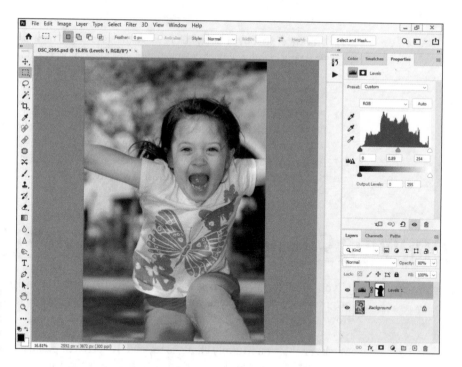

FIGURE 3-9:
Use masks
to target
adjustments to
specific areas.

Mashing Up Versions of the Same Shot

I include this technique when I just can't get a photo to shine the way I want it to using a single developed version. To work around this problem, I create one or more virtual copies of the original photo in Lightroom and then process them differently. I optimize different areas of the photo in each copy.

Quite often, this technique is helpful when working with a bright sky and a dark subject or foreground. Figure 3-10 shows a nice photo of a pasture in Oklahoma that I photographed near sunset. I could get the foreground to look good, or the sky, but not both. So I created a virtual copy and made two sets of adjustments. I exported them both and created a file in Photoshop to blend them together. Figure 3-10 shows the photo optimized for the green pasture and trees. The upper layer is turned off.

Figure 3-11 shows the upper layer turned on. The effect is dramatic. I used a mask to hide the foreground in the top photo so that the bottom layer could show through. Remember, this is the same photo. I didn't montage two shots together to create this effect.

478   BOOK 5 **Managing and Processing Your Shots**

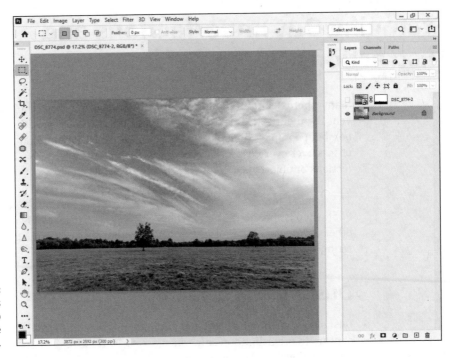

FIGURE 3-10:
Load your photos
into Photoshop
and arrange
them.

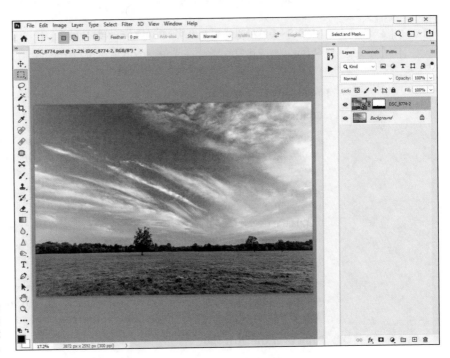

FIGURE 3-11:
Mask out areas
on a photo that
you want to hide.

Stamping Out Imperfections and Distractions

Many photos contain blemishes or distractions. It's impossible to avoid or prevent them entirely. Dust spots, specks of lint, pimples, and the occasional photo bomber pop up without asking for permission. Although I don't encourage you to obsess over every aspect of every photo you take, covering up distracting imperfections or objects is a great way to improve your shots.

The general process is called *cloning* because the tool you'll use most often in Photoshop is the Clone Stamp. The Spot Healing Brush and Healing Brush are two other useful cleaning tools. After you learn how to handle the Clone Stamp, mastering the other two is easy.

Dusting and cleaning

Dust shows up as a big blob in your photo. It's most noticeable in the sky, but also appears in other light, evenly toned areas. To remove dust spots and other small imperfections, follow these steps:

1. **Create a new layer above the photo background.**

   This is purely my preference. You can clone right on the photo layer if you want, but if you do, mistakes are far harder to correct.

2. **Select the Clone Stamp Brush.**

3. **Configure the brush.**

   If cloning on a separate layer, make sure that the Sample is set to Current & Below. This setting enables you to select a sample from a layer beneath the one you are brushing on.

   Specify a size large enough to cover the dust. In this case, the brush is 220 pixels in size. I prefer using a hardness of 0 percent when cloning dust. The soft brush blends the new material very effectively. If you're cloning over textured areas and you can see your brush strokes, you may want to increase the Hardness.

4. **Select a sample area.**

   Press Alt/Option (Win/Mac) and click an area with matching color, lightness, and texture. In this case, I selected a nearby area of the sky, as shown in Figure 3-12. Note that you may have to resample several times to get the tone just right.

5. **Paint over the dust spot.**

   If you see that things aren't matching, undo and try again. If you've obtained a good match, you'll never know that a dust spot was there to begin with. Figure 3-13 shows the final version of my photo.

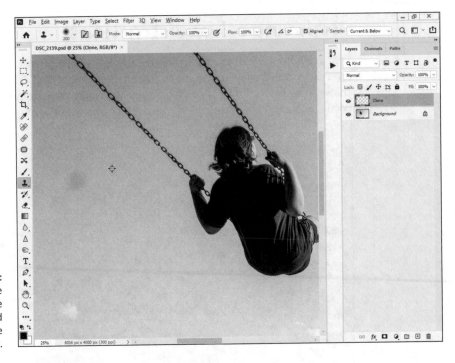

FIGURE 3-12:
Matching the
tone of the
sample and
destination is the
hardest part.

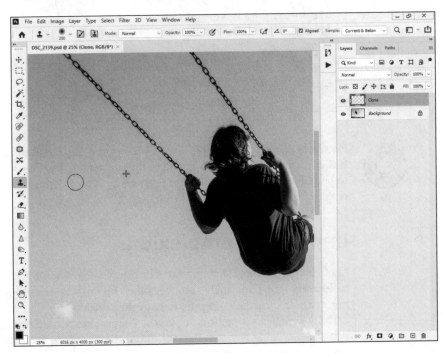

FIGURE 3-13:
The Clone Stamp
is fantastic at
removing dust
and blemishes.

Removing other distractions

Dust isn't the only distraction you can zap from your photos. Other objects can divert attention from your subject or make the scene less than desirable. Figure 3-14 shows some unsightly light posts that take attention away from an otherwise gorgeous fountain. I am in the process of removing a post in the figure.

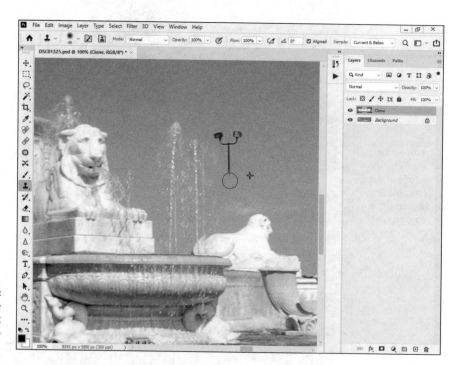

TIP

Regularly select a new sample area to hide your work. Mix it up, but pay attention. If the texture and tones don't match, the replacement will be visible. You want it to be hidden, and you don't want features to repeat. Figure 3-15 shows the final result of this small section of the photo.

Improving complexions

Another type of imperfection relates to complexion. I don't give my subjects total makeovers, but I routinely remove minor blemishes. The thing you have to be most careful of is matching the tone of the surrounding skin. The face is a wonderfully complex shape, full of curves. That makes it hard sometimes to remove zits without being obvious. I prefer to use the Clone Stamp, but the Spot Healing Brush is effective when the blemishes are not all packed together. Figure 3-16 shows an area with a handful of blemishes. I've created my separate layer and have the tool set up.

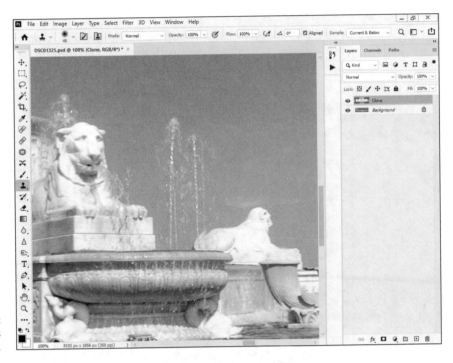

FIGURE 3-15: It's like it was never there.

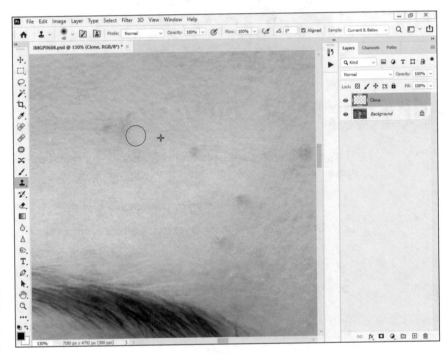

FIGURE 3-16: People will thank you for improving their complexions.

Figure 3-17 shows the final result. Although I tried to remove the most noticeable blemishes, I didn't try to smooth the skin and turn this into a glamour shot. I prefer to leave it as real as possible.

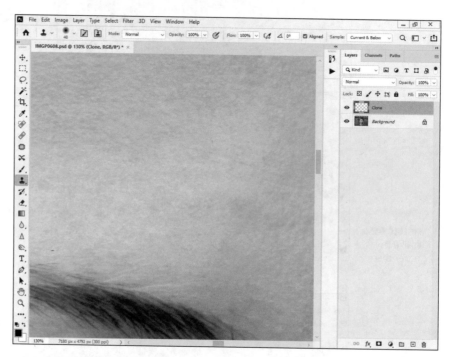

FIGURE 3-17:
The focus is on
the person
now instead of
his skin.

Adjusting Final Composition

I try to finish composing photos in Lightroom, but sometimes when it's necessary recompose in Photoshop. Here's how you can do it:

1. **Finish all the other work you want to accomplish.**

2. **Create a merged photo layer that captures your work.**

   I select everything on a visible layer, perform a merged copy, and then paste that as a new layer.

3. **Convert the merged photo layer to a Smart Object.**

   Right-click it in the Layers panel and choose Convert to Smart Object.

4. **Click the Crop tool.**

5. **Mark the area of the photo you want to preserve.**

   Mark the area by drawing a crop area with the tool, as shown in Figure 3-18. You can also drag the corner and edge handles to change the crop boundaries. I prefer to set the tool to keep the original ratio.

6. **Deselect Delete Cropped Pixels from the Options panel.**

   This action ensures that the pixels you crop are preserved. It's vital that you don't forget this step.

7. **Double-click in the crop area to commit the crop.**

8. **If you need to recompose, click the Crop tool and then click the photo in the workspace.**

   Trust me. When you click the cropped photo (having selected the Crop tool as well as deselected Delete Cropped Pixels in Step 6), the uncropped photo will appear.

You can also convert the bottom photo layer to a Smart Object before cropping.

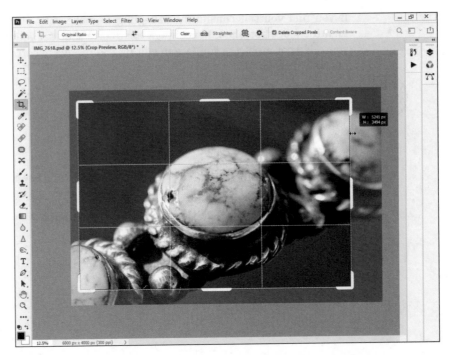

FIGURE 3-18:
Mark the crop
area with the
crop tool.

Words of Caution and Encouragement

REMEMBER

You're much more likely to ruin a photo by heavy-handed editing than by leaving it alone. As you work with your photos in Photoshop, keep these thoughts in mind:

>> **Fewer changes are better.** If you're trying to create a realistic interpretation of the photo, the less you mess with it, the better. A great-looking portrait is a perfect example. Resist the temptation to overdo something just because you can.

>> **Don't push too hard.** You run a greater risk of ruining the photo the harder you push things. A perfect example is trying to oversharpen or remove too much noise.

>> **Accept a photo.** The sensible solution is to find the spot where you can look at a photo and accept it for what it is. Not all photos are perfect. Some have noise; some have exposure problems; some have a bit of distortion. That's a reasonable life-lesson as well.

If you find yourself constantly struggling to make your photos look better in Lightroom or Photoshop, I encourage you to take a look at your photography. Ask yourself what problems you face in editing and resolve to correct them when you take the photograph.

TIP

Here are some tips:

>> Take your shots at the lowest possible ISO so that you don't have to throw noise reduction at everything you shoot.

>> Support the camera so that it doesn't jiggle or jostle, and pay attention to shutter speed. That way, not every photo is blurry.

>> Frame well-designed shots so that you don't have to crop them later.

>> Try to keep distracting objects out of the background.

>> Hold the camera straight and level so that you don't always have to straighten the photo.

>> Although no lens is perfect, use the best lenses you can.

RANTING ABOUT NOISE

I'm convinced that most dSLR photographers worry too much about noise reduction. I used to, but have successfully gotten over most of it. I'm not saying that you should stand up and cheer over your noisy photos, but the truth is that unless you're blowing up a photo to ridiculous proportions, more noise than you may realize is acceptable.

Do yourself a favor. Go get an old photography book or look online for famous older photographs. Look at their flaws and realize that they are still magnificent. Being noise free isn't what makes them great. Go take those kinds of photos, and relax about the limitations of the technology.

REMEMBER

You *can* do it. Everyone can be a good photographer by learning, practicing, observing, and identifying areas to improve in, and then correcting the things that are holding them back. Applications like Lightroom and Photoshop are wonderful tools that will help you achieve your goals!

Chapter **4**

Expressing Your Artistry

This is a "relax and have fun" chapter. Sit back, put your feet up, grab a snack, and loosen up on the reins of your life. Let your mind wander into creativity. It's amazing to see how photos transform when you process them artistically. Go crazy! Convert them from color to black and white, colorize or tint them, or apply artistic filters and effects.

You can use programs like Lightroom and Photoshop for these effects. You should also take advantage of creative processing features that are available in your camera. Although you're using modern technology, don't think these pursuits are new. Photographers of all eras have manipulated, tweaked, and perfected their photos using whatever they could get their hands on.

Why Be Creative?

I want to encourage those of you who are having trouble letting go and being creative with your photos. Don't be timid, and don't apologize. Not everyone is going to like your style, but that's the way the world works. Keep trying, learning, and improving. To borrow a phrase, "Be All You Can Be" — with the emphasis on *you*.

I've written a few reasons for expressing your creativity that might stimulate your imagination:

>> **For concealing:** Sometimes a color photo has something wrong that you can hide by converting it to black and white or colorizing. You may also be able to turn a "so-so" photo around by applying a creative filter. Don't let those photos go to waste. Turn to the "Converting to Black and White" section and jump right in.

>> **For emphasis:** You can often use artistic techniques to emphasize certain elements. Details and geometry stand out and make a photo interesting when shown from a completely different point of view. The "Experimenting with Artistic Filters" section has a lot of great ideas that can help you emphasize aspects of your photos.

>> **For mood:** It's possible to create many different moods by converting a photo to black and white or using select color tints to colorize it. Various filters may have the same effect. Create whatever mood you're after. See the "Colorizing Your Photos" section for more information.

>> **For art:** No one says you have to have a solid reason to do anything artistic. It's your art. You decide. Some photographers have developed their own sense of style over the years regardless of what anyone else thought. Figure 4-1 is a stairwell that looks as though M.C. Escher put it together. It's in the loading area of the building in Figure 4-16. The shot looks boring in color. As a black-and-white image, the lines, shapes, tones, and shadows leap out at you.

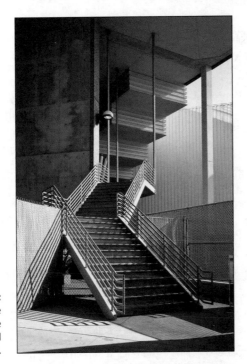

FIGURE 4-1:
Black-and-white photos have an artistry all their own.

Software for Your Artistic Endeavors

As with the other software chapters, I need to add a quick disclaimer before the action starts. I've chosen to feature Adobe Photoshop in this chapter because it represents the pinnacle of creative photo editing. It is more accessible than ever.

You can accomplish most of the tasks in this chapter using other applications, including software that comes with your camera. Specific features and capabilities will differ, however. If you're using something besides Photoshop, don't worry. The fundamentals of expressing your artistry are the same.

EXPRESSING YOUR CREATIVITY IN LIGHTROOM

You can achieve many of the same artistic effects using Lightroom that you can in Photoshop. You have to know where to look, however. Here's a quick summary of some of the tools that you can find when using the Develop module:

- **Presets:** Located in the left panel. Organized into categories like Color, Creative, and B&W. You can even create your own.

- **Black & White:** Select the Black & White treatment in the Basic panel or click Color (beside Profile) and then monochrome. Make tonal adjustments by dragging the sliders in the B & W panel.

- **HSL/Color:** Use the HSL/Color panel to selectively adjust saturation and luminance (brightness) of different hues in the photo. You can desaturate all the yellows, for instance, or increase the saturation of greens to make grass pop.

- **Split Toning:** Give shadows and highlights their own color tints using the Split Toning panel. Adjust saturation for each and tweak the balance if you like.

- **Effects:** The Effects panel contains vignetting, to darken or brighten around the edges, and film grain effects.

- **Filters:** Use the Graduated or Radial filter tools located between the Histogram and Basic panels to make selective adjustments to areas of your photo. Although they are mostly used to correct things like brightness and contrast, you can get pretty creative with these.

Despite having some very nifty tools to adjust black-and-white photos with, Lightroom doesn't have the same types of creative filters as Photoshop. You'll need to export your photo as a TIFF or open it in Photoshop from Lightroom to take advantage of them.

Converting to Black and White

Black-and-white (also known as B&W) prints evoke different kinds of feelings than their color counterparts do. In B&W, the focus is on tone, texture, and mood rather than on hue and saturation. They can be magical or somber or parts in between. This section shows you the easiest way to use Photoshop to change color photos to black and white. Conversion is different from shooting directly in black and white, which I cover near the end of the chapter. The advantage to conversion is that you have more control over how your photos are changed.

Using black-and-white adjustment layers

Not surprisingly, Photoshop has many powerful tools that change color images to black and white. Rather than try to show them all to you, I want to cut to the chase and feature the one I use the most: the Black & White adjustment layer. This technique gives you lots of control over how the final image looks and is relatively painless. For example, you can change blue skies into dark–gray shades, green grass into lighter gray, and red features to medium gray.

I encourage you to make basic adjustments to your color photo in Adobe Lightroom. These adjustments include lens corrections, overall exposure, protecting highlights and shadows, contrast, and so forth. Load the finished color photo into Photoshop. To convert color photos using Photoshop's Black & White adjustment tool, follow these steps:

1. **Click the New Adjustment Layer button and choose Black & White.**

   The button is at the bottom of the Layers panel. The Black & White option is in the middle of the second group from the bottom.

   Photoshop quickly creates the adjustment layer, as shown in Figure 4-2, and loads the default settings, as shown in Figure 4-3.

2. **Choose a different preset from the Properties panel, if desired.**

   Each preset is a predefined grayscale mix. Options include natural-looking mixes like Default, Darker, Green Filter, Lighter, as well as special mixes like Blue Filter, Infrared, Neutral Density, and Red filter. Scroll the list to find one that sounds interesting and select it. The effect on the photo is immediately updated. If you like, you can click the Auto button and see what Photoshop thinks.

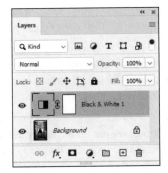

FIGURE 4-2:
The Black & White adjustment layer as it appears in the Layers panel.

3. Manually adjust the effect using the color sliders, if desired.

Photoshop adjusts the gray tones in the image based on the position of each color slider (see Figure 4-3). Dragging a slider to the left darkens the gray tone for areas of the photo with that color. Dragging it right lightens the gray tone. The numerical values range from –200 (very dark) to 300 (very light).

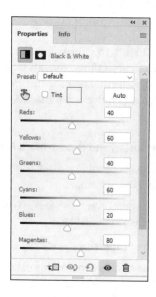

FIGURE 4-3: Each color slider affects the tonality of the black-and-white image.

These controls make it easy to lighten or darken specific areas of the black-and-white image by changing the sliders for each color.

If you're more visually inclined, you can also click the On-image adjustment tool (the small hand with the index finger extended) and click a color in the photo you want to modify. *While you hold the mouse button down*, drag left and right on the photo to darken or lighten that area. The correct color slider automatically updates the photo.

REMEMBER

You're not colorizing the image when you make changes to the color sliders. Instead, you're adjusting the *gray tone* of the specific color you choose. You can, for example, turn blues dark gray and reds light gray.

The final photo is shown in Figure 4-4. It represents a good example of how black and white can transform a photo. We put up a chair by the front door so that our cat can sit and watch traffic and birds go by. It's okay in color but looks even better when converted to black and white.

TIP

With practice, you can train yourself to see or think in black and white. You'll be able to more easily pick out potentially amazing tones, textures, and contrasts, and then bring them out as you take and process your shots.

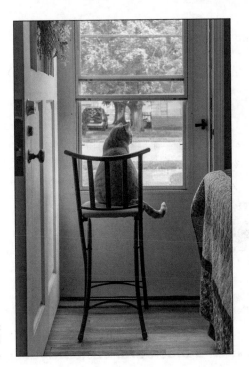

FIGURE 4-4:
The finished
conversion.

When you've finished your black-and-white adjustments, you can continue to edit the photo like any other. If you need to make contrast, brightness, or other adjustments, you can use more adjustment layers if you like.

When you're finished making adjustments, I recommend saving your Photoshop file first. Then flatten the image and save it as a TIFF. Next, import your photo back into Lightroom or other photo-management program. After it's back in the fold, so to speak, you can continue to manage, edit, print, and archive the image, along with your other photos, using Lightroom.

Photo gallery

Now that you've seen that the process of converting your photos from color to black and white in Photoshop isn't that technically difficult, it's time for a few examples.

Exploring cool presets

The presets contained in the Properties panel of the Black & White adjustment layer are good. I used the Infrared preset on the photo in Figure 4-5. It's quite stunning how the leaves of the tree in the foreground and those on the far bank of the river appear to be brightly lit. That's the effect of the preset turning yellow and green colors into bright grayscale tones. The sky and water contrast nicely with the clouds.

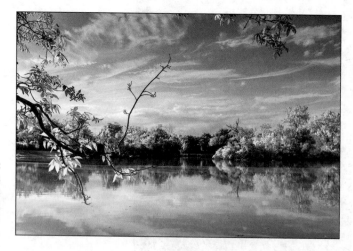

FIGURE 4-5:
Explore presets
like this
one, which
imitates infrared
photography.

Muting colors with a black-and-white layer

Don't feel as though you always have to turn a color photo fully into black and white. I like mixing things up by lowering the opacity of the Black & White adjustment layer and letting some color show through. Figure 4-6 shows the Layers panel. The adjustment layer is only 63% solid.

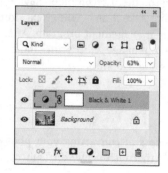

FIGURE 4-6:
Adjust the opacity
of layers to blend
color with black
and white.

Figure 4-7 shows the final result. The colors have been muted and the image looks a little bit like an old, faded postcard. I was going to convert it entirely to black and white, but as I played around with the opacity of the adjustment layer, I found that I liked it with a little color. This technique is another way to integrate black and white into your creative repertoire.

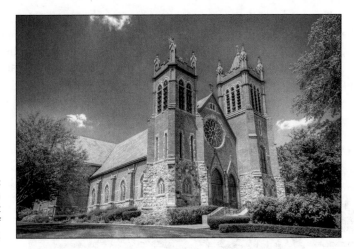

FIGURE 4-7:
Experimentation
is an important
aspect of
creativity.

Using multiple black-and-white adjustments

Expressing your creativity artistry has a lot to do with thinking outside the box. One way of doing that is to create multiple Black & White adjustment layers and mask them in such a way that each one alters a specific part of the photo.

Figure 4-8 shows the Layers panel displaying four Black & White adjustment layers. Each adjustment is masked to target a different part of the photo: the sky, the trees and grass, the plane, and the tarmac.

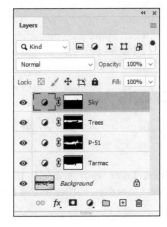

FIGURE 4-8:
Use masks
on different
adjustment layers
to target specific
areas of the
photo.

Figure 4-9 shows the finished black-and-white image. I could not accomplish what I wanted creatively with a single black-and-white adjustment. It took four, each having different goals. I wanted the sky a little darker, so that the clouds were defined but not overdone. I brightened the trees so that they didn't appear to be in shadow. I wanted the plane bright but the colorful areas on the spinner and tail dark. Finally, the concrete looked best darkened. This is the only airworthy TP-51C in existence. It was converted from a P-51C to the dual-control variant in 2003.

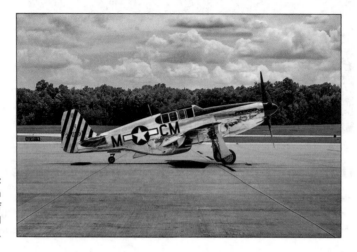

FIGURE 4-9:
A little extra effort pays off when the final photo is done.

Colorizing Your Photos

Colorizing (a.k.a. *tinting* or *toning*) black-and-white images replaces black with one, two, or more colors, resulting in unique color effects that create different moods, tonalities, or apparent age. You can approach colorizing images in several ways. I run through a few that I use regularly.

Tinting the fast and easy way

Tinting your photos as you convert them to black and white is both convenient and easy. Here's how:

1. Create a Black & White adjustment layer, as described in the "Using black-and-white adjustment layers" section, earlier in this chapter.

2. Select the Tint option on the Properties panel, as shown in Figure 4-10.

3. Click the color swatch to open the Color Picker.

4. Adjust the color to taste.

   Click in the Color Picker to select a Tint Color. You'll be able to enter numeric values for color, brightness, and saturation or use the picker to make visual selections.

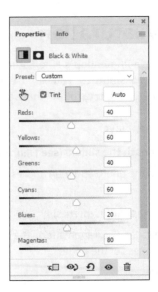

FIGURE 4-10:
Select the Tint box to colorize using the Black & White adjustment layer.

Figure 4-11 shows the finished image. (Yes, that's me. After a few days of not shaving, while posing hilariously for my wife. I rarely make it into my books. I'm normally the one taking the photos.)

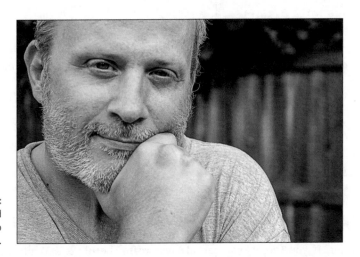

FIGURE 4-11:
Scruffy and subtle tinting go together.

Colorizing with Hue/Saturation

Another way to colorize photos is to use Photoshop's Hue/Saturation adjustment. It's a great method to quickly explore possibilities. You can use this technique for color or black-and-white photos. To give it a try, follow these steps:

1. **Create a Hue/Saturation adjustment layer.**

2. **Select the small Colorize box beneath the sliders (see Figure 4-12).**

    This option removes the color from the photo and then applies the current *hue* (a fancy name for color).

3. **Make Hue, Saturation, and Lightness adjustments.**

    To change the color, drag the Hue slider. Saturation affects the color intensity. Lightness controls the overall brightness of the photo.

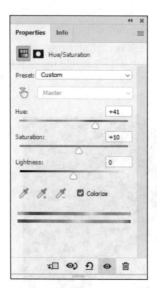

FIGURE 4-12:
Colorize also applies a single hue to a photo.

TIP

You get more control over tonality by converting the photo to black and white first. To do so, create a Black & White adjustment layer and then a Hue/Saturation layer. If you forget, you can always create the Black & White adjustment layer second and drag it below the Hue/Saturation adjustment layer in the Layers panel.

Split toning using Color Balance

Split toning enables you to apply colors to a photo's shadows and highlights. This means that you can selectively colorize black-and-white photos or create interesting special effects with color photos. The easiest way to split tone in Photoshop is to use a Color Balance adjustment layer. Here's how:

1. **Create a Color Balance adjustment layer.**

2. **In the Properties panel, select Shadows from the Tone drop-down list.**

   If you prefer working with highlights first, select Highlights from the drop-down list and adjust Shadows in Step 4.

3. **Adjust the color sliders, as shown in Figure 4-13.**

   Color Balance presents you with three color pairs: Cyan/Red, Magenta/Green, and Yellow/Blue. Drag the slider toward the color you want to increase.

   Your chosen color gets stronger while the paired color is reduced. For example, when you add cyan, red is reduced. When you add blue, yellow is reduced. You can't increase two opposing colors — magenta and green, for example — at the same time. It's an *either-or* proposition.

4. **Select Highlights from the Tone drop-down list.**

5. **Adjust the color sliders.**

   This time you're working in the highlight tonal range.

6. **Balance the effect by adjusting the opacity of the Color Balance adjustment layer.**

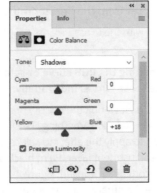

FIGURE 4-13:
Colorize by adjusting the color balance in each tonal region.

Figure 4-14 shows the effects of making the highlights in this shot of my wife magenta with yellow and the shadows a deep blue. It's quite fun to play with split toning.

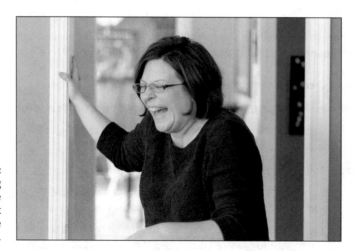

FIGURE 4-14:
Split toning gives you more options but not too many to be overwhelming.

Cross-processing with Curves

Cross-processing is a term that comes from the art of processing film with the wrong chemicals. Yikes! People made mistakes in the darkroom and realized that the color effects looked cool. Thankfully, cross-processing in Photoshop is easier than messing with smelly chemicals. To cross-process a photo (color or black and white) in Photoshop, follow these steps:

1. **Create a Curves adjustment layer.**

2. **Select the Cross Process (RGB) preset from the Preset drop-down list.**

    Figure 4-15 shows the Curves panel with the Cross Process (RGB) preset loaded.

3. **Alter the curve, if you want, by editing the RGB curve or selecting specific channels (R, G, or B) and altering those curves individually.**

    If you want to tone down the effect, try lowering the opacity of the adjustment layer. You can also change the Blend mode to something like Darken, or Soft Light, which looks good. If you want to apply the effect to select areas of your photo, use the built-in mask of the adjustment layer. Paint black on the mask to prevent the Curves adjustment from being applied. Figure 4-16 reveals the final, cross-processed photo. Notice the otherworldly tones and accentuated contrast applied to the image. That's the beauty of cross-processing.

TIP

It's possible to create a cross process look by using the Color Balance adjustment layer. Set the shadows to green and highlights to yellow. The effect may be so light that it's hard to see in other programs. You can work around this issue by split toning instead.

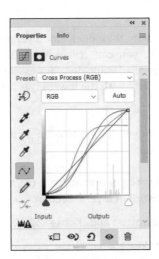

FIGURE 4-15:
The Cross
Process preset in
Photoshop.

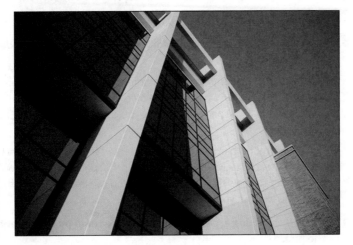

FIGURE 4-16:
This large
building
looks great
cross-processed.

Using color layers

Another approach to colorizing a photo is to use color layers. You can work with color or black-and-white photos. With this technique, add layers filled with color (either a solid color or gradient) over the photo layer. Blend the color layer with the photo layer by lowering the color layer's opacity.

This technique relies on blend modes. *Blending modes* affect whether (and how) layers on top allow other layers to show through. Normally, *opaque* (solid; the opposite of transparent) layers don't allow other layers to show through. You can change this behavior, which is what you're counting on to colorize the image.

You can use more than one color in more than one color layer and erase or blend them in creative ways. For example, you can create blue-tinted shadows and gold-tinted highlights. Some applications (Photoshop, for example) let you modify which portions of the color layer blend with the lower layer based on the tonality of either layer.

This technique isn't rocket science, but you'll have to do more work in Photoshop. To use color layers, follow these steps:

1. **Create a Black & White adjustment layer and adjust it to your liking; see the "Using black-and-white adjustment layers" section.**

2. **Click the New Adjustment Layer button and choose Solid Color.**

3. **Choose a color from the Color Picker; then click OK.**

   The Color Fill layer will appear in your Layers palette, as shown in Figure 4-17.

4. **Change the blending mode on the Layers panel to Color.**

5. **Adjust the intensity of your color layers with the Opacity slider on the Layers panel.**

   The Opacity slider controls the color intensity. Color Fill 4 layer, as shown in Figure 4-17, is set to 16 percent. The black-and-white image should show through even at 100 percent because you changed the blending mode to Color.

REMEMBER

   If you have more than one color layer stacked on top of each other, lower the opacity for each stacked layer to less than 100 percent. This allows the lower color layers to show through to the top. You can leave the bottom color layer at 100 if you like, but you can also lower it.

6. **Blend by masking areas on the color layer that you don't want to affect the photo.**

   You can also control blending by using the Layer Style dialog box. Double-click next to (not on) the color layer's name in the Layers panel to open it. Then change the Underlying Layer sliders to control what tones you want to accept the color.

7. **Add more color layers, if you want.**

   You can go all out and create duotones, tritons, quadtones, and more by adding more color layers. Have one color for tinting the shadows, another for the mid-tones, and another for the highlights. You can also use multiple colors for each.

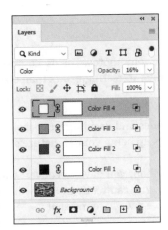

FIGURE 4-17:
Control color
strength by
lowering layer
opacity.

Figure 4-18 shows the final result. I found this old, abandoned Pontiac Executive and quickly fell in love with it. This model was in production from 1966 through 1970. Subjects like this are great to photograph. The textures in this photo are amazing when juxtaposed with the sleek P-51 in Figure 4-9. Black-and-white photos, whether toned or not, help you showcase these details.

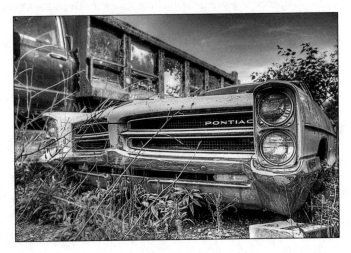

FIGURE 4-18:
Use multiple
color layers for
detailed color
toning.

If your application doesn't support color blending but has layers, blend with layer opacity.

TIP

Creating duotones

Duotones are another way to colorize your photos. The process was originally used by printers who wanted more visually interesting prints than black and white but without the cost of full color.

Have fun experimenting with duotones and deciding what looks best to you! You might create a unique look that ends up being your signature style.

REMEMBER

When you create duotones in Photoshop, you have to convert the image to grayscale and then convert it to duotone. You can't stay in RGB, which is the standard color mode of most photos. But I have a way around that.

To apply a duotone, follow these steps:

1. **Create a Black & White adjustment layer and adjust it to your liking, as shown in the "Using black-and-white adjustment layers" section.**

This converts the photo to black and white without destroying any information.

2. **Create a duplicate image with merged layers.**

Do so by choosing Image ➪ Duplicate. Check the Duplicate Merged Layers Only box in the Duplicate Image dialog box. Click OK.

Now you have a copy of your photo, converted to black and white. This is the temporary working file. You'll create the duotone with it and then copy and paste it back into your normal file.

You can close the original file for this part of the process as long as you save it in Photoshop format. You'll need it at the end.

3. **Convert the duplicate image to grayscale by choosing Image ➪ Mode ➪ Grayscale.**

When asked, choose to discard the color information. If asked, merge layers.

4. **Convert the duplicate image to Duotone by choosing Image ➪ Mode ➪ Duotone.**

The Duotone Options dialog box shows a monotone initially, or the settings from your last application.

5. **In the Duotone Options dialog box, choose a duotone from the Preset drop-down menu.**

I suggest first browsing through the extensive list of presets and applying those that you like. Figure 4-19 shows a preset loaded in the dialog box and the image visible onscreen. I selected the Warm Gray 11 bl 2 option from the Preset menu.

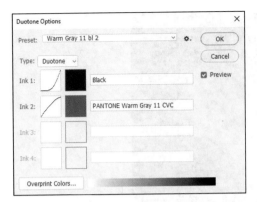

FIGURE 4-19:
Applying a
duotone preset.

When you become familiar with duotones, load a preset that's close to what you want and use it as a starting point to create your own preset. You can apply a number of inks, create specific curves for each color, and choose the colors themselves (by using the Color Picker or browsing the extensive color libraries). Experiment with the settings in the dialog box.

You can save presets that you have changed. Choose the settings you like, and then select the small drop-down menu tucked between the Preset menu and the OK button. Within this list are Save and Load Preset menus.

6. **Click OK.**

You've created the duotone using the copied image. Now it's time to put it back into your original file as a new layer.

7. **Select the layer in the duplicate image by pressing Ctrl+A/⌘+A (Win/Mac).**

8. **Copy the later in the duplicate image by pressing Ctrl+C/⌘+C (Win/Mac).**

9. **Switch to the original image file.**

Reopen it if you have to.

10. **Paste the Duotone layer into the original file by pressing Ctrl+V/⌘+V (Win/Mac).**

11. **Close the copied duplicate image. There is no need to save this working file.**

That's it. See Figure 4-20 for my final photo. Once again, this isn't a bad shot in color. However, converting the photo to black and white and then adding some tone makes Jacob the center of attention and not his t-shirt or skateboard.

TIP

If you're not working in Photoshop, create your own duotones using color layers. If using Lightroom, use the Split Toning feature or a Develop Preset that has toning.

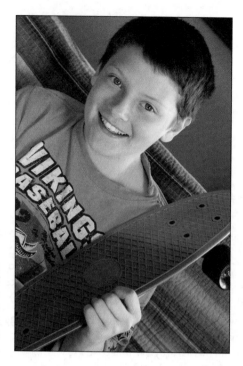

FIGURE 4-20:
A dash of duotone keeps black-and-white shots from looking too cold and gray.

Experimenting with Artistic Filters

And now for something completely creative. I could play around with artistic filters all day. I really could. They are creative, inspiring, and easy to use. Part of the fun is the journey. Enjoy experimenting to find out what looks good with your photos. Don't worry if something doesn't look good right away. The process involves a degree of trial and error.

Using the Filter Gallery

Your first stop should be the Filter Gallery, which is a special dialog box that allows you to preview and experiment with many different types of filters. To launch the Filter Gallery, follow these steps:

1. **Choose Filter ⇨ Filter Gallery.**

A large dialog box opens, as shown in Figure 4-21. A preview of the photo is shown on the left side. Click the magnification buttons at the lower-left corner to zoom in and out. You can press Ctrl+0/⌘+0 (Win/Mac) to view the entire photo.

Individual filters are grouped by categories to the right of the preview window. Click the arrow by the category name to see the filter thumbnails associated with that category.

Settings for the selected filter are shown on the right. The name of the currently selected filter appears in a drop-down list above the settings. If you prefer, you can select new filters using this list instead of the thumbnails.

Additional controls are shown in the bottom of the dialog box. You can add or remove filters, turn them on or off, and rearrange them using the controls in this area.

2. **Find and choose a filter that you want to apply.**

   Select filters from the thumbnails or the drop-down list. The thumbnails are arranged in these categories: Artistic, Brush Strokes, Distort, Sketch, Stylize, and Texture. The filters are alphabetized in the drop-down list.

3. **Experiment with the filter's settings.**

   Have fun and experiment with different settings. Filters that may seem uninspiring may turn around if you tweak the slider controls a bit. If you're in a hurry, don't feel bad about having a quick look at the default settings and moving on if the result doesn't look promising.

4. **Click OK to apply or Cancel to quit the Filter Gallery without applying.**

I show a few examples of filters from the Filter gallery in an upcoming section called "Filter fun."

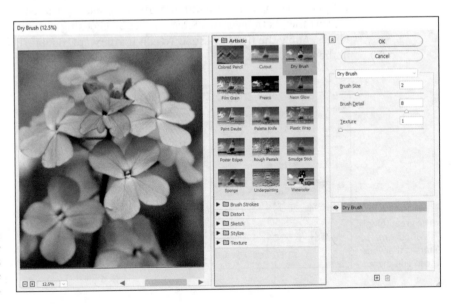

FIGURE 4-21:
The Filter Gallery dialog box is full of creative controls.

Expressing Your Artistry

Applying other filters

If the Filter Gallery doesn't have what you're looking for, the Filters menu includes additional filters. Several are grouped with the Filter Gallery in the same area of the menu. Numerous categories are listed on the bottom half of the menu. To apply one of these filters, follow these steps:

1. **Select the Filters menu.**

2. **Choose the filter that you want to apply from the menu.**

Most filters open a dialog box with one or more controls. Some, like Stylize ⇨ Find Edges, don't.

3. **Modify the filter's settings, if possible.**

Filters like Liquify open a complicated dialog box with many options and settings. Some, like Pixillate ⇨ Pointillize, are easy to understand and have very intuitive settings. Unfortunately, I don't have the room to go into all the interesting details. Although I show a few examples in the section called "Filter fun," you should take advantage of the Photoshop Help menu and manual for more details about each filter.

Smart Filters

The process I've described thus far applies the filter you've chosen, whether from the Filter Gallery or not, to the layer you have selected. You can't change the filter after it has been applied. You must Undo and then reapply the same filter or filters with new settings or use a different filter. If you want to edit filters, you should convert the photo layer to a Smart Object by choosing Filter ⇨ Convert for Smart Filters. Apply the filter as usual. To edit it afterward, double-click the filter name in the Layers panel (see Figure 4-22).

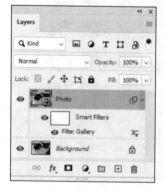

FIGURE 4-22: The great thing about Smart Filters is that you can edit them.

Filter fun

Telling you about filters is one thing. Showing you is another. I've selected several of my photos and applied interesting filters to give you an idea of the many artistic possibilities you have at your fingertips.

Extrude

Extrude is a funky filter. I love it. It's in the Stylize group of the Filters menu. When you select it, you get a few options. You can select the shape of the extrusion (blocks or pyramids) as well as the size and depth, and you can make a few other choices. Aside from boosting the depth to 120, I left the settings alone for this photo of a flower shown in Figure 4-23.

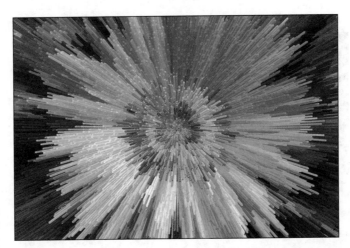

FIGURE 4-23: Extrude is mind-blowing.

Stamp

Figure 4-24 is a photo of one of my electric guitars, after having applied the Stamp filter. Located in the Filter Gallery, the Stamp filter has an important requirement. Like some of the other filters in the Sketch group, the foreground and background colors determine the colors of the stamp. In this case, I chose black as the foreground and white as the background color. It turns the black guitar mostly white.

Cutout

I took the photo shown in Figure 4-25 on a Fall retreat with our church's youth group. The camp we were at has a giant swing. It's a total thrill ride. You get strapped into your seat and then hauled up. When you pull the rip-cord, you drop a good ways before you start swinging. I looked for a unique vantage point and found one underneath the campers as they were being pulled up.

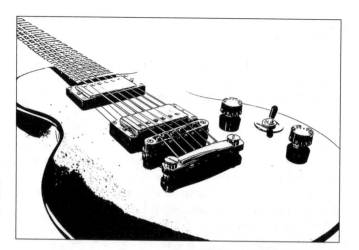

FIGURE 4-24:
Remember to set
the colors before
you apply the
Stamp filter.

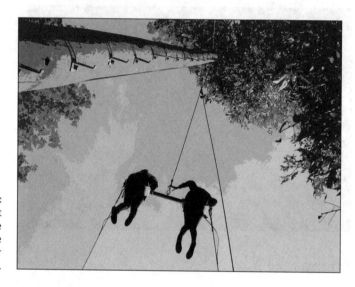

FIGURE 4-25:
The Cutout
filter imitates the
effect of a collage
made from paper
cutouts.

Poster edges

I took the photo in Figure 4-26 from inside the Gateway Arch in St. Louis. I'm at
the very top looking due west. The downtown area is prominently featured in this
photo, and the baseball stadium is visible to the left side.

This photo doesn't look like a photo anymore because I applied the Poster Edges
filter to it. You can find it in the Filter Gallery.

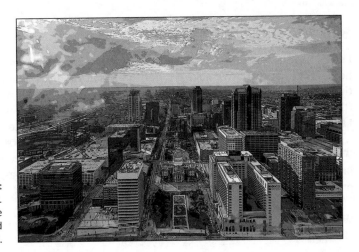

FIGURE 4-26:
Downtown St.
Louis as if it were
hand drawn and
colored.

Pointillize

Pointillize is a fun filter that I want to use on everything. It doesn't look good on everything, though, so I have to hold back some. It has one option: the size of the dots. Pointillize is in the Pixelate group of filters.

Figure 4-27 shows the filter applied to a photo of my daughter on a swing right beside a lake. I didn't have to do much to prepare the photo for the filter. I exported a TIFF from Lightroom and loaded it into Photoshop; then I applied the filter. Afterward, you can always import your work back into Lightroom to manage it.

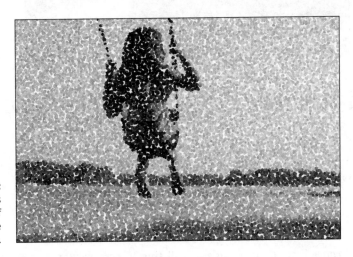

FIGURE 4-27:
Pointillize uses
small circles of
color to create
the image.

Blurring with poster edges

Figure 4-28 is a photo of my son, Jacob, getting sprayed down with the garden hose in our backyard. We have a lot of fun in our family! I applied two filters to this shot. First, I duplicated the photo layer and then blurred it with a Radial Blur (that's with the Blur filters) set to zoom. I then masked his face, which means that I hid it. This allowed the unblurred version just around his face to be visible. I then merged a copy of all the visible layers to a new target layer (Ctrl+Shift+Alt+E for Windows; ⌘+Shift+Option+E for Mac) and applied the Poster Edges filter to that layer. I couldn't use a single Smart Filter because I wanted to mask the blur effect on his face but apply the Poster Edge filter to the entire photo.

With some persistence, patience, and experimentation, you can create really cool effects like this by stacking filters and being creative with different masks.

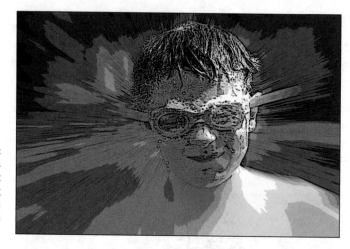

FIGURE 4-28: Have fun as you experiment by combining different filters and effects together.

Using In-Camera Creative Styles and Filters

Don't think you have to wait until you get to your computer to turn on your creativity. Start before you shoot with camera styles and continue through playback with special filters.

Using in-camera styles

Creative styles (Nikon cameras call this feature *picture control*) are a type of in-camera processing option that happens when you take the photo. They let you push photos in different creative directions without having to be an expert.

Here are some of the standard creative styles you see on most cameras:

» **Standard:** Your basic photo. Optimized for good all-round appearance.

» **Neutral:** Toned down compared to Standard. Use if you plan to process it with software.

» **Vivid:** Increases the saturation and contrast to add pop.

» **Portrait:** Optimizes for people and skin tones. May be softer than normal.

» **Landscape:** Optimizes for natural tones. May be more colorful and sharper.

» **Black & White/Monochrome:** Choose this setting (see Figure 4-29) for a classic black-and-white photo (see Figure 4-30).

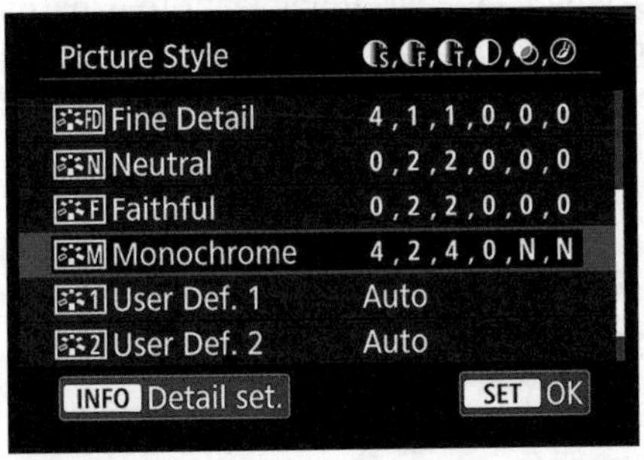

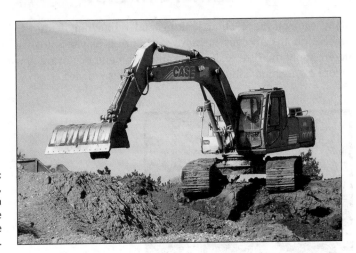

FIGURE 4-29:
You can shoot in black and white by selecting the correct style.

FIGURE 4-30:
In this case, the camera processed the black-and-white photo for me.

Here are some other options you may run across:

>> **Sunset:** Use when you're shooting into or in the sunset. This style emphasizes the reddish-orange colors.

>> **Clear:** Captures transparent colors in bright areas. Good for lights.

>> **Deep:** Colorful and solid.

>> **Light:** Bright and airy.

>> **Night Scene:** Tones down contrast to make night scenes more realistic.

>> **Autumn Leaves:** Saturates reds and yellows.

>> **Sepia:** Applies an old-school tint to a black-and-white photo.

TIP

I strongly recommend saving Raw+JPEG if you want to experiment with different creative styles. This approach gives you a finished JPEG and an unmodified Raw image to work with later if you want.

You may be able to customize the built-in styles on your camera by editing them. They most often have three or four tweakable parameters, such as contrast, saturation, and sharpness. You might even be able to download styles from the Internet and load them into your camera.

Applying in-camera filters

Many cameras have photo-editing and retouching features that allow you to process photos on your memory card during playback instead of using a computer. Apply the filter using the camera's menu or during playback, as shown in Figure 4-31. Some dSLRs let you shoot in these modes.

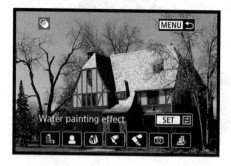

FIGURE 4-31:
In-camera filters and effects do not require a computer.

Figure 4-32 shows the image created by the camera using the Water Painting effect. As you can see, you can apply your creativity using your camera as well as a computer.

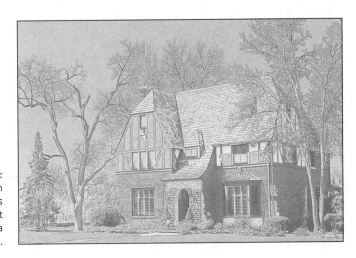

FIGURE 4-32:
Experiment with different effects to find out what works best for a particular photo.

Chapter **5**
Creating Panoramas

Shooting panoramas is fun. Panoramas look great, and the process of shooting them will provide you with a welcome break from standard photography. Point the camera at something interesting. Take a picture. Pan the camera a bit, but not too far. Shoot again. Keep going until you've taken enough photos to create a panorama. All you need is a few, but the more, the merrier! After you get back to your computer, load the photos into software that can stitch them together into a single image. This is panorama photography, in a savory nutshell.

If you're looking for affirmation, panoramas evoke oohs and aahs from everyone. It's rewarding to find a good scene that you want to capture in a format wider or taller than a standard photo and then make it happen. I show you how to take the photos and process them in this chapter.

Shooting Pan-tastic Panoramas

The main point of photographing a panorama is to capture overlapping photos of a scene that are fairly consistent in depth of field, exposure, and color.

REMEMBER

Technically, you never actually photograph *the panorama*. You take shots of individual photos that, when merged or stitched together, create the final image that is the panorama. However, most people (including myself) aren't sticklers about it and simply refer to the process, in part or as a whole, as panorama photography.

Getting your camera ready

When shooting panoramas, you have two diametrically opposed approaches to setting up the camera. They both work. Choose the one that fits your personality:

>> **Casual:** If you're interested in casually shooting panoramas, you can set up your camera however you want to. Even Auto mode works well.

I recommend, however, that you use aperture-priority mode so that the depth of field is the same between shots. Set the aperture that you want, and then let ISO and shutter speed vary.

Depending on the scene you are shooting, the camera may focus on subjects that are at different distances. If that happens, at it appears obvious, switch to manual focus. Focus on your main point of interest and don't change it between frames. This keeps the focal distance consistent from shot to shot.

>> **Controlling:** In this case, your goal is to set up the camera so that you can shoot very consistent photos from frame to frame. For maximum control over your camera and the exposure settings, use the manual shooting mode and manually focus. You should also shoot as Raw+JPEG so that you can control Raw processing yourself. Use the JPEGs for visualization. With them, you can quickly put a small panorama together to see whether you like it and want to work on the full version using the Raw photos.

Of course, you can mix and match between relaxed and controlling. There's enough middle ground there for most people.

Regardless of which approach you gravitate toward, you'll benefit by shooting Raw photos, which enables you to correct white balance issues in software easier than with JPEGs. It also alleviates the need to worry about the color space. If you save only JPEGs, set the white balance manually so that it doesn't change, and if you want the highest-quality shots, set the color space to Adobe RGB (1998).

When I use a tripod, I use a remote to trigger the shutter. It's an important part of my un-bump, anti-jostle, and de-jiggle strategy. Set the drive mode to Remote, if necessary. If you don't have a remote, set the drive to a timer. Leave the metering mode on multi-zone or pattern. You need to change metering mode only if there are obvious exposure differences between frames.

Shooting tripod-assisted panoramas

When you're ready to begin shooting, grab your camera and tripod and go find an interesting subject — the wider or taller, the better.

Then follow these steps to set up and shoot the photos:

1. Mount and level your camera on a tripod.

REMEMBER

Rotate your camera and make sure that it stays level when you point it in a different direction. If your camera has an electronic level, turn it on and use it to level the camera. You can also look through the viewfinder on the monitor if using Live View to ensure that the scene is level.

2. Determine a framing strategy.

This step may sound overly complicated, but it may take you only a moment.

- **Consider width/height:** Decide how wide or tall you want your panorama to be and then guesstimate how many shots you think it'll take to capture it with your current lens and focal length.

- **Check landmarks:** Note key landmarks along the way that will help the software stitch the frames together. Try to put them in adjacent frames.

- **Center it:** Try to center the most important elements of the scene in the middle frame of the panorama.

In Figure 5-1, I imagined making a 4- to 5-frame panorama of one of my favorite bridges. Each separate photo has important parts of the scene, and overlaps details with the photos beside it. I need them all to create the panorama.

REMEMBER

Your goal is *not* to shoot frames that perfectly border each other. It may feel weird at first, but frames or your panorama need to overlap. Features that appear in different shots helps the panorama program *stitch* (assemble) the frames together by providing good reference points. The more reference points, the greater the possibility of a successful stitch. Try to overlap each frame by about a third.

Overlapping features

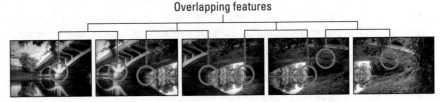

FIGURE 5-1:
Picturing a framing strategy.

3. Perform a dry run, if desired.

If you need to, visualize each shot by looking at it through your viewfinder or monitor, pan, and look at the next one. Check out the landmarks that help you identify the boundaries of your photos and how much overlap will occur.

Creating Panoramas

TIP

If you have a tripod with a compass, you can make a note of the reading for the center point of each frame.

Take a few meter readings along the way to see whether exposure varies from one side of the panorama to the other. If you like, check your camera's histogram to make sure that you're not blowing out any highlights. Decide on a final exposure if you're using manual mode.

4. Pan to one side and shoot the first photo.

You can shoot from left to right, right to left, top to bottom, or the reverse. It's all good.

5. Pan and continue shooting photos to complete the panorama.

The photography part is finished when you shoot the last shot of the panorama. The rest of the work, which is the subject of the rest of this chapter, takes place in software. Figure 5-2 shows the final panorama.

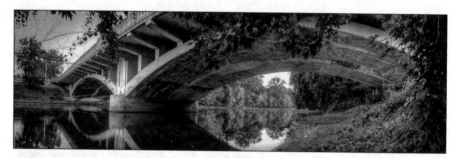

FIGURE 5-2:
The final panorama in black and white.

Shooting handheld panoramas

Shooting handheld panoramas is much more relaxed than using a tripod. You don't need the tripod, a remote shutter release, or any other equipment besides your digital SLR. I love shooting handheld panoramas. You can shoot them on the spur of the moment whether you're in the water, on the beach, or inside a famous landmark.

What you do need is a bit of hand-eye coordination and the ability to steadily pan the camera manually between shots.

I use the same basic camera settings when shooting handheld panoramas that I use for tripod work, but I pay attention to the shutter speed. Aperture-priority keeps the depth of field consistent between frames. If the shutter speeds are slow, switch to manual or shutter-priority mode so that you can set the shutter speed fast enough to keep the photos sharp. ISO may be higher as well.

Hold the camera as level as you can while panning. Pause, focus, and take each photo; then pan the camera to take the next. Pay attention to how much overlap you provide. Make sure that it's a third of a photo or more. And practice.

Stitching Photos Together

Normal panoramas don't merge themselves together. You have to use specialized software to combine, or stitch, the separate frames of the panorama together into a single, blended image. Some cameras have special panorama shooting modes that automate this process, however, which I cover later.

Creating panoramas with Lightroom

Creating panoramas in Lightroom is delightfully easy. The feature is called Photo Merge, and you can activate it in the Library or Develop modules. Here's a quick rundown on how the process works:

1. **Select the photos you want to merge into a panorama (see Figure 5-3).**

   They can be in JPEG or Raw image file format. I've created both, and while Lightroom complains that it can't access lens correction data for some JPEGs, the end result is not noticeably worse than using Raw images.

   You can develop your photos prior to merging or wait until afterward. Not all settings are carried into the panorama. Frankly, I would wait until you've created the panorama to make adjustments on a single, consolidated image.

2. **Choose Photo ⇨ Photo Merge ⇨ Panorama.**

   If using the mobile version of Lightroom, select Photo ⇨ Photo Merge ⇨ Panorama Merge.

   You can also right-click and choose Photo Merge ⇨ Panorama, or press Ctrl+M/⌘+M (Win/Win). If you have shot the panorama in HDR, select the HDR Panorama option.

   The Panorama Merge Preview dialog box opens, as shown in Figure 5-4, with a few controls and a preview of the panorama. Lightroom automatically builds a preview of the selected projection and displays it. If it can't successfully build the panorama, Lightroom tells you that it is unable to merge the photos.

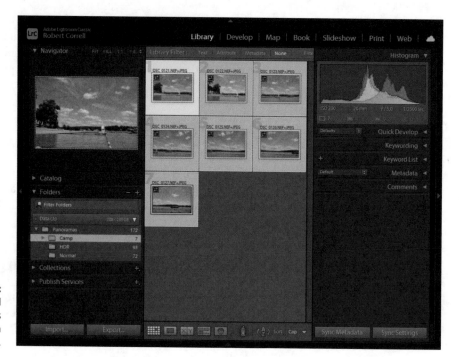

FIGURE 5-3:
I've selected seven photos to create a panorama with.

3. Select a projection type.

Panorama projection types essentially correspond to different map projections you learned when studying maps and geography in Social Studies. The source photos partially cover the interior of a globe called the *panoramic sphere.* The challenge is how to present that three-dimensional information using only two dimensions. The answer is to project it onto a flat, two-dimensional plane. You can do that in different ways, which explains why Lightroom includes three projection types:

- **Spherical:** Photos from the panoramic sphere are assigned X and Y coordinates and are mapped onto a flat surface just as latitude and longitude are on a map. This option works well on wide-angle landscape shots because vertical lines and the horizon line, or equator, are straight. Vertical distances are stretched a bit compared to horizontal. This projection type is also called equirectangular.

- **Cylindrical:** The photos from the panoramic sphere are mapped as a cylinder and then unrolled. This option also works well with wide shots. Like the spherical type, vertical lines and the horizon remain straight. Vertical distances toward the top and bottom of the photo are stretched more than toward the center.

- **Perspective:** This type of projection, also known as *rectilinear* or *flat,* simply maps the pixels on the interior of the panoramic sphere directly onto a flat plane. This is close to how we see, but isn't always the best method to choose. The center of the panorama will look fine, but the outer areas can easily distort.

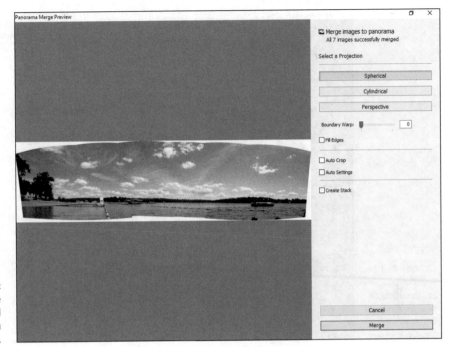

FIGURE 5-4:
Panorama Merge Preview has all the controls you need.

4. **Select Auto Crop and choose a Boundary Warp, if desired.**

   Auto Crop crops out all the white space surrounding the panorama to create a nice, clean border. Boundary Warp fills the white space with warped areas of the photo. If you max the Boundary Warp setting, you don't need to crop at all.

   A good compromise is to fill as much of the white space as you can using Boundary Warp, so long as it looks natural (you may have to try a few settings to see which one works best), and then crop the rest using Auto Crop. I've done just that in Figure 5-5.

   The Create Stacks option puts everything into a stack in Lightroom with the panorama on top after the operation is complete. Using this option helps declutter the image display area.

5. **Click Merge to create the panorama.**

   When Lightroom finishes, it creates a new, unlayered file using Adobe's Digital Negative Raw image file format (.dng) and places it in the same location as the source photos. It shows up in your Library accordingly.

6. **Edit your panorama normally, as shown in Figure 5-6.**

   Switch to the Develop module and use the controls to improve your panorama.

7. **Export the final panorama (shown in Figure 5-7) as a JPEG or TIFF when completed.**

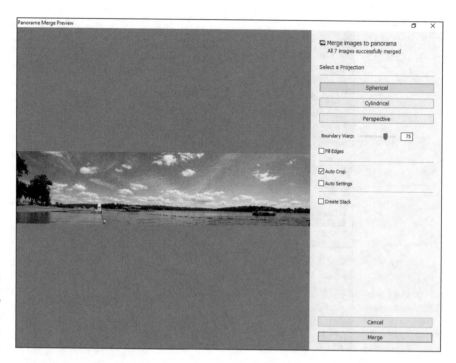

FIGURE 5-5:
I've used a combination of features in this case to get a clean border.

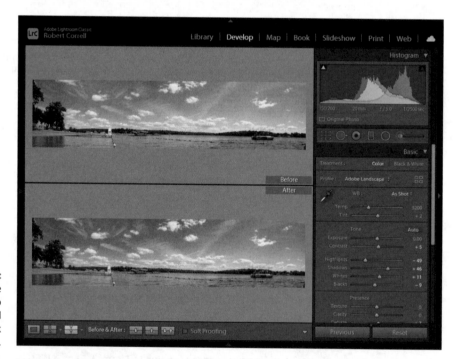

FIGURE 5-6:
Edit the panorama to spruce it up and make it look better.

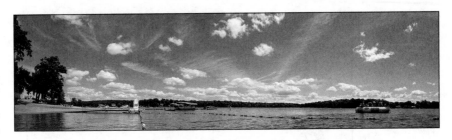

Creating panoramas with Photoshop

Stitching together panoramas in Photoshop isn't difficult. The main difference between using Photoshop and Lightroom is that Lightroom can immediately process Raw photos. Photoshop must open Raw images using Adobe Camera Raw. Select the Raw photos in the Adobe Camera Raw Filmstrip, right-click, and choose Merge to Panorama. You also have the option of creating HDR Panoramas. From this point on, the process is identical to the Photo Merge feature in Lightroom.

Photoshop has another panorama feature, called Photomerge, which works slightly differently from Lightroom or Adobe Camera Raw. You have more projection types to choose from, and you can produce a layered file that enables you to correct blending problems. The biggest downside to Photomerge is that it offers no preview of the panorama. You have to create the panorama to see it. Here's how to use Photomerge:

1. **Open the photos you want to use for the panorama in Photoshop.**

   Alternatively, you can jump to Step 2 without opening any files. When you get to Step 3, click Browse to find the source files you want Photoshop to use to create the panorama.

   You can use JPEGs, although 8-bits-per-channel TIFFs that you have already converted from Raw photos give you better results.

2. **Choose File ⇨ Automate ⇨ Photomerge.**

   The Photomerge dialog box opens (see Figure 5-8). Layout options are on the left. Source files and options are in the center. Most controls are fairly self-explanatory.

3. **Click the Add Open Files button.**

   Photoshop adds your chosen files' names to the list, as shown in Figure 5-8. If you need to add more, click Browse. If you want to remove one, select it from the central list and click Remove.

   Photoshop may prompt you to save the files. If you need to, cancel and create backup copies of the originals.

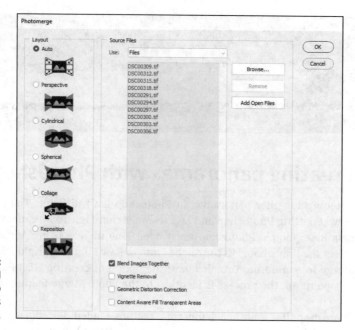

FIGURE 5-8:
I've added ten photos to create this panorama with.

4. **Choose a layout:**

   - **Auto:** This option allows Photoshop to choose between Perspective and Cylindrical layouts.

   - **Perspective, Cylindrical, or Spherical:** These three options are identical to those from Adobe Lightroom. (See the "Creating panoramas with Lightroom" section.)

   - **Collage:** Throw everything together and align it like a collage. The software rotates and scales photos as required.

   - **Reposition:** This layout aligns each photo based on matching reference points but doesn't transform them in any way. This option can produce good-looking panoramas that don't suffer from undue amounts of distortion.

5. **Select other options.**

   You can choose from these four:

   - **Blend Images Together** automatically blends the photos together. Deselect this option to perform this task manually. I recommend leaving it selected.

   - **Vignette Removal** balances the exposure of the corners of each photo with the center.

- **Geometric Distortion Correction** attempts to compensate for lens distortion.

- **Content Aware Fill Transparent Areas** automatically fills gaps in the panorama, just as Boundary Warp does in Lightroom.

6. **Click OK to continue.**

Photoshop creates the panorama and loads it into the interface as an unsaved file, as shown in Figure 5-9. Notice that each photo takes up its own layer and is masked to blend with the others. This approach is substantially different from that of Lightroom and enables you to edit each layer separately. You see the entire panorama in the main window.

7. **Save the panorama as a Photoshop (**.psd**) file.**

TIP

Use this saved file as a multilayered working file that you can use to tweak blending and make other adjustments. When finished, resize and crop, if desired, and then save a flattened copy with all the layers merged together as a TIFF or JPEG. Figure 5-10 shows the final panorama. I made a few minor adjustments to the brightness and contrast, removed my shadow, cropped the photo, and saved this flattened version.

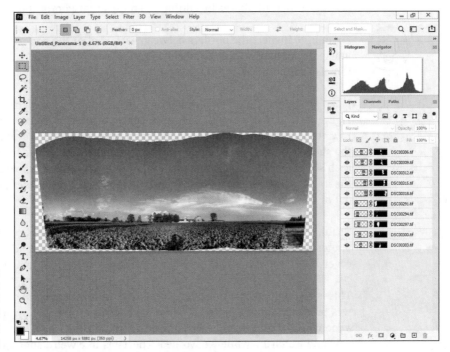

FIGURE 5-9:
Photoshop creates layered panoramas that you can continue to edit.

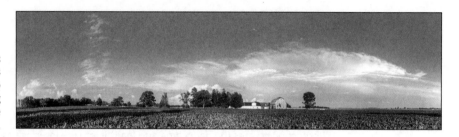

FIGURE 5-10:
Panoramas
enable you to
capture sweeping
views with little
distortion.

Stepping Up Your Game

There's nothing wrong with using what you have to shoot panoramas. Technically, you don't even need a tripod. It can be just you and your camera. However, many tools are designed to help you improve your panoramas. This section tells you about some of those tools.

Advanced blending in Photoshop

When working with panoramas in Photoshop, you can correct blending issues between different photos by editing the masks that Photoshop creates.

TIP

Zoom in to inspect the borders between each shot of the panorama. If things look unusual, you may be able to edit the mask of one or more layers to correct it. You can also soften mask edges to blend the photos better.

I had to do a lot of manual blending on the panorama of my wife, shown in Figure 5-11. I had a crazy panorama concept and convinced her to play along. I wanted to see what it would look like to photograph her several times and use the shots to create a panorama. She changed outfits and moved positions between each shot. For this panorama, blending was important. As shown in Figure 5-11, the initial panorama that Photoshop created blended one of her poses completely out of the picture.

Thankfully, I created this panorama in Photoshop, so I had access to the layered photos and masks. I had to work carefully with the masks and edit the one that covered her to put her back in. Figure 5-12 shows the final image.

This is also a good example of cropping. The working image shows that our house was pretty discombobulated because of renovations we were working on. This is a room off the kitchen that we plopped a few old couches in so that the kids could play and watch TV while we worked. The TV is in a weird spot, and you can see a blue cooler on a stand in the background. It's really a work in progress. I was able to crop all that out and make the final photo much more presentable.

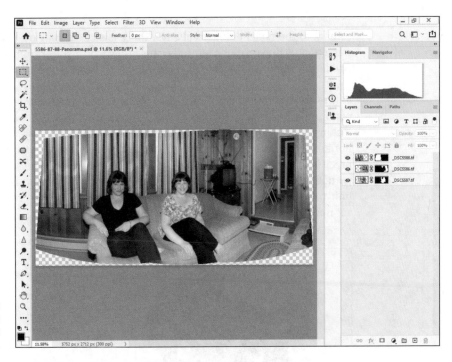

FIGURE 5-11:
There should be
three women in
this photo.

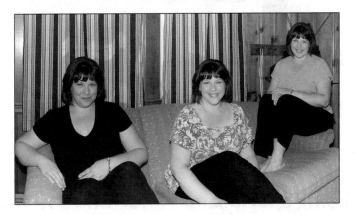

FIGURE 5-12:
Layered
panoramas
enable you to
correct some
difficult
problems.

Using a panoramic tripod head

If you really want to get into panoramas, consider buying a dedicated panoramic tripod head. For many, the extra effort is totally worth it.

TECHNICAL STUFF

When you rotate your camera on a tripod using a normal head, the camera rotates around the screw that connects them. Although this setup is generally acceptable, it's not the ideal solution. For best results, you should rotate the camera around the optical center of the lens, sometimes called the *no-parallax point,* the *entrance pupil,* or the *nodal point.* By changing the axis or rotation from the center of the camera to the nodal point (as always, there is some debate over this), your panorama photos line up much better because they won't suffer from as much parallax. *Parallax* is when nearby objects move between frames in relation to a far object.

Figure 5-13 shows a consumer-level Nikon dSLR mounted on the Nodal Ninja panoramic head (www.fanotec.com). This head is a beefy, well-made series of locking brackets that holds the camera in position whether you want to shoot horizontal or vertical panoramas. Getting the camera mounted takes a degree of precision, but after you set it up, you can quickly attach the same camera again without changing anything. One of the great things about this head is how the unit rotates in incremental steps. You take a photo and then rotate the camera a set number of clicks to reach the next position.

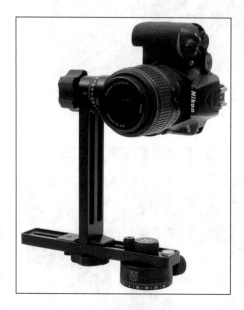

FIGURE 5-13:
A specialized panoramic tripod head enables you to shoot precise panoramas.

Using specialized panorama software

The best panorama package on the market works for both Windows and Macintosh; it's PTGui (www.ptgui.com). If you want to control just about every conceivable part of the panorama process and are considering displaying or selling your panoramas professionally, PTGui is for you.

This powerful all-in-one panorama application gives you customizable control points and significantly more projection types than most other programs. Two of the application's windows are shown in Figure 5-14. I loaded five images that I shot of a lake into the program and am in the process of stitching them together to form a panorama. You can set the horizon line as well as change many other parameters using the Panorama Editor window. If you're serious about creating HDR panoramas, download either PTGui or PTGui Pro and have a closer look for yourself. The Pro version even has its own HDR and tone-mapping features.

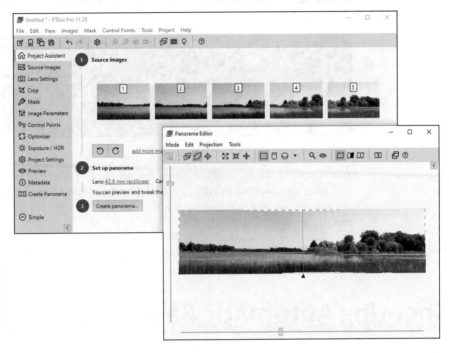

FIGURE 5-14: PTGui Pro is a fantastic application dedicated to panoramas.

Shooting HDR panoramas

High Dynamic Range photography and panorama photography go well together. They both use special software to create a final image out of component photos. HDR photography uses exposure brackets to capture a greater range of light than is possible in a single photo, and panorama photography uses the same camera settings to capture a larger scene than a single photo can.

To shoot a panorama in HDR, set up your camera to photograph exposure brackets. Shoot a bracketed sequence for each frame of the panorama, as shown in Figure 5-15. The easiest way to process the photos is to use the HDR Panorama features found in Lightroom and Photoshop, and the HDR-aware PTGui. You can also process the HDR frames separately using an HDR program like Photomatix Pro and then load the results in your panorama software. Figure 5-16 shows my finished panorama.

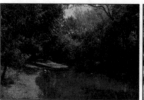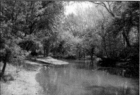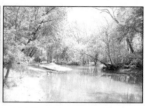

FIGURE 5-15:
These exposure
brackets create
a single frame of
the panorama.

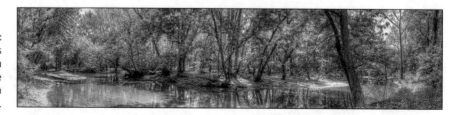

FIGURE 5-16:
HDR panoramas
enable to you
capture more
details than
usual.

You'll end up shooting three times the number of overall photos when photographing a panorama in HDR, and it takes more time to process everything and put the panorama together, but what you can accomplish by combining these techniques is amazing.

For more information on HDR photography, turn to the next chapter.

Shooting Automatic Panoramas

Some cameras, mostly Sony dSLTs, shoot and process panoramas automatically. The camera handles all the complicated processing. Sony calls the feature Sweep Panorama (formerly Sweep Shooting). It's also available in 3-D.

REMEMBER

These panoramas are saved as a single JPEG, which means that you do not have access to the individual shots that the camera used. No Raw images are saved, either. You get the finished panorama only. Sony's 3-D panoramas require two files. Figure 5-17 shows a panorama that I shot using an inexpensive Sony dSLT and ultra-wide-angle lens.

FIGURE 5-17:
The panorama
did not require
any software to
create.

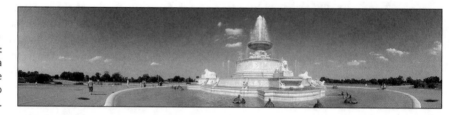

TIP

Keep these things in mind when shooting automatic panoramas:

» **Straight, level, and steady:** Panning can be hard without tilting the camera. Pay attention to the indicators in the viewfinder, on the Live View monitor, and in the scene. In addition, you have to pan at a steady speed. If you sweep too fast or too slowly, the camera will get cranky and stop the shot.

» **Stitching problems:** Automatic panoramas are awesome most of the time, but when the camera has trouble stitching the frames together, the result may be messy.

» **Keep at it:** Centering your subjects within the vertical space of the panorama can be a challenge. You may need several attempts to get a good panorama with people in the shot because you can accidentally crop their heads out or put too much space above them.

» **Zoom and inspect:** Zoom in and inspect your panoramas before moving on! It's impossible to see small errors in a huge panorama from a small thumbnail on the back of your camera. You can't possibly tell whether the shots have stitching problems without zooming in and panning around.

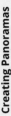

Creating Panoramas

Chapter **6**

Enjoying HDR Photography

High dynamic range (HDR) photography gets around your camera's limited ability to capture details in dark shadows and details in bright highlights in the same photo. It does this by using more than one photo to collect brightness information. Similar to shooting panoramas, HDR photography is a two-step process.

The first step is photography. Select a scene and take more than one shot with different exposure settings (see Book 3, Chapter 1 for more information about exposure). These are called exposure brackets. I explain what exposure brackets are and how to shoot them in the first part of this chapter.

The second step of HDR photography involves specialized software. You combine the exposure brackets into a single, high-dynamic range image, which you then tone map. Tone mapping is at the creative heart of the entire process. You use controls in the software that allow you to manipulate the HDR image and control how it looks. It's sort of like processing a Raw photo. You save the final result as a single, standard image file.

I walk you through each step in this chapter, and finish with a list of alternate techniques and ideas for you to try.

HDR Software

You probably knew this was coming. You'll need an application that can handle High Dynamic Range photography. As with the other chapters that rely on software to accomplish certain tasks, I've made the decision to focus on a single application.

Photomatix Pro, I choose you for this chapter! It's the leading HDR application out there. I like it. I use it. It even integrates with Adobe Lightroom as an export option. You can download a trial version at www.hdrsoft.com. The trial doesn't expire, which is nice, but it does add a watermark to the final image. I find that perfectly acceptable. It allows you to experiment with the full program for as long and as many times as you like before deciding whether to buy it.

Having said that, other applications are out there either devoted to or that dabble in HDR. If you prefer to shop around, by all means, do so!

Learning about HDR

High Dynamic Range (HDR) photography terminology can take a bit of getting used to, but the concept is easy enough to understand: It's difficult to take a photograph of many scenes without losing details in the shadows, highlights, or in both areas. The solution is to artificially enhance your camera's dynamic range by using more than one photo.

The photos that capture the additional details are called *exposure brackets*. As shown in Figure 6-1, each records the same scene but uses a different exposure. Underexposed shots capture details in bright highlights. Overexposed shots capture details in dark, shadowy areas.

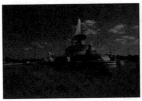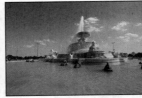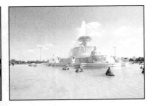

Special HDR software merges the bracketed photos into a single HDR image, which you *tone map* into a normal image. Tone mapping is a creative process. You make the decisions that affect the final brightness, contrast, color, and overall look of the image. After tone mapping, the final image is converted into a JPEG or TIFF and saved, as shown in Figure 6-2.

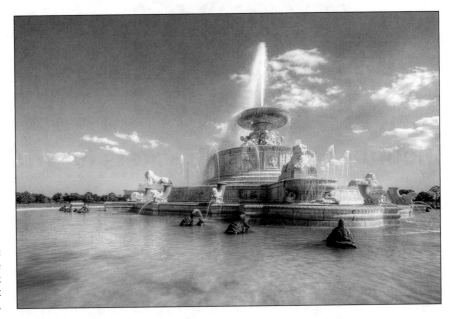

FIGURE 6-2:
HDR can preserve
details in dark
and very bright
areas.

HDR photography can seem fickle at times. Don't hesitate to try it on every scene you can, but there are certain situations in which it works best. Look for scenes with high contrast and great lighting. HDR works exceedingly well in the morning and evening golden hours. The light is more magical and the results look fantastic. It can also work inside, as shown in Figure 6-3.

Enjoying HDR
Photography

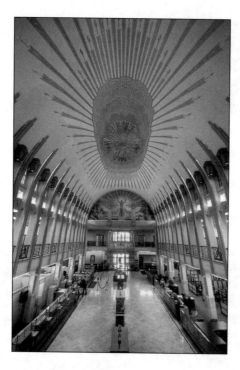

FIGURE 6-3:
Look for colorful
scenes with a
high contrast
ratio and lots of
details.

Shooting Exposure Brackets for HDR

You'll have to change a few things from your normal routine to set up your camera to shoot exposure brackets using *automatic exposure bracketing* (AEB). It's not
much, but it's important that you get it down. When ready, shooting the brackets
with a tripod or even handheld is a breeze.

Configuring your camera

You need to pay attention to only a few settings to shoot good images for HDR. Here
are my recommendations:

>> **Exposure controls:** Set your camera to aperture-priority autoexposure mode
because it ensures a constant depth of field across the different bracketed
exposures.

Set the ISO manually. You do not want to leave Auto ISO on because it can
change between shots and mess with the brackets. If you're not using a tripod, or you're photographing moving clouds, you may need to raise the base

REMEMBER

ISO so that you can get a faster shutter speed. When shooting outside with a tripod, I prefer ISO 100.

Shutter speed changes based on the exposure needed to shoot the brackets.

>> **Image quality:** Set the image quality to include Raw photos. I use Raw+JPEG so that I have the option of loading the JPEGs into Photomatix Pro to quickly see whether the scene was worth shooting.

>> **Other settings:** Set the Drive/Release mode to Continuous so that you don't have to keep pressing the shutter button.

If you will be using long shutter speeds, ensure that noise reduction is turned off. If you use JPEGs, you can, but don't have to turn off any dynamic range tricks that your camera uses to make JPEGs look better. Two Canon options that correct brightness and contrast are called Auto Lighting Optimizer and Highlight Tone Priority. Nikon has a similar feature called Active D-Lighting.

Turn off Image Stabilization if the camera is on a tripod or is otherwise solid. If you're shooting handheld, keep it on.

>> **Total control:** If you're a real stickler, switch to manual focus and set the white balance manually. Doing so ensures consistent photos across all the brackets.

>> **AEB:** You need to turn on your camera's AEB feature and set it up. See the upcoming "Setting up automatic exposure bracketing (AEB)" section for details.

>> **Tripod and remote:** I recommend using a tripod and a remote-shutter release when shooting HDR. Shooting handheld brackets is possible, but you have to be steady and not move around.

TIP

I've made just about every mistake possible shooting HDR, including using shutter–priority mode (the aperture changed between shots), forgetting to save Raw photos, leaving Image Stabilization on when using a tripod, and more. To be honest, the differences were negligible. All you really need are the brackets — however you can get them!

Setting up automatic exposure bracketing (AEB)

Autoexposure bracketing (AEB) is a feature that enables the camera to automatically shoot exposure brackets of a scene. After you configure a few details, the camera handles changing the necessary exposure settings and takes the right number of shots when you press the shutter button. It's a great timesaver and is a critical feature to have if you want to shoot handheld HDR.

Inexplicably, given the popularity of HDR, not all cameras have an autoexposure bracketing feature. If you can't find it anywhere in the menu system or hidden with the Drive/Release mode, your camera may be one of the culprits. The Nikon D3500 is an otherwise excellent camera, for example, but doesn't have AEB. If this is you, you'll have to shoot brackets manually. I talk about that in the "Manually bracketing exposures" section, later in this chapter.

For those cameras that do have AEB, setting up it is pretty easy. You simply have to set the number of brackets you want to shoot and the exposure difference (in EV) between them.

How you turn on AEB differs from camera to camera; turn to your manual for the precise details. Some cameras set the number of brackets from a different menu, which takes some time. Other cameras make you choose the number of brackets and their distance apart each time you turn on the AEB feature. Still other cameras don't let you change the number of brackets. You can modify only the EV distance between them. I'm in the process of setting up the EV distance between three brackets on a Canon camera in Figure 6-4.

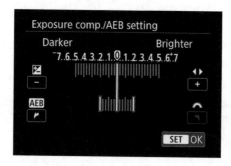

FIGURE 6-4: Setting the EV difference between three brackets.

When starting out, I recommend shooting three exposure brackets, each separated by 2.0 EV. Figure 6-5 shows how the brackets appear on the Canon Quick Control screen after setting them up. These settings capture a wide total dynamic range and don't flood you with a million and one files.

Please feel free to experiment with the number of brackets and their EV distance. I've shot everything from two to nine brackets, separated by 0.3 EV to 2.0 EV. More files, separated by a smaller amount, capture a finer exposure gradient. However, having more brackets takes more work to shoot, store, and process.

REMEMBER

Double-check your camera's manual to see what shooting modes are compatible with AEB. Depending on your camera, you may need to be in an advanced autoexposure mode or your camera's manual mode. Manual mode requires you to set the starting exposure. The bracketing feature handles the rest.

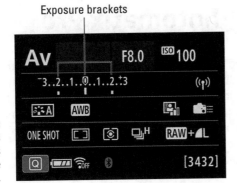

Exposure brackets

FIGURE 6-5:
The brackets
show up as marks
under the
exposure index.

Your camera may have more advanced AEB options. Look in your camera menu or manual for these features:

>> **Sequence:** Set the order the shots are taken. If you can change this setting, you can put the metered exposure first, in the middle, or last. I prefer it first so that I can spot it from the thumbnail in Lightroom faster than having to count exposures from the darkest or lightest. The other exposures tend to be taken from dark to light.

>> **Auto cancel:** Most of the time, bracketing is canceled when you turn off the camera. Some cameras restart the bracketing sequence where you left off if you turn the camera off and back on. If you have a camera like this and don't like that behavior, you may be able to turn it off.

>> **Bracketing option:** Some cameras lump several different types of bracketing together. You may have to identify that you want *exposure bracketing* as opposed to white balance bracketing.

REMEMBER

Many cameras indicate the bracket being shot in the viewfinder or on the camera back with a mark under the exposure meter.

Shooting the exposure brackets

After you configure your camera and enable AEB, shooting the brackets is ridiculously easy. Frame the scene, focus and meter normally, and then pull the trigger. If you have the Drive mode set to shoot continuously, simply hold the shutter button or remote down until the brackets are finished. If you have the Drive set to Single, press the shutter button as many times as you have brackets.

REMEMBER

When returning to normal photography, make sure to turn off auto bracketing.

Enjoying HDR
Photography

Tone Mapping in Photomatix Pro

After you prepare and shoot your exposure brackets for your HDR image, as described in the preceding sections, the next steps are in software. Load or export photos into Photomatix Pro, generate the HDR image, and then tone map it. *Tone mapping* is the process that you use to convert the high-dynamic-range image into something your computer can display normally. A finished image is shown in Figure 6-6. This scene shows the front of a dramatic stone church with blue sky and clouds. The details and lighting differences made this a great candidate for HDR.

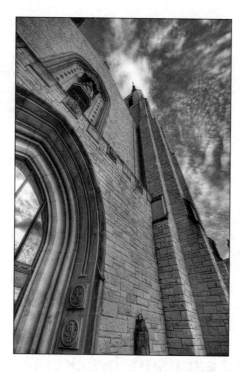

FIGURE 6-6:
The payoff for a little extra effort is an amazing image.

TIP

Tone mapping is sometimes so unpredictable that showing you how to do it well is difficult. Every HDR image is different. The key is to experiment with the controls and then practice, practice, practice.

Creating the HDR image

Before you get to tone mapping, you have to load the bracketed photos into Photomatix Pro and create an HDR image. Just follow these steps:

1. **Start Photomatix Pro.**

   Download the free trial from www.hdrsoft.com. If you like what you see and buy it, you won't have to put up with watermarks.

   When you launch Photomatix Pro, it starts out as an empty shell (see Figure 6-7).

2. **Drag your brackets and drop them on the main program window (refer to Figure 6-7).**

   If you dropped JPEGs or TIFFs onto Photomatix Pro, confirm that you want to merge the files and begin HDR processing. The program assumes that that's what you want to do if you are using Raw images.

   You can also select Browse & Load and use the Open dialog box to select your brackets.

3. **Confirm your brackets (see Figure 6-8) and click Next.**

   There are only a few options here. Deselect any photos you want to leave out of the process. Click Check Exposures to have Photomatix Pro evaluate the exposures and tell you whether you seem to have captured enough detail in the dark and bright areas of the scene. You can also have the default preset set here.

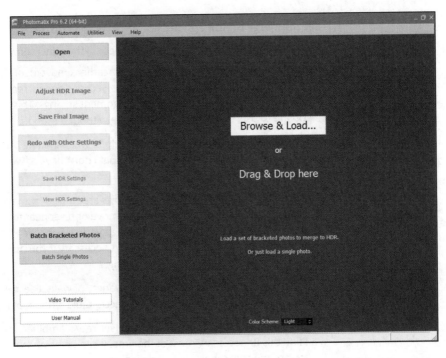

FIGURE 6-7:
The Photomatix Pro interface when you start it.

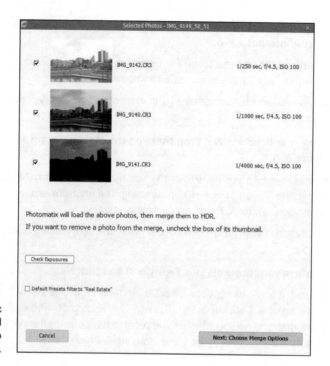

Selected Photos - IMG_9149_50_51

☑	IMG_9142.CR3	1/250 sec, f/4.5, ISO 100
☑	IMG_9140.CR3	1/1000 sec, f/4.5, ISO 100
☑	IMG_9141.CR3	1/4000 sec, f/4.5, ISO 100

Photomatix will load the above photos, then merge them to HDR.
If you want to remove a photo from the merge, uncheck the box of its thumbnail.

Check Exposures

☐ Default Presets filter to "Real Estate"

Cancel   Next: Choose Merge Options

FIGURE 6-8:
Brackets loaded
and ready to
merge.

4. **Set the Merge to HDR options.**

Select from the following options that appear in the panel shown in Figure 6-9:

- **Align source images:** Adjusts for slight camera movement. There are four presets. You can include perspective corrections and increase or decrease the maximum shift if you show the alignment settings. This is a good option to use, especially when shooting without a tripod.

- **Crop aligned images:** This is pretty helpful when loading brackets shot without a tripod. I leave it selected so that I don't have to worry about cropping in Photoshop.

- **Show options to remove ghosts:** *Ghosts* are caused by moving objects that appear in one bracket and either move or disappear from the other brackets. You can identify problem areas yourself or have Photomatix Pro handle it automatically. This option isn't necessary if you don't have people, vehicles, or tree branches visibly moving.

- **Reduce noise on:** Reduces noise in a variety of ways. Feel free to ignore this unless your final image has an unacceptable amount of noise.

- **Reduce chromatic aberrations:** Reduces red/cyan/blue/yellow fringing. I find this unnecessary most of the time. It can be helpful when shooting toward the sun, especially as evening approaches.

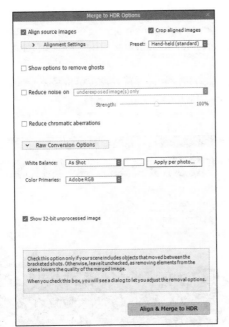

FIGURE 6-9:
These options
control how
brackets are
merged into a
single HDR image.

The following options are visible only if you're using Raw photos to generate the HDR image:

- **White Balance:** The default setting As Shot is often adequate. Change if needed.

- **Color Primaries:** Choose between sRGB, Adobe RGB (1998), and ProPhoto RGB. I prefer Adobe RGB (1998) unless I want to save a JPEG, in which case I set the option to sRGB.

Select the Show 32-bit Unprocessed Image box if you want to see the HDR image before you start tone mapping. This enables you to save it and reload in the future, bypassing the merging process.

5. **Continue.**

If you left the ghosting option deselected in Step 4, click the Align and Merge to HDR button.

If you selected the ghosting option, click the Align & Show Deghosting button. After a bit of processing, you'll see the Deghosting Options dialog box. Choose your option (selective or automatic) and then follow the instructions. When finished, click OK.

6. **Prepare to tone map.**

If you selected the option to show the HDR image, it appears onscreen. As you can see from Figure 6-10, the image isn't usable like this because your monitor is incapable of displaying photos with a wide dynamic range. You have to tone map the HDR image to make something useful out of it.

Enjoying HDR
Photography

At this point, you're ready to start tone mapping. Save the HDR image (File⇨Save As) if you can't immediately start. Then you can reload it at your leisure.

If you left the option to see the 32-bit unprocessed image deselected in Step 4, you'll immediately enter the tone mapping mode.

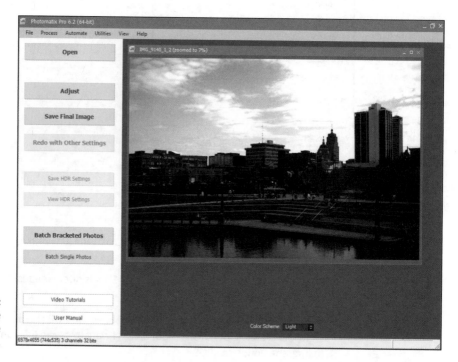

FIGURE 6-10:
The HDR image
waiting to be tone
mapped.

TIP

If you know that you want to use all the same HDR settings, try *batch processing*. You'll set up rules for Photomatix Pro to follow as it creates HDR images out of any number of bracketed sets. This feature is very nice.

Tone mapping the HDR image

I wanted to give this section a title like "The least you need to know about tone mapping your HDR images in Photomatix Pro without much fuss but with good results," but it was too long. My goal is to help you narrow down some of the features and options so that you can get started without feeling overwhelmed. Figure 6-11 shows the Adjust & Preview window in Photomatix Pro with an image being tone mapped. Here goes:

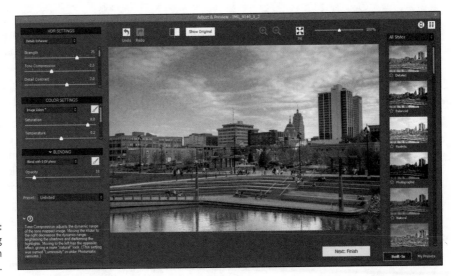

FIGURE 6-11:
Tone mapping
an HDR image in
Photomatix Pro.

1. **Select an HDR Settings method.**

   Tone mapping using the Details Enhancer is the HDR option that I cover here. Select it, if necessary, from the HDR Settings list. Use the Details Enhancer to create anything from classic HDR images to more realistic interpretations.

   Other options are available for you to choose and experiment with. They include the Contrast Optimizer, Tone Balancer, Tone Compressor, four types of Fusion, and Average. Each option has its own settings and style.

2. **Make adjustments.**

   This is where you have to play with the program. I can't tell you a single setting that can make every image look good. You can start by investigating different presets that come with the program. They are located in the Presets window.

   TIP

   You can also just wing it. For each control, move it through its entire range to see what it does when at the minimum and maximum. Continue through each one until you reach the bottom. Here are the Details Enhancer controls that have the greatest effect on the look of your photo but need a bit of explanation:

   - **Strength:** Controls the overall amount of contrast and detail enhancement applied to the image. For a dramatic effect, raise Strength toward 100. Conversely, to create a more realistic effect, reduce strength to 50 or lower.

   - **Tone Compression:** Controls how hard to squeeze the dynamic range of the image. Move the slider to the right to increase the compression, which reduces the dynamic range. Shadows are brightened and highlights darkened more to get everything to fit. Move it to the left to ease up on the compression, which increases the dynamic range. Shadows and highlights are affected less.

Enjoying HDR
Photography

- **Detail Contrast:** Accentuates local contrast. The default is 0. Higher settings amplify local contrast and darken the image. Can boost drama. Lower settings reduce local contrast and lighten the image.

- **Lighting Adjustments:** Controls the level at which contrast enhancements are smoothed out. This setting plays a large role in determining how the final tone mapped image looks. It's also responsible for much of the debate over the "HDR look," both good and bad. Smoothing comes in two modes. You control smoothing in one with a free-ranging slider. Higher values produce more smoothing, and lower values result in less. If you check the Lighting Effects box, you see discrete buttons to control the smoothing strength.

There are additional controls that address color settings, blending, and plenty of preset and viewing controls.

3. **When you are finished tone mapping, click Finish.**

Photomatix Pro cogitates, calculates, and burns some electricity as it renders your image. It appears in a Finishing Touch dialog box, as shown in Figure 6-12.

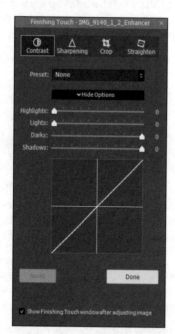

FIGURE 6-12:
You have the option of sprucing up the image before saving.

4. Add finishing touches, if desired, and press Done.

Adjust contrast, color, and sharpening to one degree or another. You can also crop and straighten. If you plan to edit the photo in Lightroom or another application later, you can dispense with this step. However, it's nice to have these features so that you can quickly spruce up your image and be done.

5. Save your image by choosing File ⇨ Save As.

Select a location and enter a new name, if desired. Change the type and select the additional options if you like. I prefer to save my tone mapped images as 8-bit TIFFs. I also save the tone mapping settings, as shown in Figure 6-13.

You can also select File ⇨ Save Image. In that case, Photomatix Pro applies the file options you have previously selected.

6. Finalize your photos.

Tone mapped images don't always look perfect when they leave Photomatix Pro. Load them into Lightroom or use Photoshop to reduce noise, sharpen, improve tone, and so forth. Figure 6-14 shows my completed image of this scene.

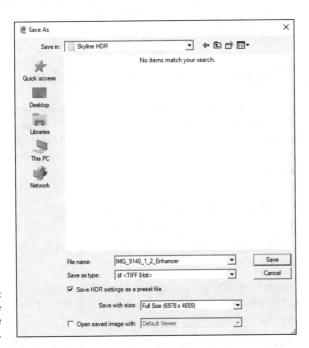

FIGURE 6-13:
I like saving the settings with the image.

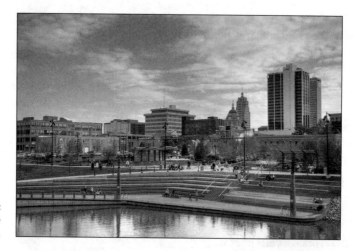

Trying Alternative Techniques

HDR photography is an immense field with many different options and possibilities. A number of different techniques might work for you. Try them to see whether you're interested.

Using your camera's HDR modes

Your camera may have a built-in HDR feature. It handles shooting the brackets, creating the HDR image, and tone mapping it, all in one go. The left image in Figure 6-15 shows the HDR Mode feature in Shooting Menu 4 of a Canon dSLR. The right image shows the options. This is a good example of what you can expect from in-camera HDR:

>> **Adjust Dynamic Range:** Set to Disable HDR by default. To turn on HDR, set to Auto or choose from one of the discrete EV ranges (from +/-1 EV to +/-3 EV).

>> **Effect:** Select an effect. Options are Natural, Art Standard, Art Vivid, Art Bold, or Art Embossed.

>> **Continuous HDR:** This is a neat option. Select 1 Shot only if you want to shoot one HDR sequence and return to normal shooting. Set to Every Shot if you want to keep shooting HDR.

>> **Auto Image Align:** Set to Enable (best when shooting handheld) or Disable (best when using a tripod).

>> **Save Source Images:** This option (not shown in the figure) may not be available on all cameras. Select All Images if you want to save all the source images, including JPEGs and RAW. I highly recommend this setting because you can use software to create your own HDR images using the source photos later, in case you don't like the camera's result. Choose HDR Image only if you want the take-it-or-leave-it solution.

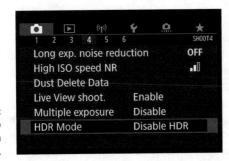 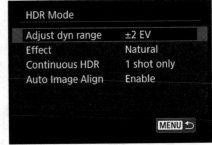

FIGURE 6-15: Setting up HDR mode on a Canon dSLR.

Preparing your images differently

You can choose one of several ways to load images into an application like Photomatix Pro to create and tone map an HDR image. The path you take depends on what files you use:

>> **Raw images directly from the camera:** You can throw your Raw photos into most HDR applications and they'll dutifully merge them into the HDR image. You'll hardly notice a thing. That's good if you're in a hurry and don't mind letting the HDR software handle it.

>> **JPEGs directly from the camera:** You can load JPEG brackets into HDR applications. None of them complain a bit, even Photoshop. JPEGs need no conversion or processing. The caveat here involves quality. The difference may be hard to notice unless the scene has a lot of wide gradients, but JPEGs don't produce the same quality as Raw exposures or TIFFs converted from Raw exposures.

>> **Converted Raw photos:** If you want the best quality and the most control over the HDR process, convert your Raw photos to TIFF files before processing them into HDR images. You can convert them to JPEGs if you like, but then you should just use the JPEGs from your camera if that's the case.

If you use Adobe Lightroom Classic, you can buy the Photomatix Pro export plug-in. It streamlines your workflow by letting you select single exposures or brackets and sending them over to Photomatix to process into HDR. You even have the option to automatically import the result into Lightroom. You don't have to convert the Raw exposures yourself with this method. Lightroom applies your development settings to the exposures as it converts them to TIFFs and sends them to Photomatix.

Trying single-exposure HDR

Many HDR applications let you tone map a single Raw photo. Although this practice is technically not HDR, I refer to it as *single-exposure HDR*. You can also think of it as an alternative Raw processing technique.

By tone mapping a single Raw exposure, you access and manipulate the total dynamic range of the shot in unique ways. The result can seem as though the shot has more dynamic range than it really does. Figure 6-16 shows the final result of processing a single Raw exposure in Photomatix Pro. I tone mapped it and then did some minor editing in Photoshop. Voilà.

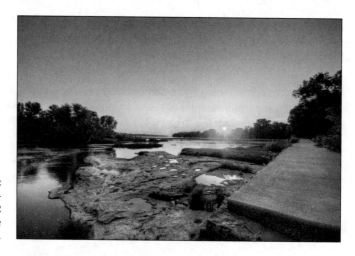

FIGURE 6-16: Use single-exposure HDR as an alternate processing tool.

Creating your own brackets from a single shot

This section is for total nerds. I keep it short and to the point. You can create your own exposure brackets from a single Raw photo. I've done this many times. You can unlock quite a bit of dynamic range from a single Raw photo and use that when tone mapping.

Use Lightroom or Adobe Camera Raw to create three partially processed versions of the same Raw photo. Separate their exposures by 2.0 EV so that you have an underexposed, a properly exposed, and an overexposed photo. Don't worry about other processing settings: Focus on the exposure differences. However, you can apply the same lens correction and transformations, including rotating and cropping, as long as you use identical settings on all three versions of the photo (although it would be interesting to experiment with wildly different settings). Export the three images as 8-bit TIFFs and load them into Photomatix Pro. Create an HDR image and tone map.

Manually bracketing exposures

If your camera doesn't have an AEB feature, you'll have to shoot the exposure brackets manually.

Frankly, manual exposure bracketing is a pain. It slows you down and makes shooting handheld HDR almost impossible. I remember having to go to the trouble of manually bracketing with my Sony Alpha 300. I suppose it was a rite of passage.

Although I would choose auto over manual brackets in most situations, knowing how to bracket manually can be a useful skill. For example, you may want to set up a shot with a number of brackets and EV difference that your camera won't shoot automatically. In those rare instances, you should resort to manual bracketing.

Now, it's not rocket science. It's just slow and irritating. Enter your camera's manual shooting mode, choose an aperture and ISO, and then meter the scene. Based on that reading, adjust the shutter speed to shoot the brackets. In contrast to my preference when using AEB, I prefer to start with underexposed photos and move progressively brighter when shooting manual brackets. I find this approach quicker to execute and less prone to error because I don't have to jump back and forth along the exposure scale.

Over time, you should be able to knock out a bracket of three to five exposures fairly quickly, assuming that the shutter speeds are reasonably fast.

Using other applications for HDR

Photomatix Pro isn't the only HDR application on the market. Other standalone HDR applications are available, and some photo editors have HDR modules. Adobe Photoshop as well as Lightroom have HDR features built into them, even for HDR panoramas. Although I don't have room to show you everything, you can load exposure brackets into their HDR workflows just as you would panorama photos.

To create and tone map an HDR image in Photoshop, load your images and then choose File ⇨ Automate ⇨ Merge to HDR Pro. Tone map the merged image using the controls in the Merge to HDR Pro dialog box, as shown in Figure 6-17. I suggest choosing a preset to see what sort of effects are possible and then tweaking individual parameters. In this case, I chose a preset with a high saturation and then fiddled around with the Radius and Strength settings until I liked the effect.

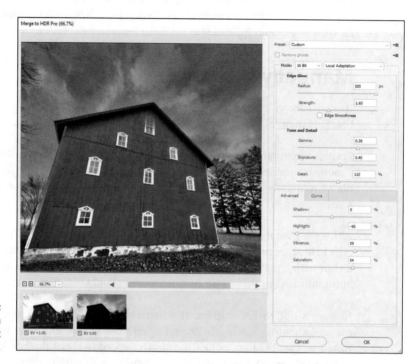

FIGURE 6-17: Photoshop has a decent HDR capability built in.

In Lightroom, select the brackets and then choose Photo ⇨ Photo Merge ⇨ HDR to launch the HDR Merge Preview dialog box. There are only a few options, as shown in Figure 6-18. You can choose Auto Align, use Auto Settings, and decide how much to deghost the images. In this case, I chose High deghosting because the water was moving a bit, which made some of the floating leaves and tree reflections blurry.

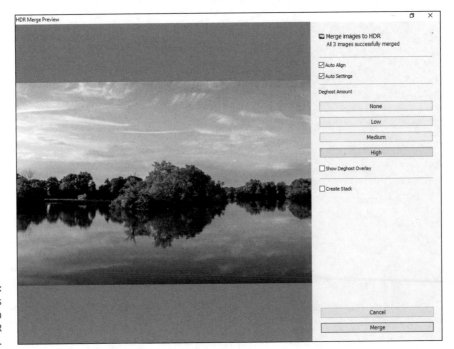

FIGURE 6-18:
Applications like Lightroom feature basic HDR processing.

6

Showcasing Different Scenes

Contents at a Glance

Chapter **1**

Portraits

Whether you like taking spontaneous shots of people or animals in every-day life or prefer setting up more formal portraits, the techniques you can use to make your shots look good are the same.

Stand back a bit from your subjects and try not to position them too close to a background. Use aperture-priority shooting mode, if possible, and open up the aperture (see Book 3, Chapter 2). Larger apertures create a shallower *depth of field*, which is the area that appears in focus. Everything else will be blurred. This effect makes your subjects stand out more from the background and look really nice.

When you or your subjects are moving, switch to shutter-priority mode and dial in a fast enough shutter speed (see Book 3, Chapter 3) to prevent blur. If the light is strong enough, you may be able to use aperture-priority mode knowing that the shutter speed will be fast. Don't be afraid of using slightly higher ISOs in this case. ISO (see Book 3, Chapter 4) often has to rise to pick up the exposure slack. If necessary, set up additional lighting or use a flash. When inside, I try to take advantage of lighting from nearby windows.

Capturing Animal Portraits

Animals are people too, right? Whether you're capturing photos of your house cat or the magnificent African Lion shown in Figure 1-1, animals make great subjects for portraits. My family and I went to our local zoo one day late in the summer for some fun. When we arrived at the lion enclosure, Bahati was lounging lazily next to the glass. It's hit and miss with the cats. Sometimes they are there and sometimes not. When the opportunity to capture this unique shot presented itself, I was very excited.

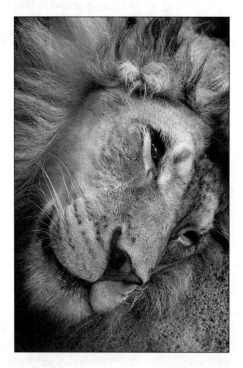

FIGURE 1-1:
Use faster shutter speeds when photographing animals.

I quickly put my mid-level Canon APS-C dSLR in shutter-priority mode and zoomed in to 55mm. With animals, you have to counter possible movement, so I set the shutter speed to 1/250 second. The aperture settled on f/5.6 and the ISO rose to 200.

I processed this photo in black and white to focus attention on the texture of the lion fur. As a bonus, the concrete he is on almost disappears.

Keys to this photo:

>> Use shutter-priority mode and relatively fast shutter speed to ensure a crisp photo.

>> Use image stabilization to help keep things steady.

>> Zoom in or step closer to frame faces.

>> Be prepared for magic moments.

Copy What Works

One day, a good friend of ours posted a new profile pic on Facebook that we really loved. She was at a café, sitting at a table with a cup of coffee. I was working with a full-frame Pentax camera, so I decided to attempt a similar photo.

I set up the shot shown in Figure 1-2 at a table in the front lobby of our church. This part of the building faces south and has floor-to-ceiling windows across the whole side. Morning and evening light in this area is fantastic. I used aperture-priority mode, set the aperture to f/4.5, and zoomed in to 63mm. The shutter speed was 1/400 second and the ISO rose to 200. Stabilization was on.

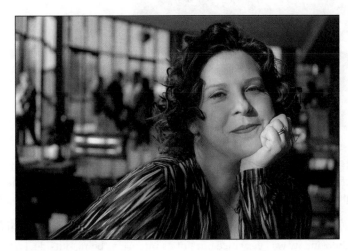

FIGURE 1-2: A great portrait, purposefully crafted.

Keys to this photo:

>> I wasn't afraid to copy something I liked but still make it my own.

>> The shot is framed off-center to include background.

>> Natural light illuminates the scene beautifully.

>> The aperture is wide enough to blur the background artistically.

Snapping Casual Portraits

I was heading out the door with a full-frame Pentax dSLR when I looked over and saw my son Sam playing at the computer. I told him to smile and took the casual snapshot shown in Figure 1-3.

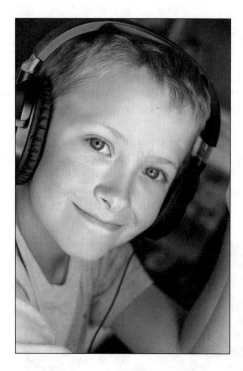

FIGURE 1-3:
FIGURE 1-3:
Kids look their
best when they
don't have to
pose.

If you have your camera with you, always be ready for action. Casual portraits that you take at a moment's notice often capture a person's natural beauty and personality better than posed shots.

The professional-level camera and lens make a difference in this shot. The light from the window was very nice but not as intense as being outside. I opened the aperture and was able to use a moderate shutter speed and slightly elevated ISO. This shot was taken using aperture-priority mode at 68mm, f/4.5, 1/100 second, and ISO 400.

Keys to this photo:

» Quick, casual shots often produce the most natural-looking portraits.

» It's hard to beat a 36.4 MP full-frame camera and quality lens.

» When inside, take advantage of natural light from windows.

Posing Group Photos

Figure 1-4 shows a group shot of my wife and three generations of women from a family we're good friends with. It's a classic group photo that I took one afternoon at a baseball game for the kids.

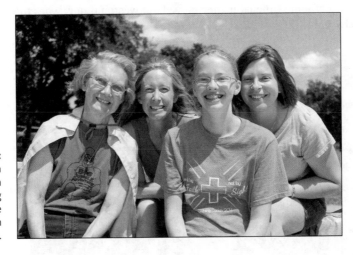

FIGURE 1-4: Pay attention to focus when photographing groups of people and position them accordingly.

I love this shot. It was bright and beautiful outside, but late enough that the sun was not directly overhead. The colors pop, and everyone is happy and smiling. I had the two on the top row lean in so that everyone would be close to the same focal plane. It's very hard to get everyone in focus if the group is spread out too far from front to back.

I shot this with a top-end consumer-level Canon dSLR and standard zoom lens. This shot was taken using aperture-priority mode at 27mm, f/4, 1/1000 second, and ISO 100.

Keys to this photo:

» Have your subjects look down at you to minimize squinting.

» Frame using the Rule of Thirds.

» Take two or three shots in situations like this and choose the best one.

» Line people up at the same distance so they are all in focus.

Say Cheese!

Our church bought a new property a few years ago. We had just taken possession and everyone was invited to come and look at it and discuss planned renovations. We were having fun in the brightly decorated kids wing when I ran across a good friend in the hallway, as shown in Figure 1-5. He would go on to marry the Kids Pastor. Some time later they moved out west and now work together at the same church.

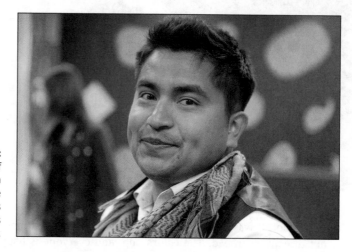

FIGURE 1-5: Great mix of focal length and aperture for a gorgeous spontaneous portrait.

I had a professional full-frame Canon camera and L-series lens on me and basically popped it up and said, "Smile for the camera!" I had already set the camera up for these situations, so it was ready: aperture-priority and f/4. I zoomed in to 85mm, which is a classic full-frame portrait focal length. The shutter speed was 1/100 second and the ISO rose to 1250. Image stabilization was engaged.

Keys to this photo:

>> Be ready for spontaneous shots.

>> This shot has a relaxed composition that features plenty of background.

>> Good portraits showcase great personality.

>> Use an open aperture for smooth backgrounds.

Chapter **2**

Landscapes

P hotographing landscapes is a fun and rewarding activity. You get to go out where the scenery is! In the process, you work with, and sometimes around, the weather, sunlight, and other environmental factors that you often have no control over. It's a great feeling when you position yourself at the right place at the right time and capture a magnificent scene with your digital SLR.

I know I won't have to twist your arm when I suggest that you take photography trips to all sorts of places, near and far. Feel free to shoot at different times, but the golden hour, which is the hour after sunrise and before sunset, is when the light is the most appealing. Over time, be sure to mix things up. The photos I've chosen for this chapter do precisely that: I took them at different times of the year, at different hours of the day, in different weather, and with different cameras. Each one is unique, but they are all landscapes.

Using an Ultra Wide-Angle Lens

On the surface, there's not much to the photo in Figure 2-1. However, I can't take my eyes off it. My family and I were visiting Detroit on a photo excursion and were in the Grosse Pointe area one afternoon. It was hot and sunny. Having discovered the beauty of Lake St. Claire, I got the camera and tripod out and took some shots.

This photo has most of the ingredients for a classic landscape: tripod, remote, and aperture at f/8.

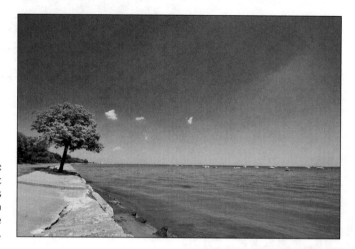

FIGURE 2-1: Classic landscapes emphasize width and maximize depth of field.

My lens choice was important for this scene. With so much to see, composing and framing landscapes is a good skill to develop. The Rule of Thirds is important. Although this is ostensibly a shot of the lake, I included the tree and shoreline on the left to provide a sense of scale. The lone tree and treeline further back provide contrast to the blue expanse of water and sky.

I took this photo with a Sony APS-C dSLT in aperture-priority mode at 10mm, f/8, 1/320 second, and ISO 100.

Keys to this photo:

» Using an ultra wide-angle lens at 10mm made this shot expansive.

» I framed the scene using the Rule of Thirds.

» I shot using a tripod and remote.

» Classic f/8 landscape aperture delivered infinite depth of field.

Getting Up Early

The bridge shown in Figure 2-2 is about a half mile from where I live. It's very cool-looking and begs to be photographed. As with many subjects, however, being beautiful does not automatically translate into being easily photographed.

Recognizing an opportunity to try something different one foggy morning, I grabbed my camera and drove over before the fog lifted.

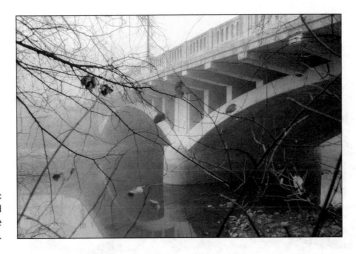

FIGURE 2-2: Don't be afraid to shoot intimate landscapes.

Although still a landscape, this shot is intimate as opposed to expansive. The main subject is fairly close, there are branches in the foreground, the fog creates a sense of mystery, and the morning light is soft and diffused. I chose a wide-angle focal length instead of ultra-wide, shot at f/4 instead of the more traditional f/8, and held the camera by hand instead of using tripod. Yet it works!

I took this shot with a Nikon APS-C dSLR in aperture-priority mode at 24mm, f/4, 1/40 second, and ISO 110.

Keys to this photo:

>> You should take advantage of different weather conditions.

>> The fog makes this scene mysterious and intriguing — and diffuses the light.

>> Look for unique angles to photograph subjects you see all the time.

>> You don't always need to use ultra-wide focal lengths to capture landscapes.

Going Different Places

You can shoot "landscapes" in the city, too. On a trip to Detroit, we went downtown several times to see the sights. One afternoon, we visited Greektown. The scene in Figure 2-3 is filled with the hustle and bustle of a district devoted to entertainment. As I looked at the scene through the viewfinder, I saw a woman walking toward me. She stood out from all the other activity, and I knew that she would make the shot special. I waited for just the right time and then took the photo.

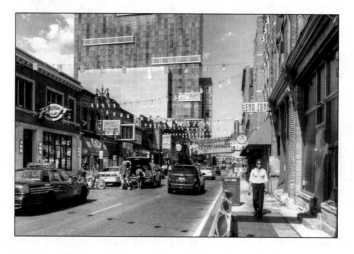

FIGURE 2-3:
Cities are human-made landscapes.

I took this shot with a Sony APS-C dSLT in aperture-priority mode at 22mm, f/8, 1/250 second, and ISO 100.

Keys to this photo:

>> I used the timing and opportunity to photograph the woman walking toward me.

>> I framed the street using the Rule of Thirds.

>> The aperture provides great depth of field while shutter speed prevents blur.

>> The wide angle makes the scene feel large.

Getting Out in the Weather

Figure 2-4 shows a winter scene that I photographed in late November. The day was cold and decidedly wintery. It snowed several inches and the wind was blowing forcefully. In a word: Perfect! I had not been up to this lake outside of the summer, so this was a perfect opportunity for fun and photography.

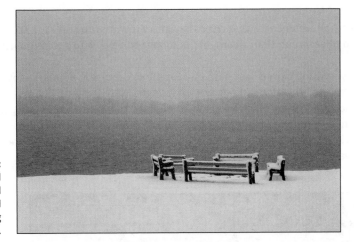

FIGURE 2-4:
Good composition and framing are vital when shooting landscapes.

I know what you're thinking: What could be more boring than a photo of a snowy beach on a day with a featureless gray sky in a snowstorm! But the benches, the lake, and the trees beyond provide just enough detail and variation in tone to make it work. On the whole, it's supposed to look desolate. There is beauty in that desolation. Although the scene is stark, the circle benches stand out. I zoomed in and used a normal focal length to make them more prominent.

I took this shot with a Canon APS-C dSLR in aperture-priority mode at 37mm, f/5, 1/200 second, and ISO 100.

Keys to this photo:

>> I was willing to make the effort to be out in the cold and snow.

>> The Rule of Thirds divides the scene nicely into fore, mid, and background.

>> A normal angle gives the benches greater importance.

>> It's a study in low-contrast, virtually monochrome beauty.

The Classic Sunset

Sunsets are a classic landscape ingredient. They are predictable, which is nice, but they can also be challenging to photograph. It can be difficult to find the right vantage point that looks toward the setting sun and has the right mix of details that you want to capture. Scout out rivers, lakes, and other scenes and pay attention to their orientation. Rivers that run north to south, for example, don't work as well as an east–west river that looks toward the sunset. Lakes are often easier to photograph than rivers, but you have to be able to access the right spot.

Everything worked out perfectly for me to capture the sunset shown in Figure 2-5. I spotted this area on our way past as we were heading out on a weekend excursion. We made plans to come back close to sunset on our way home. I built in enough time to look for a good location after we arrived and was able to set up my tripod, get the camera set up, and take some test shots. All I had to do then was wait for the right moment.

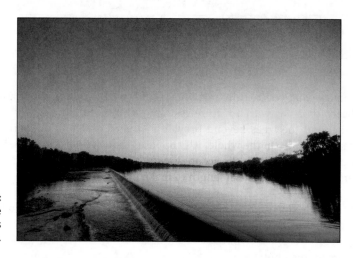

FIGURE 2-5: Sunsets make gorgeous subjects.

I took this shot with a Sony APS-C dSLT in aperture-priority mode at 10mm, f/8, 1/50 second, and ISO 100.

Keys to this photo:

>> The east-west river creates a very deep scene that extends toward the sunset.

>> A colorful sky combined with its reflection on the river contrasts with the darker riverbanks.

>> The sun is out of the frame but still illuminates the scene beautifully.

>> Ultra wide-angle focal length captures the breadth of the river and dam.

Chapter **3**

Action

I f you want to take action shots, you should make shutter speed your top priority. All else is secondary. Use the largest aperture you can and raise the ISO as much as you need to for the best exposure. A blurry action shot isn't worth printing and framing. I know. Believe me!

The other element to keep in mind is that capturing action is about motion. Put your camera in a continuous focus mode so that it keeps focusing as long as you have the shutter pressed halfway. Use a single AF point for the greatest focusing precision. If you need help tracking your subject, switch to a zone AF mode.

Tracking the Action

You can't get much more action-oriented than the photo I took of this Lockheed Martin F-22 Raptor performing a demonstration flight at an air show (see Figure 3-1). It screamed across the sky. I get goosebumps just thinking about it. To capture this sort of action, you need a fast shutter speed and the reflexes to frame and track a moving target, focus, and take the photo before you lose the shot. I used a monopod to support the heavy camera and large super-telephoto lens I was using. I took this shot with a Nikon APS-C dSLR in shutter-priority mode at 300mm, f/4.5, 1/1000 second, and ISO 125.

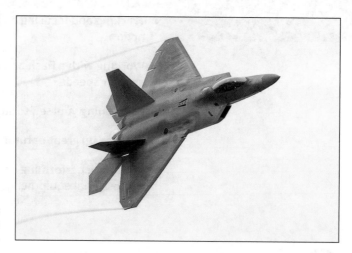

FIGURE 3-1:
This was an
awesome fly-by.

TIP

When photographing a fast subject, don't point the camera at one spot and expect to get a good photo as it moves through the frame. Instead, track and pan to follow it as best you can, using continuous focus to lock on. This technique takes some practice to get good at. Hone your skills by focusing on cars driving by, birds, or other animals that might be running around in your nearby environment.

Keys to this photo:

>> Very fast shutter speed needed to photograph the fast jet.

>> Super telephoto lens to capture action at a distance.

>> Monopod for help in supporting heavy camera and lens.

>> Fast tracking, panning, framing, and focusing skills.

Using an External Flash

I don't normally use a flash when engaged in action photography. When I do, I use an external flash. This setup enables high-speed sync, which works with faster shutter speeds than the camera's built-in flash.

This is how I captured the photo in Figure 3-2. I was at an outdoor mall with my wife and the kids taking fun shots with my Nikon APS-C dSLR and AF-S NIKKOR 24-70mm F2.8G ED zoom lens. I wanted to use a fill flash to light their faces better. I needed a fast shutter speed because I was shooting action. I connected my external flash and enabled High-Speed Sync. I took this shot in aperture-priority mode at 70mm, f/3.5, 1/1600 second, and ISO 100. The lighting was strong enough overall that I knew the shutter speed was going to be fast, so I decided to control the aperture directly.

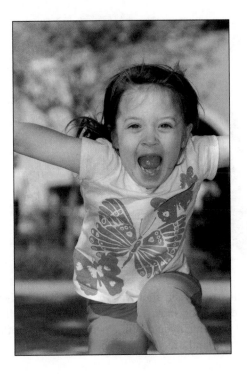

FIGURE 3-2:
Using high-speed sync for action fill flash.

Keys to this photo:

>> External flash made high-speed sync possible.

>> Very quick shutter speed froze the action perfectly.

>> Fantastic lens rendered the scene beautifully.

>> Near-telephoto focal length meant that I could stand back and not get jumped on.

Finding the Right Spot

REMEMBER

If you're going to photograph action that is predictable, choosing the right location increases your chances of capturing a great shot. For example, the photo I took in Figure 3-3 at a harness race captured horse and driver as they made the final turn and began their push toward the finish line. Although I couldn't know exactly how the scene was going to develop each time around, the distance, angle, and general action were the same each time. Knowing this, I was able to scout out a few different locations, helped me reliably capture great shots because I knew what to expect.

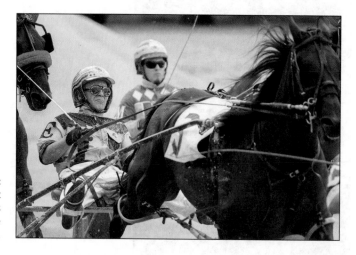

FIGURE 3-3:
Finding the right location helps you capture the right moment.

In this case, the challenge of each shot was to quickly frame the specific scene I wanted to capture and time the shot. Action is about capturing fleeting moments. It's not like a portrait for which you can line people up and tell them to hold still. Timing is very important, and practice helps quite a bit.

As with other action shots with lots of motion, this shot required a fast shutter speed. I used a Nikon APS–C dSLR and 300mm super–telephoto lens set to f/4. The shutter speed was 1/1000 and the ISO was 500.

Keys to this photo:

>> Location, location, location.

>> A sense of timing to capture the right moment.

>> Fast shutter speeds for fast action.

>> Fast shutter speeds often result in high ISO.

Great Light Is Great

My goal has been to include a wide range of shots in this book. Not everyone can go to an NFL game and photograph professional athletes in their element. For many people, backyard fun with family or friends is where the action is.

I took the photo shown in Figure 3-4 one day near the end of November. We were horsing around in the backyard. The kids were pretending to score touchdowns and then leaping up on a piece of play equipment. Sam (to the right) looks like he's guarding Jacob, but he's actually celebrating Jacob's *Lambeau Leap*. Their expressions are priceless.

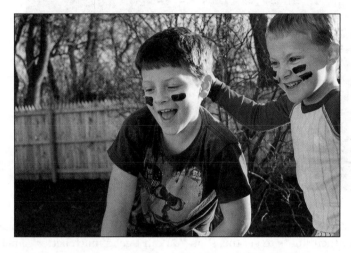

FIGURE 3-4:
Consumer-level cameras can capture beautiful photos in many conditions.

The thing that strikes me about this shot is how beautiful it is. The light enabled me to capture it with a fast shutter speed. I took this shot with a Sony APS-C dSLT in shutter-priority mode at 35mm, f/4.5, 1/250 second, and ISO 125.

Keys to this photo:

>> Great light makes capturing action easier, and your subjects will look prettier.

>> Not everything has to be 1/1000 second. Sometimes 1/250 is fine.

>> You don't always have to use a super telephoto lens. I shot this with a standard zoom lens on a Sony APS-C dSLR at 35mm.

>> Action is action, whether it's in a yard or at a professional sports venue.

Pushing to the Limits

When you're photographing people in action, especially indoors, you often have to push the camera to its limits. I took the photo shown in Figure 3-5 during a practice session of our church band. I consider this an action shot because my focus was on capturing the performer's movements. The challenge in this case was to capture those movements in relatively low light.

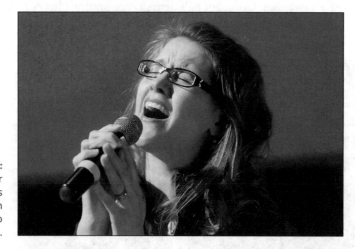

FIGURE 3-5: A superior camera and lens can shoot at high ISOs with little to no noise.

What surprised me at the time was having to push a professional camera and lens to their limits to get this shot. You can't get a much better combination than the full-frame Canon 5D Mark III and EF 70–200mm f/4L IS USM telephoto zoom lens, and they were barely able to capture this moment. The ISO rose to a staggering 12800 to take this shot at 1/250 second. I set the camera to shutter-priority mode and zoomed in to 135mm. The camera set the aperture to f/4.

Keys to this photo:

» Some conditions are a challenge even when using the best equipment.

» Professional cameras shoot much better photos at high ISOs.

» Interior lighting may look fine to your eye but not be strong enough to support fast shutter speeds.

» Use shutter-priority mode when photographing performers on stage.

Chapter **4**

Close-Ups

love zooming in and capturing close-ups. I'm always on the lookout to photograph unique details from a different perspective.

Photographing close-ups is a really fun way to express yourself as a photographer. You focus on smaller details than usual, which encourages you to grow creatively. Over time, you really do start to see things in a different light, whether the photo is of a flower, a bracelet, ice on a door, or a penny.

You don't have to have anything besides a dSLR and a typical zoom lens (see Book 2, Chapter 1) to enjoy close-up photography. However, you can invest in macro lenses and other gear that will help you capture close-ups and macros more effectively. In this chapter, I share how I captured five of my favorite close-ups.

Zoom In

Not every close-up has to look as though you shot it with an electron microscope. Close-ups can be relatively relaxed if you like, as shown in Figure 4-1. My wife was preparing food outside early one evening and the light was incredible. It was spring, and we were itching to be outside. Instead of cleaning off the table, I used her tools as props for the background. You can see a knife and a colander of radishes as well as a paper napkin strategically placed around the African violet. The placement of these items isn't accidental.

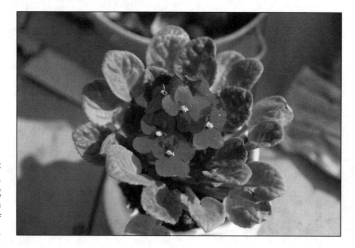

FIGURE 4-1: Quite often, shooting close-ups is just a matter of zooming in.

I used a professional Canon full-frame dSLR and lens for this photo. Overkill, possibly, but I can't complain. I zoomed in to 73mm, which is in the near/medium telephoto range for a full-frame camera. Other than that, this was very close to a normal handheld shot. The aperture was f/4, shutter speed was 1/800, and ISO was only 100.

Keys to this photo:

>> Late-afternoon light is warm and inviting.

>> I composed this shot purposefully, choosing my props and positioning them around the central subject to create the scene.

>> Near-telephoto focal length on a full-frame camera made the shot a nice close-up without looking too close.

>> No extra gear or effort required; I used what I had immediately available.

Be Ready to Grab Your Camera

When you see something interesting, be ready to get your camera and start photographing. Case in point: I noticed that ice had formed on one of our storm doors, as shown in Figure 4-2. It was December 24 and brutally cold. Fighting a bit of laziness, I put down my coffee and went to get a camera. I chose my consumer-level Nikon APS-C dSLR and put a nice 50mm prime lens on it.

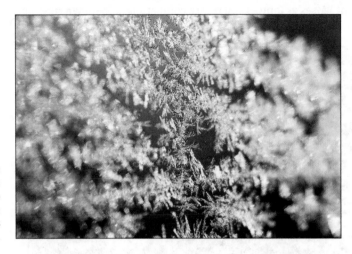

FIGURE 4-2:
Always be on the lookout to photograph unique scenes closely.

I came back into the room and took a few test shots straight on. Boring. Bracing myself, I got closer and angled the camera so that I could capture an oblique shot. Interesting! I set the camera to aperture-priority mode and dialed in f/3.5 for this shot. The shutter speed was 1/2500 and the ISO was 100.

Keys to this photo:

» Its unique perspective was captured by getting close, opening the lens, and angling the camera.

» No other special gear or equipment was needed.

» Holding the camera and using a fast shutter speed ensured a crisp shot with sharp details.

» I had to be willing to go get my camera.

Using Diopters

Now it's time to unleash some extra equipment on you. I captured the close-up of the sunflower shown in Figure 4-3 using a diopter attached to the lens of a consumer-level Canon dSLR. The lens wasn't anything fancy, just your standard 18-55mm kit lens. Diopters magnify things, just as a magnifying glass does (see

Book 2, Chapter 3). They also enable you to move closer and still focus. Diopters are easy to carry and relatively inexpensive. They also work well with step-down rings, which means that you can buy large diopters and use them on many different lenses as long as you have a compatible step-down ring. I used 77mm diopters.

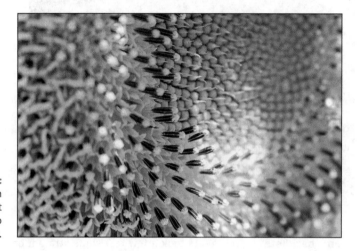

FIGURE 4-3:
Diopters are an inexpensive but effective way to magnify subjects.

I took this amazing shot late in the day when the light struck the sunflower from the side. I zoomed in to 55mm and, with a +10 diopter attached, was able to capture a unique close-up. I used shutter-priority and set the shutter speed to 1/640 second. The camera set the aperture to f/6.3. Even at f/6.3, the depth of field is very narrow because of the close focus distance made possible by the diopter. The ISO rose to 640.

Keys to this photo:

>> Diopters magnify subjects and make close-ups easier to take with a standard lens.

>> Early evening sunlight illuminates this detailed scene wonderfully.

>> Pay attention to shutter speed when shooting handheld close-ups to ensure crisp shots.

>> ISO rises to compensate for small apertures and fast shutter speeds.

Whatever Works, Works

You're going to laugh at this one. I was experimenting with reversing rings. They enable you to mount lenses on your camera backward, which turns normal lenses into close-up/macro lenses. I realize they aren't everyone's cuppa tea. You have to manually focus, aperture control can be a problem, and it's just odd. However, I have some old NIKKOR manual focus lenses that work perfectly with reversing rings. I control the aperture on the lenses and mount them on Canon dSLRs.

I was looking for interesting subjects to photograph when I grabbed the turquoise bracelet shown in Figure 4-4. I bought it for my wife one year when I was on a trip to Texas. Curious, she followed me outside to help. We went around to the back of the garage and she held the bracelet over our black trash bin. It worked fantastically as a backdrop. She was able to steady her arm on it, which helped me focus and shoot a crisp photo. I used a Canon APS-C dSLR set to shutter-priority mode with an old 50mm NIKKOR manual focus lens set to f/2. The shutter speed was 1/250 second and the ISO was 200.

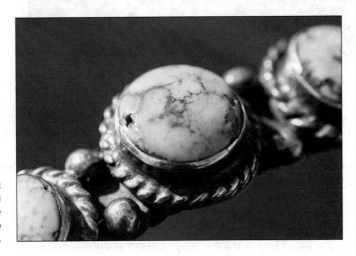

FIGURE 4-4: Use what you have to make every photo better.

Keys to this photo:

>> Reversing rings are totally cool but require some effort to use.

>> Use what you have to help capture the shot: an old lens, a bracelet, and trash bin, in this case. As long as it works, it doesn't matter.

>> Wide aperture and bright light enabled me to set the shutter speed to 1/250 to ensure a sharp photo.

Close-Ups

Focus on Small Details

Finally, I present President Abraham Lincoln (see Figure 4-5). On a penny, of course. But wow, what a penny. This one has been through some rough times. It's not the newest penny and has a lot of gouges on the surface. Those qualities make it the perfect subject for a close-up.

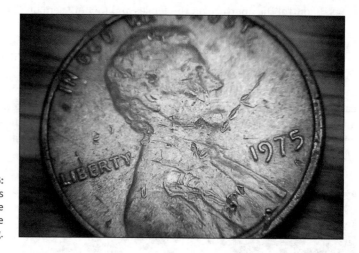

FIGURE 4-5:
The small details on this penny are what make the shot interesting.

I shot this in my studio using a consumer-level Nikon APS-C dSLR in manual mode with a digital Holga lens attached. To increase the magnification, I used the 60mm macro attachment that pops onto the main Holga lens. I mounted the camera on a tripod and moved the penny, which I placed on a piece of wood, back and forth in order to focus. I used Live View to compose the shot and raised the ISO to 3200 to brighten the scene.

Even though the Holga lens has a small aperture, the depth of field of this shot is very narrow. I focused on the word *Liberty* and the date to make them the sharpest features. I took a number of test shots at different angles, and liked this one the best.

Keys to this photo:

>> I took it with a digital Holga lens with macro attachment.

>> It was shot in my studio using Live View and a tripod.

>> Even with bright lighting, the ISO rose dramatically because of the small aperture.

>> I chose a damaged penny as a more interesting subject.

Index

A

A/Av (Aperture-Priority Autoexposure) mode, 133, 141, 147

accessing archives, 442

accessories. *See also specific accessories*

about, 33–35

for external flash units, 399–401

for macro/close-up photography, 204–211

packing, 128–129

Action mode, 137

action photography

about, 573

depth of field for, 293–294

lighting for, 576–577

location for, 574–575

pushing to the limits with, 577–578

shutter speed for, 312–313

with telephoto lenses, 219–221

tracking the action, 573–574

using external flash, 574–575

activating

built-in flash, 379–384

lens-based image stabilization, 97–98

Long Exposure Noise Reduction, 308

red-eye reduction, 387

Active D-Lighting (Nikon), 275

adapter ring, 345

adjusting

autofocus settings, 124–125

color, 338

color vibrancy, 459–460

contrast, 338

dynamic range, 552

exposure, 453–454

final composition, 484–485

lenses, 36

metering modes, 258

saturation, 459–460

tone, 338

adjustment layers, 477–478, 493–495

adjustments (Photoshop), 471

Adobe Bridge, 426, 429

Adobe Lightroom

about, 431–432, 492

creating and tone mapping HDR images in, 555–556

creating panoramas with, 523–527

using, 445–446, 468

Adobe Photoshop

about, 431–432

advanced blending in, 530–531

creating and tone mapping HDR images in, 555–556

creating files, 468–470

creating panoramas with, 523–530

features of, 470–471

using, 433, 468

AdobeRGB, 112, 471–472

Advanced Auto mode, 132

advanced blending, in Photoshop, 530–531

advanced editing, for photos, 436

advanced options, 123–126

Advanced Photo System, Classic (APS-C), 11–12

adverse weather, 65–68

AE (autoexposure) Lock, 271–274

AE Lock/FE Lock/Index/Reduce button, 41

AEB (auto exposure bracketing)

about, 274

for HDR photography, 541

setting up, 541–543

AF (Autofocus)

about, 22–23, 149

changing settings, 124–125

mid-range models, 18

professional models, 19

AF Area Selection button, 22, 42

AF DX Fisheye-Nikkor 10.5mm f/2 8G ED lens, 230

AF Fisheye-Nikkor 16mm f/2.8 lens, 230

AF (autofocus) modes, 149–150, 307–308

AF point selection/Magnify button, 41

AF (autofocus) points, 22, 150

AF-assist illuminator, 396, 397

AF-S NIKKOR 50mm f/1.4G, 286

AF-S NIKKOR 300mm f/4D IF-ED, 282

AI focus, 150

AI servo, 150

alerts, 115

ambient light. *See* lighting

A-mount (Alpha mount), 14

analyzing photos, 260–267

metering
  about, 255
  camera metering modes, 256–258
  external light meter, 259
  general methods of, 256
  mid-range models, 18
  professional models, 19
  scenes, 258–259
Metering mode
  about, 256
  changing, 258
  setting, 151
MF (Manual Focus)
  about, 149
  for in-studio shooting, 199–200
  switching between auto focus and, 95–96
  using, 96–97
Micro Four Thirds, 12, 14, 82
microphones, 40
mid-range models, 18
mini stand, 01, 405
minimum aperture, 280
mirror, 15
Mirror Lockup/Mirror Up setting, 154, 305
mirrorless cameras, 10–11
Mode button
  on cameras, 42
  on external flash units, 405
models
  about, 9–11
  mid-range, 18
monitors, articulated, 30–31, 52–53
monopods, 50, 52, 129, 330
motion blur, 307–308
mounds, in histograms, 264
mount, 87
mounting foot, 396, 397

mounting lenses, 91–93
Movie menu, 102
movies
  about, 23–24
  editing software for, 433
  options for, 114
  shooting, 366
MP (megapixels), 12
multiple exposures mode, 140
multipurpose zoom lenses, 163–165
Multi-zone metering mode, 257
muting colors, 496–497

N

naming dSLRs, 9–16
natural light, 357–364
navigating external flash units, 406
ND (neutral density) filters, 349–350
ND graduated filters, 351
near telephoto lenses, 77, 214
Nearest Neighbor (Photoshop), 439
network storage, for archiving, 441
neutral density (ND) filters, 339, 349–350
Neutral style, 515
night, shooting at, 363–364
Night Portrait mode, 138
Night Scene style, 516
Night View/Scene mode, 138
Nikon
  about, 9
  Active D-Lighting, 275
  AF points, 23
  autofocus motor, 75
  Capture NX-D, 430
  checklist for, 155

  Filter Effects, 25
  Guide mode, 135
  HDR, 275
  ISO, 322
  lens mounts, 13
  lenses, 71, 75
  picture control, 514–516
  Speedlight, 395
  tilt-shift lenses, 233
  Vibration Reduction (VR), 27–28
  wireless file transfer adapters, 426
Nodal Ninja (website), 532
noise, ISO and, 323–324
noise reduction
  about, 113, 461, 487
  setting, 153
non-CPU lens, 282
non-destructive editing, 448
noon light, 359
normal focal lengths, zoom lenses and, 168–170
normal lenses, 77, 78
normal magnetism, for memory cards, 57
normal zoom lenses, 163–165
numbers, for ISO, 321–323

O

off-camera cord, 413–414
OLED (organic light-emitting diode) monitors, 15
Olympus
  about, 10
  Flash, 395
  lens mounts, 14
  lenses, 71
one shot mode, 149
online storage, for archiving, 441

two-button controls, on external flash units, 406

types, of lenses, 75

U

ultra wide-angle lenses, for landscapes, 567–568

ultraviolet (UV) filter, 348–349, 372

ultra-wide angle lenses, 77, 81

umbrellas, 410–411

underexposed, 248

underwater, dealing with, 68

underwater gear, buying, 34

unpacking gear, 129–131

updating firmware, 122–123

upgrading software, 434

UV (ultraviolet) filter, 348–349, 372

V

valleys, in histograms, 264

variable maximum aperture, 279–280

Vello, 411

verifying

battery level, 54, 131

buttons, 131

exposures remaining, 131

knobs, 131

lenses, 131

white balance, 459

vertical distortion, in interiors, 185

vertical grips, 48–49, 170. *See also* grips

vertical orientation, 188–189

vertical perspective distortion, 461–462

vests, buying, 34

Vibrance/Saturation adjustment layer, 477

Vibration Reduction (VR), 85, 86, 304–305

video mode settings, 118

viewfinder adjustment dial, 42

viewfinder diopters, 35

viewfinders

about, 15, 37

choosing viewing modes from, 144–145

mid-range models, 18

specifications for, 26–27

viewing exposure settings from, 253, 254

viewing indices, 260

viewing modes

choosing, 144–146

exposure settings, 253–255

vignette, 180

virtual horizon, 115

Vivid style, 515

VR (Vibration Reduction), 85, 86, 304–305

W

Warning icon, 2

warnings, 115, 255

water photography, shutter speed for, 313–314

watermark, 437

weather

about, 364

adverse, 65–68

clouds, 364–365

fog, 366

landscapes, 570–571

snow, 67–68, 365

websites, 371

websites

BlackRapid, 64

Cokin's Creative Filter System, 345

depth of field calculator, 289

Dummies, 3

easyCover, 65

golden hour, 360, 371

lens rentals, 215

Lensbaby, 239

Life Pixel Infrared, 354

LumiQuest, 400

Nodal Ninja, 532

Photomatix Pro, 538

PTGui, 532

Vello, 411

weather, 371

wet weather, dealing with, 66

white balance

checking, 459

color filters for, 339

setting, 151–153

white balance cards, 34

wide-angle adapter, 01

wide-angle lenses

about, 77, 78–79, 177–178

cityscapes, 180–182

focal length categories, 77

improving wide-angle shots, 186–191

interiors, 184–185

landscapes, 179–180

portraits, 185–186

single buildings, 182–184

wide-angle photography, 165–168

wide-angle zoom lenses, 81–82

Wi-Fi, 29

About the Author

Robert Correll is an author and photographer with more than two decades of writing experience. He is the author of all four editions of the best-selling *Digital SLR Photography All-in-One For Dummies*, and has written numerous other *For Dummies* guides to popular dSLR models, including the Canon EOS 5D Mark III, the EOS 90D, 80D, 60D, and 77D, the EOS Rebel T6i, T5i, T5, and T3, and the Sony A77, A65, A55, and A35. Some of his other works include *Photo Restoration: From Snapshots to Great Shots, Digital Holga Photography, High Dynamic Range Photography For Dummies,* and *HDR Photography Photo Workshop*. Robert currently works at Purdue University Fort Wayne. He graduated from the United States Air Force Academy.

Dedication

To my family.

Author's Acknowledgments

As always, thanks to my wife and children for encouraging, supporting, loving, and sustaining me. Thank you for going with me to Michigan, Oklahoma, Indiana, Ohio, Illinois, and Missouri — including all the camps, parks, towns, zoos, national monuments, churches, cemeteries, cities, rivers, races, air shows, our backyard, and other points of interest in between — to take the photos in this book.

Many thanks to my agent, David Fugate of Launchbooks.com.

I'm grateful to have worked with so many talented people on this book. I am deeply thankful to the wonderful publishing team at John Wiley & Sons, including Steve Hayes and Susan Christophersen. I am also thankful to Mark Hemmings for his technical review.

Many other people have been incredibly supportive and helpful. Special thanks to Jacob, Don, Jane, Abby, Darwin, Christine, Tom, Byron, Bill Bailey, Gary Fong, Lensbaby, Lomography, and Roger Cicala of LensRentals.com.

Publisher's Acknowledgments

Executive Editor: Steven Hayes

Project and Copy Editor: Susan Christophersen

Technical Editor: Mark Hemmings

Proofreader: Debbye Butler

Production Editor: Mohammed Zafar Ali

Front Cover Image: Courtesy of Robert Correll